Measuring Offender Risk

Measuring Offender Risk

A CRIMINAL JUSTICE SOURCEBOOK

Dean J. Champion

GREENWOOD PRESS
Westport, Connecticut • London

In memory of my late parents,
Erma Janet Hackett Champion
and
Frank Dewey Champion

Library of Congress Cataloging-in-Publication Data

Champion, Dean J.
Measuring offender risk : a criminal justice sourcebook / Dean J. Champion.
p. cm.
Includes bibliographical references and index.
ISBN 0-313-28593-4 (alk. paper)
1. Criminal justice, Administration of—United States. 2. Risk assessment—United States. 3. Criminals—United States. I. Title.
HV9950.C453 1994
364.3'0973—dc20 93-1651

British Library Cataloguing in Publication Data is available.

Library of Congress Catalog Card Number: 93-1651
ISBN: 0-313-28593-4

First published in 1994

Greenwood Press, 88 Post Road West, Westport, CT 06881
An imprint of Greenwood Publishing Group, Inc.

Printed in the United States of America

The paper used in this book complies with the Permanent Paper Standard issued by the National Information Standards Organization (Z39.48—1984).

10 9 8 7 6 5 4 3 2 1

Contents

Preface

Forecasts of dangerousness and risk are made during every stage of the criminal justice process. Prosecutors decide whether diversion should be granted certain offenders or whether they should be prosecuted. These difficult decisions are influenced greatly by each prosecutor's personal evaluation and belief that an offender can benefit more from more lenient treatment, such as diversion, rather than from a formal criminal prosecution which may result in a conviction and criminal record. More lenient treatment for many first offenders and their success rates from participating in diversion programs are tangible evidence that at least some offenders benefit from such leniency. Defense counsel may submit psychological assessments of their clients or have private corporations prepare reports designed to show why their clients would be good candidates for diversion instead of being prosecuted. Often, these reports include results from one or more prediction instruments which purportedly indicate the offender's rehabilitative potential and the unlikelihood of reoffending.

When probation officers and others prepare presentence investigation reports (PSIs) about convicted offenders for judicial sentencing decisions, these PSIs almost always contain a probation officer's assessment of offenders and the officer's recommendation for lenient or harsh treatment. Particularly in those jurisdictions that have loosely regulated, indeterminate sentencing systems, judicial discretion varies greatly and disparities in decision making are pervasive. While judges are not bound by these recommendations in PSI reports, these documents often influence judicial decision making.

Many jurisdictions have implemented guidelines-based schemes, mandatory sentencing models, and determinate sentencing plans. While these plans have been designed, in part, to objectify judicial decision making and ensure more equitable treatment for all convicted offenders in the sentences they receive, sentencing disparities continue. Such disparities are attributable to many factors, including race, ethnicity, gender, and socioeconomic status. Other subjective elements also impact upon sentencing decisions. These elements include "attitude" or acceptance of responsibility for the conviction offenses, the quality of defense counsel, and a complex appraisal of the offender's potential for future offending. Almost every PSI contains a prediction about future offending and a recommendation from the probation officer about the most desirable punishment options. Probation officers throughout the United States frequently use risk assessment devices as a part of their PSI preparation. These instruments involve either anamnestic, actuarial, or clinical indicators about the offender's potential for future offending.

If the sentencing decision is incarceration in either a jail or prison for either specified or unspecified intervals (as in determinate or indeterminate sentencing plans), corrections departments in different jurisdictions must make a determination of where these convicted offenders should be confined. Because chronic overcrowding characterizes most prisons and jails in every U.S. jurisdiction, this placement decision making is often a matter of finding available space to accommodate these convicts. If convicted offenders are sentenced to prison for a period of years, prison officials must accept these offenders, space permitting, and assign them to an appropriate custody level. Many of the larger prisons and penitentiaries have classification divisions whose sole responsibilities are to assess incoming prisoners and determine where they should be housed relative to other inmates. Some inmates are more dangerous than others. Some inmates have communicable diseases, such as AIDS, while others are mentally ill or chronic alcoholics or drug addicts. There are murderers, rapists, robbers, larcenists, and organized-crime figures who must be classified and placed. Should check forgers, stockbrokers convicted of fraud, and petty thieves be celled with those convicted of aggravated rape, assault, or murder? Because chronic overcrowding exists in many of these prison settings, finding different cell accommodations for prisoners with basically different criminal histories and records of dangerousness may be an unattainable luxury. In any case, some attempt is made to classify and place them most appropriately.

When inmates serve sufficient time to earn early release through parole, or if they become qualified for participation in leave programs such as work release, study release, or furloughs, paroling authorities must decide whether specific offenders will be successful if paroled or if they are assigned to particular programs. Parole boards are not perfect in their decision making, and frequently, inmates are released short of serving their full sentences only to reoffend within months of being paroled. For other inmates who are not granted early release, it is likely that many of these may never reoffend, although parole boards cannot make such forecasts. Again, decisions about early release are often made from prison conduct reports and instruments which attempt to forecast an inmate's potential dangerousness and risk if released.

Most professionals agree that each of these decision-making stages is imperfect or flawed in one or more respects. For instance, a certain proportion of those diverted, placed on probation, assigned minimum-security incarceration, and granted parole or participation in work release or furlough programs will "fail." Failure is measured in different ways, but often, it means simply that some offenders reoffend or violate one or more conditions of their programs. Additionally, few professionals will disagree that many offenders who will never reoffend or pose a danger or risk to others are actually overpenalized and/or incarcerated for longer periods as the result of faulty decision making by different actors in the criminal justice system. This is the false positive/false negative dilemma, and it has moral, legal, psychological, and social implications for both offenders and the public-at-large.

The criminal justice system exists to fulfill several goals, including punishment, "just deserts," deterrence, reintegration, rehabilitation, and greater accountability through acceptance of responsibility for one's criminal actions. But fundamental fairness is a principle ideally extended and applied to all offenders. Thus, whatever decisions are made that affect any offender should be couched in the context of fundamental fairness. Does the punishment fit the crime? Does the offender receive just deserts for the crime committed? When should leniency be exhibited and when should it be withheld?

This book is an examination of instruments and methods used by the criminal justice system in diverse ways to make decisions about offenders. It seeks to evaluate these instruments and methods, to target certain common elements or components of measures that purport to measure one's dangerousness or risk to others. Therefore, all stages of the criminal justice process will be investigated to determine how decisions are made which affect the lives of offenders.

In an attempt to collect only the most current professional information about dangerousness measures and risk assessment devices used at local, state, and federal levels, over 400 letters were sent to both juvenile and adult paroling authorities, departments of corrections, courts, and prison systems in all state and federal jurisdictions. These letters solicited copies of reports, scales, and indices of risk and dangerousness, classification guidelines, and needs assessment devices currently used by each agency or authority. The response was overwhelming. With the exception of two states and the District of Columbia, the remaining forty-eight states and several federal agencies and departments supplied much valuable information, including instrumentation presently used for different types of offender decision making. Although both juvenile and criminal justice systems were contacted in all states, only about half of the state jurisdictions provided information about juvenile offender processing and dangerousness scales. Nevertheless, with the abundant information supplied, a rich data source was created for this book's development and completeness.

Chapter 1 explores the historical origins and early use of prediction instruments designed to forecast risk and dangerousness. It investigates alternative meanings which have been given to these terms in contemporary decision making about offenders at different stages of justice processing. Finally, it establishes the importance of such instruments for the criminal justice system and provides a foundation and context for the remaining chapters.

Chapter 2 illustrates the application of various risk assessment instruments at different stages in the criminal justice process. Numerous instruments have been devised over several decades. Some of these instruments have actually been created as subscales of more popular personality assessment instruments, such as the Minnesota Multiphasic Personality Inventory (MMPI) and Cattell's 16 Personality Factor Inventory (16 PF). Other instruments have been created independent of existing assessment devices. Some have relied heavily upon descriptions of the characteristics of recidivists for their composition. These actuarial devices are probably the most popular in use today by most jurisdictions. Dangerousness instruments vary widely in their sophistication and composition. Some measures consist of ten or fewer items, while more elaborate measures include numerous indicators. However, the length of prediction instruments is not necessarily indicative of the ability of the instrument to forecast dangerousness or risk. Sometimes, simple measures of risk are as effective as or more effective at behavioral forecasting than more elaborate, sophisticated, and complicated instruments. Chapter 2 also examines the philosophical bases for using risk assessment instruments, the way these instruments are used, and several contrasting implications for affected offenders.

Chapter 3 describes selective incapacitation, or selectively incarcerating certain offenders because they have been designated as dangerous by prediction instruments. Those believed to pose serious risks to others are, in effect, selectively confined, while others, considered not dangerous, are afforded probationary terms or other options (e.g., fines, community service, participation in educational, vocational, and counseling programs). This chapter also lists and assesses the characteristics of many of the current instruments used by states and the federal government in decision making about convicted offenders. Can dangerousness be accurately predicted? How should test results be interpreted? How much validity should be given to these instruments when policy decisions are made in correctional institutions and other agencies when processing criminals?

Chapter 4 describes early classificatory criteria used by prisons to segregate inmates. Those considered psychologically disturbed or mentally ill may be separated from others, space permitting. However, prison overcrowding renders such decision making a luxury in many penal institutions. Nevertheless, early typing of offenders is used also for "level-of-custody" decisions by prison officials. Such decision making is not foolproof, however, and many misclassifications occur. Sometimes, these misclassifications lead to lawsuits filed by inmates against various prison personnel, even against other prisoners. Although the success rates and payoffs of such litigation are negligible in many cases, better classification decision making would no doubt decrease the frequency of such suit filings.

Chapter 5 describes parole board decision making. Although some states, such as Maine, and the federal government have either abolished or are abolishing their respective paroling authorities, parole boards exist in most U.S. jurisdictions. Parole boards are responsible for deciding whether inmates are entitled to early release short of serving their full prison terms. Early-release decisions by parole boards are difficult decisions. Many parole boards utilize prediction instruments to supplement their own knowledge of inmate conduct and face-to-face interviews. Because some inmates are granted early release and soon reoffend, some victims or their families have filed suits against parole boards because of their "mistakes." The legal liabilities of parole boards will be examined briefly, as well as some of the alternative strategies parole boards in different states use for making their early-release decisions.

Chapter 6 is an assessment and an evaluation of existing measures of dangerousness and risk. It explores the current and future use of such instruments at all stages of the criminal justice system. It highlights some of the major moral, ethical, legal, psychological, and social issues regarding the use of risk predictors and measures of dangerousness. The book concludes with an evaluation of existing risk assessment instruments. A comprehensive bibliography is included. Selected scales from various state jurisdictions will be illustrated in the Appendix for reference and comparison. Hopefully, this book will function as an informative resource about risk predictors and dangerousness assessment devices and be of value to both practitioners and theorists.

Dean J. Champion
Minot, North Dakota

1

Risk Assessment and Dangerousness: An Historical Analysis

INTRODUCTION

In the mid-1770s, John Howard (1726–1790), a prominent English prison reformer and sheriff of Bedfordshire, visited several European countries to investigate their respective prison systems and operations. His journey to France involved a tour of the *Maison de Force* (House of Enforcement) of Ghent, where he found prisoners were adequately clothed, well fed, and lodged in separate cells at night. He was shocked by such humanity displayed toward ordinary prisoners, since his own country celled large numbers of inmates, including males, females, and children, in workhouse common rooms with straw-strewn floors. In fact, mercantile and economic interests in England and Scotland systematically exploited prisoners, getting much free labor from them. Furthermore, a portion of inmate labor profits was given to jailers who made such prison labor available. Impressed with such different prison conditions in France and elsewhere, Howard successfully lobbied in the House of Commons where the Penitentiary Act was passed in 1779. This Act made it possible for new prison facilities to be created, where prisoners could be housed separately in more sanitary cells. Prisoners were not coddled, however; they were put to work where they could learn useful skills which they could apply when released back into their communities.

At about the same time in the American colonies, prison reformers such as Dr. Benjamin Rush (1745–1813) were hard at work to change inmate conditions, which closely mirrored those of England. Quakers, philanthropists, and other prominent citizens in Pennsylvania eventually established the Philadelphia Society for Alleviating the Miseries of Public Prisons in 1787. Through their efforts, the Pennsylvania legislature authorized the construction of a new facility, the Walnut Street Jail, in Philadelphia in 1790. This jail (actually a renovation of the old High Street Jail built in 1776) was considered innovative, since it pioneered (1) the separation of prisoners according to offense seriousness, (2) the separation of inmates according to gender, and (3) the creation of solitary confinement (American Correctional Association, 1983).

These are probably the earliest recorded attempts at offender classification and placement. Admittedly, these classification schemes were crude. At the time, however, they represented pioneering events and had favorable consequences for affected inmates. Subsequently, in the United States, England, and elsewhere, more elaborate classification schemes have been devised for diverse purposes.

This book is about offender classification. Specifically, it seeks to describe the origin, development, and current state of the art of instruments and methods whereby effective offender classification may be achieved. For our purposes, *classification is differentiating among persons according to particular characteristics they possess.* This definition is closely related to measurement, where we might seek to distinguish between objects according to previously established criteria or rules. Actually, measurement is the vehicle whereby classification systems are established.

Furthermore, both qualitative and quantitative criteria are closely linked with measurement. Since those in the criminal justice system are mostly interested in offenders and offender processing, *measurement is the assignment of numbers to social, or behavioral, and psychological properties of offenders according to rules, and correlating these numbers with these properties* (Champion, 1993: 194–195; Cohen and Nagel, 1934; Stevens, 1951). Thus, measurement is the process of using numerical expressions to differentiate between offenders according to various individual and social properties. It is assumed that these properties are largely behavioral and attitudinal characteristics amenable to measurement (Champion, 1993:195). Offender classification systems are one product of the measurement process.

Other scholars have further clarified the meaning of classification by noting that it seeks to allocate persons in previously undefined classes into groupings or classes where the persons in each aggregate or class are in some way similar or close to one another (Cormack, 1971; D. Gottfredson, 1987:1). For example, we might distinguish between and classify offenders according to previously established criteria, such as felons (persons convicted of a felony) and misdemeanants (persons convicted of a misdemeanor). Or we might classify them according to whether they are violent offenders or property offenders. Obviously, offender classification schemes may be more or less elaborate. The *Uniform Crime Reports,* for example, is an annual compilation of reported crime in the United States. It divides certain index offenses into Class I and Class II categories, where the former are comparatively more serious than the latter.

The chapter organization is as follows. First, the functions and importance of offender classification schemes will be presented. These schemes often reflect offense seriousness, such as the violent/property distinction. If offenders are classified according to these particular criteria, we might make inferences about their relative dangerousness. Violent offenses include homicide, rape, aggravated assault, and robbery (involving possible injury or death to others), while property offenses include larceny, burglary, and vehicular theft (involving contact with the property of others rather than victims themselves). Therefore, "violent" offenders are, per se, more dangerous than "property" offenders. One direct result of developing classification schemes is to categorize offenders according to their dangerousness or risk to others.

Measures of dangerousness and risk are pervasive throughout the criminal justice systems of all U.S. jurisdictions. This chapter will examine the development of such instruments as well as describe the rationale for their creation and application. Perfect classification schemes and assessments of dangerousness and risk have yet to be devised, however. All of these instruments are flawed in one or more respects. Notions of perfection and "flaws" are based upon the ability of any instrument to make behavioral forecasts or predictions. While our measures are imperfect, some of our measures are better predictors than others. Thus, we will examine some of the important criteria which determine an instrument's predictive utility. A brief overview of methodological problems associated with instrument development will be presented. The chapter will conclude by considering the general question, "Can dangerousness and risk really be predicted?" Since most jurisdictions use various instruments to predict or forecast offender dangerousness and risk anyway, it seems safe to assume that some predictive utility is being realized through such applications. However, all measures are applied with varying margins of error. We will examine these margins of error and investigate whether any consistent standards of predictive acceptability are prevalent.

CLASSIFICATION: ITS IMPORTANCE AND FUNCTIONS

The Importance of Classification

Classification is of fundamental importance in the criminal and juvenile justice systems. In a technical sense, classification is used by law enforcement officers informally during their routine patrolling and decision-making activities. Their discretion when making arrests, conducting investigations, or simply patrolling city streets involves either conscious (manifest) or unconscious (latent) classifications of events and persons who are a part of these events. Whether to use weapons or verbal commands, whether to arrest or not arrest, whether to stop certain persons and ask them questions or simply pass by these same persons—each of these choices is influenced by crude and informal mental agendas based upon one's past experiences. An officer's interpretation of events or the conduct of particular persons is catalogued and classified one way or another (Morris and Miller, 1987). One interpretation or classification of the event will trigger actions by officers that would not necessarily be triggered or activated by alternative interpretations or classifications of events. This book is not about how police officers classify events or offenders, however.

Police Discretion, Booking, and Bail Decision Making. At other stages of the criminal justice system, decisions are made about different arrestees. During the booking process, for instance, decisions are made about the seriousness of offenses alleged. A judge or magistrate will decide to set a bail bond, release offenders on their own recognizance, or deny bail, depending upon the facts of each situation (Goldkamp, 1987). In a sense, these judicial officials classify those brought before them and decide the best course of action. In at least thirty-one states, laws exist for the pretrial detention of criminal defendants on the basis of the defendant's *perceived dangerousness* (Gottlieb and Rosen, 1984; Toborg, 1984). Again, this book is not about booking offenders or deciding whether to grant them bail or release them on their own recognizance.

Prosecutorial Decision Making. Similarly, prosecutors will be presented with various cases. They must decide whether to prosecute or decline prosecution. Again, informal classifications of offenders are made and prioritized. In those jurisdictions with especially high caseloads and crowded court dockets, it is unlikely that prosecutors will proceed against less serious or petty offenders. Rather, they may reserve their prosecutorial time for only the most serious offenders. Among those types of offenders who are more likely to be prosecuted are chronic recidivists and career criminals (Chaiken and Chaiken, 1987). Judges may be able to impose small fines and suspended sentences for those who have committed minor infractions. However, this book is not about prosecutorial decision making and case prioritizing.

Classifying Convicted or Adjudicated Offenders. Classification *is* particularly important, however, after offenders have been convicted of crimes or juveniles have been adjudicated delinquent (Fagan and Guggenheim, 1990; Maier, 1989; Towberman, 1992). In those cases requiring a judicial sentencing decision to incarcerate offenders or place them under some form of supervised probation or release, assessments are usually made which purportedly indicate the likelihood of their success if they are involved in one of several nonincarcerative sentencing options (Blackmore and Welsh, 1983; Campbell, McCoy, and Osigweh, 1990; Michigan Department of Management and Budget, 1986; von Hirsch, 1984; Wright, Clear, and Dickson, 1984). If offenders are sentenced to incarceration, those responsible for managing them while in custody must classify them as well (Craddock, 1987; Johnson, Simmons, and Gordon, 1983; Megargee and Carbonell, 1985; Morris, 1984; Wright, 1986b).

Inmate Classification and Management. Some offenders may require relatively little supervision, while other offenders must be confined in isolated cells and monitored closely (Apao, Haugh, and Meyer, 1988). For instance, the suicide potential among some inmates is greater than it is for others (Sperbeck and Parlour, 1986). Some inmates suffer from different types of mental illnesses and must be managed and treated differently (Danto, 1985; Mande and Covey, 1982; Morris, 1984). Other inmates may be considered violence-prone, potential escapees, and/or likely to present excessive disciplinary problems (Baird and Austin, 1986). Such decisions are influenced by various classification schemes developed by prison or correctional staffs.

Periodic Reassessments of Inmates. During the period of one's confinement, reassessments and further classifications are made periodically, since often, inmate behavior or conduct changes over time. It may be, for instance, that particular inmates who were initially classified as dangerous and placed in maximum-security prison areas are subsequently less dangerous or not dangerous at all (Brennan, 1987a). Thus, it might be safe to change their level of custody to medium-security or minimum-security status. Reclassification is done, therefore, as a means of rethinking one's original placement and deciding whether it should be continued (Bench, 1990; Hart, 1990; Wright, 1988).

Early-Release Decision Making and Parole. Under certain types of sentencing schemes, such as indeterminate sentencing, many prison inmates eventually qualify for consideration for early release or parole. Paroling authorities, such as parole boards, interview prospective parolee-applicants and decide whether to grant them early release (Baird et al., 1987; Gottfredson and Tonry, 1987). Much parole board decision making involves the use of classification schemes and assessments of their likelihood of success "on the outside," as parolees among other community residents (Wilbanks, 1985).

The Relevance of Classification for Both Adults and Juveniles. While much of this discussion focuses upon adult criminals, it is also quite relevant for many juvenile offenders who are processed by the juvenile justice system. It is well known that juvenile court judges consider the incarceration of juveniles as the "last resort" punishment or sentence (Champion, 1992:chs. 12–13). Yet annually, many juveniles are considered for secure confinement, and classification schemes are devised to assist juvenile courts in making these difficult placement decisions (Dembo et al., 1990; Feazell, Quay, and Murray, 1991). Those juveniles with drug or alcohol dependencies, or who have close gang affiliations, or who have histories as chronic recidivists, will be classified differently from those without drug/alcohol dependencies, no gang affiliations, or who are first offenders (Dembo et al., 1990). Offense seriousness is measurable as well, and it becomes an integral part of any classification scheme used by system officials (Van Vleet and Butts, 1990).

The Functions of Classification

An extensive review of the classification literature has disclosed its following functions:

1. Classification systems enable authorities to make decisions about appropriate offender program placements. In the most general sense, those charged with offenses, whether they are adult or juvenile offenders, are considered for various types of programs, depending upon their availability among jurisdictions. Thus, defense attorneys may be able to convince prosecutors that their clients deserve diversion rather than a full-fledged prosecution. Among those considered least dangerous and potentially eligible for diversion consideration are shoplifters (Royse and Buck, 1991). Between May 1986 and May 1988, a diversion program at the county level was operated for first-offender shoplifters. Although the sample sizes were not large (e.g., there were ninety-nine program participants, forty-two program dropouts, twenty-four shoplifters not admitted to the program, and eighty-seven persons arrested prior to the program's commencement), results of the study showed that those who did not complete or participate in the program had rearrest rates which were six times higher than those of program participants (Royse and Buck, 1991). Royse and Buck found that prior offenders were considered "poor risks" and were excluded from program participation. Furthermore, participants in the program were interviewed afterwards and regarded the program as personally beneficial, largely because of the nonthreatening atmosphere and therapeutic value of permitting each shoplifter to identify his or her irrational behavior and its sources.

Alternative dispute resolution is an increasingly popular option to prosecuting offenders. Alternative dispute resolution (ADR) is not an attempt to circumvent justice, but rather, it is considered a way of mediating minor law infractions involving property loss or compensation for physical injuries. In 1985, for instance, 43 counties in New York used ADR in 56,000 cases (New York State Unified Court System, 1985). Three-fourths of all cases were referrals to community dispute resolution centers by the courts. Law enforcement and district attorneys were other chief referral sources. The average time lapse between the incident and the ADR was about two weeks, and individual ADR sessions were completed in less than two hours. About 90 percent of all cases were successfully mediated through this program. This means that while all of these offenders could have been subject to criminal prosecutions, 50,400 persons had their cases resolved by civil procedures rather than criminal procedures.

Classification is useful for deciding whether to place certain offenders in an electronic monitoring program or home incarceration. In Virginia, for example, 374 participants in six different electronic monitoring programs were examined. In a follow-up of these participants, it was found that only two participants who completed the program exhibited any recidivism (Kuplinski, 1990). It should be noted, however, that those selected for participation were carefully selected and programs were effectively staffed. Kuplinski (1990) reports that although some of these offenders had relatively short prior criminal records or were major traffic violators (DWIs, DUIs, reckless driving), many participants were felony offenders. Over 90 percent of the participants completed the program successfully. The average length of time most offenders spent on electronic monitoring was about one month. Thus, jail and prison populations were substantially reduced as well as accompanying costs of incarceration, without compromising public safety (Kuplinski, 1990).

Some scholars believe that electronic monitoring is more successful as a rehabilitative or crime control medium if accompanied by one or more other programs, such as home confinement, victim compensation, or community service (Holman and Quinn, 1992). Regarding applications of electronic monitoring for juvenile offenders, other investigators agree that such monitoring should be used in tandem with other programs as well (Wood and Brown, 1989). In any case, various authorities and researchers recommend careful screening and selection of candidates for such programs in terms of both their logical and their likely therapeutic and/or rehabilitative value (Florida Department of Corrections, 1986; Hurwitz, 1987).

While incarcerated, many inmates who are eligible enroll in vocational or educational programs. While many inmates have diverse motives for such participation (e.g., some may believe that if they participate in such programs, parole boards will regard their prison record more favorably and be more inclined to grant them early release through parole), at least some research shows positive results from such participation. For instance, Schumacker, Anderson, and Anderson (1990) compared four groups of adult prison releasees from nineteen correctional institutions in a large midwestern state for 1986: 118 inmates enrolled in vocational work with some academic coursework; 107 inmates enrolled in vocational work only; 248 inmates were enrolled in academic programs only; and 287 inmates were not enrolled in any program (the control group). Compared with the control group, the program participants had a significantly lower rate of criminal activity. Not every inmate is eligible for such program participation, however. Prison officials classify inmates to determine whether they qualify, and the eligibility criteria vary among prison staffs in any jurisdiction. Furthermore, mere participation in such programs is no guarantee of no future recidivism. Nevertheless, certain positive results of classification have been realized, at least in some investigations.

Work release and furloughs are also programs for which inmates may be eligible. With some exceptions, furloughs and work release are reserved for those inmates who have less than one year to serve before their release dates. Thus, these programs are viewed as reintegrative, meaning that inmates, who have been subject to a heavy degree of regimentation while incarcerated, will have an opportunity to ease back into community living more smoothly. Work release permits some inmates to leave their prisons and perform services or particular jobs on weekends. However, they must return to prison following their work. Those who are granted furloughs may visit their families, again probably on weekends. These permit both families of inmates and inmates themselves to become accustomed to life "on the outside." Again, classification is used to determine program eligibility.

Investigators have mixed opinions about the effectiveness of both furloughs and work release as either reintegrative or rehabilitative. In Virginia, where some of the strictest eligibility criteria prevail, researchers found that in 1982, for instance, only 15 percent of the total confined felon population would meet the prevailing eligibility standard (Jones, 1982). Modestly successful results were reported (Jones, 1982). In Rochester, New York, 365 work releasees were studied from 1979 to 1982 (MacDonald and Bala, 1983). Over the duration of the work release program, seventy-four participants were dropped from the program because of one or more program violations. When all offenders were subsequently paroled or otherwise discharged from their facilities, the work release group had a recidivism rate of only 16 percent, about half that of the unsatisfactory group of seventy-four inmates who failed to complete the program successfully (MacDonald and Bala, 1983).

Furlough programs in most states and the Federal Bureau of Prisons have also been investigated. In twenty-nine state jurisdictions, for instance, the absconding rate during the first half of 1988 was less than 1 percent, based upon a total of 67,736 furloughs granted (Smith and Sabatino, 1990). Most states reported positive results from involving inmates in furlough programs. A furlough program operated by the Oahu Community Correctional Center, Corrections Division, Department of Social Services and Housing, reported a 68 percent success rate among furloughees between 1977 and 1983 (Uriell, 1984). Again, strict eligibility criteria were imposed, and not everyone was permitted into the program during the study duration. While some scholars have termed such classification as *creaming,* or selecting only the best inmates who are least likely to recidivate for program participation, there is little question that for a majority of those who participate, there are obvious long-range benefits. However, critics contend that there are too few studies of high-risk offenders who might otherwise become involved in such programs and benefit from them.

2. *Classification systems help to identify one's needs and the provision of effective services in specialized treatment programs.* Not all classification is conducted for the purpose of determining program placements or level of risk relative to others. Many persons who are charged with offenses may suffer from mental disorders or mental illness. Such illnesses may not be detected in the early stages of criminal processing, through prosecution, trial, and sentencing (Steury, 1991). There are at least three categories of inmates who create special management problems for correctional administrators: *the vulnerable* (those frequently found in protective custody); *the troublemakers* (those often found in administrative segregation or disciplinary detention); and *the mentally abnormal* (the mentally ill and retarded) (McGee, Warner, and Harlow, 1985).

An unknown number of mentally disordered defendants enter guilty pleas unknowingly in plea bargaining and are hopelessly misclassified and misplaced in jails and prisons throughout most states. Some evidence suggests that increasing importance is being given to developing classification mechanisms, even in small jail systems, where mental illness problems have historically been neglected (Brennan and Wells, 1992:48–50). Small jails, for instance, have typically defended their nonuse of classification schemes, simply because their small sizes and chronic overcrowding have seemingly rendered classification as "irrelevant" (p. 50). An observation from a 1970 Rhode Island court case is worth noting: "Classification is essential to the operation of an orderly and safe prison. It is a prerequisite for the rational allocation of whatever program opportunities exist within the institution. It enables the institution to gauge the proper custody level of an inmate, *to identify the inmate's education, vocational, and psychological needs, and to separate nonviolent inmates from the more predatory.* Classification is also indispensable for any coherent future planning" (Brennan and Wells, 1992:50–51). [Italics mine]

Various types of sex offenders may require different treatment services as well (Gordon and Porporino, 1991). For example, in Canada, the Correctional Service commenced a program in the mid-1970s geared to develop specialized treatment programs for sex offenders. Gordon and Porporino (1991:162) note that "although varying in approach and duration, each program targets particular risk factors such as low self-esteem, poor communication and social skills, unhealthy attitudes toward sexuality and women, and deviant sexual arousal patterns." Thus, these researchers suggest that all sex offenders require some form of treatment, but not all offenders necessarily need treatment of the same type (p. 162). They differentiate between rapists, pedophiles, and incest offenders among those targeted by the Canadian programs described. Other treatment programs have been identified in various U.S. jurisdictions. For instance, the Center for Behavioral Intervention in Portland, Oregon, offers a comprehensive outpatient assessment and treatment for sex offenders (Fillmore and Jewell, 1987). Court referrals are subjected to individualized therapy programs based upon psychological and behavior learning theory. In some jurisdictions, violent sex offenders are targeted and treated with a combination of group-individual therapy and major tranquilizers to suppress their sex drives (Abel, Becker, and Skinner, 1987).

3. Classification assists in determining offender custody level if confined in either prison or jail. A clear priority and objective of classification is placing inmates in an appropriate level of custody, according to their degree of dangerousness or risk toward others, even toward themselves. Inappropriate placements mean placing certain, less serious inmates in jail or prison space which should be occupied by other, more serious inmates. The higher the level of custody, the more costly the custody. For example, if we were to place numerous low-risk offenders in maximum-security space, this would be incredibly expensive for any jurisdiction. Texas is a case in point. Ann W. Richards, governor of Texas in 1992, has indicated that we must "make sure that the right people are occupying prison cells. . . . We must use the prisons to keep violent criminals off the street. . . . We must lock away the people who have no regard for the life or safety of other human beings" (Richards, 1992:13). Richards is especially sensitive to this issue, since Texas has a backlog of prison-bound offenders larger than the total prison populations of thirty-six states. Thus, Texas, like many other jurisdictions, has had to undertake a massive prison construction program which, unfortunately, will never catch up with current and projected backlogs. Strategic management of scarce prison space resources may alleviate this allocation problem to some extent, but such strategic management must be preceded by effective inmate classification. Appropriate inmate placement is a key prison governance issue among correctional professionals (DiIulio, 1987).

The development of effective inmate classification tools has been given considerable priority and significance in recent years. Entire issues of professional journals have been devoted to prisoner classification schemes and models (Posey, 1988). Many jurisdictions are currently modifying their existing classification schemes. For instance, the Colorado Department of Corrections has implemented extensive changes and revisions in its inmate classification policies and procedures. Prompting such policy changes has been the general problem of *overclassification,* where many prisoners are assigned to a higher security level than they actually require. In recent years, the Colorado Department of Corrections has implemented policies which have decreased greatly the number of offenders classified as "maximum-security" offenders, while the proportion of medium-security offenders has increased (Colorado Division of Criminal Justice, 1986).

Both larger and smaller jails are also affected by space limitations and availability for separating more dangerous inmates from less dangerous ones. Studies of small samples of jails in selected jurisdictions show that a key problem is inadequate space for the classification of prisoners (Jenson, 1984; Kalinich and Klofas, 1986). Some states, such as Michigan, have implemented innovative jail classification programs such as the Jail Inmate Classification System (JICS) (Wells and Brennan, 1992). Commenced in 1981, the JICS was subjected to tests in various pilot projects over the next eight years. By 1989, two fully automated versions of the JICS were developed, and by 1990, sixteen Michigan jails had adopted JICS (Wells and Brennan, 1992:61). Based upon a decision-tree methodology, JICS has demonstrated the utility of using standardized classification measures for inmates in both large and small jail facilities. By 1992, steps were being taken to create a statewide reporting system which would be capable of monitoring trends and patterns of all state jail space utilization (Wells and Brennan, 1992:61). Therefore, classification has proved fruitful for more effective inmate management and information exchanges among Michigan county and city jurisdictions. It is difficult to apply such standardized classification measures interchangeably between jail and prison populations, however (Brennan, 1987b).

4. Classification helps to adjust offender custody level during confinement, considering behavioral improvement and evidence of rehabilitation. Once offenders have been classified and placed in one security level or another, in either a jail or a prison, it is likely that many inmates will modify their behavior over time such that their original custody level might be changed (Johnson, Simmons, and Gordon, 1983). As we will see in subsequent chapters, many state jurisdictions to be examined here have incorporated into their planning and inmate management operations various reassessments and reclassifications of their inmate populations at designated intervals (Baird and Austin, 1986; Buchanan, 1986; Rocheleau, 1986; Wright, 1986b). Reclassifications of offenders enable prisons and jails to reallocate scarce space more effectively (Bench, 1990). Furthermore, such reassessments often prove valuable as indicators of behavioral change or prison adjustment which may necessitate a change in offenders' security classifications (Robins et al., 1986).

Interestingly, in some jurisdictions, the use of reclassification schemes has been closely associated with the social control of inmate behaviors (Craddock, 1987). In North Carolina prisons, for instance, *custody promotions,* or transfers of prisoners from medium to minimum security, were considered positive sanctions or rewards for "encouraged behavior," while *custody nonpromotions or de-*

motions were closely associated with "prohibited behaviors" and used as negative sanctions or punishments. Thus, social control considerations appeared more significantly related to classification and reclassification compared with extralegal, legal, and organizational management factors (Craddock, 1987). In many instances, jurisdictions have gravitated toward greater use of minimum-security areas for inmates as opposed to medium- or maximum-security areas, simply because of reduced costs rather than for any rehabilitative benefit (Austin, 1983).

5. While confined, inmates may be targeted for particular services and/or programs to meet their needs. Some inmates experience more adjustment problems compared with other inmates. Attempts to identify and track those inmates most likely to pose serious adjustment problems have been modestly successful (Wright, 1988). A survey of corrections directors in all states and the Federal Bureau of Prisons, together with opinions obtained from fifty-three criminal justice scholars, has indicated strong nationwide support for at least three types of shared or concurrently operated prison facilities: (1) a medical/psychiatric facility that would be capable of handling the aged or developmentally disabled; (2) a high-security facility for inmates who are assaultive and/or high escape risks; and (3) a protective custody facility for certain inmates (Lawson, 1984). Some persons may require physical separation from other inmates. Former law enforcement officers convicted of crimes or witnesses who have testified against organized-crime figures in exchange for lesser sentences may be less at risk if confined separately from other prisoners who might otherwise endanger them.

Growing numbers of physically handicapped or disabled offenders are entering jails and prisons annually. These offenders create special problems for correctional staff, because extraordinary provisions must often be made to provide for their care, custody, and control (Tiberia, 1992:31). Collectively classified as inmates with *developmental disabilities* (DD), these prisoners don't necessarily respond to correctional officers in "normal" ways, compared with inmates who do not have such disabilities. DDs suffer from mild to severe mental retardation, exhibit learning disabilities, have emotional disorders, and/or are physically limited in their ability to perform certain duties. Developmentally disabled prisoners may require specially constructed pathways from one prison area to another. Not all prisons currently are equipped with the latest state-of-the-art designs to accommodate physically impaired prisoners. In order to meet the needs of DDs more effectively, jurisdictions such as the New York State Commission on Correction have implemented a training program known as ECHO, or *Effectively Communicating with Handicapped Offenders* (Tiberia, 1992:34). This program enables correctional staff to more easily identify those with DDs and trains officers to deal with them differently and more constructively.

6. Classification may be used for offender management and deterrence relative to program or prison rules and requirements. One reason some inmates receive a maximum-security classification initially is because they have evidenced few coping skills with others. They may be violence-prone or easily moved toward aggressive acts against others. Some prisons have attempted to change such violent behavior patterns by creating programs designed to improve inmates' anger management skills. A study was conducted in 1989 of forty-three convicted murderers who were psychologically assessed as having poor anger management abilities (Napolitano and Brown, 1991). The California Men's Colony, a medium-security correctional facility, was the site of the study, where these inmates were subjected to an anger management program consisting of four stages over a twelve-week period. Training program coordinators noted that in Stage I, these inmates were initially apathetic and extremely negative upon confrontation. In Stage II, from the third to the sixth week, emerging interest in group process and content was observed, and inmates increasingly participated in the program and asked more questions. During Stage III, which lasted until the ninth week, prisoners tended to rebel against the new anger management strategies and attempted to defend their old behavior patterns and coping mechanisms. Napolitano and Brown note that during this stage, inmate participation and unity peaked, and the sessions were characterized by greater argumentativeness and debate. Finally, in Stage IV, inmates began to accept and actually practice the new anger management behaviors they had learned.

This study is significant, in part, because it shows how prison staff interventions might be useful in changing inmate interpersonal conduct. However, not all prisons are equipped or staffed with those skilled in changing inmate behaviors through programs such as anger management. Classification may be used to strategically separate the most disruptive inmates from others, or to arrange combinations of inmates who get along best through *Unit Management.* Unit Management has been used as a means of controlling violence in prisons such as the maximum-security prison, the Massachusetts Correctional Institution, Cedar Junction (MCICJ) (formerly known as Walpole State Prison) (Farmer, 1988:41).

Characterized by a history of inmate violence and a low degree of administrative control, MCICJ was a facility in need of reorganization and new administration. With the cooperation of the Federal Bureau of Prisons, which operated a facility in Oxford, Wisconsin, MCICJ staff identified key inmate leaders and transferred them to the Wisconsin federal facility prior to a planned prison riot including a "hit" list of key prison staff and correctional officers. The riot was abated, but authorities wanted to preserve their current level of control over prison inmates. One mechanism administrators used was to "threaten" inmates with a transfer to Oxford, Wisconsin, which was notorious for its extensive use of solitary confinement and lack of inmate amenities. Another more positive step was to institute Unit Management, which consisted of grouping inmates in 50–100 inmate groups. Each group was assigned a unit manager, secretary, correctional counselor, caseworker, educator, psychologist, and a health worker. Using some standardized policies and procedures, these Unit Management teams had disciplinary, classification, and programmatic authority over their respective inmate groups (Farmer, 1988:45). Prisoners were also classified and separated from one another according to *Quay,* a system of classification using personality factors and degree of aggressiveness as key determinants of how inmates should be grouped. While not all violence was eliminated, the level of violence in that facility was substantially decreased as a result (Farmer, 1988:46).

A similar effort has been reported by Leeke and Mohn (1986). The South Carolina Department of Corrections began using the Adult Inmate Management System (AIMS) in 1984 as one result of a court order to develop a better internal classification procedure within all state facilities. South Carolina prison officials eventually adopted a procedure which separated prisoners into three psychological/behavioral basic aggressiveness groupings, including the alphas, betas, and gammas. Prisoners were separated during evening hours according to their classification, with the result of an 18 percent reduction in the level of prisoner violence (Leeke and Mohn, 1986). Interestingly, Leeke and Mohn note that although 70 percent of the prisoners at the main state facility have violent offense records, the prison has the lowest protective custody population in the state. These researchers attribute much of the success of AIMS to the fact that it makes security and human service staff more accessible to inmates and greater inmate participation occurs. The origins of AIMS will be discussed later in this chapter.

Another approach to inmate control and management is to offer prisoners incentives for participating in vocational and educational programs. In most penal institutions, participation in educational programs of any kind is considered favorable behavior by administrative staff and paroling authorities. Thus, it is conceivable that if inmates know they stand a better chance of being paroled if they participate in available educational programs, at least two goals are being realized. These goals are greater inmate conformity to prison rules and increased inmate educational level and subsequent employability. Obviously, some inmates enroll in these educational programs to present a more favorable image to those in control. However, various researchers report that many inmates regard their educational experiences as personally beneficial and valuable, and believe that their lives will improve after release (Stephens, 1992).

Not all inmates wishing to enroll in various vocational/educational programs may qualify, however. And for those who qualify and enroll in such programs, there are no guarantees that all successful participants will be successful when released. For instance, a study of 526 offenders in three Wisconsin prisons during the period 1980–1985 showed mixed results for those enrolled in vocational, secondary, and elementary programs (Knepper, 1989). For instance, when offender backgrounds were controlled according to age, race, gender, previous incarcerations, prior convictions, and type of offense, program enrollees subsequently exhibited fewer adjustment problems and lower needs assessment scores compared with other releasees who did not participate in these educational programs. However, the program enrollees had slightly higher rates of recidivism compared with nonparticipants (Knepper, 1989).

In some instances, education is mandatory for all inmates. In 1991, for instance, only thirteen states had mandatory education requirements for their correctional institutions (Di Vito, 1991). Usually, those prisoners who do not meet specific, minimal educational criteria must attend educational classes for a designated period. After this compulsory period, their education may be continued, but only on a voluntary basis. In an effort to encourage these offenders to continue their education while imprisoned, authorities make it clear that their sentence lengths will be reduced if their educational level improves (Di Vito, 1991). Although some prisoners have challenged the legality of such compulsory education in these institutions, the results for a majority of inmate participants have been largely favorable. Other studies concur with Di Vito's findings. Oberst (1988) has found, for example, that Virginia's "No Read, No Release" incentive-based program has had a significant impact on prisoner conduct. Virginia authorities offer designated less-educated inmates the chance to improve their literacy achievement to no lower than the sixth-grade level. This achievement, if realized, is considered significant at the time of parole consideration. Inmates understand the nature of this incentive and it seems to work (Oberst, 1988).

7. Classification schemes are useful for policy decision making and administrative planning relevant for jail and prison construction, the nature and number of facilities required, and the types of services to be made available within such facilities. Knowing the types of offenders to be housed or accommodated and whether sufficient facilities exist for their particular needs is an important consideration for any planning body in any jurisdiction. Admissions of large numbers of alcohol-dependent or drug-dependent inmates to jails or prisons for either short- or long-term stays, or admitting those with neuroses or psychoses creates potential managerial and order-maintenance problems for the staffs of these institutions. Prisoners with problems are likely to become disruptive and unruly, perhaps injuring themselves or others by their behaviors.

Many jurisdictions, such as the New York City correctional system, screen new inmate admissions by subjecting them to different types of questions in interviews. Such screenings disclose the prevalence of mental illness among a large proportion of admittees. For example, samples of 299 males processed at the Manhattan House of Detention in the winter of 1988, 236 males admitted to the same facility in May 1989, and 151 males admitted to the Montefiore-Rikers Island methadone detoxification program in July 1990 showed that from one-fourth to one-third of all admissions suffered from some form of mental illness (Michaels et al., 1992). Many of these admittees were homeless, and homelessness itself was correlated highly with one type of mental disorder or another. These researchers recommended that mental health policy improvements be made in the following areas: improving the treatment of the disordered when they are in crisis; improving jail identification of and response to mentally disordered detainees, and developing community treatment facilities as alternatives to prison confinement to better serve the needs of mentally ill offenders (Michaels et al., 1992).

One of several facilities designed to treat mental disorders is the Patuxent Institution in Maryland (McDonald et al., 1990). This facility serves both intellectually and emotionally impaired offenders. While the effects of such facilities and treatment on offender recidivism are negligible, the manifest intent of such facilities is to provide alternative care for those with special problems. In short, the issue is whether these sorts of persons ought to be imprisoned or institutionalized in more clinical settings, where specialized treatments are more likely to be provided (McDonald et al.,1990).

8. Classification systems enable parole boards to make better early-release decisions about eligible offenders. The frequently used Minnesota Multiphasic Personality Inventory (MMPI) has assisted parole boards and other decision-making bodies in targeting the most eligible inmates for programs such as work release (Kalichman, 1988). The MMPI has also been used to differentiate between inmates who are more likely to engage in disruptive aggressive behaviors and those who are nonaggressive but make use of excessive sick calls (Wright, 1988). Although more than a few scholars caution that prediction instruments are flawed in various respects and should be used in tandem with other types of assessments, such as clinical examinations and prior records of inmate behavior (Brennan, 1987a; Monahan, 1984; Sechrest, 1987), it is likely that widespread use of such instruments and assessments will continue, if for no other reason than that they provide the bases for objective decision making in contrast with subjective and potentially biased judgments and assessments (Glaser, 1987). A particularly interesting view is expressed by Wilkins (1985), who suggests that because decisions must be made about offenders at many stages of criminal justice processing, the uncertainty inherent in prediction measures need not be disabling, particularly if we convert such uncertainty into probability. Therefore, we would gauge inmates' potential for success in program completion (e.g., work release, furloughs, halfway house residency) probabilistically, making allowances for prediction error and the failure of our schemes and classification models to detect false negatives perfectly.

Studies of the pragmatic utility of various prediction methods associated with parole risk assessment indicate many similarities in the quality of prediction when more complex measures are contrasted with simpler measures (Gottfredson and Gottfredson, 1985). Some researchers advocate the use of mathematical models or computer-simulated predictions of parolee risk, particularly in an area where improvements in the predictive utility of instruments continue to be made (Bonham, 1984; Farrington and Tarling, 1985; Wilbanks, 1985). There is evidence that presently, several valid risk assessment instruments exist for use by state parole boards. The Oregon Parole Board, for example, revised its risk assessment instrument during the mid-1980s. Based upon risk scores, various ex-inmates were tracked according to whether they had previously been identified as "excellent" or "poor" risks (Baird et al., 1987). On the basis of nearly 1,400 cases during 1984, the predictive capabilities of the new instrument were evidenced to be reliable. In fact, larger numbers of inmates classified under new scaling procedures would be regarded as "excellent" risks rather than "poor" risks. The ability of the new measures to differentiate between various classes of offenders was particularly good, especially when "success" rates (measured by subsequent recidivism of parolees) of different offender groupings were compared. Caution should be exercised, according to some authorities, when generalizing findings from one state department of corrections to other corrections departments (Wright, Clear, and Dickson, 1984). It is not always the case that prediction measures which are useful in one state will be particularly useful in other states.

Although the U.S. Parole Commission has changed the nature of federal parole into alternative forms of supervised release programs, predictive devices such as the Salient Factor Score 81 (SFS 81) have been used in the past with favorable results (Hoffman, 1983). Most jurisdictions have various screening criteria in place, however, in order to separate predictably more successful program participants from less successful ones. For instance, New Jersey has a screening board which carefully selects certain inmates for participation in an intensive parole supervision program (Talty, 1985). Similarly, the Texas Department of Criminal Justice, Pardons and Parole Division, has a Pre-Parole Transfer (PPT) program which admits predictably low-risk offenders for halfway house program participation (Eisenberg, 1990). Before certain inmates are released to halfway houses, they participate in PPT, which is an intermediate program designed to help them learn to readjust to community living. Research results suggest that PPT participants exhibit significantly lower rates of recidivism compared with non-PPT inmates who are transferred directly to halfway houses (Eisenberg, 1990).

9. Community corrections agencies can utilize classification schemes to determine those parolees who qualify for participation and those who don't qualify. A broad range of programs have been classified as *community corrections* primarily because offenders either remain in their communities or are reintegrated into their communities depending upon their probation or parole status. Community corrections programs are often community-operated and provide a variety of services for participating offenders. These services may include individual or group counseling, job placement assistance, temporary living quarters, and other amenities. Parolees are normally obligated to comply with several program conditions, such as curfew, avoidance of wrongdoing, avoidance of drugs and alcohol, and maintenance of employment.

Space availability in many community corrections programs is limited, and therefore, classification is once again used to determine participant eligibility. A basic objective of virtually all community corrections programs is offender supervision and/or control, especially where high-risk offenders are paroled (Clear and O'Leary, 1983). In recent years, many community corrections programs have escalated the degree of offender accountability required of program participants (Benekos, 1990). Thus, citizen anxieties have been reduced somewhat as greater offender control mechanisms have been implemented. Currently, many scholars regard community corrections as sufficiently punitive and functional as an alternative to incarceration.

Community corrections programs are not necessarily for all types of offenders, however. Some convicted offenders do not seem amenable to any type of rehabilitation or intervention strategy. Many scholars believe that it is possible to distinguish between those offenders who are amenable to rehabilitation and those who are not (Armor et al., 1989). For example, two samples of Alabama prisoners in the work release unit of the Hamilton Correctional Facility were compared. One group was comprised of those who volunteered for group counseling or some other rehabilitative program, while the other group consisted of nonvolunteers. Using discriminant function analysis, significant differences were identified between the two inmate groups, and it was concluded that it is possible to forecast offender amenability to rehabilitation (Armor et al., 1989). Similar forecasts have been made successfully with large numbers of prison inmates regarding their chronicity of offending behavior (Decker and Salert, 1986).

It should be noted that simple program participation by itself is no guarantee that parolees and others will refrain from committing new offenses when released. Often, intensive supervision is required for many of these offenders for a period following their release. Requiring inmates to comply with various parole conditions enables them to practice conforming behaviors in their communities and improve their own chances for success in "going straight."

10. Classification systems enable assessments of risk and dangerousness to be made generally in anticipation of the type of supervision best suited for particular offenders. A direct benefit of classification is that it enables authorities at all stages of the criminal and juvenile justice systems to assess clients in terms of their risk or dangerousness. Because a more extensive discussion of this classification function is presented in a subsequent section of this chapter, it is sufficient for the present to note that ordinarily, the level of supervision or monitoring required for different types of offenders may be determined by evaluating their future risk or dangerousness to others. Those who present greater risks and are considered more dangerous to the public and/or themselves are supervised more closely than others.

Child sexual abuse and molestation is currently receiving much media attention, and known child sexual abusers are often closely monitored when released from custody. Because not all child sexual abusers are alike and behave in identical ways, a common supervisory model might be inappropriate or inapplicable to the broad class of these offenders. Various risk assessment devices have been created to anticipate whether some convicted child sexual abusers are more inclined to reoffend than others. Efforts by researchers to devise valid and reliable risk assessment instruments for such offenders have been modestly successful, and differential supervision of these types of criminals appears warranted on the basis of the predictive utility of these scaling devices (Prentky, 1990).

11. Classification schemes assist in decision making relevant for community crime control, the nature of penalties to be imposed, and the determination of punishment. For those offenders who are released short of serving their full prison or jail sentences, and for those who are placed on probation within their communities, it is considered important to match each with an appropriate set of conditions as a part of his or her overall parole or probation program. Those offenders with prior histories of drug or alcohol dependencies may be required to submit to random drug testing by paroling or other authorities at any time. Curfews might be imposed, as well as restitution, community service, victim compensation, home confinement, and/or electronic monitoring. These conditions of probation or parole are considered a part or a continuation of the punishment process.

Former gang members may require frequent face-to-face visits and monitoring by parole or probation officers for the duration of their sentences. Gainful employment and/or school attendance may be mandatory program components as well. In effect, classification schemes enable authorities to tailor each program to match offender needs and behavioral requirements.

12. Classification may enable authorities to determine whether selective incapacitation is desirable for particular offenders or offender groupings. A highly controversial approach to crime control is *selective incapacitation* (Decker and Salert, 1986; Gottfredson and Tonry, 1987; Gottlieb and Rosen, 1984; Monahan, 1984; Tonry, 1987). Selective incapacitation means to incarcerate or incapacitate certain offenders on the basis of their likelihood of reoffending. Those considered less likely to reoffend are conditionally released into various community programs or unconditionally released back into their communities. Among selective incapacitation's critics are Morris and Miller (1985) and von Hirsch (1985), who argue that the present predictive utility of our dangerousness instruments and risk scales simply does not justify punishing offenders for crimes they have not, as yet, committed. Thus, greater interest seems to be controlling undesirables, while the condemnatory features of punishment are downplayed and little interest is exhibited in offenders as persons. Thus, there is a propensity among officials to overpenalize certain offenders and subject them to undeserved punishment.

Conrad (1985) concurs with these views and suggests that, subject to some leeway for mitigation or aggravation, felons who commit the same crimes and have the same records of recidivism should be treated alike. Morris (1984) observes that no punishment should be imposed, nor the term of punishment extended, by virtue of a prediction of dangerousness, beyond that which would be justified as a deserved punishment independently of that prediction.

One positive measure used to guard against arbitrary and potentially unfair and disparate sentencing practices is the creation of sentencing guidelines. Guidelines-based sentencing schemes are aimed at reducing the subjectivity inherent in indeterminate sentencing among criminal court judges and creating more equitable treatment for those with similar criminal histories who have been convicted of similar offenses, regardless of race, gender, or socioeconomic status. However, despite the fairness intended by such guidelines sentencing schemes, some room for judicial discretion in sentencing remains. Therefore, sentencing disparities are not entirely eliminated by any particular sentencing method we have created thus far.

As related to classification, selective incapacitation may lead to unfairness for many offenders. Further, improper applications of classification may inadvertently increase public risk. For example, some offenders may be classified as being more likely to reoffend than other offenders. Whatever assessments are made of them, they are believed to pose a definite threat to society by indicators which stress the high likelihood of their reoffending potential. However, some of these targeted offenders who are considered dangerous or highly likely to recidivate and are given longer sentences or denied early release may, in fact, never reoffend. These are *false positives* and are unfairly penalized because of their suspected criminal propensities. There are also some offenders who are believed safe to society and unlikely to reoffend, again based upon criteria from the same instruments which purportedly forecast dangerousness or society risk. However, a portion of these "safe" offenders may commit new offenses, even violent offenses, if released. These are considered *false negatives* and pose some danger or risk to society. While false positives and false negatives will be discussed in more detail in Chapter 2, they underscore some of the many problems confronting investigators who devise classification schemes. We are never 100 percent confident of our prediction schemes, and not all persons classified particular ways will exhibit subsequent behaviors consistent with how they have been classified. False positives are the ones who stand the greater chance of being treated unfairly by classification schemes. They are more often deprived of liberty when they shouldn't be deprived of it. Some of the more important issues involved in selective incapacitation will be discussed in greater depth in Chapter 3.

DANGEROUSNESS, RISK, AND NEEDS ASSESSMENTS DEFINED

The concepts of *dangerousness* and *risk* are often used interchangeably. Dangerousness and risk both convey *propensities to cause harm to others or oneself.* What is the likelihood that any particular offender will be violent toward others? Does an offender pose any risk to public safety? What is the likelihood that any particular offender will commit suicide or attempt it? Risk (or dangerousness) instruments are screening devices intended to distinguish between different types of offenders for purposes of determining initial institutional classification, security placement and inmate management, early release eligibility, and the level of supervision required under conditions of probation or parole. Most state jurisdictions and the federal government refer to these measures as *risk instruments* rather than *dangerousness instruments* (Illinois has a dangerousness designation) (Illinois Department of Corrections, 1988). There is considerable variance among states regarding the format and content of such measures. An example of one of the less elaborate versions of a risk assessment instrument is one used by the State of Iowa shown in Form 1.1.

Needs assessment devices are instruments that measure an offender's personal/social skills, health well-being and emotional stability, educational level and vocational strengths and weaknesses, alcohol/drug dependencies, mental ability, and other relevant life factors, and which highlight those areas for which services are available and could or should be provided. Needs assessment devices, measures, scales, or inventories identify the types of services offenders might require

Form 1.1
Iowa Department of Corrections Assessment of Client Risk

Client Name ______________________________ ICBC# ____________
Last First MI

Date of Assessment ____________________ Officer's Name ____________________

Offense ____________________

Instructions: Score items and add total score.

Item		SCORE
1. Age at Classification	28 or older = 0 27 or younger = 1	☐
2. Age at First Adult Conviction/Juvenile Adjudication (Include Deferreds)	24 or older = -2 20 to 23 = 0 19 or under = 2	☐
3. Prior Juvenile Commitments	None = 0 One or more = 2	☐
4. Prior Probation/Parole Supervisions (Adult or Juvenile Adjudications)	None = 0 One or more = 2	☐
5. Number of Prior Probation/Parole Revocations (Adult or Juvenile Adjudications)	None = 0 One = 2 Two or more = 3	☐
6. Felony/Misdemeanor Convictions (Include present offense, deferreds, & Juvenile Adjudications Circle applicable and add for score. Do not exceed a total of 3.)	Burglary or Robbery = 1 Theft, Forgery, FUFI, Fraudulent Practices = 1 Assault, Weapons Public Order Offenses = 1 None = 0	☐
7. Misdemeanor Conviction History (Simple & Serious Misdemeanors Only) (Include present offense, deferreds, & Juvenile Adjudication)	None or one = 0 Two or more = 1	☐
8. Sex	Female = 0 Male = 2	☐
9. Alcohol Usage Problems	No interference = 0 Occasional abuse = 1 Frequent abuse = 2	☐
10. Drug Usage Problems	No interference = 0 Occasional abuse = 1 Frequent abuse = 2	☐
11. Number of Address Changes in last 12 months (prior to incarceration for parole)	None = -1 One or more = 1	☐
12. Companions	No adverse relationships = 0 Associations occasionally negative = 1 Associations almost completely negative = 2	☐
13. Employment	Satisfactory one year or longer = -2 Secure or not applicable = 0 Unsatisfactory, or Unemployed, Unemployable = 2	☐
	TOTAL SCORE	☐

Clients are assigned to the highest level of supervision indicated on the following scale:

RISK
25 to 15 Intensive
14 to 8 Normal
7 to 2 Minimum
1 to -5 Administrative

LEVEL OF SUPERVISION
1 Intensive
2 Normal
3 Minimum
4 Administrative

REASON FOR OVERRIDE
0 Assaultive offense
1 Severity of offense
2 Special conditions set by parole board, court, or district
3 Client not available for active supervision
4 Force field indicates high needs
5 Other ____________________

Comments: ____________________

Level ☐

Revised level ☐

Override reason code ☐

____
override approval/date

if incarcerated. If some offenders are illiterate, they may be placed, either voluntarily or involuntarily, into an educational program at some level, depending upon the amount of remedial work deemed necessary (Oberst, 1988). Psychologically disturbed or mentally ill offenders may require some type of counseling or therapy. Some offenders may require particular medications for illnesses or other maladies. Some offenders are alcohol- or drug-dependent, thus requiring some aggressive treatment from institutional services. If offenders are to be paroled, the paroling authority may assess their needs and target them for placement in the most appropriate community programs where they can receive assistance deemed vital to their successfulness on parole (Schumacker, Anderson, and Anderson, 1990). The same is true for probationers commencing their probationary sentences. Judges want to know if they require special services or should be made to involve themselves in various community organizations and activities. A good example of an offender need assessment is one used by the Indiana Department of Corrections shown in Form 1.2.

Risk and need assessments may also be referred to jointly and contained in a longer inventory or measure, labeled a *risk-need assessment.* An inspection of

Form 1.2
Indiana: Proposed Adult Needs Assessment Instrument

Indiana Judicial Center
101 West Ohio Street, Suite 1110
Indianapolis, Indiana 26204-1989

	Factor Score		Relationship to Criminal Behavior		Total
Probationer's Name ______ **Cause No.** ______ **Probation Officer** ______ **Date Completed** ______					
1. Academic/Vocational Skills 0 Adequate skills; able to handle everyday requirements 1 Skill level causing moderate adjustment/functioning problems 2 Skill level causing serious adjustment/functioning problems	___	+	___	=	___
2. Employment/Means of Support 0 Satisfactory employment or means of support for one year or longer 1 Unsatisfactory employment or means less than adequate for support 2 Unemployed and no means of support	___	+	___	=	___
3. Substance Use 0 No know interference 1 Some disruption 2 Serious disruption	___	+	___	=	___
4. Emotional/Mental Stability 0 No problems 1 Moderate problems 2 Serious problems	___	+	___	=	___
5. Financial Management 0 No current difficulties 1 Situational or minor difficulties 2 Severe difficulties; may include garnishment, bad checks or bankruptcy	___	+	___	=	___
6. Family/Marital Relationships 0 Stable 1 Some disorganization or stress 2 Major disorganization or stress	___	+	___	=	___
7. Peer Relationships 0 No adverse relationships 1 Occasional adverse/negative relationships 2 Associations are almost completely negative	___	+	___	=	___
8. Health 0 No problems 1 Illness or physical condition interferes with functioning 2 Serious physical condition or chronic illness interferes with functioning	___	+	___	=	___
9. Other, Must Explain: (0, 1 or 2) ______ ______	___	+	___	=	___

Comments ______
______
______

Supervisor's signature: (Optional) ______

Relationship to Criminal Behavior Scores:
0 No relationship
1 Moderately related
2 Directly related

If one or more individual categories total score is 3 or above, then the 3 most serious needs should be prioritized and a supervision plan developed.

these devices and the individual items included within them will indicate which factors seem to have the greatest priority and predictive utility. Both of these scales assign different weights, depending upon the value of the predictive utility of the item for forecasting either risk or needs. For instance, in Form 1.1, the Iowa Assessment of Client Risk scale assigns the weight of up to "3" for the number of previous probation/parole revocations, while the "number of address changes in last 12 months" receives a maximum point value of "1." This item also includes a "– 1" value if the offender had no address changes. Thus, greater community stability (as measured by how much one moves from place to place) is rewarded. In the Indiana Adult Needs Assessment in Form 1.2, all factors have maximum weights of "2" and are weighted equally.

Depending upon an offender's cumulative score or raw point total, interpretive tables are usually consulted to determine the *level of needs* and *types of needs* which should be addressed with one or more services. These services might include alcohol or drug abuse treatment programs, vocational/educational training, employment counseling, or individual/group therapy (Robins et al., 1986). Those areas most indicative of greatest weaknesses or needs are typically those with the largest score weights.

Because of various flaws inherent in such instruments, there are grounds for some skepticism. Sechrest (1987) has found that often, classification schemes that match certain offenders with specific treatment programs lack theoretical coherence. Thus, while classifications of offenders result in separate categorizations destined to receive certain treatments and services, considerable variation exists among individual offenders within each category. Therefore, there are frequent mismatches between classification systems and the treatment programs prescribed. For example, one or two points in either direction can make a great deal of difference to those offenders who complete the needs assessment scale in Form 1.2. If we were to challenge the theoretical coherence of this scale, we might raise such questions as why *age at classification* has a "0" and "1" point breakdown, while *companions* has a "0," "1," and "2" point breakdown. What theoretical justification exists for including specific items initially, as well as for assigning different item weight patterns for these items?

It is not considered unusual to see jurisdictions use both risk and needs assessment measures simultaneously. Many jurisdictions have and use both types of scales. While the scales vary in content among these jurisdictions, almost all of these devices have the same objectives. Furthermore, it has been found that an offender's needs correlate highly with conformity or nonconformity with program requirements and conditions. In short, needs assessment scales or devices also may be indicators of offender propensity to recidivate and potential program failure. For instance, Banks (1984) studied 487 probationers in the Georgia Department of Offender Rehabilitation. Of these 487 probationers, 90 subsequently had their probation revoked for one or more probation program violations. Banks found that the 18 percent of probationers who recidivated and had their probation revoked also had the highest needs scores among all probationers studied. In this particular study, the recidivist sample exhibited much higher illicit drug use and abuse, which had been disclosed earlier on a needs assessment device. Banks found no predictive utility associated with race, gender, and age, however. Furthermore, probation officers and others in charge of offender management are not always able to personally diagnose probationer needs based upon direct client interactions and impressions. Banks also found low correlations between offender needs scores and officer assessments of offender needs.

In addition to initial risk and needs assessments used for offender classification and treatment, *reassessment measures* also exist and are applied for periodic readjustments, such as changing custody level from maximum-security to medium- or to minimum-security. Reassessment devices may also be used to gauge whether sufficient improvement has occurred among inmates or clients diagnosed with various needs requiring intervention, treatment, or special services. A good example of a risk reassessment scale is the Iowa Department of Corrections Reassessment of Client Risk shown in Form 1.3. In the following section, we will discuss briefly the rationale for and early use of risk/needs measures.

THE RATIONALE FOR AND EARLY USE OF RISK/NEEDS MEASURES

Risk assessment measures have been devised and are used largely for the purpose of determining probabilities that offender-clients will engage in dangerous or maladjusted behaviors (Joyce, 1985:78). These probabilities are subsequently used for placement, program, and security decision making (Joyce, 1985:78). Needs measures and instruments enable corrections personnel and administrative staffs to highlight client weaknesses or problems which may have led to their convictions or difficulties initially. Once problem areas have been targeted, specific services or treatments might be scheduled and provided.

Credited with establishing early prisoner classification systems in the eighteenth century are various Christian reform movements (American Correctional Association, 1983:194). Behavioral scientists, especially psychiatrists and psychologists, conducted research during the period 1910–1920 and found that custody-level placements of inmates as well as other program assignments could be made by using certain psychological characteristics as predictors (American Correctional Association, 1983:196). These classification schemes were often influenced by prevailing criminological theories, however, and had diverse consequences for offender management and treatment.

For example, Charles Darwin's *The Origin of Species* profoundly influenced several social and psychological theories of criminal behavior by highlighting physical features as potentially useful in classifying people. Writing several decades after Darwin's evolutionary work was completed, Cesare Lombroso described the physical characteristics of criminals in great detail (Lombroso, 1911). Lombroso promoted the idea of phrenology, where criminal types could presumably be identified by their skull shapes. Other theorists believed that

Form 1.3
Iowa Department of Corrections Reassessment of Client Risk

Client Name ______________________ ICBC# __________
Last First MI

Date of Reassessment ______________ Officer's Name ______________

Offense ______________

Instructions: Score items and add total score. **SCORE**

Item	Response	Score
1. Age at first Adult Conviction/Juvenile Adjudication (Include deferreds)	24 or older = -2 20 to 23 = 0 19 or younger = 1	
2. Prior Juvenile Commitments	None = 0 One or more = 2	
3. Prior Probations/Parole Supervisions (Adult or Juvenile Adjudications)	None = 0 One or more = 2	
4. Number of Prior Probation/Parole Revocations (Adult or Juvenile Adjudications)	None = 0 One or more = 2	
5. Felony/Misdemeanor Convictions (Include present offense, deferreds, Juvenile Adjudications Circle applicable and add for score. Do not exceed a total of 3.)	Burglary or Robbery = 1 Theft, Forgery, FUFI, Fraudulent Practices = 1 Assault, Weapons Public Order Offenses = 1 None = 0	
6. Misdemeanor Conviction History (Simple & Serious Misdemeanors Only) (Include present offense, deferreds, & juvenile adjudications.)	None or one = 0 Two or more = 1	
7. Sex	Female = 0 Male = 1	
8. Alcohol Usage Problems	No interference = 0 Occasional abuse = 1 Frequent abuse = 2	
9. Drug Usage Problems	No interference = 0 Occasional abuse = 1 Frequent abuse = 2	
*10. Employment	Satisfactory one year or longer = -2 Secure or not applicable = 0 Unsatisfactory, or Unemployed, Unemployable = 2	
*11. Companions	No adverse relationships = 0 Associations occasionally negative = 1 Associations almost completely negative = 2	
*12. Problems with Current Living Situation	Relatively stable relationships and/or address = 0 Moderate disorganization or stress = 1 Major disorganization or stress = 2	
*13. Response to Supervision Conditions	No problems of consequence = 0 Moderate compliance problem = 1 Frequently unwilling to comply = 3	
*14. New Arrests	None = 0 One or more arrests = 3	
*15. Use of Community Resources	Not Needed = 0 Productively Utilized = 0 Needed, but not available = 1 Utilized, but not beneficial = 2 Client rejected referral = 3	

*Since last classification

TOTAL SCORE ____

Clients are assigned to the highest level of supervision indicated on the following scale:

RISK
31 to 15 Intensive
14 to 8 Normal
7 to 2 Minimum
1 to -5 Administrative

LEVELS OF SUPERVISION
1 Intensive
2 Normal
3 Minimum
4 Administrative

REASON FOR OVERRIDE
0 Assaultive offense
1 Severity of offense
2 Special conditions set by parole board, court, or district
3 Client not available for active supervision
4 Force field indicates high needs
5 Other ______________

Comments: ______________

Level ____

Revised level ____

Override reason code ____

____
override approval/date

TS 8/92

criminal conduct was hereditary, transmitted genetically. Thus, some state corrections institutions sterilized certain inmates during the early 1900s. Despite considerable research to the contrary later, some of these early ideas about criminal behavior were still being applied more recently (Cortes and Gatti, 1972; Epps and Parnell, 1952). For an excellent discussion of the early history of classification schemes, see Don Gottfredson (1987:3–10).

Subsequently, criminologists and criminal justice scholars have become increasingly involved in devising risk assessment inventories and needs indices, using combinations of psychological, social, socioeconomic, and demographic factors and related criteria to make dangerousness forecasts and behavioral predictions. It is generally acknowledged that formal, paper-pencil risk and needs instruments began to proliferate during the 1960s (Spieker and Pierson, 1989:6). Some of this instrumentation work was used initially with juvenile offenders. Subsequently, numerous behavioral and psychological instruments were devised and used for the purpose of assessing client risk or inmate dangerousness. The Minnesota Multiphasic Personality Inventory (MMPI), consisting of 550 true-false items, was originally used in departments of corrections for personality assessments. While this instrument is still applied in many correctional settings, some researchers, such as Edwin Megargee, have extracted certain items from the MMPI for use as predictors of inmate violence and adjustment (Megargee and Carbonell, 1985). Classifications such as Megargee's are often designated as *MMPI-based assessments or classifications*. Applications of scales such as Megargee's have received mixed results and evaluations. In at least some studies, such scales have demonstrably low reliability (Johnson, Simmons, and Gordon, 1983; Megargee and Carbonell, 1985).

Preceding Megargee was the work of Quay (Quay and Parsons, 1971). Quay devised a relatively simple typology of delinquent behavior, classifying delinquents into four categories: Undersocialized Aggression, Socialized Aggression, Attention Deficit, and Anxiety-Withdrawal-Dysphoria. Juveniles would complete a self-administered questionnaire and their personality scores would be quickly tabulated. Depending upon how particular juveniles were depicted and classified, different treatments would be administered to help them. Later, Quay devised a scale which he called AIMS, or the Adult Internal Management System (Quay, 1984). Again, Quay used a self-administered inventory, the Correctional Adjustment Checklist and the Correctional Adjustment Life History (Sechrest, 1987:302–303). His adult typology consisted of five types of inmates: Aggressive Psychopathic, Manipulative, Situational, Inadequate-Dependent, and Neurotic-Anxious. Sechrest (1987:303) and others (Spieker and Pierson, 1989) consider AIMS more of an inmate management tool than a rehabilitative or treatment-centered one, however.

Another system used with some frequency is the I-Level Classification, referring to the Interpersonal Maturity Level Classification System. This system was originally developed by Sullivan, Grant, and Grant (1957) for use with juvenile offenders. It is based on a mixture of developmental and psychoanalytic theories and is administered by psychologists or psychiatrists in lengthy clinical interviews (Spieker and Pierson, 1989). Clients are classified as being at particular "I-levels," such as I-1, I-2, and so on, up to I-7. Each I-level is a developmental stage reflecting one's ability to cope with complex personal and interpersonal problems. The higher the I-level, the better-adjusted the client, according to its proponents. Juvenile delinquents often have low I-levels, between I-1 and I-3. Psychiatric assessments of juvenile as well as adult offenders are expensive and time-consuming, regardless of their predictive utility and assistance for inmate management and treatment. Unfortunately, the relation of this system to particular forms of treatment has never been fully articulated. Sechrest (1987:300–303) notes that I-Level Classification applications have been limited in adult settings, even in juvenile ones. No doubt one explanation for this is the prohibitive cost of administration and interpretation. Further, many existing scales and indices are tailored for men rather than for women. Thus, in recent years, several jurisdictions have devised special risk assessment devices for females (Spieker and Pierson, 1989:7–8). For instance, Illinois developed and implemented a female initial classification instrument in January 1984 (Illinois Department of Corrections, 1988). Actually, the instrument devised for female offender classification is very similar to the one used to classify male offenders in Illinois, with minor variations. Both of these instruments may be examined in Appendix A. The female classification instrument has more elaborate vocational and educational categorizations, contains information about tickets issued within the last six months, and has fewer classification levels compared with the male classification instrument.

It was not until the 1980s, however, that state corrections departments began to create and apply risk assessment schemes with some regularity. For example, Arizona created its first Offender Classification System manual in 1986 (Arizona Department of Corrections, 1991). Instrumentation for risk assessment was established in Illinois in the mid-1980s (Illinois Department of Corrections, 1988). Tennessee sought requests for proposals in 1987 to devise risk measures for its inmate population. Missouri introduced a variation of AIMS for use in its Department of Corrections in 1988 (Spieker and Pierson, 1989). Iowa's Risk/Needs Classification System was implemented in December 1983 and revised extensively in 1992 (Iowa Department of Correctional Services, 1992). Many jurisdictions are currently revising or have recently revised their risk and needs instruments.

SOME APPLICATIONS OF RISK/NEEDS MEASURES

We have already discussed several of the many potential applications of risk/needs instruments and measures. One convenient way of highlighting the most common applications of these instruments by the different states is to examine their own utilization criteria and objectives. The following state utilization criteria are not intended to represent all other states or to typify them. Rather, they have been highlighted because of their diversity of objectives. For example, Iowa's Classification Risk Assessment Scale is used for the following purposes:

1. program planning;
2. budgeting and deployment of resources;
3. evaluating services, programs, procedures, and performances;

4. measuring the potential impact of legislative and policy changes;
5. enhancing accountability through standardization;
6. equitably distributing the workloads; and
7. improving service delivery to clients (Iowa Department of Correctional Services, 1992:6).

Iowa officials elaborate further by noting that their Client Management Classification is to assist in assigning levels of supervision and changing supervisory levels. Further, this instrument will yield a risk level which will "tell you how often you need to see offenders . . . [as well as] . . . tell you what you need to do with offenders when you see them" (Iowa Department of Correctional Services, 1992:5).

Arizona's Offender Classification System (OCS) is designed to assign all offenders to an appropriate institutional setting based on required levels of security/custody and the needs of offenders for productive work, education, and treatment during their incarceration (Arizona Department of Corrections, 1991). Additionally, risk prediction tools, as utilized by the Colorado Parole Guidelines Commission (1988), are for the purposes of

1. concentrating secure management and/or program resources on a specific group of "high need" offenders without reducing public safety;
2. promoting greater understanding of the statistical management of the parole release process;
3. significantly improving predictive accuracy over case-review or clinical methods; and
4. addressing offender needs as they relate to reoffending in the community.

The above goals for Iowa, Arizona, and Colorado are couched in the context of initial placement decisions and closely related to management objectives, including allocating scarce resources most profitably in view of system constraints. Theoretically, if the system's processual features are optimized, offender management is also. Presumably, the quality of services available to offender-clients would also be improved. But as we have seen, risk assessments serve several purposes. For instance, the Ohio Parole Board uses a guideline system for determining early releases of certain offenders through parole or furlough. This guideline system incorporates a risk assessment instrument and has the following objectives:

1. to provide for public protection by not releasing those inmates who represent a high risk of repeating violent or other serious crimes;
2. to provide an appropriate continuum of sanctions for crime;
3. to cooperate with correctional management in providing safe, secure, and humane conditions in state correctional institutions;
4. to recognize the achievement of those inmates with special identifiable problems relat-

ing to their criminal behavior who have participated in institutional programs designed to alleviate their problems; and

5. to make the decision-making process of the Adult Parole Authority more open, equitable, and understandable both to the public and to the inmate (Ohio Parole Board, 1992:2).

Ohio's parole board guideline system objectives differ substantially from those of Iowa and Arizona. The Ohio risk assessment objectives are more offender-oriented, with emphases upon the appropriateness of sanctions and identification of offender-client needs which may be met by particular services. There are also greater concerns for public safety and greater community comprehension of the parole decision-making process. Although we might attribute much of the variation in risk assessment objectives among these states to the fact that different uses are made of the risk instruments (e.g., initial classification of inmates and parole decision making), the contents of the various instruments do not differ dramatically. Most states distinguish between offender evaluations for the purpose of determining their *institutional risk* and their *public risk.* Again, the device contents are often identical or very similar. An examination of the utilization criteria for other state risk assessment devices yields similar diversity of instrument goals.

It is possible to group these diverse objectives according to several general applications. Thus, we may conclude that for most states, the following general applications are made of risk assessment instruments at different client-processing stages:

1. to promote better program planning through optimum budgeting and deployment of resources;
2. to target high-risk and high-need offenders for particular custody levels, programs, and services without endangering the safety of others;
3. to apply fair and appropriate sanctions to particular classes of offenders and raise their level of accountability;
4. to provide mechanisms for evaluating services and programs as well as service and program improvements over time; and
5. to maximize public safety as well as public understanding of the diverse functions of corrections by making decision making more open and comprehensible to both citizens and offender-clients.

AN OVERVIEW OF SELECTED PROBLEMS WITH RISK/NEEDS ASSESSMENTS

While a more detailed discussion of criticisms of risk assessment instruments will be presented in Chapter 2, a brief overview of selected problems associated with such devices will be provided here. It is generally acknowledged that no risk assessment device is foolproof or perfect. However, virtually every state and the federal government utilizes risk assessments in one form or another for various offender-related purposes. Such widespread use of assessment tools is evidence of their acceptance and utility, despite the fact that some offender misclassification occurs and is anticipated. Four major stages of offender processing are of particular interest to us here. These include: (1) initial classification for risk, needs, and institutional placement; (2) institutional reassessment for possible reclassification; (3) evaluating one's parole eligibility and potential for success; and (4) assessments of offenders in post-incarcerative supervision and community-based correctional programs.

Initial Classification for Risk, Needs, and Institutional Placement

The general kinds of problems typically encountered by institutional officials as the result of administering risk and needs assessment instruments to groups of entering offenders all focus around misclassification.

1. Some inmates will be "overclassified" and assigned to closer custody, such as medium- or maximum-security levels; actually, these inmates do not require close custody and would do well in a less-secure custody level with other inmates.
2. Some inmates will be "underclassified" and assigned to minimum-security blocks; actually, these inmates pose adjustment problems and/or are incapable of getting along with others; they are dangerous to others or themselves.
3. Some inmates with debilitating illnesses or psychological problems will not be targeted by needs instruments for special services; thus, their personal and/or interpersonal problems will remain untreated; conceivably, interactions with other inmates in close custody may, in fact, aggravate their original problems to the point where they will be exploited by other inmates or where they will endanger other inmates by their behaviors.
4. Some inmates may be placed in programs or receive special services when, in fact, they do not need such services; thus, scarce program space is allocated to the wrong inmate-clients and the effectiveness of the institution as a rehabilitative medium is undermined.

It should be noted that classification and placement decisions are not wholly dependent upon paper-pencil risk assessment instruments. Provisions are almost always in place for administrative overrides. These overrides involve changes in classification different from what the raw scale scores indicate. Corrections officers and others may override a scale score, but usually, they must provide a written rationale for doing so. Also, some overrides are mandatory, depending upon how an offender was sentenced. Thus, an inmate might be classified one way by a risk assessment instrument, but the court may have imposed a more or less stringent punishment (e.g., solitary confinement, maximum-security placement) which prison officials are obliged to follow. Of course, some of these overrides are warranted if scale scores suggest that certain offenders are more dangerous or pose greater risks than their other behavioral criteria might indicate. Also, some inmates may require special handling for their own protection from attacks by other prisoners (e.g., child sexual abusers, pedophiliacs, assassins of popular persons, and organized crime figures).

Institutional Reassessment for Reclassification

Reassessments of inmates while in custody are generally made at six-month intervals. For example, the Arizona Department of Corrections provides for a Reclassification Review 180 days following an inmate's admission to its penal facilities. Furthermore, continuous 180-day reviews and reassessments are made of all Arizona inmates, generally to determine whether their present level of custody should be changed and/or whether their treatments/services/programs should be continued or terminated. Some inmates are initially diagnosed as having high suicide potential and are closely supervised subsequently. Following their initial adjustment to prison life, their suicide potential is likely to diminish. Thus, it would be both costly and unproductive to continue their high custody level following apparent adjustment.

In contrast, the Pennsylvania Department of Corrections must administer reclassification instruments every twelve months (Commonwealth of Pennsylvania Department of Corrections, 1992:B1). Alternatively, the Alaska Department of Corrections conducts reclassifications of its offender population every six months. An inspection of most state classification and reclassification criteria discloses that the six-month standard seems most popular in view of its more frequent use. Six-month re-evaluations are arguably better than twelve-month evaluations, since many offenders with short-term problems may not need a full year of treatment or institutional services. Thus, inmate recoveries are more quickly detected when the re-examination interval is shorter rather than longer. The "down" side of shorter testing intervals and reassessments is that more paperwork is involved. But considering the potential for diverting scarce services and programs to those most in need of them, the additional paperwork limitation may be easily offset (Brennan, 1987b; Johnson, 1987).

Many states, such as Colorado, Iowa, Minnesota, and South Carolina, have significantly revamped their classification and risk/needs assessment tools in recent years. At least one of these states, Colorado, has undertaken such instrument revisions because of overclassification problems (Colorado Division of Criminal Justice, 1986; Posey, 1988). One major result of dramatically changing the Colorado Department of Corrections classification policies and practices has been a significant reduction in the proportion of offenders designated as maximum-security inmates. Larger portions of offenders now are classified as medium-security inmates. Despite these drastic changes in policy and instrumentation, Colorado officials believe that some overclassification continues to persist (Colorado Division of Criminal Justice, 1986).

All of the problems articulated under initial risk assessment above also are associated with reclassifications of inmates. Some inmates are good actors and may fool program staff. Thus, the problems of overclassification and underclassification continue. Also perpetuated are some of the initial problems relating to ineffective or inaccurate diagnoses of inmate needs (Sechrest, 1987). Accurate assessments of mental well-being or mental health are also difficult to make for particular individuals at particular times in their institutionalization (Mande and Covey, 1982). In contrast, certain inmate behaviors must be either rewarded or punished. Reclassification and reassessment may accomplish either objective. Some inmates may assault other inmates or staff, or participate in riots. Other institutional infractions may be exhibited. Some Massachusetts prisons, for example, have Departmental Segregation Units, or DSUs, which are comparable to solitary confinement. Prisoners who misbehave are reclassified and placed in these DSUs for disciplinary purposes (Rocheleau, 1986). Other offenders who successfully complete certain educational or vocational programs or who are diagnosed as "cured" of some debilitating problem, such as drug or alcohol dependency, may be rewarded by being given a level of custody with greater freedom of movement and more privileges.

Evaluating Parole Eligibility and Success Potential

Public risk is a key consideration in early release or parole decision making. Every state parole board attempts to minimize public risk by carefully assessing the dangerousness potential of all prospective parolees. Most of us are familiar with the cases of Sirhan Sirhan (convicted of assassinating Robert Kennedy) and Charles Manson (convicted of murdering several persons in a mass-murder rampage, including actress Sharon Tate). These notorious murderers have been eligible for parole for many years, yet they are consistently denied early release. It is unlikely that they will ever be paroled, particularly in view of public sentiment and the nature and seriousness of their crimes. By the same token, most of us are aware of incidents involving paroling dangerous offenders who subsequently commit new and serious offenses. More than a few parolees have committed murder, rape, or aggravated assault while participating in a parole program. Thus, it is expected that greater public interest and scrutiny are directed at parole boards and their actions rather than focused upon prison officials who engage in offender management.

Parole boards have dual responsibilities, however. They have responsibilities both to the public and to inmates who become eligible for possible early release. But they must balance their concern for public safety against whatever is the best action to be taken in any prospective parolee case. These decisions are not always easy, and as we have seen, mistakes are often made. Among other states, Oregon has recently modified its parole risk assessment criteria (Baird et al., 1987). The latest version of the risk assessment instrument, a history/risk scale, has resulted in fewer inmates being classified as "poor risks" compared with previous devices used. Baird et al. (1987) indicate that in general, low-risk cases involve inmates who have served longer terms than "poor-risk" cases. One factor associated with being a low-risk candidate for parole is model behavior as an inmate while confined. Misconduct is often correlated with parole failure, although not all inmates who exhibit misconduct are necessarily future program failures if paroled (Bonham, 1984; Goetting and Howsen, 1986).

For prospective parolees, decisions made by parole boards are crucial, since their freedom is at stake. If parole boards decide not to grant certain inmates early release on the basis of predictive criteria showing them to be public risks or likely program failures, they will continue to be imprisoned until their next parole hearing. Parole hearings are conducted at different intervals, depending upon the jurisdiction. Some states conduct them annually, while other jurisdictions conduct them more or less often. Critics, such as von Hirsch (1984) and Wright, Clear, and Dickson (1984), suggest that incapacitating offenders because of actions they have not, as yet, exhibited (e.g., reoffending or harming others) might be premature if not wrong. Selective incapacitation is premature to the extent that the prediction instruments used have not been validated or have low levels of reliability. It is wrong to the extent that most offenders are penalized for things they haven't done. The issue of selective incapacitation will be explored in greater detail in Chapter 2. Presently, it is sufficient to note that this is a particularly troublesome problem plaguing parole boards.

Assessments of Offenders for Community-Based Correctional Programs

Regardless of whether offenders are probationers or parolees, in many instances they will be assigned to community-based correctional programs. These programs offer a wide variety of services, such as employment assistance, vocational/educational training, individual or group therapy and counseling, and financial aid. Because almost all offenders who become involved in community corrections programs are permitted freedom and the mobility to move about within their respective communities, the public safety issue is an important one. Few residents of any community would knowingly want dangerous persons roaming their neighborhoods unrestricted or unmonitored. However, many community-based programs have formerly dangerous persons as clients. At what point does a violent, dangerous offender become nonviolent and nondangerous? We have no magical indicators of definite or dramatic personality or interpersonal changes, whenever they might occur. Rather, we most often base our impressions of offender candidacy for involvement in these programs on prior behaviors and expressed attitudes. Clinical assessments by psychologists and psychiatrists are also used as predictors of success potential (Hanson et al., 1983; Johnson, Simmons, and Gordon, 1983; Mande and Covey, 1982; Megargee and Carbonell, 1985; Megargee, Carbonell, and Bohn, 1988; Miller, 1984; Steadman, 1985).

SUMMARY

Crude attempts at offender classification and placement are at least traceable to the Walnut Street Jail, established in Philadelphia, Pennsylvania, in 1790. Classification is differentiating among persons according to particular characteristics they possess. Classifications according to dangerousness or risk posed to others are important at various stages of the criminal and juvenile justice systems, although the primary importance of classification is associated with corrections and offender placement decisions. Other stages of the justice process, such as parole board decisions, utilize offender classification schemes to estimate or predict offender likelihood of success if granted early release from jail or prison. Both juveniles and adult offenders are subjected to risk and needs assessments to determine their level of custody, program eligibility, and mode of rehabilitation.

Functions of classification include determining offender eligibility for particular prison or community corrections programs, such as work release or halfway house candidacy; identifying offenders' needs and placing offenders where they can receive treatment or assistance in meeting these needs; determining offender custody level if incarcerated; adjusting offender custody level after a period of incarceration; constructing more adequate systems of offender management; making better policy decisions relating to prison and jail construction; and enabling parole boards to make more informed early-release decisions about inmates eligible for parole. Frequently related to risk assessments are needs assessments, which enable officials to focus upon an offender's weaknesses and strengths and determine the proper remedial or therapeutic action to be taken. Needs assessments are more relevant in those geographical areas where a wide variety of offender services exists. No risk or needs instrument is without flaw, however. Thus, it is expected that some misclassification occurs. Offender misclassifications mean that some convicts or adjudicated delinquents will be overpenalized, while others will be underpenalized. Some may not receive the proper services they require. In the next chapter, we will look at both the criminal and juvenile justice systems and various applications of risk/needs assessments at crucial stages of offender processing.

2

The Criminal Justice System and Predictions of Risk: Variations in Instrumentation

INTRODUCTION

The use of risk and needs instrumentation is widespread throughout all facets of the criminal and juvenile justice systems. This chapter provides a brief overview of both the criminal and juvenile justice systems. It highlights those phases of each system where risk and needs measures are most likely to be applied. Whether those phases involve juvenile intake officers, prosecutors, and judges, or whether they involve criminal prosecutions, convictions, and corrections, risk assessments help to guide decision making by particular authorities or bodies. Probably the most prominent application of risk instruments is found in corrections, where jail and prison officials attempt to classify entering inmates. Later, parole boards will use risk assessments as important data or criteria to justify or disapprove early releases. Earlier in the juvenile and criminal justice systems, probation officers prepare either predispositional reports or presentence investigation reports for judges.

An additional purpose of this chapter is to examine the criteria these actors and bodies use for making their recommendations and decisions. Risk prediction is flawed, however. In almost every instance, there is a tendency for these instruments to both overpredict and underpredict, to the extent that some offenders deemed to be dangerous or to pose risks to others are actually harmless and will eventually pose no risks. Other offenders will be designated as nondangerous and unlikely to pose serious public risks. But when released, these offenders commit new crimes which harm others in serious ways. Basically, this is the recurring problem of *false positives* and *false negatives.* This problem will be examined in the context of instruments presently devised.

AN OVERVIEW OF THE CRIMINAL AND JUVENILE JUSTICE SYSTEMS

The Criminal Justice System

The criminal justice system is an interrelated set of agencies and organizations designed to control criminal behavior, to detect crime, and to apprehend, process, prosecute, punish, or rehabilitate criminal offenders. Figure 2.1 is a diagram of the criminal and juvenile justice systems. The juvenile justice system is portrayed in the lower branch of this figure.

The common elements of the criminal justice system include law enforcement, prosecution and courts, and corrections, although law-making bodies such as the legislatures of states and the federal government are sometimes included. The use of the word *system* is somewhat misleading, since it implies a degree of planned coordination between these components. In reality, however, various criminal justice components are not particularly integrated and coordinated. While it is true that a division of labor between components is generally apparent, each is independent of the others. The word *process* is often preferred, since it depicts how offenders move through the various phases of the system and are "processed." A system exists, but it is a loosely integrated one. Law enforcement officers, for example, seldom ask prosecutors and the courts if they have arrested too many criminals for the system to manage. Also, prosecutors and the courts seldom consult with prison or jail authorities about whether there is sufficient space to accommodate those sentenced to incarcerative terms. Below are descriptions of the various criminal justice system components and a brief overview of each process component.

Legislatures. Criminal laws originate largely as the result of legislative actions in most jurisdictions. Jurisdiction refers to the power of courts to hear cases, although we generally think of jurisdictions as political subdivisions, including townships, cities, counties, states, or federal districts. When criminals cross state or county lines, for instance, they leave the state or local jurisdictions where violations of the law occurred. Under certain circumstances, these jurisdictional boundaries may be crossed by pursuing authorities. At the federal level, any federal agency may enforce certain federal laws in any state, territory, or U.S. possession.

The Congress of the United States passes criminal laws that are enforceable by various federal agencies, including the Federal Bureau of Investigation (FBI), Drug Enforcement Administration (DEA), and the Criminal Investigation Division (CID) of the Internal Revenue Service. State legislatures enact criminal laws that are enforced by state and local law enforcement officers. At the community level, city and county governments determine specific criminal laws, statutes, and ordinances that should be enforced, depending upon the circumstances of the locality. Some local ordinances target juvenile conduct. These ordinances include laws relating to curfew, truancy, and incorrigibility, where parents or guardians cannot control the behaviors of their children.

Figure 2.1
The Criminal Justice System

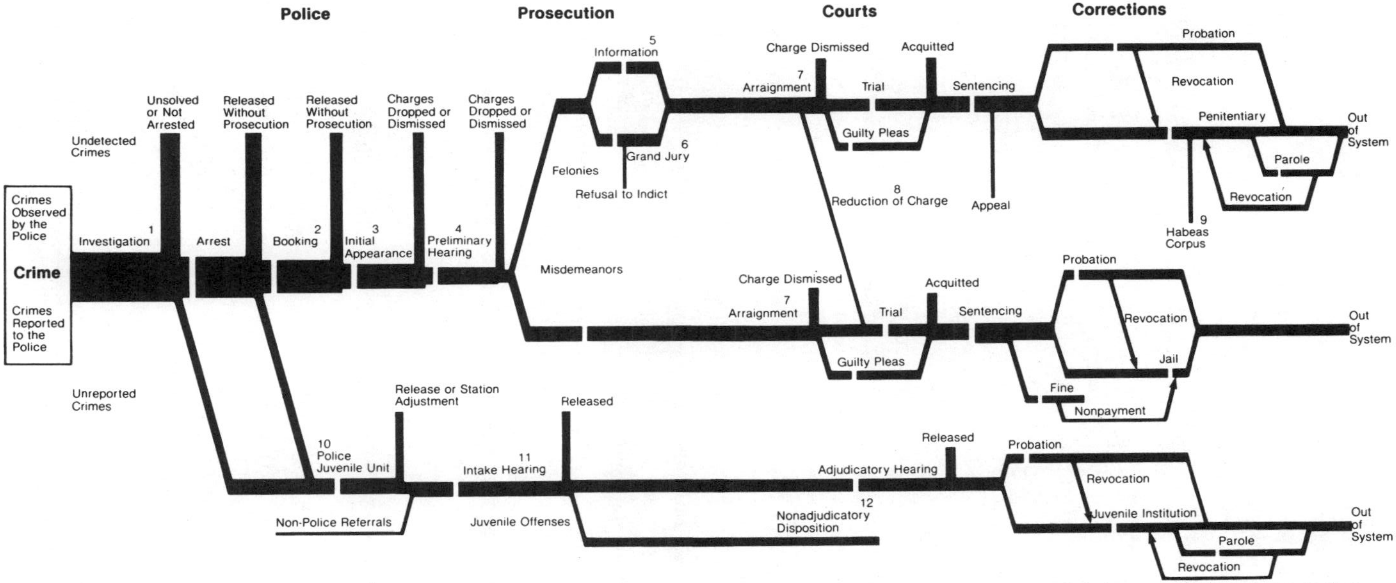

1. May continue until trial.
2. Administrative record of arrest. First step at which temporary release on bail may be available.
3. Before magistrate, commissioner, or justice of peace. Formal notice of charge, advice of rights. Bail set. Summary trials for petty offenses usually conducted here without further processing.
4. Preliminary testing of evidence against defendant. Charge may be reduced. No separate preliminary hearing for misdemeanors in some systems.
5. Charge filed by prosecutor on basis of information submitted by police or citizens. Alternative to grand jury indictment. Often used in felonies, almost always in misdemeanors.
6. Reviews whether government evidence sufficient to justify trial. Some states have no grand jury system; others seldom use it.
7. Appearance for plea. Defendant elects trial by judge or jury (if available). Counsel for indigent usually appointed here in felonies, often not at all in other cases.
8. Charge may be reduced at any time prior to trial in return for plea of guilty or for other reasons.
9. Challenge on constitutional grounds to legality of detention. May be sought at any point in process.
10. Police often hold informal hearings or dismiss or adjust many cases without further processing.
11. Probation officer decides desirability of further court action.
12. Welfare agency, social services, counseling, medical care, etc., for cases where adjudicatory handling not needed.

Source: President's Commission of Law Enforcement and Administration of Justice, *The Challenge of Crime in a Free Society* (Washington, D.C.: U.S. Government Printing Office, 1967).

Law Enforcement. There are over 20,000 law enforcement agencies in the United States (U.S. Department of Justice, 1988). These are distributed throughout the local, state, and federal governmental levels. Approximately 500,000 employees in these agencies are law enforcement officers (Jamieson and Flanagan, 1989). The most visible law enforcement officers are uniformed police officers in local and state governments. While federal authorities may become involved in federal crimes allegedly committed by juveniles, most of the time their work is focused upon apprehending adult offenders. Often, federal agents and other federal officers who apprehend juveniles will deliver them to local authorities for processing. Direct federal processing of juveniles is relatively rare (Miller et al., 1985; Rossum, Koller, and Manfredi, 1987).

Prosecution and the Courts. When criminal suspects and others are arrested by law enforcement officers or are otherwise taken into custody, they are usually booked. Booking involves obtaining descriptive information from those arrested, including their names, addresses, occupations (if any), next of kin, photographs, and fingerprints. Booking varies in formality among jurisdictions. Essentially, the booking process is a formality as well as an account or written report of the arrest or detention. Police may consult other law enforcement agencies through a computer network to determine whether those arrested have prior records of arrests or crimes. Interested agencies such as the Bureau of Justice Statistics within the U.S. Department of Justice may collect this statistical information later to profile those admitted to jails and other places of confinement.

Figure 2.1 shows other stages of processing in the criminal justice system subsequent to the arrest and booking of suspects. Adult offenders will likely move forward to the initial appearance stage. The initial appearance of defendants or those charged with crimes is before a magistrate or other court official, usually to advise defendants of the charges against them and to determine the amount of bail necessary to obtain their release. Bail or a bail bond is a surety in the form of money or property that may be posted by either a bonding company or others, including defendants themselves, to obtain their temporary release from custody and to ensure their subsequent appearance at trial. Under the Eighth Amendment, only those entitled to bail may receive it. Bail is not an absolute right under the Constitution. Ordinarily, those not entitled to bail are considered either very dangerous to others or highly likely to flee the jurisdiction to avoid prosecution for their crimes. Because of serious jail overcrowding problems and other considerations, bail is often waived in minor cases, and defendants are released on their own recognizance, or ROR. Usually, persons placed on ROR are not considered dangerous or likely to flee the jurisdiction. Between the defendant's arrest, booking, and initial appearance, prosecutors representing the state's interests must decide whether to prosecute this person for the crime(s) alleged.

Depending upon the circumstances, prosecutors may follow through with charges against defendants and take their cases to trial. A "worst case" scenario will be used for the defendant, where one or more crimes are alleged and a "not guilty" plea is entered. All defendants charged with crimes are entitled to a preliminary hearing or its equivalent. A preliminary hearing is a proceeding where both the prosecutor and the defense counsel may present some evidence against and on behalf of the defendant. Preliminary hearings establish whether probable cause exists. Probable cause is the determination or reasonable suspicion that a crime has been committed and that the defendant likely committed it. These hearings are not trials and do not establish the defendant's guilt or innocence. They are intended to determine whether sufficient evidence exists to proceed further (i.e., probable cause). In about half of all state jurisdictions, grand juries are used for essentially the same purpose as preliminary hearings. Grand juries "indict" persons or find that there is sufficient evidence to support the criminal charges against them. Let's assume that probable cause has been established and the case moves forward to the next stage.

Subsequently, the defendant is arraigned. An arraignment is a proceeding where (1) a list of specific charges is made available to defendants and their attorneys, (2) a formal plea to the charges is entered by the defendant, and (3) a trial date is established. Trials are adversarial proceedings where a defendant's guilt or innocence is established. We will assume that the defendant is tried and eventually convicted of one or more crimes alleged.

When defendants are convicted of any crime, they must be sentenced by the judge. Criminal court judges consider all circumstances and information available, and on the basis of their experience and judgment, together with statutory provisions mandated by legislatures, they impose sentences. Sentences do not necessarily involve incarceration. In many states, judges are permitted wide latitude in the sentences they may give convicted offenders. Judges consider factors such as the offender's leadership role in the crime and whether physical injuries were inflicted on victims during the crime's commission. Such circumstances are aggravating circumstances, and they intensify the punishment convicted offenders receive. Other factors are considered, including whether offenders furnished helpful information to police that enabled them to apprehend others connected with the crime. An offender's youthfulness would be considered as well. Whether offenders were mentally ill when they committed their crimes would also be important. These factors are considered mitigating circumstances, and they often mitigate the severity of punishment imposed. Judges often rely on presentence investigation reports prepared by probation officers. These documents contain much valuable background information about the defendant, the crime circumstances, and the risk or dangerousness the defendant might pose to society if released on probation. Judges consult these documents and often rely on their contents to justify whatever punishment they apply. Some risk and/or needs instruments may be administered to convicted offenders and included as a part of the investigation.

Because of serious prison and jail overcrowding problems in most jurisdictions, however, judges often impose probation as a punishment. Probation is a conditional nonincarcerative sentence, where the offender is under the management of probation department personnel or probation officers. Probation is most often used for first offenders who have been convicted of minor crimes. However, evidence of its growing use in the United States annually for more serious crimes (e.g., felony probation) is well documented (Champion, 1988). There are many correctional options available for judges to impose besides probation and incarceration. A vast array of intermediate punishments has been described by McCarthy (1987). Intermediate punishments are sanctions that exist somewhere between incarceration and probation on the continuum of criminal penalties (McCarthy, 1987:1). Intermediate punishments might include electronic monitoring, house arrest or home confinement, or community-based correctional alternatives such as halfway houses or intensive supervised probation or parole. Many of these options are available to juvenile as well as adult offenders. Regardless of whether convicted offenders receive probation or a sentence involving incarceration for designated terms, offenders move to the final component of the criminal justice process—corrections.

Corrections. Corrections consists of all agencies and personnel who deal with convicted offenders after court proceedings. As noted earlier, some convicted offenders may receive probation, or conditional sentences in lieu of incarceration. The use of probation in the United States is widespread. In 1990 over 2.7 million offenders were on probation (Jankowski, 1991:1). Other offenders may be confined in jails or prisons, again depending upon the seriousness of their offenses, the jurisdiction where the conviction occurred, and the availability of jail or prison space. Over 408,000 offenders were in jails in 1990, while 330,000 were in prisons in the United States (Cohen, 1991; Stephan and Jankowski, 1991).

Generally, jails are short-term facilities that are locally or state-operated by city or county governments (Mays and Thompson, 1991). In a few instances, jails are state-operated. Most jail functions include but are not limited to detaining those arrested for various offenses who are awaiting trial; maintaining witnesses in protective custody pending their testimony in court; providing confinement for short-term, petty offenders serving sentences of less than one year; and accommodating overflow from state or federal prisons in instances where chronic prison overcrowding exists (Mays and Thompson, 1991). Ordinarily, jails are not equipped for long-term confinement of prisoners. They have few, if any, recreational facilities and few services. As we have seen, jails are often sites where juveniles are taken when they are first apprehended. Various dispositional arrangements are made pertaining to them once police officers and others have investigated the circumstances of their arrests.

In contrast, prisons are long-term facilities. Most prisons have recreational yards, hospitals, work programs, and a host of other facilities to accommodate inmates who are confined for lengthy periods. Prisons are usually reserved for more serious offenders who have received incarcerative sentences of one year or longer from judges. It is highly unusual for misdemeanants who are sentenced to short incarcerative terms to be situated in prison facilities. There simply is no space available in most jurisdictions to accommodate them. Priority is given to long-term and more dangerous offenders, although each jurisdiction exhibits differences in the composition of its prison population. In certain areas where chronic prison overcrowding exists, it is not unusual for the courts to order prison inmates confined to local jail facilities to serve a portion of their incarcerative terms. This is a primary means of alleviating prison overcrowding, although it often creates or contributes to chronic jail overcrowding in the process. In Chapter 1, we saw how risk and needs measures were applied to classify offenders sentenced to prison to determine their custody level and type of treatment prescribed.

In many jurisdictions, inmates of prisons and jails may be released short of serving their full sentences. Under an indeterminate type of sentencing scheme, this is usually accomplished through parole. Parole is a conditional release from incarceration for a designated period, usually the remainder of the original sentence. Thus, if offenders were sentenced to a ten-year term, they might become eligible for parole after serving only four or five years. A parole board would consider their parole eligibility and grant them early release from prison. In parole situations, parolees are supervised by parole officers. In 1990, 531,407 offenders were on parole in the United States (Jankowski, 1991:1). Parole boards utilize risk instruments to assess an inmate's likelihood of succeeding "on the outside" if paroled. Needs instruments may also be helpful to assist parole boards in determining any conditions which they feel should accompany parole. Parole is always conditional, in that parolees are expected to abide by certain rules. However, they may be required to participate in mandatory educational programs, receive psychological counseling or group therapy, or become involved in a vocational school activity to acquire skills to make them more employable.

Besides parole and under a determinate sentencing scheme, prisoners can obtain early release automatically through the accumulation of good-time credits. Good-time credits are numbers of days subtracted from the original sentence. These are accumulated on the basis of the amount of time served. For instance, for every thirty days served, a prisoner may acquire fifteen, thirty, or even forty-five days good-time credit. In federal prisons, federal inmates can accumulate fifty-four days per year as good time, which is subtracted from their original sentences. Under these circumstances, once offenders have served their time (less good-time credits), they are released from the criminal justice system without further obligation.

The Juvenile Justice System

In many ways, the juvenile justice system mirrors the criminal justice system. But it is much more simplified. Police officers or others either arrest juvenile offenders or refer them to juvenile court for processing. This processing includes intake, detention, prosecution, juvenile court adjudication, and juvenile corrections.

Juvenile Arrestees. It is estimated that annually, 479,000 juveniles are locked up in adult jails in the United States (Dale, 1988:46). About 10 percent of these are actually held for serious offenses. About 20 percent are status offenders. About 19,000 youths have been jailed, often on suspicion, even though they haven't committed offenses of any kind (Dale, 1988:46). States such as Illinois have recently passed laws to prevent police officers from detaining juveniles in adult jails for periods of more than six hours (Huskey, 1990:122). For example, in 1988 in Illinois, more than 1,200 juveniles spent more than six hours in jails and lockups, while more than 100 were in jail for nearly three weeks (Huskey, 1990:122). Most of these jailed youths were nonviolent offenders. Huskey (1990:122) notes that 700 of those jailed included status offenders, and about 1,000 were between the ages of ten and thirteen.

Classification, Preliminary Disposition, and Intake. Whenever youths have been taken into custody and are determined to require special care, are needy or dependent, or are otherwise unsupervised by adults or guardians, social welfare agencies or human service organizations may be identified as destinations for their removal from jails. Verification of a youth's identity and contacts with parents may result in verbal warnings by police and return of the youth to the parents. These actions are preliminary dispositions. Those juveniles who are actually arrested will eventually appear at an intake proceeding. Intake varies in formality among jurisdictions. Intake is a screening procedure conducted by a court officer or a probation officer, where one or several courses of action are recommended.

In most jurisdictions, intake normally results in one of six actions, depending, in part, upon the discretion of intake officers: (1) dismissal of the case, with or without a verbal or written reprimand; (2) remand youths to the custody of their parents; (3) remand youths to the custody of their parents, with provisions for or referrals to counseling or special services; (4) divert youths to an alternative dispute resolution program, if one exists in the jurisdiction; or (5) refer youths to the juvenile prosecutor for further action and possible filing of a delinquency petition.

The Prosecution and Adjudication of Juvenile Offenders. Most serious juvenile offenders are referred to juvenile prosecutors for further action. Juvenile court prosecutors have broad discretionary powers. If they wish, they may drop prosecutions of cases against alleged offenders. Much depends upon the docket load or case activity of their own juvenile courts. Prosecutors further screen cases by diverting some of the most serious ones to criminal court through waiver, transfer, or certification.

Prosecutors either file petitions or act on the petitions filed by others (Laub and MacMurray, 1987). Petitions are official documents filed in juvenile courts on the juvenile's behalf, specifying reasons for the youth's court appearance. These documents assert that juveniles fall within the categories of dependent or neglected, status offender, or delinquent, and the reasons for such assertions are usually provided (Rogers and Mays, 1987:571). Filing a petition formally places the juvenile before the juvenile judge in many jurisdictions. But juveniles may come before juvenile judges in less formal ways. There is considerable variation in different jurisdictions about how juvenile courts are conducted. Increasingly, juvenile courts are emulating criminal courts in many respects (Feeney, 1987; Krisberg, 1988; Springer, 1987). Most of the physical trappings are present, including the judge's bench, tables for the prosecution and defense, and a witness stand.

In most jurisdictions, juvenile judges have almost absolute discretion in how their courts are conducted. Juvenile defendants alleged to have committed various crimes may or may not be granted a trial by jury, if one is requested. Few states permit jury trials for juveniles in juvenile courts, according to legislative mandates. The doctrine of *parens patriae* is very much in evidence in juvenile courtrooms. After hearing the evidence presented by both sides in any juvenile proceeding, the judge decides or adjudicates the matter. An adjudication is a judgment or action on the petition filed with the court by others. If the petition alleges delinquency on the part of certain juveniles, the judge determines whether the juveniles are delinquent or not delinquent. If the petition alleges that the juveniles involved are dependent, neglected, or otherwise in need of care by agencies or others, the judge decides the matter. If the adjudicatory proceeding fails to support the facts alleged in the petition filed with the court, the case is dismissed and the youth is freed. If the adjudicatory proceeding supports the allegations, then the judge must sentence the juvenile or order a particular disposition. Numerous sanctioning options are available to juvenile judges if youths are adjudicated delinquent. These are generally divided according to nominal, conditional, or custodial options.

Nominal dispositions are the least punitive of the three major courses of action available to juvenile judges. These include either "verbal warnings" or "stern reprimands." The nature of such verbal warnings or reprimands is exclusively a matter of judicial discretion. Release to the custody of parents or legal guardians completes the juvenile court action against the youth. Most often, those youths who are first offenders or low-risk offenders are subject to these minimal sanctions. More serious juvenile offenders and chronic recidivists merit some form of conditional punishment, even out-of-home placement, such as incarceration in a nonsecure or secure facility.

For all practical purposes, all *conditional dispositions* are probationary options. Youths are placed on probation and required to comply with certain conditions during the probationary period. Conditional options or dispositions usually provide for an act or acts on the part of juveniles to be fulfilled as "conditions" of the sentence imposed. Or these conditions might be placements in programs or community facilities where assorted treatments may be applied. If juveniles have been adjudicated as "delinquent" and if the delinquency involved damage to a victim's property or bodily harm, restitution to victims may be required to pay for the property or medical bills. Many jurisdictions provide for community services of various kinds to be performed by juveniles. They may be required to cut lawns in city parks, clean debris from local highways or public areas, or perform other services (e.g., painting, maintenance work, carpentry work). Which services should be provided different youths? Do some youths pose greater risks to themselves or society than other youths? At this crucial stage, risk assessments, together with determinations of juveniles' needs, may be made. Risk and needs assessments enhance decision making about subsequent placements and/or program involvements of juveniles which are ideally designed to meet their needs and/or manage their behaviors with varying degrees of administrative control.

Some youths may be required to take courses or therapy at various community service agencies. If they are alcohol- or drug-dependent, they may be required to take steps toward recovery from their dependencies. Another option available to judges is to sentence youths to custodial terms and suspend their sentences in favor of probation for a designated period such as six months or one year. In certain jurisdictions, some youths may be permitted to live at home and attend their schools, but they must wear electronic anklets or wristlets as a part of an electronic monitoring program. Such programs are designed to keep electronic tabs on offenders. Offenders wear devices that emit electronic signals that can be received at some central location, such as a juvenile probation department. Or youths may be reached by special telephonic devices and must place their electronic wristlets into receptacles that enable the sender to verify the offender's presence at home. Again, not all youths are necessarily eligible for such types of programs with low levels of direct supervisory control. Some youths require secure placement or incarceration, where their behaviors are continuously monitored and their movements restricted.

Custodial options are divided according to nonsecure custody and secure custody. Nonsecure custody includes out-of-home placements in foster homes, group homes, camps, ranches, or schools. These are often temporary measures designed to allow officials to determine more permanent arrangements for juvenile placements later. Juveniles have freedom of movement, and they may participate in school and other youthful activities. If they are assigned to group homes or are placed in camps or ranches, they must observe curfews and comply with camp or ranch rules of conduct. It is assumed that if they are in the care of others, such as foster homes or shelters, curfews will also be imposed.

The "last resort," according to juvenile court judges, is for the most serious juvenile offenders to be placed in secure custody—either short- or long-term (*Criminal Justice Newsletter,* 1988:5–6; Krisberg et al., 1986). Judges are reluctant to imprison youths, in part because of overcrowding in secure juvenile facilities, the potentially adverse effects of labeling from "prisonization," and the possible availability of intermediate punishments through community-service agencies. Community services designed to manage juvenile offenders are often termed *community corrections.* Both risk and needs assessments may be used to classify juveniles at this stage, because institutional authorities want to separate more serious offenders from less serious ones. Initial screenings of entering youthful inmates enable preliminary distinctions to be made much like those in adult institutions.

Unfortunately, large numbers of juveniles who are not among the worst juveniles are placed in secure facilities. In Oregon, for example, substantial numbers of runaways, youths with mental health problems, drug abusers, and child abuse victims have been institutionalized primarily because of few available community-based treatment programs (Bakal and Krisberg, 1987). According to a fifty-state survey of juvenile judge sentencing dispositions issued by the National Conference of State Legislatures (1988), judges in some states may impose weekend confinement in secure facilities for some youths as a punishment. In eight states (Alaska, Arkansas, Illinois, Kansas, Montana, New Mexico, Texas, and Vermont), courts commit those adjudicated youths to the relevant youth corrections agencies, and those agencies decide what types of placements are appropriate (*Criminal Justice Newsletter,* 1988:5). However, several states have acted aggressively to ensure that only the most serious juvenile offenders receive secure institutionalization (*Criminal Justice Newsletter,* 1988:5).

Influencing judicial decision making are predispositional reports about certain juveniles which are prepared by juvenile probation officers. These reports are similar to presentence investigation reports for adult offenders. They include much valuable background information about juvenile offenders, their weaknesses and strengths, abilities and limitations. Probation officers also make their own assessments and recommendations based upon their analysis and observation of the juvenile and the juvenile's record. Ordinarily, these predisposition reports are not mandatory for all juvenile delinquency adjudications. Juvenile court judges have the right to request such reports if they believe the appropriateness of their sentencing decision making might be enhanced. Most institution-bound offenders will have such reports completed by probation officers. The contents of these reports may be made available to officials in charge of secure institutions in order to make the best placement decisions.

Juvenile Corrections. The range of juvenile corrections is almost as broad as that existing for adult offenders convicted of crimes. Many juveniles adjudicated as delinquent may be placed on probation. Depending upon juvenile probation officer caseloads in various jurisdictions, this probation may be more or less intense, commensurate with intensive supervised probation for adults (Baird, 1987; Colley, Culbertson, and Latessa, 1987). Placement in different types of probationary programs is dependent upon how the youth is originally classified (Baird, 1985).

Probation, either standard or intensive, may also be conditional and involve restitution to victims and/or community services. In 1990, there were over 75,000 juveniles on probation in various state jurisdictions (American Correctional Association, 1992). Juveniles may be placed in community-based residential programs or exposed to various therapies and treatments or training. Also, there are many types of intermediate punishments, including several community-based interventions, home confinement, electronic monitoring, and intensive supervised probation. Risk instruments may be used to determine whether certain juvenile offenders qualify for entry into one or more of these community programs. The clear intent of using such instrumentation would be to protect community residents from dangerous juveniles who may pose risks for them.

Confinement in state industrial schools is the juvenile equivalent of incarceration in a state prison for adults. This type of confinement is considered "hard time" for many juveniles. The California Youth Authority operates various facilities to house growing numbers of juvenile offenders in secure confinement. Lengths of commitment vary for offenders, depending upon the seriousness of their adjudication offenses. In 1990, there were over 90,000 juveniles in public and private correctional facilities in the United States (Flanagan and Jamieson, 1991). Three-fourths of those in secure confinement are male (Flanagan and Jamieson, 1991).

When juveniles are first admitted to either public or private detention facilities, they are administered a battery of tests. These tests attempt to assess their educational level, reading ability, and other personal qualities. Risk and needs assessment inventories are also administered to determine the level of custody each juvenile should receive as well as the nature of his or her program involvement. Some of these instruments are designed to determine how well juveniles adjust to their new incarcerative surroundings (Kochis, 1992).

After juveniles have served a portion of their incarcerative sentences, they are paroled by a juvenile parole board to the supervision of an appropriate state or community agency. In 1990, there were over 50,000 juveniles on parole in various state jurisdictions (Flanagan and Jamieson, 1991). In Utah, for instance, a seven-member board, the Utah Youth Parole Authority, makes early-release decisions over large numbers of incarcerated youths monthly. Operated by the Utah Division of Youth Corrections, this board consists of three citizens and four staff members. In one thirty-seven day period, the board conducted approximately 300 parole hearings (Norman, 1986). Although the board appears to be guided by certain eligibility criteria, a juvenile's institutional behavior while confined is considered quite important as an indicator of the youth's future community reintegration (Norman, 1986). Increasingly, juvenile paroling authorities are using risk and needs assessment devices to objectify their decision making. One reason for greater use of such instrumentation is widespread criticism from many quarters about the subjectivity, unfairness, and disparities exhibited generally by previous parole board actions.

TYPES OF RISK PREDICTION INSTRUMENTS

Three basic categories of risk classifications have been identified (Morris and Miller, 1985:13–14):

1. Anamnestic prediction. This is a prediction of offender behavior according to *past circumstances*. The circumstances are similar now, therefore, it is likely the offender will behave the same way now. For example, a presentence investigation report may show that an offender was alcohol- and drug-dependent, unemployed, inclined toward violence because of previous assault incidents, and

poorly educated. Recidivists convicted of new crimes may exhibit present circumstances similar to those that prevailed when they were convicted of their earlier offense. Thus, judges and others might rely heavily upon the *situational* similarity of past and present circumstances to measure offender risk. However, if some offenders have made a significant effort between convictions to obtain additional education or training for better job performance, or if they are no longer alcohol- or drug-dependent, other types of behavioral forecasts will have to be made. This is because different circumstances exist now compared with previous circumstances.

2. The actuarial prediction. This type of prediction is based upon the *characteristics of a class of offenders* similar to offenders being considered for probation, parole, or inmate classification. This prediction considers others like them, situated as they are, and how they behaved in the past. Therefore, it is likely that those persons who exhibit similar characteristics to the general class of offenders considered for these different sanctioning and classification options will behave in ways similar to that particular class. In effect, this is an aggregate predictive tool. For instance, assume we have targeted a large sample of persons placed on probation and track them over a two-year period. We determine that 65 percent of these probationers did not complete their probationary periods satisfactorily. We describe these "failures" as follows: they are predominantly young, black, unemployed or underemployed, lack a high school education, were victims of child abuse, and are drug-dependent. Now, whenever young, black, unemployed, less educated, drug-dependent, former child-abuse victims are considered for probation, parole, inmate classification, or some intermediate sanctioning option, their chances of being placed in one program or another, or of being classified one way or another, may be influenced greatly by the general characteristics of previous program failures. Interestingly, it seems that program "failures" are more often described and used to structure risk instruments than are program "successes."

3. The clinical prediction. This type of prediction is based upon the predictor's professional training and experience working directly with the offender. Based upon extensive diagnostic examinations, the belief is that the offender will behave in a certain way. The subjectivity inherent in clinical prediction is apparent. The skills of the assessor are prominent. However, such prediction is more expensive, since each clinical prediction is individualized. Both anamnestic and actuarial prediction respectively utilize situational factors and general characteristics of offenders in forecasting their future risk. Interestingly, the highest degrees of validity are associated with actuarial and anamnestic predictions (for instance, those currently used by parole boards), and they are considered very reliable. In contrast, clinical prediction is most accurately described as an art and rests upon the past successes of the predictor (Floud and Young, 1981:29). Predictors in clinical predictions are usually psychiatrists or psychologists with extensive clinical training and experience with deviant conduct and criminal behavior.

Any prediction tools which are used, and any claims about their validity and reliability, and/or the recommendations concerning their applicability to specific offender situations, are subject to certain limitations. Because they are fallible instruments, they should not be relied upon completely for determining one's life chances as a probationer, parolee, or for any other important classification decision. For instance, Morris and Miller (1985:35–37) have suggested three guiding principles for parole boards to consider when making early-release decisions:

1. Punishment should not be imposed, nor the term of punishment extended, by virtue of a prediction of dangerousness, beyond that which would be justified as a deserved punishment independently of that prediction.
2. Provided this limitation is respected, predictions of dangerousness may properly influence sentencing decisions and other decisions under criminal law.
3. The base expectancy rate of violence for the criminal predicted as dangerous must be shown by reliable evidence to be substantially higher than the base expectancy rate of another criminal with a closely similar criminal record and convicted of a closely similar crime but not predicted as unusually dangerous, before the greater dangerousness of the former may be relied on to intensify or extend his/her punishment.

SOME USES OF RISK ASSESSMENT IN CRIMINAL AND JUVENILE JUSTICE

Risk assessments made of offenders may range from unstructured, subjective observations of their behaviors to elaborate, carefully constructed instruments. Applications of such structured devices are most prevalent in corrections. However, prosecutors and judges must make frequent assessments of offender risk as well. For instance, prosecutors exert considerable influence in pretrial release decision making (Siddiqi, 1991). Should an alleged offender be granted pretrial release or bail? Prosecutors can ask that offenders be released on their own recognizance pending trial (ROR); they can ask for a high bail to help ensure a defendant's appearance in court later; or they can ask that particular defendants be held without bail. Factors such as crime seriousness and perceived offender dangerousness or risk posed to the community affect their decisions. Often, prosecutorial decisions about bail or no bail recommendations rest upon the particular circumstances surrounding a case. Prosecutors in federal jurisdictions frequently screen their cases to determine those most eligible for pretrial release (Garner, 1991). In some cases, psychiatric reports of alleged offenders are consulted before making these decisions. Whether situational, actuarial, or clinical criteria are used, the intent of predicting risk in these cases is to make more informed decisions (Zimmerman and Cohen, 1990). In some cases, prosecutors may seek civil commitments of alleged offenders based upon data gathered from ward charts, arrest and community mental health center records, and other behavioral components (e.g., type, object, frequency, weapons/means, and severity of outcome) (Hiday, 1990).

Assessments of dangerousness and risk are also made of juvenile offenders by prosecutors, intake officers, and others. In New York, for example, prosecutors in juvenile courts have often relied upon assessments of public risk or dangerousness to place juvenile offenders in prevention detention or preventive incarceration (Fagan and Guggenheim, 1990). A fifty-state survey was conducted to determine the current state of the art in juvenile risk assessment. It was found that most states had some semblance of risk assessment for juvenile offenders, but only a minority of states have formal risk instruments (Towberman, 1992). Predominant risk factors in these few states include offense severity, past history of offending, offender age, psychological measures, use of community resources, peer group association, family problems, substance abuse, and absconding (Towberman, 1992). These findings are consistent with the juvenile risk assessment data gathered for this book. Less than half of all states furnished juvenile risk assessment instruments on the basis of a request from a comprehensive mail survey.

In yet other jurisdictions, juvenile detainees might be tested for drug use while being held at detention centers awaiting their court adjudication (Dembo et al., 1990). Studies of urine testing for drugs among 399 youths entering the Hillsborough Regional Detention Center in Tampa, Florida, have disclosed that those testing positive for cocaine were older youths, age sixteen or seventeen. Furthermore, 51 percent of those testing positive for drugs were subsequently rearrested or referred by juvenile authorities for new offenses within ten to fifteen months of their original adjudications. Recidivism among those testing negative for drugs was about 33 percent for the same time interval (Dembo et al., 1990). Thus, simply knowing whether certain juvenile offenders test positive for drugs causes prosecutors to regard them as greater risks for future offending compared with those youths who do not use drugs. In these instances, drug use or nonuse might function as one crude indicator of future offending and might adversely affect a juvenile's adjudication outcome. Apart from these applications, screening instruments might be used proactively to determine high-risk juveniles to target for delinquency prevention programs (Wieczorek, Welte, and Mirand, 1991).

Judges and Risk Assessment

Compared with prosecutors, judges rely more heavily on risk assessments of convicted offenders. Typically, judges rely upon numerical indicators of risk (and needs) assessments in order to make more objective sentencing decisions (Lovegrove, 1989). These quantitative aids help to avoid inconsistencies and disparities in the imposition of prison sentences and the length of imprisonment. In many states, sentencing decisions represent a degree of uncertainty. Judges attempt to manage this uncertainty by developing patterned responses that are a product of an attribution process involving assessments of an offender's likelihood of committing future crimes (Albonetti, 1991). Should offenders be placed in available community programs or incarcerated (Jengeleski, Labecki, and Kayser, 1992)? Actuarial predictions are most often made by judges in their sentencing decisions. The magnitude of probation is such that in 1990, 2,670,234 offenders were under some form of probation supervision (Jankowski, 1991:1). In all, over 4.7 million offenders were under some form of correctional management that same year (Jankowski, 1991:1).

Presentence Investigation Reports. Also assisting judges in their sentencing decisions are probation officers who prepare presentence investigation reports (PSIs). PSIs are written summaries of information obtained by the probation officer through interviews with the defendant and an investigation of the defendant's background (Drass and Spencer, 1987:280). These documents are structured to the extent that they require probation officers to fill in standard information about defendants. PSIs also contain narratives, or summaries or accounts of the crime, highlighting certain information about defendants and containing sentencing recommendations from probation officers (Drass and Spencer, 1987:280). Sometimes, especially for recidivists, these probation officer recommendations are more severe than those contemplated by the judge (Campbell, McCoy, and Osigweh, 1990). Space may also be available for the defendant's version of the crime and why it was committed.

Federal district judges order PSIs prepared within a sixty-day period following the defendant's conviction. Federal district judges order PSIs conducted by U.S. probation officers under the authority of 18 U.S. Code, Sec. 3552(a, b, and c) and 18 U.S.C. Federal Rule of Criminal Procedure 32(c)(1) (1993). Extensions of time beyond the sixty-day period may be granted if further study of the defendant is desirable, with judicial approval. Usually, this is an additional sixty-day period. This time interval permits the court to obtain psychiatric examinations of the defendant or reports from psychological examiners. These materials are helpful in deciding the most appropriate sentence for the offender. State and local requirements for the submission of PSIs vary greatly from those prescribed by federal rules. Some states, such as California, require PSIs to be prepared within a ten-day period following a defendant's conviction.

There is no standard form for a PSI common to all jurisdictions. However, most PSIs contain similar information. A presentence investigation report is a document prepared, usually by a probation agency or officer, which provides background information on the convicted offender including name, age, present address, occupation (if any), potential for employment, the crime(s) involved, relevant circumstances associated with the crime, family data, evidence of prior record (if any), marital status, and other relevant data.

Federal PSIs are required for all convicted criminal offenders (unless offenders waive the PSI with court permission and if the conviction is plea bargained) (U.S. Code, Rule 32(c), 1993). F.R.Cr.P. 32(c) specifies in substance that

> The probation service . . . shall make a presentence investigation and report to the court before the imposition of sentence or the granting of probation unless, with the permission of the court, the defendant waives a presentence investigation and report, or the court finds that there is in the record information sufficient to enable the meaningful exercise of sentencing discretion, and the court explains this finding on the record. . . . the report

shall contain any prior criminal record of the defendant and such information about his characteristics, his financial condition and the circumstances affecting his behavior as may be helpful in imposing sentence or in granting probation or in the correctional treatment of the defendant, and such other information as may be required by the court.

Kentucky, Virginia, and Tennessee are some of the many states that have PSI provisions in their criminal statutes. For example, Tennessee's PSI statute, T.C.A. 40-35-207 (1989), requires probation officers to obtain the following information:

1. The characteristics and circumstances of the offense committed by the defendant;
2. The defendant's physical and mental history and condition, family and social situation and background, education, occupation and personal habits;
3. Information about mitigating or aggravating circumstances associated with the offense;
4. The defendant's prior record, if any;
5. Information about whether the court should prescribe probation and the conditions associated with probation, if granted;
6. Any information about the capability of the defendant to pay restitution to crime victims or to support the defendant's own dependents;
7. Any statement volunteered by the victim(s) of the crime to supplement the report; and
8. Information to assist the court in determining whether to sentence the offender to a community-based alternative or incarceration.

The narrative in PSIs is an especially important component and is often persuasive in sentencing severity. Probation officers have much discretion whether to influence the favorableness or unfavorableness of these reports for offenders. One important factor is the probation officer's judgment of the degree of public risk posed by the offender if placed on probation. Thus, probation officers attempt to predict the offender's future behavior (Clear, Clear, and Burrell, 1989; Cohn and Ferriter, 1990; Frishtik, 1988). This is one of the most difficult tasks associated with probation work.

The Functions of PSIs. The functions of PSIs are

1. to provide the sentencing judge with an adequate analysis of the offender's background and prospects for rehabilitation;
2. to assist probation officers in their officer/client planning; such planning may involve community service, restitution to crime victims, assignment to community-based corrections agencies, house arrest/electronic monitoring, or some other nonincarcerative alternative; PSIs disclose information to sentencing judges about any mitigating circumstances that would lessen the harshness of the sentence;
3. to classify and categorize offenders into various risk categories;
4. to assist parole boards in determining early release and the conditions accompanying the granting of parole (Weintraub, 1987:26);

5. to permit probation officers or other supervisory authorities greater monitoring capability over offenders sentenced to some form of probation; and
6. to provide research material for scholars to conduct investigations of crime patterns, parole board decision making, judicial sentencing trends, and other related phenomenon.

The Contents of PSIs. Whether a PSI report contains the defendant's version of the offense should be determined on the basis of the best interests of the offender. This is why the assistance of counsel is important. If offenders decide to appeal the conviction later, a written statement prepared by them about their version of the offense could be used by the court to impeach them and cause the appeal to fail. Thus, as some critics have said, there are "countervailing reasons why [defense] counsel often advises against submitting a 'defendant's version of the offense' following a conviction after trial" (Weintraub, 1987:26).

Whether PSIs are used for sentencing, community supervision, inmate classification, or parole/release decision making, they share many of the following contents: offender's criminal record, including numbers of parole/probation revocations, numbers of adult and juvenile arrests, age at first arrest, nature of arrest crimes, number of adult and juvenile convictions, age at first conviction, nature of prior convictions, repeat conviction types, number of previous felony sentences, number of previous probation sentences, number of juvenile incarcerations, number of jail terms served, number of prison terms served, age at first incarceration, length of current term, total years incarcerated, nature of current crime, whether victim injury occurred, current age and educational level, employment history, mental health status, drug use, living arrangements, alcohol use/abuse, address changes in past year, prison infractions, program participation, release plans, escape history, attitude, and financial status (Gottfredson and Tonry, 1987:158).

An alternative to PSI reports suggested in recent years and implemented in selected jurisdictions is the Criminological Case Evaluation and Sentencing Recommendation (CCE-SR) (Gitchoff and Rush, 1989). This is a document that provides the judiciary with in-depth background information and offers creative sentencing options. The CCE-SR is a privately commissioned document prepared for the defense attorney or the court. It might advocate therapy and community service in lieu of imprisonment. One long-range implication of CCE-SRs is that they might enhance offender classification for correctional facilities. Thus, correctional officials might make more informed decisions for inmates in the prison classification process, in sentence modification proceedings, or in an attempt to transfer the client to an institution better suited for rehabilitation (Gitchoff and Rush, 1989).

Corrections and Risk Assessment

Prisoners in state and federal institutions cannot be lumped into a common category in terms of offense seriousness or risk posed to others. There are rapists, murderers, thieves, robbers, terrorists, gang members, drug dealers, ex-stock market insider traders, embezzlers, con artists, pimps, and child sexual abusers. Additionally, the differences among them include the nature and seriousness of their conviction offenses, age, and psychological or medical problems. In order to cope more effectively with meeting the needs of such diverse offenders, prisons have established different confinement facilities and levels of custody, depending upon how each prisoner is classified.

Prisoner Classification. Early Christian reform movements have been credited with establishing the first prisoner classification systems in the eighteenth century (American Correctional Association, 1983:194). The Philadelphia Walnut Street Jail in 1790 attempted to segregate prisoners according to age, gender, and offense seriousness. Subsequent efforts were made by penal authorities to classify and separate inmates according to various criteria in many state and federal prison facilities. It is generally acknowledged that adequate classification schemes for inmates have yet to be devised (Craddock, 1987; Austin, 1986; Austin and Pannell, 1986). Classification schemes are based largely on psychological, behavioral, and sociodemographic criteria. The use of psychological characteristics as predictors of risk or dangerousness and subsequent custody assignments for prisoners were stimulated by research during the period 1910–1920 (American Correctional Association, 1983:196). Psychologists and psychiatrists became increasingly involved in devising classificatory schemes for prisoners, especially those with mental problems (Metzner, 1992). Devices were eventually created based on a wider variety of personal and social criteria (Fink, 1992).

Today, all prisons in the United States have classification schemes of one type or another for differentiating among prisoners and assigning them to particular accommodations. The use of such schemes has varying utility depending on the purpose for the initial classification such as identifying those likely to engage in assaultive or aggressive disciplinary infractions (Clark, Canales-Portalatin, and Weth, 1992; Wright, 1986a). But regardless of the type of classification scheme employed by corrections officials in screening their inmates, prisoners are eventually channeled into one of several fixed custody levels. These are minimum, medium, and maximum security. It should also be noted that while many prisons and penitentiaries may be generally classified according to these three designations, it is also likely that a single prison or penitentiary will have three or more separate sections designated as such within the same facility. Thus, a prison often has a minimum-security area, a medium-security area, and a maximum-security area.

Minimum-Security Prisons. Minimum-security prisons are facilities designed to house low-risk, nonviolent first offenders. These institutions are also established to accommodate those serving short-term sentences. Minimum-security state facilities include a subsidiary of the New Jersey State Prison at Jones Farm in West Trenton; the Medfield, Massachusetts, Prison Project where inmates work in hospital wards in various capacities; and the Chillicothe, Missouri, Correctional Center for female offenders. Minimum-security housing is often of a dormitory-like quality, with grounds and physical plant features resembling a university campus rather than a prison. Those assigned to minimum-security facilities are trusted to comply with whatever rules are in force. Because of the greater trust administrators place in inmates in minimum-security institutions, these sites are believed to be most likely to promote greater self-confidence and self-esteem among prisoners. The rehabilitative potential of minimum-security inmates is high, while those in more secure detention facilities are considered more hard-core offenders and less likely to reform. The emphasis is upon prisoner reintegration into society. Usually, a wider variety of programs is available to inmates of minimum-security facilities. Also, there are generally fewer restrictions associated with familial visits.

Medium-Security Prisons. Approximately 60 percent of all state and federal prisons in the United States are medium- and minimum-security institutions (Carney, 1989). According to the American Correctional Association (1987), a majority of state and federal prison facilities are designed to accommodate medium- and minimum-security inmates. As of 1988, of the six U.S. penitentiaries, all but the one in Atlanta, Georgia, were classified as maximum-security. However, each of these federal institutions operates minimum-security satellite camps to house short-term and low-risk offenders. These minimum-security camps include dormitories, a dispensary, a medical center, and other conveniences. These camps are located adjacent to federal prisons and not directly within them (American Correctional Association, 1987:407).

The Federal Bureau of Prisons currently uses a six-level scale ranging from Level 1 to Level 6, with Level 1 being a minimum-security facility such as the Federal Prison Camp in Big Spring, Texas, and a Level 6 being a maximum-security facility such as the Marion, Illinois, Penitentiary. The prisons or penitentiaries in many states use similar classification schemes for describing inmate custody. Visitation privileges are tighter, compared with minimum-security institutions, and privileges, freedom of movement, and access to various educational, vocational, and/or therapeutic programs is more restricted. However, medium-security facilities at both state and federal levels sometimes offer inmates opportunities for work release, furloughs, and other types of programs that increase their freedom of movement.

Maximum-Security Prisons. About 40 percent of all U.S. prisons are maximum-security institutions. Those sentenced to maximum-security facilities are considered among the most dangerous, high-risk offenders. Those who have prior records of escape and who are violent crime recidivists often are sentenced to maximum-security institutions. Maximum-security prisons are characterized by many stringent rules and restrictions, and inmates are isolated from one another for long periods in single-cell accommodations. Prisoners in their cells or work areas are closely monitored by correctional officers with the use of closed-circuit television monitors. Visitation privileges are greatly restricted. There is no rehabilitation objective, with the principal function of these institutions being strictly custodial (Israel, 1983).

Maxi-Maxi Prisons. The most serious and dangerous federal prisoners are housed at the federal penitentiary at Marion, Illinois. This facility is one of the newer federal penitentiaries, constructed in 1963. It is designed to house only 574 inmates, and those incarcerated at Marion are considered the very worst prisoners in the system. Those sentenced to Marion are the most dangerous and violence-prone. Further, they are quite inclined to escape whenever the opportunity arises.

Typically, there is less violence in minimum-security facilities, while medium- and maximum-security institutions report greater amounts of inmate violence. This is due, in large part, to the fact that minimum-security inmates are considered less dangerous and pose the least risk to the safety of correctional officers or other inmates. Therefore, prison officials are most interested in empirical criteria that enable them to make the best inmate placements which will enhance inmate management and reduce violence. Each state and the federal system uses different types of inmate classification schemes for this purpose. Further, most states provide for reassessments of inmates after incarcerative periods of six months or one year. This is seen as one possible reward for good conduct among prisoners, if there is a chance they might be reclassified to a lower level of custody later. Lower levels of custody usually mean more privileges. And those prisoners held in lower custody levels acquire a greater degree of trust among prison officials. Often, this low classification level impacts favorably on early release or parole decision making.

No single scheme for classifying offenders is foolproof, although several have emerged as popular. Four of the most popular inmate classification systems used today include the National Institute of Corrections (NIC) Custody Determination Model; Quay's Adult Internal Management System; the Federal Model used in the Bureau of Prisons; and the California Model (Mason, 1992). The Megargee Inmate Typology purports to measure "inmate adjustment to prison life" (Megargee and Carbonell, 1985). Another type of inventory has been devised by Edwin Megargee. Megargee and his associates selected items from the Minnesota Multiphasic Personality Inventory (MMPI), a psychological assessment device, to define ten prisoner types and to predict an inmate's inclination to violate prison rules or act aggressively against others. Basically a psychological tool, the Megargee Inmate Typology has been adopted by various state prison systems for purposes of classifying prisoners into different custody levels. The successfulness and predictive utility of this instrument is questionable, however, as are all classificatory devices for assessing inmates (Louscher, Hosford, and Moss, 1983; Johnson, Simmons, and Gordon, 1983). One problem Megargee himself detected was that prisoner classification types based on his index scores change drastically during a one-year period, such that the reliability of this instrument may be challenged.

Others besides Megargee have sought to devise useful inmate classification criteria, but they have not been particularly fruitful (Gottfredson and Gottfredson, 1988; Farrington and Tarling, 1985; Goetting and Howsen, 1986). For example,

Goetting and Howsen (1986) found that inmate misconduct is highly correlated with being young, black, and male; having a relatively high number of prior convictions; having been unemployed prior to incarceration; and having been imprisoned for a long period. But descriptions of those who engage in prison misconduct are difficult to apply in screening stages to decide the level of custody inmates should be assigned. Should we place in high levels of custody all young, unemployed, black males with prior records and long sentences? Classifications according to these criteria would quickly be challenged as racist and discriminatory, which they would be. This is one major fault with actuarial prediction schemes.

The controversy over the development and use of inmate classification devices is heightened by those researchers reporting favorable outcomes when such devices are used on selected inmate populations. For instance, the Louisiana Department of Corrections tested two devices designed to predict an inmate's escape risk. Using race, juvenile arrest history, employment history, and selected subscales from the MMPI, researchers found that 54 percent of the escapees and 76 percent of the nonescapees were correctly identified. These are not bad percentages, considering the general nature and inadequacy of behavioral forecasting. The report suggested that this escape prediction device could be useful as a screening instrument for evaluating inmate escape risk (Shaffer, Bluoin, and Pettigrew, 1985). Additionally, Robins and others (1986) have described the use of the Initial Classification Analysis for classifying female offenders at the Missouri Diagnostic Center in 1983 according to their educational, custodial, vocational, and medical/health care needs. This instrument was found to have fairly high reliability. Similar instruments have been devised in other countries, such as Canada (Motiuk, Motiuk, and Bonta, 1992).

Challenging inmate classification schemes on moral and legal grounds are several critics (Decker and Salert, 1986; Gottfredson and Tonry, 1987; Morris, 1984; von Hirsch, 1985). How inmates are initially classified and subsequently accommodated while in prison may influence directly or indirectly their parole chances (Hoffman, 1983; Gottfredson and Gottfredson, 1988). An inmate classified as "maximum-security" may not deserve such a classification, which implies that the inmate is considered dangerous. Furthermore, inmate opportunities for personal development and rehabilitation are adversely influenced by such classifications. On the other hand, those inmates classified as minimum-security have access to a wider variety of prison benefits and programs. They are not monitored as closely and are not considered particularly dangerous. When these inmates face parole boards, their custody levels may be assets or liabilities. Prisoners who have been maintained under minimum-security conditions can argue that they have "proven" themselves worthy of release through the trust granted them initially by prison officials. Inmates maintained under maximum-security conditions will likely prejudice parole boards because they have not been granted extensive prison privileges.

Classification instruments vary in their stability and predictive utility, often lacking generalization to prisoners in different jurisdictions, lacking instrument validation, and posing serious questions about the current state of the art in statistical risk prediction (Wright, Clear, and Dickson, 1984). Since these risk prediction devices are frequently employed for deciding inmates' levels of custody while incarcerated as well as influencing their parole chances, it seems reasonable that challenges should be made about the quality of these instruments and their use by prison authorities and others.

Just because a risk assessment instrument is more technologically sophisticated, this does not necessarily mean that it is any better as a predictor than a simpler instrument. Five prediction methods involving linear additive models, clustering models, and multivariate contingency tables were examined in the context of their respective parole risk assessment for 4,500 parolees released from federal prisons in 1970–1972 (Gottfredson and Gottfredson, 1985). Researchers found that simpler and more easily understood prediction methods worked about as well as more sophisticated schemes based on advanced statistical techniques.

Parole Board Early-Release Decision Making and Risk Forecasts

Parole Boards and Their Diversity. Parole boards are diverse entities. Each state has different criteria for selecting or appointing parole board members. No graduate schools in the United States offer degrees in parole board membership. Often, parole board members are political appointees, many of whom have little or no correctional experience. Parole board members may be university professors who teach criminal justice. Physicians, psychiatrists, and lawyers might be parole board members. Ministers also qualify. Because of few, if any, standards that qualify persons as parole board members, parole boards are often blamed for "incorrect" early-release decision making. Some parolees may commit murder or rape. Media attention is given to such events, and parole boards are soundly criticized by the press and others. Interestingly, parole boards are often blamed for early releases of inmates beyond their direct control. For example, as one result of sentencing reforms in many states, mandatory, early mandatory, determinate, and presumptive sentencing provisions permit offenders early release if they accumulate sufficient good-time credits that result in deductions of time from their original sentences. When one's time is served, one is released. Automatically. There is no early-release decision to be made. Therefore, when some inmates walk out of prison, the parole board might take the heat although it had absolutely nothing to do with the inmate release.

Parole Board Decision Making. Exerting a tremendous impact on how corrections professionals do their jobs is chronic prison overcrowding. Substantial increases in numbers of parolees and the intensity of their supervision have been observed in recent years, but at the same time, the number of parole revocation hearings has skyrocketed (Burke, 1987:74). The aims of parole boards are similar to those of sentencing: treatment, incapacitation, deterrence, and deserts (Gottfredson and Gottfredson, 1988:230). However, parole boards appear to receive more criticism from the public about the decisions they make compared with earlier similar judicial decisions. The significant question for parole boards is *when to release inmates rather than whether to release them* (Gottfredson, Wilkins, and Hoffman, 1978).

Parole board decision making includes determining the date for first parole consideration, fixing the dates for subsequent hearings, fixing minimum terms served, waiving minimum terms, modifying earlier decisions, fixing parole dates, denying further parole consideration, awarding good-time credits, fixing the length of sentence to be served in prison and/or parole, or setting special conditions of parole, including requirements of supervision or treatment programs (Gottfredson and Gottfredson, 1988:236). In the State of Washington, for example, judges may set a minimum term, but the parole board may waive this minimum term (O'Leary and Hanrahan, 1976; Gottfredson and Gottfredson, 1988:236).

Apart from parole board decision making, several states have legislated emergency-release provisions to ease prison overcrowding. Such provisions override any parole board decision. States such as Michigan and Illinois have adopted such emergency provisions. In 1980, Michigan adopted the Prison Overcrowding Emergency Powers Act (Gottfredson and Gottfredson, 1988:214). Therefore, if the prison population exceeds the rated maximum capacity for thirty days, the governor declares an emergency whereby a mandatory ninety-day reduction in the sentences of those prisoners serving minimum statutory terms is created. This policy remains in effect until the prison population is reduced to 95 percent capacity (Gottfredson and Gottfredson, 1988:214). The judiciary may become involved in contributing to rising parole rates. For instance, between 1980 and 1990, the Texas Department of Criminal Justice has lowered the prisoner population to about 95 percent of its capacity (Bodapati and Marquart, 1992). Much of this inmate population reduction was attributable to court mandates.

Most states had changed their sentencing provisions by 1988. In many instances, these sentencing provision changes reduced substantially the discretionary power of parole boards to grant early release to prisoners. This was part of a "get tough on crime" trend among several states (Martin, 1983). Martin (1983) says that among the states severely curtailing sentence commutation are Colorado (1982), Illinois (1980), and Oklahoma (1982). An example of the effects of the "get tough" policy occurred in Pennsylvania, where reductions in sentence commutations dropped from 128 in 1977 to 2 in 1981.

The National Institute of Corrections has received many requests for and provided technical assistance to parole boards in making more objective early-release decisions (Burke, 1987:74). These and other similar consultations have resulted in the formulation of explicit guidelines and policies to govern release or revocation decisions (Burke, 1987:76). Parole boards have been encouraged to focus on at least five major areas:

1. Policy making. How does policy making differ from individual decision making? How does it relate to individual discretion? What steps are involved? Who must participate? How can policy be made operational?
2. Management. What management needs exist? How can board and staff roles for management be clarified?
3. Roles of research. How can research be used to inform policy making and decision making? What role must policy makers play in developing risk instruments? How can parole decision makers communicate effectively with technical staff?
4. Criminal justice system issues. How can the critical overlaps between parole and other agencies be identified? What are viable mechanisms for cooperation? How do other agencies' policies and practices influence workload?
5. Strategies. What are effective strategies for handling and building effective working relationships with the various public interests that are of importance to parole? (Burke, 1987:78)

Among corrections professionals, especially parole board members, it is generally accepted that their primary concerns are fulfilling their objectives and demonstrating a high degree of accountability to the general public (Callanan, 1986:76). Professionals contend that parole fails only when it is allowed to fail through "neglect, ignorance, and political expediency" (Atkinson, 1986:56). Other experts disagree and say that the general question of parole board effectiveness is meaningless (Gottfredson and Gottfredson, 1988:235). These critics argue that because of the diversity of goals and objectives of U.S. parole boards, legal sanctioning systems and procedures, virtually *any* statement about parole is in danger of being shown to be false.

Some experts say that "a strong parole system does not release inmates who pose an undue risk to public safety or who would be unlikely to benefit from rehabilitative services to the community" (Atkinson, 1986:54). How such risks can be predicted in advance is a highly controversial subject. An interesting twist on the theme of parole board effectiveness is a parole board decision to release a poor-risk inmate. Subsequently, because of a minor technical parole violation (e.g., curfew, drinking), the technical parole violator is returned to prison. Because some minor technical rules were violated, it was demonstrated that the parolee was in danger of committing new, more serious, offenses, and thus, a crime prevention function was performed by revoking parole. The success of the parole decision–parole supervision system was demonstrated by the parolee failure (Gottfredson and Gottfredson, 1988:234).

Yet other professionals suggest that it might be wise to grant release to a poor risk about to be released anyway, because release without parole officer supervision would mean no supervisory control (Gottfredson and Gottfredson, 1988:234). At least some control would be provided, if even for a brief period, and this might assist the offender's reintegration into society. Parole denial to the poor risk would be dysfunctional in this instance. Furthermore, significant legal issues concerning the due process requirements that must prevail at parole board hearings are also raised (Metchik, 1992).

Parole Board Orientations. Parole board decision making has been classified into at least six different categories, each with its own value system: (1) the jurist, (2) the sanctioner, (3) the treater, (4) the controller, (5) the citizen, and (6) the regulator (Gottfredson and Gottfredson, 1988: 231–233; O'Leary and Hall, 1976). The jurist value system sees parole decisions as a natural part of the criminal justice system where fairness and equity predominate. Emphasized are an inmate's rights, and parole board members strive to be sensitive to due process. The sanctioner value system equates the seriousness of the offense with the amount of time served. In some respects, this is closely connected with the "just deserts" philosophy.

Rehabilitation is stressed by the treater orientation, and decisions are made in terms of what benefits offenders the most if parole is granted. Therefore, participation in various educational or vocational programs, therapy or encounter groups, restitution, and other types of conditions might accompany an inmate's early release. The controller orientation stresses intensive parole supervision and monitoring. Conditions that increase the degree of control over the offender are created. Electronic monitoring or house arrest might be a part of the parole program. Regardless, the controller value system sees offender incapacitation or severe restrictions of freedom while on parole as desirable. The controller value system is most concerned with the risk posed to the public by an offender's early release.

The citizen orientation appeals to public interests by ensuring that community expectations are fulfilled by making appropriate early-release decisions. What will the likely public reaction be if certain types of offenders are released short of serving their full terms? Is the public good best served by such decisions? Community harmony and social order should be preserved, and parole board decisions should be made which promote community harmony and order. In view of mixed public sentiment and current dissatisfaction with parole board decision making generally, this is seemingly an impossible task. Finally, the regulator orientation emphasizes inmate reactions to parole board decisions. Control over inmates is maintained, in part, by the existence of a reward system. This reward system says to inmates that good behavior will lead to more favorable parole board decisions about their early release, when they become eligible for it. If parole board decision making is cavalier, unfair, subjective, or inconsistent, then inmates will be distrustful of the system and its promised rewards for rule compliance. Will the parole supervision system be undermined or enhanced as the result of parole board decision making? If prison officials wish to maintain a relatively high degree of harmony within their prisons by using the possibility of parole as a reward for good behavior, then the credibility of parole board decision making cannot be brought into question (O'Leary and Hall, 1976; Gottfredson and Gottfredson, 1988:231–232). To do so would undermine inmate confidence in the system and possibly lead to more frequent and dangerous disruptions and inmate misconduct.

When parole board decision making is considered in these diverse and sometimes conflicting contexts, it is easier to understand why extensive variability exists among parole boards in different jurisdictions. Each parole board member possesses one or another of these value systems. It is not likely that an entire parole board is closely connected with one view exclusively. Rather, these different values explain in part why apparently inconsistent decisions about the early release of similar inmates are made, even by the same parole boards, at different points in time.

Developing and Implementing Objective Parole Criteria. With such diversity among parole board members and the values they espouse, is it possible to establish objective parole criteria to govern all parole board decision making? Theoretically, objective parole criteria would immunize parole board members from accusations of racism as the result of releasing disproportionately large numbers of offenders of particular races or ethnic backgrounds. Parole board member liability would be limited in instances where offenders who are granted early release are especially dangerous and pose substantial danger to the community.

Some objective parole criteria have been compared with determinate sentencing policies, while traditional parole criteria have been equated with indeterminate sentencing systems (Lombardi and Lombardi, 1986:86). Following are some advantages of objective parole criteria:

1. Inmates know their presumptive release dates within several months of their incarceration.
2. The paroling authority is bound or obligated to meet the presumptive release date.
3. The paroling authority uses scores consisting of an inmate's criminal history and offense severity to determine time ranges for parole release.
4. The paroling authority uses a composite group score representing criminal histories of similar offenders to predict parole success (Lombardi and Lombardi, 1986:86–87).

These objective parole criteria have sometimes operated to restrict the discretionary power and flexibility of parole boards. While fairness to offenders and parole board accountability are increased by making the parole/release decision-making process more explicit and consistent, there are occasional undesirable, unanticipated consequences (Lombardi and Lombardi, 1986:87; Gottfredson, Hoffman, Sigler, and Wilkins, 1973). The Florida Parole Commission, for instance, implemented new objective parole criteria in 1980 (Lombardi, 1981). Before 1980, Florida's prison inmates had filed approximately 400 lawsuits annually. After the objective criteria went into effect, the number of lawsuits filed increased to about 1,800 annually.

These Florida inmate lawsuits primarily involved four basic issues. First, inmates said that objective scoring system errors led to unfavorable classifications and unjustifiably longer incarcerative terms. Second, they claimed that they had originally been placed in the wrong level of offense severity, usually resulting from an incorrect interpretation of their plea bargain agreements. Third, they claimed that parole board members extended or shortened their incarceration lengths in inconsistent ways by either considering or failing to consider certain aggravating circumstances such as using a weapon during the commission of the crime or causing serious injury to victims. Finally, the inmates said that the parole board failed to consider mitigating circumstances that would lessen the length of incarceration (Lombardi, 1981). All of these issues seemingly could be remedied by close monitoring of all parole board decision making and insistence on consistency in their standards. However, seldom do provisions exist to govern parole board decision making and accountability.

Actually, interest in devising consistent and objective early-release criteria is probably as old as parole itself. Most of the popular and more scientific methods for devising predictive criteria have been developed since the late 1960s, however. In 1972, the U.S. Parole Commission started to use an actuarial device in predicting parole success of federal prisoners (Hoffman, 1983). By the early 1980s, every state had either devised a system or was using one originated by another jurisdiction whereby parole decision making could be objectified (Gottfredson and Tonry, 1987).

Corrections experts currently contend that the technology exists that can classify offenders accurately on the basis of their potential risk to public safety; social service, educational, and vocational needs; and individual behavioral profiles. However, these experts also charge that many paroling bodies have not as yet fully exploited this technology in a cooperative and systematic manner (Atkinson, 1986:56). At the same time, other experts caution that the current state of the art in statistical risk prediction is such that many developed models are unstable when applied to various prisoner populations from one state to the next (Wright, Clear, and Dickson, 1984). Furthermore, insufficient validation of prediction instruments has occurred. When a parole risk assessment device was developed by Wisconsin officials for parole board decision making, for example, the device became popularly applied in several other states, especially after being recognized as a useful instrument by the National Institute of Corrections. However, the Wisconsin instrument appeared to lack validity when applied to a sample of New York parolees (Wright, Clear, and Dickson, 1984). This strongly suggests the need to devise measures that are applicable for selected inmate populations on a state-by-state basis.

The American Correctional Association (ACA) has had a continuing interest in the improvement of parole board integrity regarding classifications of prisoners and early-release recommendations. In 1984, the ACA established a policy statement relating to identifying and matching offender needs with existing correctional resources. Among other recommendations, the ACA policy statement encouraged all personnel involved in the classification process to be trained to assess and interpret classification instruments as well as their validation.

Parole boards must consider whether eligible inmates can observe the requirements of their parole if early release is granted. Therefore, these boards look at different inmates from the standpoint of parole agreements. Parole agreements are contracts between the offender and the state. Parole officers are responsible for ensuring offender compliance with the conditions set forth in the contract. If one or more conditions of this agreement are violated, the discretionary power of the parole officer is invoked. The parole officer may choose to overlook the violation, depending upon its seriousness. Or the officer may decide under the circumstances to recommend parole revocation. Parole revocations are not arbitrarily determined by parole officers. Parolees alleged to have violated one or more parole agreement conditions are entitled to a two-stage hearing to determine (1) if there was probable cause that their contract was violated, and (2) which punishment should be imposed. Return to prison is one alternative, but it is not automatically selected. Often, parole boards simply assign parole violators to a more intensively supervised parole program.

For instance, the Connecticut Parole Board has several standards which govern each early-release decision. These standards include

1. The nature and circumstances of inmate offenses and the inmate's current attitudes toward them.
2. The inmate's prior record and parole adjustment if paroled previously.
3. Inmate's attitude toward family members, the victim, and authority in general.
4. The institutional adjustment of inmates, including their participation in vocational/educational programs while incarcerated.
5. Inmate's employment history and work skills.
6. Inmate's physical, mental, and emotional condition as determined from interviews and other diagnostic information available.
7. Inmate's insight into the causes of his/her own criminal behavior in the past.
8. Inmate's personal efforts to find solutions to personal problems such as alcoholism, drug dependency, and need for educational training or developing special skills.
9. The adequacy of the inmate's parole plan, including planned place of residence, social acquaintances, and employment program (Connecticut Board of Parole, 1974).

All parole boards establish criteria to govern their parole decisions similar to those developed by Connecticut. Occasionally, psychiatric reports or examinations are prepared at the time of an inmate's sentencing. Another document is the PSI report. This report is often consulted in order to assist board members in making the best early-release decisions. Finally, parole boards may sometimes rely on victim testimony at parole hearings. Several states currently permit victim participation in parole board consideration for specific inmates. Victims may offer either written or oral testimony at these parole hearings, and parole boards weigh such written or oral testimony accordingly (Parsonage, 1992).

Consistency of Parole Board Decision Making. Parole boards strive for consistency. This is highly desirable in the application of any parole criteria (Gabor, 1986:19). Many inmate lawsuits involve allegations of inconsistent application of parole eligibility guidelines. The U.S. Parole Commission has stressed consistency in the application of its own standards. In 1982, a sample of 100 initial parole hearings was selected, 20 from each of five U.S. Parole Commission regions. Hearing examiners and various panels of research experts agreed on the appropriate guideline range in 86 percent of the cases. Disagreements were attributable to lack of guideline clarity, inadequate file information, or plain error within the hearing panel itself (Beck and Hoffman, 1985).

Ernest W. Burgess of the University of Chicago devised a weighting system for parole prognosis in 1928 (Glaser, 1987:256). However, more contemporary objective parole decision making and guidelines formulation can be traced to the pioneering work of Don Gottfredson and Leslie Wilkins, leaders of the Parole Decision-Making Project in the early 1970s (Goldkamp, 1987:106). The National Council on Crime and Delinquency and the U.S. Parole Commission (originally the U.S. Board of Parole) were interested in parole decision making and asked social scientists to help them determine relevant criteria involved in early-release decisions (Goldkamp, 1987:106). One fruitful result of the Parole Decision-Making Project was the adoption of a set of guidelines that provided parole board members with specific criteria to assess the successfulness of granting parole to various offenders. Several categories of offenders were established by these guidelines and based, in part, on a ranking of offense severity as well as a *salient factor score* (Gottfredson, Wilkins, and Hoffman, 1978). A salient factor score is a numerical classification that supposedly predicts the probability of a parolee's success if parole is granted.

Salient factor scores (SFS) were originally designed to assist parole board members to make fair, objective, and just parole decisions. Departures from these guidelines by parole boards were to be accompanied by written rationales outlining the reasons for such departures. In 1973, the U.S. Parole Commission formally adopted these parole decision guidelines, and SFSs were used in all federal parole hearings (Goldkamp, 1987:106). This was largely the result of a federal court order for the U.S. Board of Parole to articulate specifically its policies for granting parole (*Childs v. United States Board of Parole,* 1973). More than a few states were encouraged by the use of SFSs and either adopted the federal format or developed their versions.

The salient factor score previously used by the federal government consisted of seven criteria; its 1976 refinement was known as the *SFS 76*. In 1981, the salient factor scoring instrument was revised to yield a six-factor predictive device known as the *SFS 81* (Hoffman, 1983). A comparison of the revised SFS 81 with the SFS 76 was made to determine their relative validity, stability, simplicity, and scoring reliability. Both instruments appeared to have similar predictive characteristics, although the revised device possessed greater scoring reliability (Hoffman, 1983). More importantly, the SFS 81 weights heavily the extent and recency of an offender's criminal history (Hoffman, 1983). Seven possible points may be earned by having no prior convictions or adjudications (adult or juvenile), no prior commitments of more than thirty days, and being twenty-six years of age or older at the time of the current offense (with certain exceptions). Other points could be earned by not being heroin/opiate dependent and by not being a probation/parole/confinement/escape status violator. Lower scores meant that offenders would be considered "poor risks," while higher scores meant that they would be regarded as "good" or "very good" risks. The actual SFS 81 previously used is shown in Form 2.1.

It is important to understand that classification systems, such as the SFS 81

Form 2.1
The Salient Factor Score (SFS 81) Index

SALIENT FACTOR SCORE INDEX

1. Prior convictions/adjudications (adult or juvenile):
   None (3 pts)
   One (2 points)
   Two or three (1 point)
   Four or more (0 points)
2. Prior commitments of more than 30 days (adult or juvenile):
   None (2 points)
   One or two (1 point)
   Three or more (0 points)
3. Age at current offense/prior commitments:
   25 years of age or older (2 points)
   20-25 years of age (1 point)
   19 years of age or younger (0 points)
4. Recent commitment free period (three years):
No prior commitment of more than 30 days (adult or juvenile) or released to the community from last such commitment at least three years prior to the commencement of the current offense (1 point)
Otherwise (0 points)
5. Probation/parole/confinement/escape status violator this time:
Neither on probation, parole, confinement, or escape status at the time of the current offense, nor committed as a probation, parole, confinement, or escape status violator this time (1 point)
Otherwise (0 points)
6. Heroin/opiate dependence:
No history of heroin/opiate dependence (1 point)
Otherwise (0 points)

Total score = ___________

Source: U.S. Parole Commission, *Rules and Procedures Manual.* Washington, DC: U.S. Parole Commission, 1985.

Scores on the SFS 81 ranged from "0" to "10." The following score ranges and prognoses were generated:

Score Range	Parole Prognosis
0 - 3	"Poor"
4 - 5	"Fair"
6 - 7	"Good"
8 - 10	"Very Good"

instrument, are simply models. These models are assigned names such as the National Institute of Corrections Prison Classification Model or the Iowa Risk Assessment Model (Rans, 1984:50). Some authorities have outlined some important and desirable characteristics of such predictive models:

1. The model should be predictively valid.
2. The model should reflect reality.
3. The model should be designed for a dynamic system and not remain fixed over time.
4. The model should serve practical purposes.
5. The model should not be a substitute for good thinking and responsible judgment.
6. The model should be both qualitative and quantitative (Rans, 1984:50).

Parole boards would consult tabled offense characteristics consisting of categories of varying offense severity. Adult ranges, expressed in number of months served, are provided for each category and are cross-tabulated with the four-category parole prognosis above. Thus, a parole board can theoretically apply a consistent set of standards to prisoners committing similar offenses. When the board departs from these standards, especially when parole is possible for an offender but denied, a written rationale is provided for both the prisoner and the appellate authorities.

The U.S. Parole Commission revised its existing rules and modified its classification system in 1985. These new guidelines are somewhat less severe than those established in 1981. Comparing figures pertaining to time served before parole eligibility occurs shows many similarities, although in several instances, fewer months must be served for different offense severity levels. In any case, a parole board may depart from these guidelines and either shorten or lengthen the amount of time to be served (*Yamamoto v. U.S. Parole Commission,* 1986; *Lynch v. U.S. Parole Commission,* 1985; *Robinson v. Hadden,* 1983; *Stroud v. U.S. Parole Commission,* 1982). But written justification must be provided (*Myrick v. Gunnell,* 1983). And inmates have the right to appeal decisions of parole boards to a higher authority such as the National Appeals Board (18 U.S.C. Sec. 4215, 1993).

Predictions of dangerousness or risk have played vital roles in decision making throughout the criminal justice system (Morris and Miller, 1985:2). However, no predictive model is problem-free. Offenders are often misclassified, salient factor scores may not accurately reflect offenders' true parole potential, or the instrument, although applicable in one jurisdiction, may not be suitably applied in another jurisdiction. Although some studies report fairly accurate and predictable results with various risk instruments (i.e., parolees who are successful) (Eisenberg, 1986; Banks, 1984; Iowa Office for Criminal Justice and Juvenile Justice Planning, 1983; Iowa Statistical Analysis Center, 1985), other studies are less positive and recommend interpretive caution and further validation of the devices used (Beck and Hoffman, 1985; Robins et al., 1986; Sepejak, Webster, and Menzies, 1984; Zwetchkenbaum-Segal, 1984).

For example, the case of *Jones v. United States* (1983) involved the civil commitment issue of confining the defendant, Jones, to a term in a hospital (on the grounds of his future dangerousness) longer than that otherwise imposed had Jones been sentenced and held as a prisoner. Jones had earlier pleaded not guilty to a criminal act by reason of insanity. The U.S. Supreme Court held that Jones could, indeed, be detained beyond the limits of a criminal sentence, because his dangerousness was presumed on the basis of his original plea (Morris and Miller, 1985:30). In *Barefoot v. Estelle* (1983), a more serious case involving the possible imposition of the death penalty for a convicted murderer, Thomas A. Barefoot, testimony of an examining psychiatrist was permitted under the Texas death penalty statute which allows capital punishment if there is a finding that "there is a probability that the defendant would commit criminal acts of violence that would constitute a continuing threat to society" (Morris and Miller, 1985:31). The U.S. Supreme Court upheld the Texas statute.

In attempting to administer the affairs of parole boards equitably, a chief concern of most members is to minimize both the frequency of false positives and false negatives (Gabor, 1986:12–13). Predicting dangerousness and denying parole to an inmate who is not likely to be dangerous or to recidivate is probably as serious as granting parole to someone predicted not to be dangerous but who turns out to be dangerous anyway. But in the context of fairness or "just deserts," basing punishment and parole decision making on the gravity of the offense itself or on the blameworthiness of past criminal acts may be the most equitable solution in the long run (von Hirsch, 1985).

Programs for Parolees. The programs available to parolees parallel those available to probationers. In most states and in the federal system, parolees and probationers report regularly to the same persons. A distinction is often made between probationers and parolees in that probationers are considered less dangerous and have been sentenced to a nonincarcerative alternative. Obviously, there are numerous parolees who are considered unlikely risks to public safety or are not dangerous either. Parolees have served time in prison, however. Some persons may consider this factor significant in distinguishing between the potential dangerousness of parolees and probationers. Furthermore, older parolees may be perceived as less threatening than younger parolees (Hall, 1992).

Depending upon the particular types of assessment devices used in a jurisdiction, prospective parolees may be eligible for one or more parole plan options. Not all of these options are available in all jurisdictions. But all of these options have in common the fact that they seek to reintegrate offenders into their communities. They facilitate the transition from a highly structured, regimented prison environment to loosely regulated community living. Initially, some inmates have trouble making this transition. Thus, agencies and programs have been created to provide them different kinds of assistance during this transition period. Some of these programs, such as furloughs and work/education release, are designed for inmates who are to be released within a short time, such as six months. Some inmates may be permitted outside-of-prison work or educational opportunities during days or weekends, or they may be allowed to stay with their families on weekends. But eventually they must return to prison until their parole is officially invoked. Work release and furlough programs allow participating inmates to establish trust. If they can maintain this trust prison authorities have granted them, this virtually guarantees their parole chances.

Other programs, such as halfway houses, are for those who have been paroled. They provide temporary housing, employment assistance, and psychological counseling for parolees, if needed. Some parolees who exhibited serious problems when they first entered prison may need greater supervision when released on parole. For these offenders, various forms of intensive supervised parole (ISP) programs have been created. Some of these programs include electronic monitoring and/or home confinement. Frequent visits from parole officers at their workplaces or homes characterize ISP.

As we have already seen, parolees are granted early release from incarceration by parole boards or some other paroling authority. This does not mean that they will be removed entirely from custody, however. There are several different kinds of programs catering to particular types of parolees and requiring varying levels of parolee custody. This last section examines four of these programs. These included furloughs, work release, halfway houses, and intensive supervised parole. Several of these programs are closely associated with community-based services extended to probationers. Sometimes in some jurisdictions, both parolees and probationers will share these same services.

Furloughs are authorized, unescorted leaves from confinement granted for specific purposes and for designated time periods (McCarthy and McCarthy, 1984:163). The aim of furloughs is consistent with most other pre-release programs in that offender reintegration is stressed. Officially originating the furlough concept in the United States was Mississippi in 1918 (Marley, 1973). The growth of furlough programs in the United States was fairly rapid during the 1950s and 1960s, paralleling the dominant correctional philosophy of that period: rehabilitation. In 1965, the Federal Prisoner Rehabilitation Act was passed which authorized the Federal Bureau of Prisons to permit certain offenders to participate in furlough programs. In 1986, fewer than 100 federal offenders were participating in furlough programs, however.

The purposes of furloughs are several. Offenders are given a high degree of trust by prison officials and are permitted leaves to visit their homes and families. Interestingly, such furloughs are beneficial to both prisoners and their families, because they permit the family members to get used to the presence of the offender after a long absence through incarceration. Sometimes, prisoners may participate in educational programs outside of prison as a type of study release (Sigler and Johnson, 1989). They can arrange for employment once paroled, or they can participate in vocational training for short periods. Furloughs also provide officials with an opportunity to evaluate the offender and determine how he/she adapts to living with others in the community. Thus, the furlough is a type of test to determine with some predictability the likelihood that the inmate will conform to society's rules if eventually released through full-fledged parole. Occasional setbacks, such as the notorious Willie Horton episode in Massachusetts, have generated some controversy for furlough programs, however (Massachusetts House of Representatives, 1988). Horton, a convicted first-degree murderer, was granted a furlough and committed several serious crimes that incensed citizens. In general, however, furlough programs appear to be achieving their intended objectives (Smith and Sabatino, 1990).

Furloughs also function for some prisoners as incentives to conform to prison rules and regulations, because only prisoners who have demonstrated they can control their behaviors in prison will be considered by officials for temporary releases. Usually though not always, prisoners selected for participation in furlough programs are nearing the end of their sentences and will eventually be paroled or released anyway. They are good risks because the likelihood they will abscond while on a furlough is quite remote. A July 1988 survey of forty-seven directors of U.S. state departments of corrections showed that for the first half of 1988, out of 67,736 furloughs which were granted, there were only 366 offenders who absconded—less than 1 percent of all furloughees (Smith and Sabatino, 1990).

Work release encompasses any program that provides for (1) the labor of prison or jail inmates in the community, (2) under conditions of relaxed or no supervision, and (3) for which inmates are paid adequate wages (adapted from McCarthy and McCarthy, 1984:159–160). Also known as day pass or day parole, work release was informally adopted in the United States in the State of Vermont in 1906 (Busher, 1973). At that time, county sheriffs issued passes to certain low-risk inmates to work in the community during daytime hours, but they were obligated to return to jail at a particular curfew period.

Work release programs have several purposes which are designed to

1. Reintegrate the offender into the community.
2. Give the offender an opportunity to learn and/or practice new skills.
3. Provide offenders with the means to make restitution to victims of crimes.
4. Give offenders a chance to assist in supporting themselves and their families.
5. Help authorities to more effectively predict the likelihood of offender success if paroled.
6. Foster improvements in offenders' self-images or self-concepts through working in a nonincarcerative environment and assuming full responsibility for their conduct.

While work release programs are beneficial to offenders, in part because they permit participation in various educational and vocational/technical programs, some observers claim that inmates may not be receiving the type of training best suited for community reintegration. One expert says that of the technologies currently in place today, 50 percent of these will change completely in the next few years (Nelson, 1985:70). High technology is the primary reason for this change. Therefore, it is imperative that vocational programs that emphasize traditional trades of woodworking, metalworking, and other familiar shop skills also make available to offenders more broadly based technical skills suitable for work in a high-tech environment (Nelson, 1985:70). One criticism generally made of parole is that it has failed to prepare parolees to perform relevant jobs on the outside. However, independent studies have shown that work releasees who enrolled in vocational coursework had higher rates of employment and lower rearrest rates compared with those not enrolled (Schumacker, Anderson, and Anderson, 1990).

Halfway houses are transitional residences for inmates released from prison (Wilson, 1985:152, emphasis added). Not only is there extensive variation in the level of custody for clients, ranging from providing simple shelter on a voluntary basis to mandatory confinement with curfew, there are also many different services extended. These might include alcohol or drug-related rehabilitation facilities with some hospitalization on premises, minimal or extensive counseling services, and/or employment assistance (Latessa and Allen, 1982; McCarthy and McCarthy, 1984:201). Halfway houses are intended to serve as transitional residences, located within the community, where these former inmates of prisons can eventually adjust to life outside of prison. Occasionally, a requirement or condition associated with parole is to reside in a halfway house for a predetermined period. The offender benefits by being provided basic necessities such as food, clothing, and shelter, as well as employment opportunities which serve to defray the costs of maintaining these homes (McCarthy and McCarthy, 1984:202).

The halfway house concept is closely related to the reintegrative goal of corrections. Two hyphenated versions of the term exist. One is the halfway-out house, a facility designed to serve the immediate needs of ex-prisoners. The other is the halfway-in house, which identifies services for probationers in need of some limited supervision and confinement (McCarthy and McCarthy, 1984:154–155). Wilson (1985:155) lists several important functions of halfway houses:

1. To reintegrate ex-convicts into their communities by providing a temporary shelter and limited monitoring.
2. To provide counseling, if needed.
3. To provide job placement or employment assistance, and/or to function as an ex-inmate's spokesperson if problems on the job should arise.
4. To provide medical treatment, if needed, in the case of alcohol abuse or drug dependency.
5. To provide emergency aid or paralegal assistance if an ex-offender is rearrested or becomes involved in a police matter.
6. To provide skill or vocational training, or assistance in locating where such training can be obtained.
7. To provide crisis management services when needed.
8. To provide pre- and post-natal care for pregnant ex-offenders.
9. To provide temporary foster care for youthful offenders.
10. To monitor offenders who are expected to perform some public service/restitution to/for community/victims.

11. Assisting ex-offenders with rehabilitative plans (National Alliance of Business, 1983; Dowell, Klein, and Krichmar, 1985).

Most parolees are standard parolees, in the sense that they are obligated to adhere to certain standard early-release agreements formulated by paroling authorities. In 1987, the U.S. Sentencing Commission implemented new guidelines which included the following policy statement of recommended conditions of probation and parole supervised release:

1. The defendant shall not leave the judicial district or other specified geographical area without the permission of the court or PO [parole officer].
2. The defendant shall report to the PO as directed by the court or PO and shall submit a truthful and complete written report within the first five days of each month.
3. The defendant shall answer truthfully all inquiries by the PO and follow the instructions of the PO.
4. The defendant shall support his dependents and meet other family responsibilities.
5. The defendant shall work regularly at a lawful occupation unless excused by the PO for schooling, training, or other acceptable reasons.
6. The defendant shall notify the PO within seventy-two hours of any change in residence or employment.
7. The defendant shall refrain from excessive use of alcohol and shall not purchase, possess, use, distribute, or administer any narcotic or other controlled substance, or any paraphernalia related to such substances, except as prescribed by a physician.
8. The defendant shall not frequent places where controlled substances are illegally sold, used, distributed, or administered, or other places specified by the court.
9. The defendant shall not associate with any persons engaged in criminal activity, and shall not associate with any person convicted of a felony, unless granted permission to do so by the PO.
10. The defendant shall permit a PO to visit him at any time at home or elsewhere and shall permit confiscation of any contraband observed in plain view by the PO.
11. The defendant shall notify the PO within seventy-two hours of being arrested or questioned by a law enforcement officer.
12. The defendant shall not enter into any agreement to act as an informer or a special agent of a law enforcement agency without the permission of the court.
13. As directed by the PO, the defendant shall notify third parties of risks that may be occasioned by the defendant's criminal record or personal history or characteristics, and shall permit the probation officer to make such notifications and to confirm the defendant's compliance with such notification requirement.

Currently, *intensive supervised probation or parole* (ISP) means that offenders will have more frequent face-to-face visits with their probation/parole officers (POs), more frequent curfew and employment checks, and more conditions associated with the probation/parole programs. ISP might also involve electronic monitoring, home confinement, and random alcohol/drug testing. The intent of

ISP is to heighten offender accountability and compliance with program rules and to protect the community. An ISP program has been implemented in the federal northern district of Ohio under the auspices of the U.S. Parole Commission. The goal of this program is to provide increased community protection through more effective offender supervision. Although parole revocations in this program have been fairly high, this suggests strict enforcement of rules. Presently, findings are inconclusive about this program's effect upon offender behaviors. Nevertheless, officials are satisfied that they are fulfilling both the needs of the public and their ISP clients (Powers, 1992).

SOME DANGERS ASSOCIATED WITH ATTEMPTING TO ASSESS AND PREDICT RISK

Social scientists are interested both in predicting behavior and in understanding it. Much research is reported involving experiments where social conditions are changed and participants are closely observed. Supervisory styles are deliberately modified in the work setting and worker reactions are observed. Subsequently, a parallel is drawn between supervisory style and worker reaction, perhaps to the extent that one causes or significantly influences the other. Supervisory policies may be invoked that change employee reactions, such as greater satisfaction with work or lower labor turnover.

Prosecutors, judges, and probation officers are also interested in behavioral prediction. They must attempt to predict future offender behaviors, and whether certain offenders should be incarcerated or assigned to some community program. In any real or practical sense, it is impossible to incarcerate all convicted criminals. There is simply insufficient space presently in all U.S. jails and prisons to accommodate all convicted offenders. And it is debatable among corrections experts whether certain offenders should be incarcerated anyway (Rosecrance, 1986; Walker, 1985:65). The incarcerated offender population is less than a fourth of all convicted offenders who are under some form of supervised release today. If we *wanted* to lock up all offenders tomorrow, we would have to suddenly build four times as many prisons and jails that presently exist. This is an impossible task for many reasons that are beyond the scope of this book. Therefore, since many offenders *will be* returned to the community instead of incarcerated, risk predictions and risk instruments are essential to many persons, such as probation officers, prosecutors, and judges. They are also relevant for parole boards.

Criteria such as age, prior record, gender, type and seriousness of offense, offender attitudes, and psychological factors are used as criteria that impact one way or another upon sentencing decisions. Classification schemes are usually devised which enable probation officers and the court to rely on scores and other numerical information to impose appropriate penalties or punishments. But it is also generally acknowledged that we have no foolproof prediction devices to make perfect sentencing or early-release decisions. But many prediction devices and schemes exist and are used for these purposes.

False Positives and False Negatives

In a 1972 study of 4,146 delinquent youths in the California Youth Authority, an attempt was made by researchers to predict violence and nonviolence among the juvenile offenders. Four categories were created. The objective of the study was to predict "true positives" and "true negatives." True positives are persons predicted as violent who subsequently commit a new violent offense. True negatives are those offenders predicted as nonviolent who do not commit further offenses. Table 2.1 shows the results of a study conducted by the National Council on Crime and Delinquency in 1972 (Wenck, Robison, and Smith, 1972).

So-called error cells in Table 2.1 include false positives, or offenders (either adult or juvenile) predicted to commit new violent offenses who do not eventually commit them, and false negatives, those offenders predicted to be nonviolent who commit new offenses that are violent. Ideally, true positives should be closely monitored and supervised, even incarcerated, while true negatives should be placed on probation or diverted from the justice system entirely. False positives (404 persons in the study results presented in Table 2.1) are those offenders who are needlessly incarcerated (Walker, 1985:57). False negatives are those of most concern to criminologists and others. These are offenders who it is believed will not commit new violent acts but subsequently do commit them.

SUMMARY

Both the criminal and juvenile justice systems rely heavily on various measures of offender risk as a means of determining the offender's subsequent disposition. The criminal justice system or process consists of law enforcement, the prosecution and courts, and corrections. The juvenile justice process also manifests these components, but on a smaller and more informal scale. In both processes, risk assessments are most apparent in the latter stages of offender processing. Prosecutors sometimes use risk devices to determine whether defendants should be denied bail. Judges consult presentence investigation reports as a way of objectifying and justifying the sentences imposed. When offenders are delivered to correctional facilities for placement, risk devices are again utilized for determining their custody levels. During their incarcerative term, reassessments are made

Table 2.1
Positive and Negative Predictions of Violence

	Predicted Violent (*N*)	**Predicted Nonviolent (*N*)**
Actual violent	True Positives (52)	False Negatives (52)
Actual nonviolent	False Positives (404)	True Negatives (3638)

Source: Wenck, Robison, and Smith, 1972.

which may result in changing their levels of custody. Finally, risk instruments are frequently used by parole boards to assist in making early-release decisions about eligible inmates.

Risk prediction instruments are either anamnestic, actuarial, or clinical. Actuarial risk assessments are most commonly applied, especially in inmate classification and parole eligibility. Judges and parole boards often rely upon presentence investigation reports, which frequently contain numerical results of risk indicators or other applicable criteria that would assist them in making more objective decisions. Parole boards and parole board diversity are such that many different kinds of paroling criteria are used among jurisdictions. Although paroling authorities attempt to make informed decisions about early release, there are inherent flaws in virtually every risk instrument. Thus, some overprediction and underprediction occur, where some inmates are denied parole who should be granted it, while others are granted parole who should be denied it. Respectively, these aggregates are false positives and false negatives. Parolees are eligible for a variety of community programs, including furloughs, work release, halfway houses, and intensive supervised parole. Current attempts to develop classification schemes to predict offender future behavior, such as the potential for public risk, remain at best an unstable business in all dimensions of the criminal and juvenile justice system (Wright, Clear, and Dickson, 1984).

3

Selective Incapacitation and Recidivism: An Examination of the Issues

INTRODUCTION

Approximately two-thirds of all criminal offenders are recidivists (Greenfeld, 1985; Klein and Caggiano, 1986). That is, they continue to offend and commit new crimes despite one or more previous criminal convictions. Many of these offenders commit new crimes while on probation, parole, or some other form of conditional release. What should be done about recidivists? Some persons have advocated that we lock up *all* criminals. But in Chapter 2, we saw how difficult it would be to incarcerate all offenders, even for brief periods. Logistically, we would need at least four or five times the current prison and jail space to accommodate all criminals. The cost of such prison and jail construction is so prohibitive that it makes this possible solution a very unlikely one.

Well, then, if it is financially prohibitive or otherwise impractical to incarcerate everyone who commits crimes, why not lock up only those who are the most serious offenders and those who are most likely to reoffend? Some criminal justice analysts and experts have promoted *selective incapacitation* as a proactive method of crime control. Essentially, this means that some offenders who are determined to be greater societal risks than other offenders will be incapacitated, and for longer periods. Thus, predesignated high-risk offenders can be removed from society temporarily and placed in prisons or jails, where their behaviors can be monitored and controlled. Other low-risk offenders will also be dealt with selectively, either by being granted probation more frequently or by being placed in some community program in lieu of incarceration in a prison or jail facility. But is it fair to impose greater punishments on certain offenders and not on others, strictly on the basis of their likelihood of reoffending? Is it fair to punish them in advance, for crimes they have not, as yet, committed?

This chapter is about selective incapacitation. Selective incapacitation is a controversial method for achieving crime control. It is difficult to examine selective incapacitation without also examining the phenomenon of recidivism. This is because high recidivism rates mean repeat offenders. And repeat offenders are most troublesome for the criminal justice system. If we can somehow prevent persistent offenders from reoffending, then we stand a good chance of decreasing the crime rate. At least, this is one underlying assumption of the selective incapacitation philosophy. Another assumption is that persistent offenders can be identified in practical ways and targeted for special treatment by the courts and corrections.

First, selective incapacitation will be defined and its controversial nature will be discussed. Next, we will examine recidivism and how it is conceived in the research literature. Recidivism has numerous definitions. Since recidivism is frequently used as the measure of correctional program (and crime control) success or failure, it is important to become familiar with these alternative meanings associated with the term. Furthermore, assessments of risk are often constructed from the descriptive information gleaned from the collective characteristics of recidivists. Thus, those most likely to recidivate, as identified by these risk assessment tools, can conceivably be treated differently (e.g., selectively incapacitated) from those determined to be least likely to recidivate.

SELECTIVE INCAPACITATION DEFINED

Selective incapacitation means incarcerating certain offenders designated as high risks for reoffending. Visher (1987:514–515) defines incapacitation generally as "a strategy for crime control involv[ing] the physical isolation of an offender from the community, usually through imprisonment, to prevent the offender from committing future crimes." She further indicates that research about incapacitation is concerned with the *incapacitation effect,* or the reduction in crime that can be attributed to imprisoning persistent offenders.

Visher also distinguishes between two types of incapacitation—*collective incapacitation* and *selective incapacitation.* Collective incapacitation means to reduce crime by using traditional offense-based sentencing, where offenders who commit identical crimes are punished with identical sentences. The greater the crime seriousness, the more severe the sentence imposed. Selective incapacitation is tailoring sentencing decisions according to individual offenders . . . thought to pose the greatest risk of committing future crimes (Visher, 1987: 514–515).

Struckhoff (1987:30) notes that the history of selective incapacitation as it is currently being used may be traced to the work of Marvin Wolfgang at the University of Pennsylvania in 1972 (Wolfgang, Figlio, and Sellin, 1972). Briefly, Wolfgang and his associates described two cohorts of youths born in 1945 and 1958 respectively. Follow-ups of these cohorts revealed that of those born in 1945, 6 percent accounted for 52 percent of the known criminal offenses committed by the entire cohort. For those born in 1958, a similar finding emerged. It was found that 7.5 percent of the cohort accounted for 68 percent of all index offense arrests for the entire cohort. The primary conclusion derived by Wolfgang and his associates was that only a few offenders were accounting for a disproportionately high amount of crime. Subsequent critics and justice experts tagged the small numbers of high-rate offenders as chronic recidivists and the "chronic 6 percent." Theoretically, if we could identify these offenders in advance and incapacitate them, we could greatly reduce crime.

Indeed, more than a few criminal justice scholars and experts share this idea, at least in theory. For example, Gottfredson (1984:84) suggests that "if such high-rate offenders could be identified beforehand and confined longer, it would be the key to an effective crime reduction policy." More recently, Miranne and Geerken (1991:514) say that "if high-rate offenders could be accurately identified and distinguished from low-rate offenders, sentencing the former to a longer period of incarceration than the latter could possibly increase cost-effectiveness." Interestingly, some recent research has provided strong support for Wolfgang's original findings. Between 1986 and 1989, the New Jersey Juvenile Delinquency Commission provided an updated profile of chronic juvenile offenders in New Jersey (New Jersey Juvenile Delinquency Commission, 1991). On the basis of an examination of juvenile court records of 118,000 youths entering the Family Court for the period 1986–1989, it was found that chronic offenders accounted for about 13 percent of all docketed youths. However, this small offender aggregate was responsible for 46 percent of all charges and an even larger percentage of all serious offenses alleged. Thus, it would seem that a small core of delinquents continues to account for a large proportion of offenses, at least in New Jersey.

The Rand Corporation has done much to develop selective incapacitation strategy. Rand researcher Peter Greenwood devised a classification scheme in 1982 that purportedly would enable practitioners to determine which offenders should receive long, incapacitating sentences, and who should be sentenced to alternative correctional programs (Blackmore and Welsh, 1983). Arguing that "modest gains are better than none," some investigators say that selective incapacitation, despite its drawbacks (e.g., legal, moral, and ethical implications), seems partially successful as "the latest theory for controlling crime" (Forst, 1983). Other researchers reject this position by citing the ineffectiveness of selective incapacitation as a deterrent to certain felons such as burglars (McGriff, 1985). Before we argue the relative merits of selective incapacitation as an effective crime control strategy, we need to explore its short- and long-range objectives.

GOALS OF SELECTIVE INCAPACITATION

The goals or objectives of selective incapacitation are (1) crime prevention and reduction; (2) reduction in prison and jail overcrowding; (3) provision of more adequate treatment; (4) promotion of public safety; (5) maintenance of institutional discipline and control; (6) promotion of respect for the law and "just deserts"; (7) punishment/retribution; and (8) increasing the cost-effectiveness of incarceration. These objectives have not necessarily been listed in the order of their importance. Also, these objectives are predicated on the idea that existing instrumentation is such that high-rate offenders can be identified.

Crime Prevention and Reduction

The most frequently cited goal of selective incapacitation is to reduce or prevent crime by incapacitating high-risk offenders who are most likely to reoffend. This feat may be easier said than done. For instance, Struckhoff (1987:32) gives us an example from the Joliet, Illinois, Police Department. The department says that there are about twenty-three "high-rate offenders" out of a population of 80,000. Their impressions of precisely who the high-rate offenders are come from informants and/or the offenders themselves. Thus, the police are in the awkward position of thinking they know who are the high-rate offenders, but they're not certain. Further, Struckhoff says, when judges look at a convicted offender's rap sheet, the odds are that half of the crimes an offender has committed are not reported, and that half of the reported crimes are not on the sheet because of either processing, legal-technical restrictions, or due process rights (Struckhoff, 1987:32). Finally, there are those offenders who commit crimes badly. That is, they get caught every time they commit a crime. In short, there are no perfectly reliable ways of estimating how much crime reduction would occur if we were to suddenly identify all high-rate offenders and incapacitate them. The only sure thing is that those offenders who are incapacitated cannot commit crimes against the public while imprisoned.

Reduction in Prison and Jail Overcrowding

One popular long-range objective of selective incapacitation is that prison and jail overcrowding would be reduced significantly. This is so because we would give high-rate offenders longer incarcerative sentences, and low-rate offenders would receive shorter incarcerative sentences. Thus, prison space would be reserved primarily for high-rate offenders or chronic recidivists. However, Struckhoff (1987:32) describes the negative side of such a policy. Using incarceration figures for Ohio, Struckhoff cites research showing that if a mandatory five-year prison term were given all second-felony offenders, then this would mean an increase of 500 or 600 percent in the Ohio prisoner population during the next five years. Numerically, the Ohio inmate population would jump from 13,000 to over 65,000 in a five-year period, using selective incapacitation as it is presently advocated (Struckhoff, 1987:32).

Provision of More Adequate Treatment

If high-rate offenders were selectively incapacitated for longer terms, then it is logical to expect that they would have a greater opportunity to receive necessary treatment. Prison settings with established rehabilitative programs could meet certain inmate needs more fully, since those selectively incapacitated would be exposed to such programs for longer time periods. However, critics such as Samuel Walker (1985) suggest that the rehabilitative value of prison life and its accompanying vocational/educational programs is at best questionable.

Promotion of Public Safety

Promoting public safety through selective incapacitation is obvious. With more high-rate offenders off the streets, the public safety is enhanced. However, as Struckhoff (1987) and others (Gottfredson, 1984) have noted, we are not sure how much public safety would be increased through such an incapacitation policy. Again, we would be deterring a specific aggregate of high-rate offenders. Assuming a continuous flow of new-generation, high-rate offenders into all communities, however, the long-range effect of selective incapacitation as a crime control strategy might be negligible. Also, some researchers contend that intervention programs aimed at offender reintegration, such as furloughs and community-based corrections, may be more important deterrents to future criminality and better public safety strategies than individualized incapacitation plans based largely upon the social and psychological profiles of selected inmates (LeClair and Guarino-Ghezzi, 1991:28–32).

Maintenance of Institutional Discipline and Control

Selective incapacitation of certain offenders fosters a more clearly defined aggregate of institutional clientele. Organizational theorists might argue that a more standardized inmate population would permit officials to define offender risk more accurately, and to adjust security measures to deal with these high-risk inmates. But we must not forget the fact that selective incapacitation is designed primarily for chronic recidivists who may or may not be dangerous, in the sense that they would injure or kill others. Chronic recidivists include burglars, larcenists, forgers, insider-traders, and auto thieves, as well as murderers, rapists, and robbers. Therefore, institutional discipline and control are achieved as a direct or indirect result of better inmate management. This accrues from more informed inmate classification decisions, where offenders may be housed so as to maximize supervisory effectiveness and control.

There is a "down" side relating to inmate discipline and control, however. Moriarty (1987:3–4) suggests that selectively incapacitating the most serious offenders might create conditions under which no correctional officer would like to work. She further contends that this environment of the worst offenders would not be conducive to rehabilitation. Rather, the environment would not be conducive to anything except punishment. But institutions such as the maxi-maxi federal penitentiary at Marion, Illinois, profess to do nothing more for inmates than maintain them, away from the community, for a period of years. Spokespersons for the Federal Bureau of Prisons as well as for the Marion facility have made such statements repeatedly. Gary Henman, warden of the Marion facility in 1988, has indicated that Marion's mission is to provide a correctional setting for the most hostile, assaultive, and escape-prone inmates in the Bureau of Prisons (Henman, 1988:93). Inmates are housed, under lockdown, for twenty-two hours a day in individual cells. He says that those who come to Marion have proven that they cannot conform to rules in other institutions, and that they have earned their way into this facility by proving they cannot live peacefully with fellow inmates at other facilities (Henman, 1988:94). Inmates must maintain a record of good behavior for one year before they are permitted more liberal meal, shower, and recreational privileges. The average length of an inmate prison term at Marion is three to four years. Inmates are subsequently transferred to other institutions, primarily because they have manifested good conduct and a willingness to get along with others and conform to institutional rules.

The federal facility at Marion is probably the most extreme example of total control over inmates. Five-man teams equipped with full riot gear are used to transfer recalcitrant inmates from one cell to another. Remarkably, no inmate or correctional officer injuries have occurred during these cell transfers after a general lockdown went into effect in 1983, following an inmate rioting incident where two correctional officers were killed. Lockdowns at state and federal prisons are usually temporary conditions, where the administrative staff can regain control of the prison from inmates. However, the facility at Marion is under permanent lockdown, thus ensuring total inmate control.

Promotion of Respect for the Law and "Just Deserts"

One possible consequence of selective incapacitation is a greater respect for the law among those sanctioned with longer incarcerative terms. One position taken by selective incapacitation advocates is that those identified as high-rate offenders have earned enhanced punishments and more severe treatment dispositions. Theoretically, those offenders who are incarcerated longer and supervised more closely during the terms of their incarceration will be less likely to reoffend or recidivate when ultimately released. Quite simply, those who receive greater prison terms and/or are supervised and controlled more closely because of their high-risk status will learn that crime doesn't pay. Ideally, they will refrain from reoffending in the future. However, a general analysis of studies of recidivism according to length of time served in prison provides little or no support for this contention (Gottfredson and Gottfredson, 1988:206–213). In fact, indications are that recidivism rates may be higher for those serving longer prison terms than for those who serve shorter prison terms. But factors such as drug use, offender age, race/ethnicity, and gang membership are often uncontrolled. Their presence or absence, if known, might significantly influence these differences.

But it should be remembered that selective incapacitation is used primarily for those offenders who exhibit the characteristics of high-rate offenders with a propensity to reoffend. The manifest intent of selectively incapacitating these offenders is to remove them from circulation and place them under forms of control where they cannot reoffend for some period of time. Naturally, if we subsequently release high-rate offenders who have a propensity to reoffend, they will probably reoffend now just as we expected they would do at an earlier point in time. Thus, viewed in this light, selective incapacitation is a specific and highly individualized deterrent. It removes specific offenders from society for a designated period, thus guaranteeing that they cannot commit new crimes while incarcerated.

Punishment/Retribution

A direct aim of selective incapacitation is to punish offenders who are disposed to chronic recidivism. This view has received fairly strong support in the research literature (Blackmore and Welsh, 1983; LeClair and Guarino-Ghezzi, 1991; Miranne and Geerken, 1991; Moriarty, 1987). Since those targeted for selective incapacitation are incarcerated primarily on the basis of the likelihood of their reoffending, the primary function served, besides deterrence, is punishment. And enhanced punishments against specific offenders and not against others is a form of retribution.

Increasing the Cost-Effectiveness of Incarceration

Cost-effectiveness is often measured according to the expected amount of crime reduction accruing from incapacitating certain offenders. If controls are exerted over the chronic recidivists and most dangerous, high-rate offenders, then a considerable reduction in crime is attained, simply by removing these offenders temporarily from their communities. Therefore, a policy of incarcerating only the most chronic recidivists and/or high-rate offenders, whether they are serious or nonserious criminals, ideally maximizes the cost-effectiveness of incarceration. This cost-effectiveness is maximized by confining those with high capacities to reoffend and who otherwise would commit numerous additional crimes if released together with other, low-rate offenders. It is not especially cost-effective to incarcerate large numbers of offenders with low propensities to reoffend.

The maxi-maxi federal facility at Marion, Illinois, is supposedly cost-effective, since it houses the most escape-prone, chronic recidivists among inmates throughout the federal prison system. Theoretically, removing the most troublesome or problematic inmates from other institutions will make those other institutions more manageable. One problem most state and federal prison officials have is the presence and influence of gangs within their facilities. In fact, considerable institutional control is often in the hands of inmates themselves. This control is facilitated in large part through gang-related connections. However, at Marion, Warden Gary Henman reports that although some of those inmates are gang members, the influence of gangs at Marion is negligible.

Peter Greenwood and his associates have figured prominently in the selective incapacitation issue. On the basis of a survey of jail and prison inmates who furnished information about their criminality through self-reports, Greenwood has proposed a strategy of selective incapacitation which would extend the time served for crimes (such as burglary and robbery) committed by high-rate offenders and decrease the time served by criminals considered low-rate offenders (Greenwood and Abrahamse, 1982; Gottfredson, 1984:1). In theory, at least, Greenwood projected that crime reductions would occur without seriously affecting the natural growth of prison populations. Thus, the cost-effectiveness of prisons would be maximized through more efficient use of prison space.

Contrary views suggest that selective incapacitation will greatly expand the actual numbers of incarcerated offenders, thus requiring greater prison construction expenditures. This presumes mandatory confinement of high-rate offenders for fixed terms, such as three, four, or five years. Struckhoff's (1987) notions about this possible consequence have already been presented above, utilizing an example from the Ohio prison system. Regarding the research of Greenwood, critics have noted that at least some offenders would be targeted for selective incapacitation because of alcohol or drug dependencies or unemployment status, factors often beyond their control. Also, the veracity of those disclosing their crimes through self-reports has been questioned, since no independent corroboration of Greenwood's findings has been conducted on new samples to determine the original study reliability (Blackmore and Welsh, 1983; Blumstein, 1983c; Decker and Salert, 1986; Gottfredson, 1984:84). Thus, we cannot estimate precisely how much crime reduction would occur, since we do not know for sure how much actual crime would be committed by high-rate offenders if they were permitted freedom within their communities. This means that the cost-effectiveness of selective incapacitation cannot be accurately calculated, only crudely estimated.

MORAL/ETHICAL AND LEGAL PROBLEMS OF SELECTIVE INCAPACITATION

The moral/ethical and legal problems of selective incapacitation are (1) punishing offenders for crimes they have not as yet committed; (2) unfairly individualizing punishments; (3) the relatively low levels of accuracy associated with risk prediction instruments; and (4) increased punishment and/or intrusion of the state into the lives of those predicted to be more dangerous (Tonry, 1987: 367–369).

Punishing Offenders for Crimes They Have Not Yet Committed

The primary criticism of selective incapacitation is that certain offenders designated as "high-risk" eventually are punished in advance for crimes they have not yet committed (Fogel and Hudson, 1981; Gottfredson and Gottfredson, 1988;

Moriarty, 1987; Tonry, 1987; von Hirsch, 1984). More than a few researchers have cited gross inaccuracies of risk prediction arising from faulty instrumentation (Farrington and Tarling, 1985; Monahan, 1984; Morris and Miller, 1985; Wilkins, 1985). Conrad (1985) argues vigorously for even-handed treatment of felons who commit similar crimes and who have similar prior records. However, he allows for some sentencing disparity to the extent that such disparity is dependent upon mitigating or aggravating circumstances. Morris (1984) also advises against using dangerousness forecasts as the bases for differential sentencing and treatment.

Unfairly Individualizing Punishments

When punishments for offenders are individualized, the sentencing disparity issue is raised. Are offenders being punished for crimes they have recently committed, or are they being inordinately punished for vague predictions of their propensity to recidivate in the future (Blumstein, Cancla-Cacho, and Cohen, 1990; Capune, 1988; Clear and Barry, 1983; Cohen, 1983; Danto, 1985; Davis, 1990; Jackson, 1989; Morris and Miller, 1987; Stone, 1985; von Hirsch and Gottfredson, 1983)? Individualized punishments as contemplated by selective incapacitation would seem to run afoul of the "equal protection" and "due process" clauses of the Fourteenth Amendment. However, Tonry (1987:374–375) argues that Amendment violations do not occur as the result of making differential sentencing decisions with risk instruments where a rational basis for classification has been established. In any case, critics claim that the differential treatment of offenders on the basis of their anticipated future conduct is fundamentally unfair and premature, in view of current state-of-the-art risk instrumentation (Baird and Austin, 1986; Champion, 1990b; Hughes, 1985; Webster, Dickens, and Addario, 1985; Wenck, Robison, and Smith, 1972; Wood, 1991; Zenoff, 1985).

The Relatively Low Predictive Utility of Risk Prediction Instruments

Much has been made of the fact that the current level of sophistication of risk instrumentation leaves much to be desired (Brennan, 1987a; Stephen D. Gottfredson, 1987; Farrington, 1987; Gottfredson and Gottfredson, 1990; Haapanen, 1988; Joyce, 1985; Menzies, Webster, and Sepejak, 1985; Monahan, 1984; Morris and Miller, 1985, 1987; Robins et al., 1986). Even when psychiatrists' diagnoses of large numbers of offenders are considered in terms of which offenders are most likely to exhibit future dangerous behaviors, at least one study has shown an incorrect prediction rate of 40 percent among these professionals (Sepejak, Webster, and Menzies, 1984). Other investigators have challenged the adequacy of clinical predictions of violent or antisocial behavior on clinical grounds (Flint, 1987). Whether clinical or actuarial prediction schemes are used for risk prediction, the fact is that existing instruments are more than a little inaccurate (Wright, Clear, and Dickson, 1984).

Increased State Intrusion into the Lives of High-Risk Offenders

It has been asserted that the use of selective incapacitation is an unwarranted intrusion by the state into the lives of offenders (Gottfredson and Gottfredson, 1988; Gottfredson and Tonry, 1987). However, much of this intrusion is justified on the basis of more effective inmate management and institutional policy (Glaser, 1987; Wright, Clear, and Dickson, 1984). Morris and Miller (1985) advise, however, that individual sentencing dispositions based upon risk prediction tools should retain punishment severity within a reasonable range of "deserved" sanctions. Preferring actuarial predictions of risk over psychiatric evaluations, these critics contend that the use of predictions of dangerousness to alter individual dispositions should be allowed only to the extent that such dispositions would be justified as deserved independent of these predictions. Thus, these principles would strike a balance between individual autonomy and state authority (Morris and Miller, 1985).

Some Generalizations about the Legal Implications of Classifications of Risk

Tonry (1987:374–375) observes that the following generalizations about predictions and classifications of risk/dangerousness are legally applicable, in accordance with U.S. Supreme Court interpretations of the U.S. Constitution:

1. Classifications based directly on race, ethnicity, political beliefs, or religion are generally prohibited; reliance on one of these factors must usually be shown to be justified by a "compelling state interest"—a probative standard that is difficult to meet.
2. Classifications based on sex are often prohibited, and attempts to justify such classifications must be substantially persuasive.
3. Classifications based directly on other factors are nearly always permitted because all that must be shown is that there is "rational basis" for the classification; the courts defer to legislative and executive classifications, and it is accordingly very difficult to show that classification lacks a rational basis.
4. Classifications that result in differential impacts on racial or ethnic groups, but indirectly and without the intention to achieve that result, are nearly always permitted (unless a statutory scheme—e.g., an equal employment opportunity law—is deemed to forbid both intended and unintended differential impacts).
5. Official actions taken before trial involving jail conditions, on the basis of predictions, will generally be sustained even if they infringe on liberty unless they can be shown to be "intended to be punitive."
6. Official actions taken after conviction on the basis of predictions of dangerousness will generally be sustained so long as the sanctions or conditions imposed are within the range authorized by law.
7. Judges (at least; probably all criminal justice system officials) may rely on predictions in making decisions irrespective of the scientific integrity or credibility of the predic-

> tive evidence adduced unless they expressly declare that they are relying on evidence that is patently frivolous.

Tonry (1987:374–383) summarizes the principal legal issues of selective incapacitation as centering on (1) equal protection (e.g., strong correlations of race with various "risk" elements); (2) due process ("fixed and mechanical" instruments; "arbitrary and capricious" applications of instruments); and (3) cruel and unusual punishment. Basically, those selectively incapacitated are not treated equally, under the law. As we have seen, this problem is overcome by applying risk tools which have a rational basis and which serve administrative interests principally. Almost all risk assessment devices, such as those presented in the Appendix, have provisions for administrative overrides. That is, while scores may be generated in a "fixed and mechanical" fashion, subjective judgments by administrative staff and correctional officers can overrule preliminary inmate placements, with written justification.

The "cruel and unusual" punishment issue is mostly about whether fundamental fairness is served as the result of differential processing and sentencing. For instance, the death penalty as applied in *Furman v. Georgia* (1972) was not acceptable because of the fact that large numbers of blacks were being executed for noncapital offenses, such as rape, whereas large numbers of whites convicted of the same offense were not being executed. Thus, for those blacks convicted of rape, the application of the death penalty was interpreted as "cruel and unusual" punishment to the extent that it was being differentially applied to blacks and whites. Subsequently, in *Gregg v. Georgia* (1976), the application of the death penalty became acceptable and constitutional, since a fairer sentencing scheme and bifurcated trial proceedings were implemented in exclusively capital cases.

In a similar vein, is it cruel and unusual punishment to provide longer prison terms for those offenders considered greater risks than other offenders? Possession of a prior record, a history of drug abuse and/or alcohol dependency, a low amount of education, and a history of chronic unemployment figure prominently into risk assessment schemes. Offenders with many of these characteristics would stand a good chance of being incarcerated for longer periods, despite the fact that several of these status factors are beyond their immediate control. Should these offenders be treated or assisted instead of incarcerated? The fact is that these factors correlate highly with race and social class. The inequitable result is that more blacks than whites are disenfranchised of their liberty indirectly, as the result of apparently legal applications of risk instruments whose intent is not to discriminate on the basis of race or ethnicity.

From a crime control standpoint, selective incapacitation has considerable appeal. Ideally, only those most likely to reoffend are targeted. Selective incapacitation is discriminatory in its application, and the ethics and fairness of predictive sentencing are frequently called into question (von Hirsch, 1984). Professionals who deal with violent persons on a regular basis, mental health professionals and psychiatrists, also question the accuracy of dangerousness indices, especially when such devices are used for justifying confinement (Monahan, 1984).

One of the better discussions of the limitations of dangerousness and risk assessment instruments and their use by various actors in the criminal and juvenile justice systems has been provided by Morris (1984). He suggests several useful principles, particularly when applied in tandem with judicial sentencing and probation officer PSI recommendations:

1. Clinical predictions of dangerousness should not be relied upon other than for short-term intervention.
2. Decisions to restrict offender autonomy should be made by considering the actual extent of harm that may occur and how much individual autonomy of offenders ought to be limited.
3. Predictions of dangerousness are "present condition," not predictions of particular results.
4. Sufficiency of proof of dangerousness should not be confused with proof beyond a reasonable doubt, clear and convincing evidence, or on a balance of probability.
5. Punishment should not be imposed or extended, by virtue of a dangerousness prediction, beyond that justified as "deserved" punishment independent of that prediction.
6. Provided the previous limitation is respected, dangerousness predictions may properly influence sentencing decisions.
7. The base expectancy rate of criminal violence for the criminal predicted as dangerous should be shown by reliable evidence to be "substantially higher" than the rate for another criminal, with a closely similar crime, but not predicted as unusually dangerous, before greater dangerousness of the former may be relied on to intensify or extend the punishment (Morris, 1984).

Regardless of the quality of predictability associated with risk assessment instruments used by criminal justice personnel, such as probation officers, for classifying offenders and making judicial sentencing recommendations, what does seem to work as a deterrent to future crime is intensive supervised probation, particularly considering its cost-effectiveness compared with incarceration (Latessa, 1986:70–71). One continuing dilemma, however, is selecting those offenders who are best suited for higher levels of supervision and are least likely to recidivate (Latessa, 1986:70).

RECIDIVISM DEFINED

Existing measures of recidivism complicate rather than simplify its definition. It is important to pay attention to how recidivism is conceptualized in the research literature, since probation or parole program failures or successes are measured by recidivism rates (Wilson, 1985:160–161; McCarthy and McCarthy, 1984:116–118; Petersilia, 1987:89). A general standard has emerged among professionals establishing that a failure rate above 30 percent means that a probation or parole program is ineffective (Vito, 1986:17; Allen et al., 1985:260–261). However, a consistent definition of effectiveness has not been established.

Barry Nidorf, Chief Probation Officer for Los Angeles County, believes that recidivism doesn't necessarily reflect on the soundness or effectiveness of rehabilitation programs involving probationers or parolees (Petersilia, 1987:89). He says that if rehabilitation is the probation or parole program goal, then recidivism rates seem appropriate measures of program success or failure. "However, if control and community protection are [program] goals, then a 'success' might be viewed as the identification and quick program revocation of [offenders] who are committing crimes. After all, the police are in the business of surveillance and control, and they judge an 'arrest' a success, whereas we deem it a 'failure.' If community safety is the primary goal, then perhaps an arrest and revocation should be seen as a success and not a failure" (Petersilia, 1987:89). Nidorf's argument is persuasive, from the standpoint that critics should consider *how* they want program success to be measured. Recidivism seems relevant particularly when we consider the rehabilitative value of programs. However, many programs involving intensive supervision of parolees and probationers seem focused primarily on crime control rather than true rehabilitation (Petersilia, 1987:89).

ALTERNATIVE MEANINGS OF RECIDIVISM

Common meanings of recidivism include (1) rearrest, (2) parole or probation revocation or unsatisfactory termination, (3) technical parole or probation rule violations, (4) conviction for a new offense while on parole or probation, (5) return to prison, (6) having a prior record and being rearrested for a new offense, (7) having a prior record and being convicted for a new offense, (8) any new commitment to a jail or prison for sixty days or more, (9) presence of a new sentence exceeding one year for any offense committed during a five-year parole follow-up, (10) return of released offenders to custody of state correctional authorities, (11) return to jail, (12) reincarceration, (13) the use of drugs or alcohol by former drug or alcohol abusers, and (14) failure to complete educational or vocational/technical course or courses in or out of prison/jail custody (Maltz, 1984). The most common meanings of recidivism are *rearrests, reconvictions, revocations of parole or probation,* and *reincarcerations.*

Rearrests

Rearrest probably is the most frequently used indicator of recidivism, particularly as it relates to recidivism among probationers and parolees. However, rearrests are misleading, particularly if we depend upon them as indicators of program successes or failures. The most apparent flaw of using rearrests is the uncertainty that the offender actually committed a new crime. Some probationers and parolees may be in the wrong places at the wrong times. Thus, circumstances may suggest they are either guilty of something or have a knowledge of someone else's culpability. Probationers or parolees may be released after police discover that these ex-offenders have alibis or can otherwise account for their whereabouts. Nevertheless, a rearrest is often considered "evidence" that an offender has somehow reoffended. This conclusion is questionable. It is always possible that these probationers or parolees actually committed new crimes alleged. But this is a fact to be proved subsequently in court, and beyond a reasonable doubt. Furthermore, not all probationers and parolees who are rearrested for new crimes are subsequently prosecuted for those crimes. Instead, they may be sent to prison or back to it (Megargee and Bohn, 1979:151).

An investigation of 3,257 releasees from Delaware prisons during 1980–1982 used rearrests as the measure of recidivism (Delaware Executive Department, 1984). Investigators tracked offenders from the time of their release to the date of their first rearrest, or September 30, 1983, whichever came first. Over half of the releasees were rearrested during this time interval (51.4 percent), and 75 percent of these rearrests were within their first year of release.

This study is important, not only because of the way officials chose to define recidivism, but because of those factors which were subsequently determined to be causally linked with recidivism. Delaware officials found no significant differences in rearrest rates for offenders who had been released because of good-time credits or meritorious conduct. Also, the longer the time served by a released inmate, the more likely the inmate would be rearrested for a serious crime. Third, they found that recidivism decreases with age. Indeed, it is conceded by most researchers that recidivism declines with advancing age. Significantly less criminal activity occurs among older offenders than among younger ones. This inverse relation between age and criminal activity is practically linear.

It may be that rearrests of parolees are not related to their earlier prison behavior. Furthermore, it might be argued that inmates who served longer sentences before being paroled were probably convicted of more serious crimes earlier compared with those paroled after serving shorter periods of incarceration. Therefore, when rearrests of these more serious paroled offenders occurred, the rearrests involved more serious charges than those of offenders rearrested but previously convicted of less serious crimes. This is only speculation. However, one important limitation of the Delaware study is that it did not examine the proportion of rearrests resulting in convictions for new offenses or the extent to which paroles were revoked for technical reasons, according to various offender characteristics.

A considerable discrepancy exists between the numbers of arrests reported by police and the number of convictions that result from these arrests. The *Uniform Crime Reports (UCR),* which is compiled by the Federal Bureau of Investigation (FBI), presents much statistical material about the prevalence of crime in the United States annually. One potentially troublesome statistical summary is *crimes cleared by arrest.* For any given year, "crimes cleared by arrest" means simply that *someone* has been arrested for the reported crime. It doesn't mean that these arrests are of the actual perpetrators, or that they will necessarily result in convictions. In fact, the FBI clearance rate for *all* crimes is about 26 percent. If we take unreported crime into account, then this "clearance" figure drops appreciably to about 10 percent (Walker, 1985:26). Conviction rates for all crimes "cleared by arrest" are about 20 percent (Walker, 1985:26). Accordingly, we should view rearrest figures with caution, especially when evaluating the effectiveness of probation or parole programs and/or assessing offender rehabilitation.

Reconvictions

Probably the most reliable indicator of recidivism is reconviction for a new offense. This means that an offender has committed at least one new crime while on probation or parole, and the court has determined offender guilt beyond a reasonable doubt. Some experts say that any failure to observe probation or parole conditions or placing oneself in a position of increasing the likelihood of arrest (e.g., violating curfew or associating with other offenders) is evidence that the offender has not been rehabilitated.

Researchers at the Rand Corporation studied approximately 16,500 males who were sentenced to either prison or probation in seventeen of California's largest counties (Petersilia, Turner, Kahan, and Peterson, 1985:vi). Of these 16,500 males, a 10 percent subsample of 1,672 felony probationers who were sentenced in Los Angeles and Alameda counties were tracked for forty months, with recordings made of arrests, filings, convictions, and incarcerations. During this follow-up period, investigators found that 65 percent of these probationers (1,087) were rearrested and 51 percent (853) were reconvicted for one or more new offenses. Using the violent-nonviolent crime distinction, however, most (82 percent) of these new convictions involved nonviolent crimes (e.g., burglary and larceny). Rand researchers also found that 34 percent (568) were reincarcerated. Interestingly, 285 reconvictions (17 percent) resulted in a continuation of probation. Many of the reconvictions involved misdemeanor offenses.

Another study of recidivism partially replicated the methodology of the Rand researchers. Vito studied 317 felony probationers from three Kentucky judicial districts in 1982 (Vito, 1986:18). Vito used a thirty-six-month follow-up and found that 70 (22 percent) probationers were rearrested, 56 (18 percent) were reconvicted, and 37 were reincarcerated. About 7 percent (22) were incarcerated as probation violators. Thus, Vito's Kentucky study is very similar to the one conducted by Rand. The important issue of representativeness was raised in both of these studies by researchers. That is, to what extent do these offenders compare in their characteristics with offenders in other jurisdictions? Did the recidivism figures reported in the forty-month Rand study differ significantly from recidivism figures reported in the thirty-six-month follow-up Kentucky study by Vito? According to the 30 percent recidivism standard, both studies are well within the effective program range (Vito, 1986:24).

Revocations of Parole or Probation

A probation or parole revocation means that parolees or probationers have violated one or more of their program conditions. These conditions may involve harmless technical violations, such as curfew, or such serious violations as committing and/or being convicted of a felony. Many factors may influence a parole or probation revocation decision. Prison or jail overcrowding is one of them. The seriousness of the violation is also considered. A third factor is the recommendation of the PO. One important problem with violating technical parole or probation program requirements, however, is that often, these violations are unrelated to any type of crime. Thus, a probation or parole revocation based solely on technical grounds is irrelevant as a crime control strategy. Also, a revocation of probation or parole does not automatically mean imprisonment or a return to prison. Depending upon the grounds for the revocation and other factors, offenders may be placed in a different probation or parole program with new and higher levels of supervisory control. This is one important reason why probation and parole revocations cannot be equated with reincarceration.

Reincarcerations

Using reincarceration as a measure of recidivism is as misleading as counting the numbers of probationers and parolees who are rearrested or who have their probation or parole revoked. Reincarceration, per se, does not specify the *type of incarceration*. After probation is revoked, a probationer may be placed in a state or federal prison. After a federal parolee's status has been revoked, the parolee may be placed in a city or county jail for a short period rather than returned to the original federal prison. Both types of offenders may be placed in a community-based correctional program to be reintegrated into their communities. In these instances, the level of their supervision will usually be increased.

Some research involving 9,549 offenders released from North Carolina state prisons in 1979–1980 showed that 32.7 percent (3,123) were returned to prison within thirty-six months of their release. However, 6.5 percent or 620 of these offenders were technical parole violators (Clarke and Crum, 1985). This figure is similar to that in the Kentucky study reported earlier, where 7 percent of the reincarcerations were due to technical parole violations (Vito, 1986). It is evident that much variation in meaning surrounds the concept *recidivism*. Many studies of this phenomenon have occurred, but presently, no consensus exists about recidivism and its definition. The most frequent usages of recidivism include rearrests, reconvictions, and reincarcerations, although many other meanings have been given it. Arguably, it seems that the most relevant connotation applied to recidivism is a reconviction for a new criminal offense as opposed to a simple rearrest or parole revocation, both of which might be grounds for reincarceration. Reincarceration as a measure of recidivism is unreliable as well because it fails to distinguish between the true lawbreaker and the technical rule violator.

RECIDIVISM AND HIGH-RATE OFFENDING

High-rate offending is directly indicative of recidivism. In fact, it is more accurately indicative of *chronic* recidivism. Generally, however, recidivists may or may not be chronic. Also, they may or may not reoffend at high rates. Thus, it would be misleading to characterize *all* recidivists as high-rate offenders. Considerable descriptive information exists about recidivists. Numerous evaluative studies are conducted annually of various offender programs, and virtually all strategies for dealing with offenders are examined and re-examined. No matter the cure proposed, the illness remains. Treatments are rarely pure, however, and therefore, their evaluations are necessarily complicated (Gottfredson and Gottfredson, 1988:197).

An interesting dilemma exists concerning recidivism. Criminologists and other experts can recite lengthy lists of characteristics describing recidivists. On the basis of these general characteristics, risk assessment instruments are constructed. Subsequently, these risk assessment devices will be used to make crucial decisions about an offender's freedom. For example, if parole boards use a salient factor score to predict an offender's degree of success on parole, some inmates who are eligible for parole will be denied it, since their scores define them as poor parole risks. However, other inmates who are eligible for parole may exhibit scores which indicate that they are good or safe parole risks. "Poor risks" are consistently denied parole, while "good risks" are consistently granted it. Therefore, parole boards have inadvertently established two large offender aggregates—"poor risks" and "good risks."

Often, only one or two points separate these two aggregates of offenders on risk assessment instruments. Therefore, some parole-eligible inmates who are, in fact, *good risks* for parole may be denied it because their risk assessment scores define them as *poor risks.* By the same token some parole-eligible inmates who are, in fact, *poor risks* for parole may be granted it when their risk assessment instrument scores define them as *good risks.* As we saw in previous chapters, these two types of prediction peculiarities respectively have been labeled as *false positives* and *false negatives.*

Whenever parole-eligible false positives are denied parole, we say that they are overpenalized or subject to punishments and penalties they do not deserve. Whenever parole-eligible false negatives are granted parole and go on to commit new and serious offenses, then we say that these persons have been underpenalized. The public is outraged, the parole board is embarrassed, and the integrity of test developers and the validity of risk prediction instruments are questioned. When judges sentence certain offenders to probation and incarcerate other offenders, they also run the risk of either overpenalizing or underpenalizing them. In both types of cases, judicial sentencing decision making and parole board decision making, references are most often made to numerical scales as *objective criteria* to justify those decisions. It is not necessarily the case that these scales are superior to personal judgments by judges or parole boards. But references to numbers seem to objectify or lend credence to probation-granting or early-release decisions as opposed to making subjective appraisals of offenders and using subjective interpretations of their backgrounds contained in PSIs and/or impressions gleaned from interviews with them.

CHARACTERISTICS OF RECIDIVISTS

The following is a partial list of recidivist characteristics. It is important to note that each characteristic has been gleaned from previous research and is more or less grounded empirically. However, each characteristic considered by itself or in particular combinations with other characteristics lacks high and/or consistent predictive utility (Champion, 1990c:196–198).

1. Males are more likely than females to recidivate (Greenfeld, 1985; Wilson, 1985; Delaware Executive Department, 1984).
2. Younger felons are more likely to recidivate than older felons (Chown and Davis, 1986; Delaware Executive Department, 1984).
3. Recidivism declines with advancing age (Clarke and Crum, 1985; Delaware Executive Department, 1984).
4. Higher recidivism rates occur among those with less formal education compared with those with more formal education (Roundtree, Edwards, and Parker, 1984).
5. The longer the time served in prison, the more likely a person will be to recidivate when released (Delaware Executive Department, 1984).
6. Most recidivism occurs within the first three years of release from prison or placement on probation (Beck and Shipley, 1987; Petersilia, 1985a).
7. The greater the number of prior arrests, the more likely the recidivism (Roundtree, Edwards, and Parker, 1984).
8. Violent offenders on parole are rearrested more often than nonviolent offenders on parole (Chown and Davis, 1986).
9. Blacks tend to recidivate at a higher rate than whites and others (Beck and Shipley, 1987; Delaware Executive Department, 1984).
10. The earlier offenders begin their criminal careers, the more likely the recidivism (Wilson, 1985).
11. Felony probationers are more likely than parolees to recidivate because they usually have longer probationary periods to serve compared with parole lengths (Roundtree, Edwards, and Parker, 1984).
12. Recidivism decreases as participation in furloughs, work study, and other pre-release activities increases (LeClair, 1985).
13. Property offenders are more likely to recidivate than violent offenders (Wallerstedt, 1984).
14. Those offenders with previous stable employment records recidivate less frequently than offenders with less stable employment records (Eisenberg, 1985b).
15. Prisoners with more disciplinary reports while incarcerated recidivate more frequently than those paroled who have fewer or no disciplinary reports filed against them (Eisenberg, 1985a).
16. Releasees who have a record of one or more juvenile arrests or convictions will recidivate more frequently than those releasees without juvenile arrests or convictions (Eisenberg, 1985b; Wallerstedt, 1984: Boudouris, 1983).

17. The younger the age when a person is released, the more likely the recidivism (Wallerstedt, 1984).
18. Parolees who recidivate do so for similar crimes for which they were originally imprisoned (Oregon Crime Analysis Center, 1984).
19. Substance and alcohol abusers have higher rates of recidivism than those who do not use drugs or alcohol (Eisenberg, 1985b).

However,

1. Recidivism is not related to age when paroled (Beck and Shipley, 1987).
2. Persons paroled for violent crimes are less likely to recidivate than persons paroled for property crimes (Beck and Shipley, 1987; Wallerstedt, 1984; Boudouris, 1983).
3. The length of time served in prison has no effect on recidivism (Beck and Shipley, 1987).
4. Race and recidivism are not related (Roundtree, Edwards, and Parker, 1984; Boudouris, 1983).
5. Males do not recidivate any more frequently than females (Roundtree, Edwards, and Parker, 1984).
6. Participation in prison rehabilitative or vocational/technical programs or nonparticipation in such programs has no influence on recidivism (Eisenberg, 1985b).
7. An inmate's good-time credits earned in prison are not related to recidivism (Delaware Executive Department, 1984).
8. Drug abuse and recidivism are not related (University of Hawaii–Manoa, 1984).
9. Employment record is unrelated to recidivism (Roundtree, Edwards, and Parker, 1984).
10. Parolees who recidivate commit offenses different from the ones they originally committed (Wallerstedt, 1984).

One impression we might glean from inspecting these statements is that studies of recidivism are mixed in their conclusions. This fact should cause us to proceed with caution, especially in formulating policy or making decisions that involve recidivism characteristics. One possible explanation for this apparent lack of study continuity is that each study examines a particular offender aggregate. These samples may alternatively consist of probationers who are first offenders; low-risk parolees involved in work or study release; traffic offenders; former alcohol and drug abusers who have been paroled from a federal penitentiary; state correctional center inmates; work releasees; and released inmates with histories of mental illness. These studies also use different methodological strategies for answering the research questions raised. Further, there are variations among definitions of the same terms from these different studies.

Virtually every study concluded by noting that additional research is needed. Further, these authors acknowledged certain methodological and theoretical weaknesses of their research. While these standard research precautions and safeguards are certainly important and encourage a degree of tentativeness on our parts regarding interpreting research findings, it is true that many corrections officials, parole boards, and judges are influenced by whatever these findings suggest. Thus, conceivably improper policy conclusions are sometimes based on studies that use unusual methodological strategies or definitions of concepts (Maltz, 1984).

Regardless of the variation among studies regarding characteristics associated with recidivism, how useful are these characteristics in predicting recidivism? Can we construct an accurate profile of *typical recidivists?* Can parole boards identify with great accuracy inmates who will become recidivists? We know, or at least we think we know, that recidivists are mostly male, black, younger, less educated, and have prior records. In fact, prior records are more consistently related to recidivism than these other attributes. Therefore, should it be official judicial or parole board policy to deny probation or parole to younger, less educated, black males with prior records? What about those younger, black male prior offenders with less education who will never commit new crimes? Surely there must be some of these among our probation-eligible or parole-eligible offender populations. Can we identify these as well?

Our main problem is that while these and other characteristics describe the general category of recidivists, these characteristics are also found among many nonrecidivists. Thus, prediction measures, based upon relevant information about offenders, must be devised and tested to improve their validity and discriminatory power (Gottfredson and Gottfredson, 1988:200). A related problem is determining whether serious recidivism has occurred, not just a series of minor, technical violations. This means that some degree of agreement needs to be established about what true recidivism is and how it ought to be measured.

AVERTABLE AND NON-AVERTABLE RECIDIVISTS

One way of distinguishing between different kinds of recidivists is whether they are avertable or non-avertable. A survey of 153,465 male felony offenders admitted to state prisons in 1979 was conducted and sponsored by the Bureau of Justice Statistics (Greenfeld, 1985). Of these felons, 94,134, or 61 percent, had been incarcerated previously in either a state prison (59 percent), jail (28.4 percent), juvenile detention (10 percent), or federal/military facility (3 percent). First offenders accounted for 38.7 percent, or 59,331, of new prison admissions. One of the innovative aspects of the study was the classification of those recidivists with prior records of incarceration into *avertable recidivists* and *non-avertable recidivists.* Avertable recidivists are those offenders who would have still been in prison serving their original sentences in full at the time they were confined in 1979 for committing new offenses. Non-avertable recidivists are those offenders whose prior sentences would not have affected the commission of new crimes.

Some examples of avertable and non-avertable recidivists are illustrated as follows. Consider Jane Doe as a new 1979 prison admission. Doe was previously incarcerated in 1975 for armed robbery and given a two- to fifteen-year prison sentence. The parole board released Doe in 1978, whereupon Doe committed several burglaries. She was apprehended by police and eventually convicted of burglary in 1979. Had she still been in prison serving her entire fifteen-year sentence, those burglaries she committed never would have occurred. Doe is called an avertable recidivist, because her crimes occurred within the maximum range of her original sentence (i.e., 1975–1990).

Jane Doe's brother, John, was convicted in 1971 of vehicular theft. John was sentenced to three years. John served his time and was eventually released. John obeyed the law for several years, but in 1979 he was arrested for and convicted of stealing another automobile. Since he had already served his maximum sentence of three years for the original vehicular theft conviction from 1971 to 1974, the maximum range of his original sentence no longer applied. John is considered to be a non-avertable recidivist. Both he and his sister, Jane, are recidivists, because both of them are criminal offenders who have been convicted of one or more previous crimes. But Jane's new crimes might have been averted had Jane been forced to serve her maximum sentence. This doesn't rule out the possibility that when Jane finally served the maximum fifteen-year sentence for armed robbery, she could commit new crimes and therefore be classified as a non-avertable recidivist like her brother.

Non-avertable recidivists accounted for 34.8 percent of the 200,189 crimes, avertable recidivists accounted for 24.4 percent of them, and first offenders made up the remaining 40.8 percent. Non-avertable recidivists accounted for substantially higher percentages of crimes than did avertable recidivists in virtually every crime category. Also, non-avertable recidivists compared with first-timers accounted for substantially smaller percentages of violent crimes and drug offenses but somewhat higher percentages of property crimes (with few exceptions). The percent of offenses committed by avertable recidivists theoretically represents the proportion of crimes that would not have been committed by these offenders had they been obligated to serve out their entire sentences. This is somewhat misleading, however, because it ignores the fact that when many of these crimes were committed, other criminals were involved. Thus, the potential absence of the conspiratorial involvement of these avertable recidivists may or may not have prevented these crimes.

The same study of 1979 state prisoners identified selected characteristics of offenders. These prisoners were profiled according to the non-avertable recidivist, avertable recidivist, and first-timer distinctions. At least 50 percent or more of all 1979 admissions, regardless of admission type, were twenty-six years of age or less. Again, by age category, 1979 prison admissions decline with advancing age, with an average of 91 percent of all admissions being forty or less. Two-thirds of all admissions had not completed high school, while about half had never married. Different from what we might expect, 63 percent of all 1979 admissions were employed full-time prior to their arrest. About a third had one or more family members who had been previously incarcerated, and about the same proportion was under the influence of drugs when the offense occurred. About half of these admissions had been drinking at the time of the crime, and a third were drunk.

At the time these offenders committed the crimes leading to their 1979 incarceration, about two-thirds of the avertable recidivists were on parole, while about a fourth of the first-timers and non-avertable recidivists were on probation. An important point emphasized by these researchers is that nearly half of the recidivists who entered prison in 1979 were avertable, and they would have still been in prison during 1979 and unable to commit those new crimes if they had fully served the maximum term of their last confinement sentence (Greenfeld, 1985:6). It is likely that if the avertable recidivists had never been paroled, the prison inmate population would have risen greatly. Overcrowding would be an even greater problem than it is presently. Thus, a trade-off occurs, where the early release of future recidivists triggers more crime, but continuing the incarceration of recidivists aggravates prison overcrowding. Little is known about how many inmates would not have been recidivists if they had been paroled. Thus, while selective incapacitation seems an appropriate strategy for those who will become recidivists, we have not, as yet, devised accurate measures that will predict recidivism among prospective probationers or parolees with a high degree of precision.

One additional argument is that the characteristics of some offender aggregate are used to make decisions about individual probationers or parolees. Predictions based upon aggregate phenomena are suspect when applied to individual cases. Each sentencing decision is an individual one. Each parole board decision is an individual one. Groups of offenders do not ordinarily appear before judges to be sentenced categorically. And inmates do not appear in groups before parole boards.

RECIDIVISM AND PUBLIC POLICY

In view of the sentencing reforms enacted by various states and current trends, these figures have apparently been persuasive or at least influential in changing sentencing policies and parole criteria. The study conducted by the Bureau of Justice Statistics (BJS) is one of the larger surveys of recidivists and their characteristics. But each year, new generations of offenders enter jails and prisons. The profile of these inmates changes daily. However, some general patterns are apparent, not only from the BJS analysis but from other research as well. According to the BJS survey, using reconviction as an indicator of an adult recidivist, recidivists appear to share the following characteristics:

1. Recidivists tend to be male.
2. Recidivists tend to be younger (under thirty), and recidivism declines with advancing age.

3. Recidivists tend to have an educational level equivalent to high school or less.
4. Recidivists tend to have lengthy records of arrests and/or convictions.
5. Recidivists tend to be under no correctional supervision when committing new offenses.
6. Recidivists tend to have a record of juvenile offenses.
7. Recidivists tend to commit crimes similar to those for which they were convicted previously.
8. Recidivists tend to have alcohol or drug dependency problems associated with the commission of new offenses.
9. Recidivists tend not to commit progressively serious offenses compared with their prior records.
10. Recidivists tend to be unmarried, widowed, or divorced.
11. Recidivists tend to be employed, either full-time or part-time, when committing new offenses.

It is important to note that these characteristics may be intrinsically useful for helping us to spot "problem offenders." But we must be cautious when attempting to profile those who are most likely to commit new crimes in the future if placed on probation or parole. Parole boards might use this information as background or supplemental when interviewing parole-eligible inmates. Also, judges might use this information when deciding the appropriate sentence for a convicted offender. The odds probably favor future offender behaviors consistent with previous offender behaviors. The odds probably *increase* as the number of characteristics associated with recidivists (and possessed by probation-eligible or parole-eligible offenders) increases. But we can never be certain that specific offenders will commit new crimes. Our schemes seem more effective when large numbers of offenders sharing similar characteristics are aggregated, but parole boards and judges make decisions about individual offenders, not groups of offenders (Morris and Miller, 1987:4).

States have a considerable interest in sentencing reforms directed away from rehabilitation and toward justice with greater certainty of punishment. This interest stems, in part, from public dissatisfaction with how the courts and corrections have dealt with offenders in recent decades. Recidivism statistics stimulate public concern about parole and probation programs. The U.S. Department of Justice says that 65 percent of released prisoners will return to prison within two years, and most of these returns will occur within one year from their release. Parole may hold down prison populations, but there may be a trade-off through increased street crime (Petersilia, 1987:vi). Therefore, greater certainty of incarceration, together with longer terms of confinement for offenders, is advocated by corrections experts and scholars as a viable solution for reducing and controlling crime. However, no research has ever demonstrated conclusively that longer prison sentences make ex-offenders less likely to commit new crimes (Petersilia, 1987:vi). In fact, we have seen just the opposite outcome of long sentences in some research reported earlier in this chapter. "Getting tough" on crime is best illustrated to the public by imposing harsher and longer sentences on convicted offenders. Again, the deterrent value of lengthy incarceration is questionable. In view of public sentiment favoring longer prison sentences for offenders, we may conclude that the primary goal achieved by longer incarcerative sentences is not deterrence, but rather, incapacitation and control.

PROBATIONERS AND PAROLEES COMPARED

Few studies have actually compared probationers with parolees directly regarding their recidivism. As has been seen, there is an abundance of research about recidivists and their characteristics, but few investigators have focused upon probationers and parolees simultaneously to see whether two reasonably matched sets of offenders differ in their recidivism rates and other related characteristics. However, Rand Corporation researchers utilized an existing data base of 16,500 males convicted of felonies in several California counties in 1980 in order to compare probationers and parolees regarding their recidivism (Petersilia, Turner, and Peterson, 1986).

The Rand offender data base consisted of persons convicted of robbery, assault, burglary, larceny/theft, forgery, and drug sale/possession. These crimes were selected because offenders convicted of them may be sentenced to either prison or probation (Petersilia, Turner, and Peterson, 1986:9). Offenders were compared according to characteristics including age, race, gender, employment, juvenile/adult criminal history, and several other salient factors. Eventually 511 probationers and 511 parolees were roughly matched according to several criteria. The probationers tended to be more serious probationers than probationers in general, while the parolees were among the least serious offenders imprisoned. In short, Rand researchers selected the least serious offenders from the more serious offending group, while they selected the most serious offenders from less serious offending group. On this basis, Rand researchers argued that the two offender samples were generally comparable in terms of their offense seriousness (Petersilia, Turner, and Peterson, 1986:12).

Several important characteristics of the two samples of 1,022 offenders were described. Probationers and parolees were fairly evenly matched according to number of prior adult convictions, prior prison terms, number of conviction counts, and the percent under drug influence when crime was committed. A higher proportion of parolees had been on adult parole, on juvenile parole, were armed with a gun during the crime, and were classified as drug addicts. However, a higher proportion of probationers knew their victims, caused serious injury during the crime, and used a weapon. Both samples were about the same age when they started serving their sentences (Petersilia, Turner, and Peterson, 1986:15).

While their study examined more dimensions of offender behaviors than are reported here, the Rand researchers found that parolees recidivated more quickly compared with probationers. These investigators used rearrests, charges filed, reconvictions, and incarceration as various recidivism dimensions. In virtually every category, parolees had higher recidivism scores compared with probationers, although these differences were not that dramatic for all categories. For example, 19 percent of the probationer sample was incarcerated in prison compared with 26 percent of the parolees. Another comparison showed 72 percent of the parolees were rearrested compared with 63 percent of the probationers.

Rand researchers concluded that at least for their sample, parolees had higher recidivism rates than probationers, although their new crimes are not more serious (Petersilia, Turner, and Peterson, 1986:21). These investigators also found little influence of incarceration on recidivism. Interestingly, incarceration tended to increase recidivism rates slightly, especially for property offenders who historically have higher recidivism rates anyway (1986:24). Finally, serving longer prison terms did not influence significantly the rate of recidivism for most offense categories, although a slight decrease in recidivism occurred with longer prison terms.

These findings are consistent with similar research sponsored by the U.S. Department of Justice. Between 1979 and 1986, although the average lengths of regular prison sentences increased by 32 percent, the rate of parole revocations for both technical violations and major crimes doubled for parolees during the same period (Abt Associates, Inc., 1987:2). And of more than 20,000 federal offenders leaving probation and parole between July 1, 1985, and June 30, 1986, more than one in five had committed a new crime or violated the technical conditions of their release (Abt Associates, Inc., 1987:2). Again, incarceration seemed to make little difference. When this factor did make a difference, it tended to increase recidivism rates.

PRISON VERSUS PROBATION

Whether the greater cost of confinement in jail or prison was worth the small differences in recidivism rates observed between prisoners and probationers was a question guiding the Rand study. Rand researchers showed that probation/parole programs are about half the cost of incarceration. One example is the fact that the average costs per offender on probation in California for the samples they studied were $11,600 compared with $23,400 for incarcerated offenders (Petersilia, Turner, and Peterson, 1986:34).

Rand researchers concluded that (1) public safety would clearly benefit from somehow incapacitating a larger proportion of the felons represented in the study's matched sample of prisoners and felony probationers; (2) building more prisons can move toward accomplishing this goal, but cannot fully realize it; (3) relying on only one form of incapacitation necessarily limits society's ability to respond to the overall crime problem; in addition to imprisonment, other means of incapacitating felony offenders may be necessary to control the threat of serious crimes from felony offenders released to the community from prison and on probation, and (4) intensive probation supervision, electronic monitoring, house arrest, and other intermediate sanctions are untested, but promising new ways to ease prison overcrowding while better incapacitating felony offenders who now receive traditional probation sentences (Petersilia, Turner, and Peterson, 1986:37).

CAN RECIDIVISM BE PREVENTED?

Recidivism rates can be reduced. Short of incarcerating offenders, recidivism cannot be prevented, regardless of the program examined. However, different programs offer alternative strategies for reducing recidivism. Some programs are able to show lower recidivism rates than other programs. To this extent, they are more or less successful in achieving program goals. Some of these programs have solutions that include greater use of intensive supervised probation/parole, greater reintegration of offenders into their communities, and more technologically complex monitoring methods (e.g., electronic monitoring). More intensive monitoring of offender behaviors through various community corrections programs tends to reduce recidivism. However, no strategy is completely free of any recidivism.

The fact that 50 percent or more of all offenders, incarcerated or on probation, will recidivate in the future at some unspecified time is evidence of the rehabilitative failure of any program, including incarceration. However, one influential but conservative voice favoring incapacitation is James Q. Wilson, who argues that while imprisonment may not rehabilitate offenders, it does keep them off the streets away from the general public. And this may be the most effective means of crime control (Wilson, 1985). Another controversial solution recommended by some experts is selective incapacitation (Struckhoff, 1987:30).

Some research conducted by the National Council on Crime and Delinquency (NCCD) has examined parolee recidivism in California and reported that parolee failures have increased from 23 percent in 1975 to 53 percent in 1983 (Austin, 1987). Furthermore, administrative parole revocations have jumped from 5 to 35 percent since 1975, but the proportion of parolees being returned because of new felony convictions while on parole increased by only 5 percent. Parolee failures do not seem directly related to new criminality, however. Rather, technical and administrative factors are largely to blame in many of these parolee failure situations. The NCCD cites the following as contributing significantly to the growing numbers of administrative parole revocations: (1) declining levels of financial assistance and narcotic treatment resources for parolees; (2) increases in parole supervision caseloads; (3) a shift in public and law enforcement attitudes regarding parolees and law violators in general; (4) jail overcrowding; and (5) a more efficient law enforcement/parole supervision system (Austin, 1987:i).

Recidivism rates might be reduced through more effective probation/parole programs, smaller caseloads for POs (probably resulting in more frequent contact with probationer or parolee clients), and increasing the capacity of delivery systems (i.e., greater funding) to meet the specialized needs of offenders such as those with drug dependency problems or alcoholism. The NCCD findings and corresponding recommendations are shared by other researchers as well (Petersilia, 1987; Blumstein, 1983c). Paradoxically, more frequent contact between POs and their clients may make POs more aware of client technical violations of their program requirements. This doesn't mean that PO clients are committing more program violations, but rather that POs are in the position of observing their clients more frequently and that the likelihood of observing program infractions is increased.

Recidivism studies are almost always conducted from the viewpoint of practitioners. Seldom are the actual offenders directly involved. Investigators describe various programs, their costs and benefits, successes, and offender characteristics. But what do offenders themselves think about the programs imposed upon them? Do offenders view programs the way administrators of those programs intend for them to be viewed? An investigation was conducted in 1983 involving 106 federal probationers selected from the U.S. Probation and Parole Office in Chicago, Illinois (Allen, 1985:69). Probationers were asked by researchers to indicate what the probationers believed to be the purpose in placing them on probation. They were also asked about the probation officer's role in relation to them. Included in this inquiry were requests for opinions about how the probation system could be improved, what services could be provided, and who should provide these services (Allen, 1985:67).

Each probationer was interviewed shortly after completing the probation term. Ex-probationers were presented with four models of probation practice and asked to react to them. These four models of probation practice include the traditional rehabilitation model, the deterrence model, the desert ("just deserts") model, and the justice model. Respondents were asked to react to each of these models as possible goals of probation. Considering the recent emphasis given "just deserts" and justice in sentencing reforms, the study results were somewhat surprising.

Former probationers expressed the belief that rehabilitation was the primary aim of their probation programs. However, they also believed that deterrence was ideally the ultimate objective of their probation. The rehabilitative goal of probation was reinforced by program emphases on education and employment assistance, and plea bargaining efforts prior to sentencing. A majority of probationers believed that probation officers sincerely wished to assist them, but these offenders were split concerning the value of probation officers in providing assistance in working out personal problems (Allen, 1985:72). The small sample nevertheless highlighted certain weaknesses of existing delivery systems. Generally, these offenders were satisfied with their programs, although several believed that certain logistical and administrative changes were in order. For instance, they suggested that probation officers should strive to be more client-centered. This could be achieved through lower caseloads and closer contact with probationers. Also, they felt probation officers should be permitted more authority to act on their own, to increase their contact level. More home visits by POs were suggested as well.

Another belief was that probation programs should offer incentives or rewards for good conduct, such as early termination of probation for rule compliance. Probationers agreed that their probation should benefit the community directly. Also, their view of the program influenced directly their view of the PO role. Rehabilitation-oriented probationers saw their POs in a support role, while deterrence-oriented probationers saw their POs as serving a monitoring function (Allen, 1985:73).

According to the investigator, the real value of this study is demonstrating that offenders are willing to provide input and they have something to say (Allen, 1985:74). Each program for probationers and parolees will vary in its effectiveness, and administrators and others will evaluate the successfulness of these programs. But offenders may be an important source of feedback as well. Administrators may be able to remedy existing program defects (or at least some of them) by listening to those involved in these programs. In a sense, this is reminiscent of the participation hypothesis pertaining to employers and workers: employees will produce more and generally be more cooperative to the extent that they are involved in decisions affecting their work. This does not mean that offenders should be placed on parole boards or in advisory capacities to judges during the sentencing process. But it does suggest that corrections officials can learn much from offenders about how programs can be improved. And if the offender suggests certain improvements, there is the chance that other offenders will benefit from those improvements eventually. This may not eliminate recidivism, but it may function to reduce it.

SUMMARY

One controversial strategy for reducing crime is to incapacitate offenders selectively on the basis of those most likely and least likely to recidivate at some future time. This is selective incapacitation, and it basically penalizes those suspected of becoming recidivists and committing new offenses after having been convicted of earlier offenses. The goals of selective incapacitation include preventing and reducing crime; reducing prison and jail overcrowding by making space available only to the most serious and chronic offenders; providing more adequate treatment for those most in need of such treatment; promoting public safety; maintaining institutional discipline and control; promoting respect for the law and creating an atmosphere of "just deserts" where appropriate sanctions will be applied for those most deserving of those sanctions; punishment and retribution; and increasing the cost-effectiveness of incarceration.

Opponents of selective incapacitation believe that there are serious moral/ethical and legal questions that should be raised before implementing selective incapacitation on a large scale. One argument is that selective incapacitation is unfair because it individualizes punishments. This creates sentencing disparities where offenders who are convicted of similar crimes receive widely disparate sentences. Currently, risk assessment tools have relatively low predictive utility, and it is not possible to identify all would-be recidivists in advance with absolute certainty. Also, there is greater state intrusion into the lives of offenders designated by instrumentation to be "high-risk." The legal dimension of selective incapacitation raises the issue of whether it is fair to penalize offenders for crimes they have not, as yet, committed.

Closely connected to selective incapacitation is recidivism. Recidivism is the act of committing new crimes where offenders have been convicted of prior crimes. Not all researchers accept or use this definition, however. In fact, at least fourteen different definitions of recidivism have been provided (Maltz, 1984). The most popular definitions of recidivism include rearrests, reconvictions, probation or parole revocations, and reincarcerations. Probably the most accurate indicator of true recidivism is the number of reconvictions, since this means that offenders have previously been convicted of earlier offenses. Chronic recidivists are targets of selective incapacitation. However, not all chronic recidivists are dangerous offenders. When we consider the harm convicted offenders may inflict upon their communities if released, we must consider whether the crimes these persons are likely to commit will involve crimes against persons or property. It is difficult to forecast who will or will not be good probation or parole "risks" based upon current instrumentation. A disturbing number of false positives and false negatives suggest persistent imperfections in our research and prediction tools. Perhaps it is safest to say that recidivism can never be prevented, short of complete incapacitation through incarceration. But different programs, such as intensive supervised probation or parole, community corrections involving house arrest and/or electronic monitoring, and closer relations between probationer/parolee clients and their POs, exhibit different rates of recidivism. The closer these offender-clients are monitored, usually the lower the rate of recidivism. Opinions expressed by probationers and parolees themselves are to the effect that they will be more compliant with program rules to the extent that they believe their officer-supervisors have a continuing interest in their importance and welfare.

4

Classification in Correctional Settings: Risk as a Determinate of Level-of-Custody Decision Making

INTRODUCTION

The largest professional utilization of risk assessment measures is in the broad area of corrections. Specifically, risk assessment devices are used extensively for the purpose of classifying and categorizing prisoners according to various criteria. According to how offenders are classified by correctional management, initial placements will be made whereby new inmates are assigned to one classification level or another. These classifications are relevant for both adult and juvenile inmates as well as for male and female offenders.

In this chapter we will examine risk assessment tools as applied in correctional settings, such as jails and prisons. Most jails, prisons, or penitentiaries have articulated strategies by which their inmate populations can best be managed. The use of objective classification instruments facilitates inmate management. The first part of this chapter describes the need for risk assessment instruments in correctional institutions. What purposes are served by using these instruments, and how do both inmates and correctional staff benefit? A second important part of the chapter investigates the classification decision, how it is made, and how different actors in the correctional system affect inmate custody assignments during periods of their incarceration. What are the criteria used by these different institutions that influence how offenders are treated? Depending upon their particular custody-level assignment, prisoners may or may not have certain privileges or access to different institutional areas or services.

One consequence of inmate classification and subsequent placement is that some inmate interactions may foster violence. Violence is frequently aggravated by misclassifications of certain inmates. In short, inmates who should be placed in more secure prison areas are originally misclassified and placed in less secure areas where their behaviors are maximally disruptive. Further, those inmates who incur greater restrictions than other inmates may oppose the decision-making process resulting in their current classifications and institutional placements. Thus, the potential exists for lawsuits emanating from prisoners themselves against prison officials for various reasons. Often, the lawsuits are either the direct or indirect result of how inmates are originally classified and situated. A subsequent part of this chapter explores the nature of legal liabilities of correctional personnel arising from inmate unrest and discontentment.

The chapter concludes by describing the current problem of prison/jail overcrowding. Institutional overcrowding is a persistent problem and interferes with effective inmate management. Prison/jail officials attempt to minimize inmate problems resulting from misclassification by conducting periodic reassessments of inmate behavior. Therefore, measuring inmate risk is a continuing phenomenon. Also, classification decisions about inmates at different stages of their incarceration impact significantly upon subsequent parole board decision making. Thus, the stage is set for a detailed examination of decision making by parole boards subsequently presented in Chapter 5.

CORRECTIONAL INSTITUTIONS AND THE NEED FOR RISK ASSESSMENT

Types of Correctional Facilities

Before we examine the need for risk assessment, we must first examine briefly the nature and types and characteristics of correctional facilities most commonly available to house low- and high-risk offenders. There are many types of correctional institutions. For adult offenders, institutions exist that are exclusively designed to house either male inmates or female inmates. Many correctional facilities house both male and female offenders in separate areas. Yet other institutions provide co-correctional housing, where male and female inmates share many of the institution's services, including educational or vocational training and/or recreational areas. Also, these institutions may be designed to operate either as short-term or as long-term confinement facilities. For instance, jails have traditionally been viewed as short-term institutions, since they are designed to accommodate defendants awaiting trial and/or those convicted, low-risk misdemeanants serving short sentences of less than one year. Jails are most often locally operated, either by cities or counties. Some states have state-operated jail facilities (Welsh et al., 1990).

Largely because of their short-term nature and purpose, jails have often been constructed without many of the amenities found in large prison systems. Most jails do not have extensive recreational facilities, and many have few inmate services. Various types of rehabilitative programs, such as educational/vocational training and individual or group counseling, are simply not an integral part of jail design. However, most prisons and penitentiaries do provide extensive amenities and a wider variety of educational and social/psychological services for inmates.

Typically, more serious and/or dangerous offenders serving longer sentences (one year or longer) are confined in prisons and penitentiaries.

Court-Mandated Inmate Population Reductions

During the last two decades, however, court-ordered reductions in state and federal prison and penitentiary inmate populations have necessitated using any available jail space in given jurisdictions to house prison inmate overflows. The primary intent of these court-ordered inmate population reductions was to obligate these correctional facilities to comply with minimal health, safety, and security standards in view of their rated and actual population capacities (McMurray and Wilson, 1991; Orrick, 1989; Sechrest, 1989). Therefore, many small and large jails currently hold both short- and long-term offenders, usually in different confinement areas. While a discussion of the various financial and logistic merits for counties or cities of using their jail space in this fashion is beyond the scope of this book, it is clear that many jails suffer the same as prisons from chronic overcrowding. Sechrest (1989:87–88) notes, for instance, that jail population growth increased by 89 percent between 1978 and 1987. In fact, he indicates that 33 percent of those jails with large inmate capacities were also under court orders to reduce their inmate populations in 1987. Jail inmate population growth continues presently unabated.

Minimizing Institutional Disruption

One widely documented correlate of jail and prison overcrowding is inmate violence, which promotes serious institutional disruption (Wooldredge, 1989). Both prison and jail overcrowding are often conceptualized according to the density of the inmate population (Sechrest, 1989:87–88). Jail and prison officials have more than a vested interest in minimizing violence among inmates of their respective institutions. They wish to furnish all of their inmates with safe environments, hopefully rehabilitative ones. Furthermore, all inmates have the right to avoid victimization from other, more powerful inmates.

It is probably the case that at least in the near future, chronic jail and prison overcrowding will continue despite our best efforts to prevent it. It is not difficult to acquire this pessimistic perspective, particularly if we consider a state such as California, which presently has one of the largest prison-construction budgets in the nation. Despite the fact that California corrections authorities will have eight or nine new correctional facilities during the next few years as the result of this extensive construction, already there are more convicted felons than these new facilities will be able to accommodate. This is one reason that California places approximately 70 percent of its convicted felon population on probation annually instead of incarcerating them (Petersilia, 1985a). Therefore, many corrections officials and legislators are giving serious consideration and priority to proposals aimed at more effective inmate management (Orrick, 1989). Like several other states, North Carolina has recently established a Jail Population Management Plan as the result of the efforts of the Governor's Crime Commission (McMurray and Wilson, 1991:36). A key aim of this plan is to develop strategies to reduce jail overcrowding within existing systemic constraints without compromising public safety.

With this factual information in mind about present jail and prison inmate populations and problems, we may now consider the relevance and importance of risk assessment and inmate classification schemes. Craddock (1987:1) notes that during the late 1970s, many states began to develop systematic, "objective" models of inmate classification in response to federal court mandates. Despite these efforts and the development of numerous classification instruments and descriptive criteria, Craddock indicates that little empirical research occurred simultaneously to gauge the predictive utility of these measures (Craddock, 1987:1). In subsequent years during the 1980s and early 1990s, many state jurisdictions, such as Colorado, as well as the Federal Bureau of Prisons, sought to overhaul their existing inmate classification schemes and substitute more reliable instrumentation (Colorado Division of Criminal Justice, 1986). This statement has been independently confirmed. Indeed, when the appropriate state officials were contacted to solicit their risk assessment measures for inclusion in this book, more than a few of these administrators said that their jurisdictions were currently in the process of re-evaluating their existing assessment criteria and measures. A safe estimate is that by early 1993, at least twenty state departments of correction were in the process of overhauling their risk assessment devices and inventories.

The Need for Risk Assessment

Among the various state and federal jurisdictions, a common set of goals or classification objectives exists. While there may be minor variations in definition from one state to the next, the Delaware Bureau of Prisons has provided us with a succinct understanding of what is meant by classification. Delaware defines classification as a "process by which inmates are subdivided into groups based on a variety of considerations which include (1) determination of and assignment to appropriate custody and security levels; (2) program placement based on inmate needs and available services—medical, mental, health, vocational, educational, and work; (3) designation to proper housing placement within the institution; and (4) scheduled review of assignments to reassess an inmate's needs and progress" (Delaware Bureau of Prisons, 1992:5).

At the outset, it is important to distinguish between initial classifications and reassessments of initial classifications. Initial classifications are preliminary screenings and separations of incoming inmates according to general criteria, such as might be provided or included in a presentence investigation report. Reassessments of initial classifications are periodic re-evaluations of inmate conduct over a period of months, based upon past institutional behaviors and presently assigned custody levels. Both initial classifications and reassessments of initial classifications utilize numerical criteria extensively which result in particular inmate placements. However, provisions for executive overrides exist in most instances for both types of assessments. This means that whatever the numbers prescribe for an inmate's placement within the facility (e.g., maximum security, medium security, minimum security), senior correctional officers or prison administrators may disagree with and override this numerical value, provided they furnish a written rationale for doing so. The nature of the override is to either increase, decrease, or not interfere with an inmate's present custody level. For instance, an inmate's numerical risk assessment score may indicate placement in a maximum-security prison area. A correctional officer's observation of inmate conduct or interviews with the inmate may indicate a lower level of placement, such as medium- or minimum-security custody. Also, lower-level placements may be overridden if authorities believe a higher custody level is warranted on the basis of relevant information not immediately apparent from numerical figures on risk scales.

This important difference between initial classifications and reassessments of initial classifications is highlighted by the Michigan Department of Corrections (Kosinski, Knapp, and Daman, 1989). The researchers who devised the Michigan initial classification screen indicate that "overall, results of the study indicate that security classification is a valuable tool in the placement and management of inmates in the Michigan correction system. *Although the initial classification screen does not show strong overall predictive utility, it does effectively differentiate between the best and worst of incoming prisoners with regard to the probability of serious institutional misconduct*" (Kosinski, Knapp, and Daman, 1989:2 [Italics mine]).

Probably this is what many departments of corrections expect to achieve with their initial classification instruments. If they can discriminate initially by making general distinctions between incoming inmates according to commensurate "best" and "worst" categories, then they have minimized the likelihood of institutional disruption that might occur without an initial classification screening tool in place for preliminary inmate placements. Subsequently, they can fine-tune these earlier placement decisions with reclassifications or reassessments of inmate risk. But this time, they benefit from a knowledge of previously exhibited behaviors from inmates under various levels of custody. Accordingly, they can more effectively gauge where particular prisoners ought to be housed, in view of the variety of existing institutional placement options.

The Delaware Bureau of Prisons has also outlined several fundamental goals for its correctional classification system. These goals, worth replicating here, are to:

1. support agency goals of public safety and humane treatment;
2. provide information for population management and planning;
3. assign proper security and custody levels;

4. identify required programs and services for programming and budgeting purposes;
5. monitor the success/failure of classification designation;
6. monitor classification designation by classifying unit and classifying counselor;
7. monitor service delivery for "special needs" groups;
8. monitor identification and handling of dangerous inmates; and
9. monitor inmate initiated actions, appeals or litigation, objecting to classification decisions (Delaware Bureau of Prisons, 1992:5).

A close inspection of these classification goals indicates that Delaware officials not only want to place their inmates most effectively in the types of custody conditions best suited to their behaviors, but they also want to keep track of offender classification through periodic reassessments. Furthermore, officials are equally concerned with providing inmates with services and special programs designed for their self-improvement. It is noteworthy that these officials have committed to writing the objective of assisting inmates in their appeals or court litigation prompted by their disagreements with initial classification decisions. Also important is the fact that both public safety and humane inmate treatment are stressed. Therefore, Delaware administrators have created a well-balanced list of classification goals, striving to achieve institutional needs as well as to target and remedy inmate deficiencies and weaknesses. These diffuse objectives are not necessarily sought by all other corrections departments, however. For instance, New York initial classification instruments are almost exclusively concerned with institutional security. More than a few state jurisdictions work collaboratively with universities by establishing computerized inmate tracking systems. These systems are designed to maximize existing services or to establish new services, and to make them available to the widest possible inmate audience. Metzner (1992) says that collaborative relationships between prisons and universities exist in over half of all prison systems, although only ten states have reported system-wide computerized tracking systems.

As noted by the National Council on Crime and Delinquency (1990b:1), offenders representing very different levels of risk enter correctional systems. Some of these offenders will never commit new offenses, while others will reappear frequently throughout the criminal justice system at different stages. Those inclined to recidivate upon their release from prison are also among those most likely to be troublesome while incarcerated. For both jails and prisons, administrators attempt to manage their inmate populations in such a way that public and institutional safety is preserved to a high degree. Effective inmate management accrues largely as the result of utilizing appropriate screening mechanisms when offenders first enter the system.

A Distinction between Institutional and Public Risk

New York correctional authorities have devoted considerable time to developing risk assessment instruments that will enable them to evaluate an incoming inmate's potential risk (Alexander, 1980). An early version of their security classification guideline stressed two types of risk: institutional risk and public risk. Institutional risk is the likelihood that an inmate will be violent or disruptive to other inmates and staff. Public risk is a combination of the likelihood that an inmate will escape and the likelihood that he will be violent if he does escape (Alexander, 1980:1–3). The New York guideline is exclusively confined to the security issue, which is posed by different, incoming male inmates. Alexander (1980:1) says that the guideline is not concerned at all with punishment, rehabilitation, or deterrence. He notes that inmates with a prior incarceration may actually score lower as risks than inmates who are convicted and incarcerated for the first time. The rationale is that previously incarcerated offenders have proven themselves under incarcerative conditions, whereas first-time inmates have not proven themselves. Furthermore, inmates who will benefit from a camp program are no more likely to be classified as "minimum-security" than inmates who will not benefit from such a program. Finally, he says that the goal of deterrence is set aside to the extent that a more serious crime in the eyes of the law, such as Grand Larceny (a Class C felony), may well score lower than a less serious crime in the eyes of the law, such as Robbery 3rd (a Class D felony).

Although the Delaware initial classification goals spelled out above are fairly broad, at least one additional goal should be mentioned. Institutional security is influenced to a degree by the kinds of adjustments inmates make when entering prison. Some inmates react poorly to confinement and pose immediate problems for staff. Adjustment to conditions of confinement is especially difficult for incoming juvenile offenders. This is one reason why many jurisdictions utilize psychological measures as a part of their initial assessment instrument battery for incoming inmates. One popular psychological inventory used in both juvenile and adult corrections is the Minnesota Multiphasic Personality Inventory, or MMPI. Discussed in an earlier chapter, the MMPI is a broadly applicable tool. In fact, certain of its subscales have been incorporated in whole or in part in various other risk devices, such as Megargee's Inmate Typology (Kalichman, 1988; Megargee, Carbonell, and Bohn, 1988; Wright, 1988).

Four conceptual goals of inmate classification, especially initial classification decision making, have been articulated by Holt, Ducat, and Eakles (1981:1). These include the following:

1. All inmates should be placed in the lowest custody level consistent with public safety.
2. Inmates should be ciassfied on the basis of objective information and objective criteria.
3. The process must be applied uniformly, so that similarly situated inmates receive similar custody assignments.
4. The system must provide for centralized control over the process.

These researchers believe that the custodial classification of inmates is the core of corrections. Although initial classifications of incoming inmates have been made formally since the 1950s, it is evident that no single classification device or instrument has been foolproof in proper inmate placements. In California, for instance, Holt, Ducat, and Eakles (1981:26) report that in the late 1970s, early inmate ratings preceding their ultimate placement included the following background variables: (1) escape history; (2) prior incarcerations; and (3) length of sentence (which is also offense severity). The various California penal institutions were ranked into four groups according to the actual count or numbers of minimum-, medium-, and maximum-custody beds. Interestingly, when a validation study was conducted by matching offenders (and their history) and bed space according to custody level, institutional group assignment of new inmates was predicted accurately in only 26 percent of the cases, whereas random assignments of inmates would have predicted 25 percent of these accurately. Subsequently, more elaborate classification instruments were created which led to more accurate predictions of inmate placements.

One problem reported by Holt, Ducat, and Eakles was that the nature and type of available prison space did not match perfectly the nature and types of prisoners who fit a particular level of custody. Thus, even under optimum conditions, California authorities still were faced with a significant number of prisoners who were in custody levels other than those fitting their particular custody-level scores on initial classification devices. However, the four conceptual goals outlined above specify that generally, inmates should be assigned to the lowest possible custody level, depending upon space availability. Eventually, the California Department of Corrections implemented a new custody classification system based upon a quantitative score derived from a simple additive checklist. Validation research pertaining to the new classification system occurred during the next ten months. Officials reported that the new system has demonstrated considerable promise as a way of rationally managing correctional resources toward the goal of maintaining each inmate at the lowest custody level, commensurate with the safety of the public and members of the correctional community (Holt, Ducat, and Eakles, 1981:30).

Jail Use of Risk Assessment

Besides prisons, many jails have developed fairly elaborate classification criteria for the purpose of more effectively managing incoming inmates. Besides specific architectural and managerial modifications that affect inmate management, many city and county jail facilities have established classification systems for better inmate confinement decision making. More modern jail facilities in many jurisdictions have implemented a direct supervision style of inmate management. Slack and Dixon (1990:45) report that the numbers of assaults by inmates against jail staff and even other inmates have dramatically declined as one important result of direct supervision changes. Sites reporting decreased incidents of disruptive inmate behaviors include jails in Multnomah County, Oregon, and Pima County, Arizona.

Slack and Dixon (1990:45–46) have described a fairly new inmate classification approach known as B.A.C.I.S., which is an acronym for Behavioral Alert Classification Identification System. They note that B.A.C.I.S. is a new and total approach to classifying, housing, and identifying the inmate population confined in a direct supervision jail. This system combines intake assessment, risk analysis, in-custody behavior, and psychological behavior instruments. It works in concert with an Alpha identification system to facilitate the management of the jail inmate population.

The B.A.C.I.S. is essentially a four-phase complex classification system, including the following phases: (1) intake assessment; (2) risk analysis; (3) admissions/orientation; and (4) primary housing. The first phase, intake assessment, screens medically and mentally ill inmates from the main population, and isolates assaultive, high escape risk, and extreme protective custody inmates from the others (Slack and Dixon, 1990:45). Using basic objective risk analysis, B.A.C.I.S. further separates incoming inmates into a seventy-two-hour classification holding modular called the Admissions and Orientation Unit (1990:46). It is during this seventy-two-hour period that jail staff report on inmate in-custody behavior, administer psychological behavioral instruments, evaluate prior risk assessments made, and establish a recommended classification code. These researchers report that the B.A.C.I.S. was implemented in the Women's Facility in Santa Clara County, California, in November 1987. One immediate effect was that about 20 percent of the women were reclassified to a lower housing level than they were previously. This percentage has subsequently increased appreciably (Slack and Dixon, 1990:46). This procedure has freed up numerous high-security beds. Furthermore, the system has provided significant rewards for those inmates exhibiting positive behavior following their lower security placements.

THE CLASSIFICATION/RECLASSIFICATION DECISION

The classification/reclassification decision is an important one. While jurisdictions vary in their procedures for processing incoming inmates, most funnel new inmates through a screening or classification unit initially. Personnel staffing these diagnostic centers or classification units have the responsibility of evaluating each inmate according to reasonably objective criteria and recommending a particular level of custody on the basis of their evaluations. For example, the Alaska Department of Corrections has a unit known as Central Classification staffed by a Classification Committee. This committee consists of a group of individuals who convene regularly to review and assess a prisoner's security, custody, and program needs and make a classification recommendation. The committee decides custody placements for (1) unsentenced prisoners; (2) long-term sentenced prisoners; and (3) short-term sentenced prisoners (Alaska Department of Corrections, 1986:2).

The custody status of any prisoner is based upon a matrix score attained on particular classification forms. These scores dictate the degree of security staff supervision required to appropriately monitor and control prisoner conduct and behavior within the context of correctional management (Alaska Department of Corrections, 1986:2). The initial classification is the first classification committee hearing that a prisoner receives at a designated institution upon entering it. Alaska correctional policy requires that all prisoner custody statuses and program needs be reviewed and assessed on a scheduled basis. Similar to New York and California correctional objectives, Alaska officials strive to place offenders in the least restrictive level of security in the context of sound correctional management (Alaska Department of Corrections, 1986:3). The Alaska Department of Corrections policy relating to when such classifications are made of prisoners specifies that these classification decisions must be made within thirty days of a sentenced prisoner's arrival at the designated institution, or within sixty days after sentencing and commitment, whichever occurs first.

The Delaware Bureau of Prisons also has a classification committee known as the Institutional Based Classification Committee (Delaware Bureau of Prisons, 1992:14). This committee consists of a minimum of four staff members of the institution. Each institution establishes its own policy and criteria to govern the movement of inmates into and out of treatment programs, work assignments within the institution, and movement from one security level to another (Delaware Bureau of Prisons, 1992:14). The specific responsibilities of this committee are to

1. Approve/disapprove/modify all inmate treatment plan(s) and make modifications that are in the mutual interest of both the inmate and the Bureau;
2. Approve/disapprove/modify movement in and out of institutional/facility work assignments (inside and outside on grounds);
3. Approve/disapprove/modify movement in and out of treatment program(s) within the institution. If the program participation requires an institutional transfer, the case is to be forwarded to the Central Institutional Classification Board;
4. Approve/disapprove/modify all changes in custody level assignments within security levels;
5. Approve/disapprove/modify security level decisions including changes in security levels which comply with the criteria established in this procedure; security level changes that are exceptions to these criteria must be approved by the Central Institutional Classification Board; and
6. Review/modify recommendations for early changes in security levels, parole and reduction in sentence requests and forward to the Central Institutional Classification Board for decision (Delaware Bureau of Prisons, 1992:14).

It should be noted that occasionally, some judges may impose particular custody levels for certain convicted offenders at the time they are sentenced. Especially dangerous offenders convicted of serious crimes may be directed to serve time in a maximum-security area of some prison in the jurisdiction. Provisions for judicial recommendations are given in the program statement of the Federal Bureau of Prisons (1992: Ch.2:3). These provisions are to the effect that "a Court may recommend a specific institution or program. When consistent with Bureau of Prisons' policies or when such actions are consistent with sound correctional management, the Bureau of Prisons attempts to satisfy judicial recommendations. When this is not feasible, the Court is notified in writing with an explanation outlining the reasons for not satisfying that recommendation. When the judicial recommendation is the deciding factor causing placement outside normal guidelines, this management variable shall apply." It is significant that the Federal Bureau of Prisons has addressed this issue by referring to judicial sentencing decisions as "judicial recommendations" and saying that "attempts [will be made] to satisfy judicial recommendations." This leaves the Federal Bureau of Prisons in control of the situation, where decisions about prisoner security placements will be made with the priority of "sound correctional management" in mind. In any case, the option exists for trying to accommodate judges and their sentencing pronouncements in individual convicted offender cases.

It is not particularly common for judges to do this, however, since primarily prison administrators are in the best positions to assess existing space and appropriate allocation of that space. Thus, the "hands-off" policy regarding offender classification and placement is practiced by many judges, and prison wardens and their staff are charged with all classification and placement responsibilities.

The Federal Bureau of Prisons (1992:Ch.1:1) has four custody levels similar to those of Delaware and other states. It includes *maximum, in, out,* and *community.* In "maximum" custody, inmates require maximum control and supervision. This classification is for individuals who, by their behavior, have identified themselves as assaultive, predacious, riotous, serious escape risks, or seriously disruptive to the orderly running of an institution. Accordingly, quarters and work assignments should allow maximum control and supervision. The "in" custody level involves inmates who are assigned to regular quarters and are eligible for all regular work assignments and activities under a normal level of supervision but not for work details or programs outside the institution's secure perimeter. "Out" designees are inmates who are assigned to less secure housing outside the institution's perimeter with a minimum of two-hour intermittent staff supervision. Finally, the "community" designation applies to prisoners who are eligible for the least secure housing, including any which is outside the institution's perimeter, may work on outside details with minimal supervision, and may participate in community-based program activities if other eligibility requirements are satisfied.

CRITERIA INFLUENCING THE CLASSIFICATION/RECLASSIFICATION DECISION

The criteria for determining an inmate's custody level vary according to each institution and department of corrections. Delaware's Department of Corrections, for instance, has defined four security levels:

1. Maximum security is for inmates who present an escape risk and/or are severe internal management risks;
2. Medium security is for inmates who present escape risks but who are not severe internal management risks;
3. Minimum security is for inmates who do not present an escape risk and who are not management problems; and
4. Community security is for inmates who are assigned to educational release, or work release according to eligibility standards established by the Bureau of Prisons (Delaware Bureau of Prisons, 1992:6–16).

Besides these security levels, there are several different custody levels, including

1. High custody—designed for those inmates who require the highest level of supervision within the designated security level;
2. Low custody—designed for inmates who can function under low degrees of supervision within the designated security level;
3. Close custody (see Maximum Security Custody Level definition); and
4. Protective custody (see Maximum Security Custody Level definition) (Delaware Bureau of Prisons, 1992:7).

According to Delaware authorities, these security and custody-level designations are guidelines that are reasonably comprehensive and provide for placement of inmates in the least restrictive security and custody level within an institution while simultaneously meeting various inmate treatment/program needs.

Delaware has also established several important criteria to be used by institutional staff in determining which security and custody levels are most appropriate for particular inmates. Below are the various criteria for the four security levels listed above.

Maximum Security Criteria

1. Risk of Escape:
   a. Escape from a maximum or medium security level within the past three years with a weapon and/or involving physical injury.
   b. Escape from a minimum or community security level within the past year with a weapon and/or involving physical injury.
   c. Escape or attempted escape from a maximum or medium security level within the past year without a weapon and not involving physical injury.
2. Threat of Violence:
   a. For initial classifications only, a documented history of community violence, or
   b. A documented pattern of violent institutional conduct within the past three years.
   c. One or more Class I conduct offenses within the past one year.
   d. Eight or more Class II conduct offenses within the past six months.
   e. Documented history of highly unpredictable behavior that is dangerous to the individual, group, or community.

Medium Security Criteria

1. Risk of Escape:
   a. Escape from a minimum security level within the past year without a weapon and not involving physical injury.
   b. Escape from a minimum or community security level and incurring new charges of Class A or B felony.
2. Threat of Violence:
   a. No documented history of institutional behavior within the past one (1) year involving Class I conduct offenses.
   b. Four to six Class II conduct offenses within the past six months.
   c. No documented history of dangerous or unpredictable institutional behaviors within the past year.

Minimum Security Criteria

1. Risk of Escape:
   a. No escapes or attempted escapes from a higher security level within the past three years.
   b. Escape from Community Security within the past one year.
   c. Charged with escape from Community Security for program violations and/or absconding within the past six months.
2. Threat of Violence:
   a. No documented history of Class I conduct offenses within the past six months.
   b. Three or less Class II conduct offenses within the past six months (Delaware Bureau of Prisons, 1992:7–10).

Community Security is for inmates who are assigned to educational release or work release according to eligibility standards established by the Bureau of Prisons.

The Delaware Bureau of Prisons (1992:10) specifies that "inmates may be considered for security level placements for which they otherwise do not meet the stated criteria if the recommendation is supported by documented evidence that this placement would not present a threat to the inmate, institution, or community. There can be no exceptions to statutory prohibitions, unless authorized by the sentencing judge. However, if there is a substantial reason necessitating immediate placement of an inmate at a higher security/custody level, the warden or deptity warden must approve the assignment. This decision can be made if (1) the inmate's attitude or conduct indicates that continued presence in the general population poses a serious threat to life, property, self, staff members, other inmates or the threat of escape; or (2) when the inmate is pending a hearing for a violation of institutional rules; or (3) pending investigation or trial for a criminal act; or (4) pending transfer or is in a holdover status during transfer.

Criteria for security and custody classifications are ordinarily listed by different state departments of correction. For instance, the criteria used by the Alabama Department of Corrections include

1. History of institutional violence
2. Severity of current offense
3. Prior assaultive offense history
4. Escape history
5. Time to earliest release
6. Alcohol and drug abuse
7. Current detainer
8. Prior felony convictions
9. Stability factors (Alabama Department of Corrections, 1987:Appendix J-2).

On the basis of pre-printed scores for these items, a point total is computed which indicates the point security level as well as the recommended security level, if different. Further, Alabama Department of Corrections officials provide recommendations for particular institutions in individual inmate cases. A Central Review Board convenes and reviews all recommendations for inmate placements.

Incoming inmate processing is fairly uniform among jurisdictions as well. The procedures followed by the Arizona Department of Corrections seem reasonably typical of most corrections departments regarding how incoming inmates are processed. For example, the reception of offenders committed to the Arizona Department of Corrections is ideally a uniform process for both men and women (Arizona Department of Corrections, 1991:11). With the exception of the sites where men and women are initially processed, their treatment throughout the system is fairly uniform. Men are processed at the Alhambra Reception and Treatment Center, while women are admitted at the Arizona State Prison Complex—Perryville Santa Maria Unit. Youths are processed at the Arizona State Prison Complex—Tucson Rincon Minors Unit. At all three facilities, inmates are received by a Reception Center Administrator (Arizona Department of Corrections, 1991:11–12).

When offenders arrive at these centers, their personal effects are inventoried, and they are given an opportunity to dispose of other property not permitted by the institution. Offender identity is verified, identification cards are issued, and fingerprints and photographs are obtained. Each inmate is interviewed by an intake officer to verify the legality, completeness, and accuracy of the commitment documents. For Arizona, at least, each inmate admission must be accompanied by a correctly certified copy of the commitment order and a copy of the PSI (presentence investigation report prepared earlier by a probation officer). Subsequently, inmates are screened in terms of their medical and health histories.

Eventually each inmate is assigned to a Correctional Program Officer who will supervise the inmate's initial adjustment to the prison, will provide the offender with counseling services, if needed, and will perform an initial assessment of each case for Initial Classification. Inmates are administered the Wide Range Achievement Test (WRAT), the 16 Personality Factor Test, and the Culture Fair IQ Test. Following these test administrations, each inmate is interviewed with all available documentation. Items covered in this interview include the circumstances of the offense, the social and criminal history, the enemies, gang affiliation, and/or other protective segregation issues, and institutional program needs and projected release date (Arizona Department of Corrections, 1991:12).

Finally, inmates are rated according to an Initial Classification Score Sheet for the purpose of developing an inmate's Correctional Classification Profile (CCP). CCP factors include the offender's level of public risk, institutional risk, medical and health care needs, mental health care needs, education needs, vocational training needs, work skills, alcohol/drug abuse and treatment, sex offense treatment, and proximity to residence. These ten factors yield a profile upon which the offender's eventual placement is based.

Initial classification and institutional assignment procedures for South Carolina inmates are somewhat different from those of Alabama, although there are some similarities. For instance, South Carolina Department of Corrections officials compile a Summary Admission Report, which identifies both risks and needs of incoming offenders. The criteria used in the administered assessment instruments include the following (criteria with an asterisk [*] are also found on the Alabama initial classification instrument):

1. Risk Assessment
    *a. Severity of current offense
    b. Sentence length in years
    c. Detainers, holds or notifies
    *d. History of escapes, attempts, or escape-related offenses
    *e. History of violence
    *f. Number of prior convictions over 90 days
    g. Number of offenses in current commitment
    *h. Current age of the inmate [a stability factor]
    *i. Alcohol/drugs associated with current offense
    j. Mandatory time to serve before parole eligibility or release
2. Needs Assessment
    a. Court recommended treatment
    b. Assessment recommendations (South Carolina Department of Corrections, 1992:10–2).

In contrast, a third set of criteria involved in initial assessments of incoming inmates is provided by the Pennsylvania Department of Corrections. These criteria are indicated below (criteria asterisked once [*] are also found in the Alabama initial classification instrument, while criteria asterisked twice [**] are also found in the South Carolina initial classification instrument):

*, **1. Severity of current offense

*, **2. Severity of criminal history

*, **3. Escape history

4. Prior institutional adjustment
5. Number of prior commitments

*, **6. Time to expected release

**7. Age

8. Marital status (may be in Alabama "stability factors")
9. Employment (may be in Alabama "stability factors") (Pennsylvania Department of Corrections, 1992).

Among other state departments of corrections that provided information for this book, most of their initial classification instruments disclosed criteria more or less similar to those outlined above for Alabama, South Carolina, and Pennsylvania. At least four common elements are identified on these three instruments. These include (1) severity of the current offense; (2) severity of criminal history; (3) escape history; and (4) time to expected release date. These same criteria are also found on most other available state initial risk assessment tools.

Interestingly, both "severity of current offense" and "severity of criminal history" assess whether any particular inmate has aggressive propensities, based on previous criminal conduct, which would pose dangers for other inmates or staff. Crimes against persons or violent crimes are inherently more violent than burglary, larceny, auto theft, or embezzlement. These latter offenses are passive, not requiring or involving the immediate presence of victims. It would not be likely that inmates with pasts as burglars or embezzlers would be inclined toward violence. However, those convicted previously of aggravated assault, armed robbery, aggravated rape, or homicide would be anticipated to be more dangerous per se.

The other criteria, "escape history" and "time to expected release," focus directly upon whether any particular inmate would have the motivation to escape, under existing circumstances. Obviously, someone who has escaped from custody or has attempted to escape from custody, particularly someone who has a "history" or pattern of escape behavior, might be expected to escape again or attempt it. Furthermore, someone who is facing a long incarcerative sentence would be more interested in escaping confinement than someone who has served most of his or her sentence and has only a few months left to serve. Someone who has served nine years, six months of a ten-year sentence would be completely free of the criminal justice system by serving the remaining six months. If that person were to attempt an escape or actually succeed in escaping, the penalty would be severe upon his or her apprehension. Those convicted of escape might be given a new sentence of five years or more. Thus, it is reasonable to assume that the shorter the time interval to the expected release date, the less likely an inmate would be to escape or attempt it. It is logical to see how both violent propensities and escape history/time to serve before release would be included on classification and reclassification instruments.

Some examples of initial screening devices employed by different state prisons are provided at the end of this chapter. Form 4.1 is a classification form used by the Colorado Department of Corrections to determine security risk and custody level. All inmates are advised of this action through a subsequent classification hearing.

Alaska uses a form known as an "Agenda and Procedural Opportunities Afforded a Prisoner at a Classification Hearing." Inmates are notifed in advance and advised of the meeting's purpose. They are afforded an opportunity to appeal any action taken or any designation imposed as the result of the hearing. Inmates are advised to read this form and sign it. In the event that they are unable or unwilling to sign the form, an officer indicates this refusal and also signs the form as an administrative witness. Inmates are subsequently furnished with a Notice of Designation. Notices of Designation are not appealable. Inmates are requested to sign these forms, and officers indicate whether inmates have duly complied with these requests.

Many jurisdictions include information about inmates' physical and mental health in their initial classification screenings. For instance, Hawaii uses both mental health and medical status screening documents together with security designation forms. Form 4.2 shows a Short-Term Inmate Security Designation used by the Hawaii Department of Corrections. Forms 4.3 and 4.4 respectively show a Mental Health Intake Screening form and a Medical Admission Screening form also used by this department.

A third initial classification tool is shown in Form 4.5. This is the Tennessee Department of Corrections Initial Classification Custody Assessment Form. A slightly more elaborate initial classification inventory used by the Idaho Department of Corrections is illustrated in Form 4.6.

Form 4.7 shows an initial interview form/admission summary used by the Alabama Department of Corrections. This form includes a classification instrument, an institutional security level score sheet and an institutional recommendation page for review by a Central Review Board.

Finally, Form 4.8 shows an initial security classification guideline instrument used by the Illinois Department of Corrections to classify female offenders. Probably a majority of jurisdictions use a common instrument for both male and female incoming inmates, however.

Reclassification

Almost every jurisdiction that uses risk assessment instruments for determining inmate security risk and custody level provides for periodic reassessments of inmates. These reassessments or reclassifications enable authorities to move inmates from one custody level to another. It is a vested interest of prison officials to move inmates to lower custody levels where appropriate, since most state policies specify providing the least restrictive security for any incoming inmate, without jeopardizing institutional and public safety. Reclassifications of inmates are usually regulated according to some time interval, such as six months or one year. Thus, inmates in some jurisdictions will be reassessed and reclassified every six months, while inmates in other jurisdictions might be reassessed annually. Some examples of reassessment instruments used by different jurisdictions are shown in Forms 4.9 through 4.12.

Major and Minor Infractions

For instance, the New York Department of Corrections conducts semiannual reclassification reviews to determine whether prisoners should be transferred (New York Department of Corrections, 1988:II–58). However, the Alabama Department of Corrections provides that inmates shall be incarcerated at a particular custody level for twelve months before a reclassification is conducted and a different custody level is considered. When inmates are considered for transfer to a new level of custody, a significant factor influencing this decision is their conduct for the previous six- or twelve-month period. Those inmates with more infractions than others stand a good chance of remaining in their present level of custody, perhaps a good chance of being moved to a higher custody level. However, those who have few, if any, infractions stand a good chance of being moved to a lower level of custody. Some examples of major and minor infractions from the Alaska Department of Corrections (1986:3–5) are listed below.

Major Infractions:

Assault upon a staff member or visitor
Assault of one prisoner by another
Escape or evasion from custody
Any felony offense
Fire setting
Homicide
Possession or use of weapons or other escape implements
Rioting
Stealing, destroying the property of others
Threatening or intimidating any witness in an official proceeding

Moderate Infractions:

Adulteration of food or drink
Bribes
Possession of contraband
Counterfeiting, forging, or unauthorized reproduction of any document
Demonstrating
Extortion, blackmail, or protection
Disguise, wearing a mask
False statement
Spitting, throwing urine or fecal matter, on or at some staff member
Tampering with blocking a locking or security device
Work stoppage
Refusal or failure to participate in court-ordered treatment program

Minor Infractions:

Failure to keep medical or health care appointment
False statement
Feigning illness, malingering
Indecent exposure
Unauthorized use of mail or telephone
Obscene language
Nuisance, kicking, shouting, or banging
Threatening damage to personal property of others
Tattooing or self-mutilation, other than attempted suicide
Threats to another of bodily harm
Being in unauthorized area
Failure to abide by posted sanitation rules
Failure to keep one's person and quarters in accordance with posted rules (Alaska Department of Corrections, 1986:3–5).

An example of a review schedule when inmates are considered for reclassification is provided by the Delaware Bureau of Prisons (1992:21). A Multi-Disciplinary Team conducts an inmate review within the following time frame:

1. Review reclassification review within two weeks following the inmate's transfer from another institution within the system.
2. Review every three months for inmates serving terms of 18 months or less.
3. Review every six months for inmates serving terms of 18 months and one day to five years.
4. Annual review for inmates serving terms of five years or more.
5. Maximum (high-close and protective custody) inmates will be reviewed every 3 months (Delaware Bureau of Prisons, 1992:21).

This detailed variation in the frequency with which reviews are conducted is sentence-dependent. Thus, inmates serving shorter sentences are reviewed for reclassification and reassignment to a different custody level more frequently than inmates serving longer sentences. Not all state jurisdictions have this detail relating to reclassification procedures and the time intervals prescribed for them.

Not all reclassification is directed toward changing an inmate's level of custody, however. Reclassifications of offenders are also conducted periodically to determine whether their needs have changed. Most institutions provide an array of social and psychological services as well as vocational/educational programs meriting inmate participation. At some point, inmates may no longer require treatment, special services, or vocational/educational training. In order to maximize these services for other eligible inmates, reassessments are regularly conducted to discontinue these programs or services for some inmates and commence them for other inmates.

IMPLICATIONS OF CLASSIFICATION SCHEMES FOR INMATES: ACCESS TO DIFFERENT INMATE PRIVILEGES

We have seen that the general intent of inmate classification schemes is to maximize public and institutional safety. A secondary intent is to promote prisoner safety by separating more dangerous offenders from less dangerous ones. Also, distinctions among inmates may be made according to various programs and treatments in view of their needs scores and eligibility. Periodic reassessments of inmates are conducted, however, and some inmates may be moved from one custody level to another.

Objectives of Reclassification

The primary reasons for reclassification are twofold: punishment and reward. Classifications that result in maintaining one's custody level (if high) or changing one's custody level from a lower level to a higher level are regarded as punitive or punishment-centered. This form of punishment is in direct response to an inmate's lack of conformity to prison rules and regulations. Committing one or more infractions between reclassification periods will result in either no change in custody level or an increase in custody level. However, conformity with institutional rules and regulations often results in being reclassified to a lower custody level.

The immediate benefit of a lower custody level is a greater access to institutional freedoms and privileges. A long-range benefit is that inmates retained in the lowest levels of custody are "proving" themselves worthy of special consideration whenever they become eligible for parole. In those systems not using an early-release scheme such as parole (in the case of determinate sentencing), "good-time" credit accumulation is maximized. According to a 1990 survey conducted by *Corrections Compendium,* more than forty states award good-time credit to inmates, while only six states do not have such provisions (Davis, 1990:4). Michigan, for example, previously awarded inmates up to twenty-two days per month of disciplinary credits. These were credits given inmates who exhibited no institutional infractions. After April 1987, Michigan changed this good-time provision to "up to 7 days a month" to be earned as disciplinary credits (Davis, 1990:4).

Good-Time Credits

Good-time credits vary greatly among jurisdictions. The Federal Bureau of Prisons enables federal inmates to earn up to fifty-four days per year as good-time credit to be applied against their original sentences. Prior to November 1, 1987, federal inmates could earn up to fifteen days a month of good-time credit. Of those states with good-time provisions, Missouri has the lowest, with five days per month of good-time credit, while Alabama has the most generous good-time provisions. In Alabama prisons, inmates may earn up to seventy-five days per month of good-time credit to be applied against their original sentences. Thus, an inmate incarcerated for ten years will serve less than three years, with good behavior. [Three years served in Alabama equals seven years, six months, or 3 years × 2.5.] Interestingly, Davis (1990:4) observes that about half of these state systems deduct the good-time credit up front, whenever inmates enter the system. But in the other half of these prison systems, credits are not applied until they are earned. Yet other systems use both forms of good-time credit applications.

A unique variation in the administration of good-time credits has been provided by New Hampshire. In 1982, the New Hampshire legislature passed a "truth in sentencing" law whereby 150 disciplinary days would be added to the minimum term of incarceration (under a minimum-maximum scheme). Good-time credits could be earned by prisoners at the rate of twelve and one-half days per month to be applied against these 150 days. Thus, offenders failing to earn the good-time credit must serve the additional days added to their sentences. As of 1990, the following states had good-time provisions at the rates shown below:

More than 30 days per month: Alabama, Colorado, Illinois, Mississippi, North Carolina, Oklahoma, South Carolina, and Texas

30 days per month: Arkansas, California, Florida, Indiana, Louisiana, Montana, New Mexico, Virginia, West Virginia

20 days per month: Iowa, Massachusetts, Nevada, New Jersey, and Ohio

15 days per month: Arizona, Connecticut, Delaware, District of Columbia, Kentucky, Maine, Minnesota, Nebraska, Rhode Island, South Dakota, Vermont, Washington, and Wyoming

Less than 15 days per month: Alaska, Federal Bureau of Prisons, Michigan, Missouri, New Hampshire, New York, North Dakota, and Oregon

No good time given: Georgia, Hawaii, Idaho, Pennsylvania, Utah, and Wisconsin (Davis, 1990:5)

Besides benefiting inmates through earlier release dates, good-time provisions also benefit prison officials. Davis (1990:4–5) says that good-time credits enable prison administrators to reduce their degree of overcrowding. Meritorious good-time credits may also be awarded by prison administrators. In Florida prior to June 1988, this was known as administrative gain time and was used by prison authorities to alleviate their overcrowding problems. However, Florida law changed whereby provisional credits are now earned by inmates rather than administrative gain time. In other jurisdictions, such as the District of Columbia, officials are vested with the power to declare "states of emergency" and reduce minimum or mandatory release dates whenever their prison system exceeds the rated design capacity for thirty consecutive days or longer (Davis, 1990:4–6).

LEGAL LIABILITIES OF PRISON OFFICIALS AND STAFF AND CLASSIFICATORY CRITERIA: SOME IMPLICATIONS

Generally, prison officials have a considerable amount of discretion over how offenders are classified and situated in their institutions. Almost every state and federal prison has administrative regulations governing initial classification decision making, reclassification decision making, and inmate placements relative to these decisions. Furthermore, it is the responsibility of prison and jail officials to operate orderly systems and to ensure that inmates comply with policies and rules. Because of the inherently coercive nature of prison and jail settings, differences of opinion and disagreements between prisoners and prison staff over the policies, rules, and conditions of confinement are inevitable. Prison and jail staff try to control the flow of contraband, because inmate access to various forms of contraband is potentially disruptive and might pose safety problems for other inmates. Regulations exist that authorize routine official body and cell searches for the purpose of discovering and seizing any illegal materials. Body cavity searches and X-rays have disclosed drugs, weapons, and other materials potentially lethal to prison staff or other inmates. Officers frequently conduct shakedowns of inmate cells where items considered threatening to inmate discipline are confiscated.

The Inequalities in Different Custody Levels

However, different levels of custody create conditions of inherent inequality, since those placed in minimum-security facilities usually have a greater array of privileges and more freedon than those in higher custody levels. It is expected, therefore, that more than a few inmates will challenge their particular custody level and whether they deserve such treatment compared with other inmates. Therefore, administrative hearings are available to inmates who feel that their classification and placement is wrong, cruel and/or unusual, or detrimental to their welfare, for whatever reason. If internal administrative hearings fail to resolve the matter to any inmate's satisfaction, inmates have the right to legal action against prison officials. However, the successfulness of this legal action against prison officials by inmates is not impressive. Inmates usually lose.

Conditions of Older Facilities

Prisons and jails have low priority in local, state, and federal budgets. As a result, many jails are old and dilapidated. Large numbers of prisons in the United States are considered deplorable according to court standards. Hundreds of prisons and jails are currently under court order to improve their physical plants and other facilities so that minimal health and safety standards can be attained (Hall, 1987). Furthermore, many prisons are currently operating according to minimally acceptable health and safety standards. No court has ever ruled that prisons and jails must be comfortable, but numerous inmate lawsuits have been filed because of relatively poor cell conditions. But because of the coercive nature of an inmate's confinement and the tight discipline that must be maintained by prison or jail officials, inmates suffer deprivations, indignities, and other forms of treatment alien to their lives outside of institutional settings. Therefore, prisons and jails are prime sites for inmate grievances and legal action. It is difficult to achieve a balance between the responsibilities of prison and jail officials to maintain orderly premises and a reasonable social system ensuring acceptable inmate conduct and seeing that inmate constitutional rights are fully observed.

Misclassifications of Inmates

The legal cases arising from alleged misclassifications of prison and jail inmates are extensive. While it is beyond the scope of this book to detail all or even a large portion of these legal cases, it would be insightful to review a few of them to see how courts have considered and dealt with assorted inmate allegations relating to conditions of confinement and classification decision making. It is generally the case that inmate suits against prison officials most often involve allegations of Constitutional Amendment violations by prison staff, administrators, or both. Many of these suits are frivolous. Sometimes, certain inmates file large numbers of suits on behalf of themselves and other inmates. The case of *In re Green* (1981) is relevant here. Green was a prison inmate who filed 600–700 lawsuits on behalf of himself and other inmates during the 1970s. The courts consistently found his suits to be "frivolous, irresponsible, and unmeritorious," and one court even suggested that Green hoped to force his own release from custody by swamping the court with these frivolous suits (Anderson, 1986:14; Knight and Early, 1986:15). Large numbers of frivolous filings by inmates damage their credibility in the courts of any jurisdiction.

Historically, prison and jail inmates have been treated as second-class citizens and given little or no standing in U.S. courts, largely in view of the judicial declaration that prisoners were "slaves of the state" in *Ruffin v. Commonwealth* (1871). The *Ruffin* case did much to establish the "hands-off" doctrine practiced by U.S. courts during the next seventy years. During that period, the courts consistently refused to intervene in the management and operation of prison affairs. The "hands-off" doctrine was based on two rationales: (1) that correctional facilities were managed by the executive, and that under the "separation of powers" doctrine the judiciary should not interfere with that management, and (2) that judges were not experts in correctional administration, and therefore should not interfere with the experts who ran such facilities (Coles, 1987:49–50).

Authorities of prisons and jails determined penal policies and prescribed the means whereby these policies would be implemented. However, the case of *Ex parte Hull* was decided in 1941. At that time, prison and jail officials were screening all outgoing inmate mail, including legal documents and petitions addressed to the state or federal courts. Inmate petitions to the court for virtually any grievance or complaint, founded or unfounded, were often conveniently trashed by prison officials who claimed that these petitions were improperly prepared and thus ineligible for court action. This was because existing prison and jail policies permitted discarding such materials. However, in *Ex parte Hull* (1941), the U.S. Supreme Court said that no state or its officers may abridge or impair a prisoner's right to have access to federal courts. The court, not prison or jail officials, would determine whether petitions were properly prepared. While the original *Hull* decision pertained to a particular class of legal petitions, it was eventually extended to include categorical access to the courts (Knight and Early, 1986:24). The *Hull* case involved a *habeas corpus* petition (see the discussion of *habeas corpus* relief in the following section). Another important case was decided in 1944 which extended *habeas corpus* relief to include the "conditions of confinement" in addition to the fact of confinement. This was the case of *Coffin v. Reichard* (1944). The *Coffin* case is significant because it is the first instance that a federal appellate court declared that prisoners do not lose their civil rights as the result of entering confinement (Coles, 1987:48–49).

Forms of Inmate Relief

At least three avenues exist whereby jail and prison inmates can petition the courts concerning their classification and its consequences. These include (1) Section 1983 actions, (2) Section 2241 *habeas corpus* claims, and (3) Section 2674 Tort Claims.

Section 1983 Civil Rights Actions. The most widely used avenue is Section 1983 of Title 42 (the Civil Rights Act), which holds that "every person who, under color of any statute, ordinance, regulation, custom, or usage, of any State or Territory, subjects, or causes to be subjected, any citizen of the United States or other person within the jurisdiction thereof to the deprivation of any rights, privileges, or immunities secured by the Constitution and laws, shall be liable to the party injured in an action at law, suit in equity, or other proper proceeding for redress" (Palmer, 1985). Section 1983 actions challenge the conditions of confinement, but the fact and length of incarceration are not within this section's purview (*Preiser v. Rodriguez,* 1973).

Section 2241 Habeas Corpus *Actions.* Prisoners can challenge their imprisonment in court, but they must file a *habeas corpus* petition under Title 28, Section 2241, the Federal Habeas Corpus Statute (28 U.S.C. Section 2241, 1993; Haas and Alpert, 1986). *Habeas corpus* petitions challenge (1) the fact of confinement, (2) the nature of confinement, and (3) the length of confinement. However, the U.S. Supreme Court has determined that these writs shall only be used whenever inmates have exhausted their state remedies. Thus, state prisoners planning to file *habeas corpus* writs in federal district courts must first demonstrate that they have pursued their grievances in state courts. Otherwise, district judges will direct these suits to appropriate state courts for action. Direct filings of these types of petitions can also be made in the federal district courts, although federal judges prefer that prisoners first exhaust all possible state remedies.

Challenges about the nature of confinement (based on classification and subsequent placement in a particular level of custody) within the context of the federal *habeas corpus* statute must allege that by virtue of that confinement, prisoners are deprived of some right to which they are entitled despite the confinement, and that the deprivation of this right makes their imprisonment more burdensome (Palmer, 1985:222–223). *Habeas corpus* relief might be sought by state or federal prisoners being incarcerated in a local jail, where the jail has contracted with the state or federal government to house a portion of prison overflow to ease overcrowding. Compared with prisons, jail facilities are particularly inadequate. State and federal prisoners rightfully feel deprived of various vocational and educational programs and other benefits otherwise available to them if they were housed in long-term prison settings. But the courts have not been particularly sympathetic with prisoners about this issue.

Section 2674 Tort Actions. A third avenue is through Title 28, Section 2674 (the Federal Tort Claims Act of 1946), which provides that "the United States shall be liable, respecting the provisions of this title relating to tort claims, in the same manner and to the same extent as a private individual under like circumstances, but shall not be liable for interest prior to judgment for punitive damages." The U.S. Supreme Court decided in 1963 that inmates of federal prisons could file petitions against prison administrators and guards under the Federal Tort Claims Act in the case of *United States v. Muniz* (1963). Before this Supreme Court action, prison officials had sovereign immunity from suits by prisoners alleging damages or injuries through administrative negligence. Officials have some qualified immunity excepting them from suits under this section alleging "any claim arising out of assault, battery, false imprisonment, false arrest, malicious prosecution, abuse of process, libel, slander, misrepresentation, deceit, or interference with contract rights" (28 U.S.C. Sec. 2680, 1993).

First Amendment Violations. Inmate legal actions are also distinguishable in terms of specific Constitutional Amendment violations alleged. Sparking the most inmate legal action have been the First, Fourth, Eighth, and Fourteenth Amendments. For instance, inmates may allege that prison officials violated their First Amendment rights by forcing them to eat certain types of prison food, to trim their hair, and/or to refrain from growing beards. Some prisoners might allege that these prohibitions or institutional requirements violate their right to freedom of religious worship, where specific types of foods (e.g., meat or fish) are either required or prohibited, or where specific types of hair styles are recommended or required for religious reasons. The First Amendment states that "Congress shall make no law respecting an establishment of religion, or prohibiting the free exercise thereof; or abridging the freedom of speech, or of the press; or the right of the people peaceably to assemble, and to petition the government for a redress of grievances." One aspect of this Amendment involves letter or telephonic communications with others outside of prison as well as the receipt of communications from others. Censorship of an inmate's mail is justified to the extent that the letter "jeopardizes security, order, or rehabilitation, and the regulations may be only as broad as is necessary to meet those goals. However, officials may not censor mail simply to eliminate unflattering opinions, factually inaccurate statements, or inflammatory racial, political, or religious views" (Bronstein, 1980:30; *Procunier v. Martinez,* 1974).

Prior to the *Procunier* holding, inmate mail was inspected, both leaving and entering these institutions. Officials determined which pieces of inmate mail would be forwarded. Some of this correspondence was between inmates and their attorneys. Subsequently, a particular case focused upon this issue. This was the case of *Wolff v. McDonnell* (1974). The *Wolff* case dealt with the question of whether letters determined or found to be from attorneys may be opened by prison authorities in the presence of the inmate or whether such mail must be delivered unopened if normal detection techniques fail to indicate contraband. The U.S. Supreme Court did not add a great deal of clarity to this issue in its decision. The Court indicated that attorneys must clearly identify themselves by placing their names and addresses in plain view on envelopes and that the letters should show that they came from lawyers. In any case, prison authorities may inspect and read any document leaving and entering the institution in an effort to determine whether inmates are abusing their rights by communicating about "restricted matters" (Bronstein, 1980:29–30).

Communications between prisoners within and between different penal institutions are a different matter. The policies of many prisons and jails prohibit written communications between inmates in different institutions. Thus, if a New York state prisoner in Attica wishes to correspond with a federal prisoner in New Mexico, prison rules exist that prohibit these types of exchanges. Courts have consistently upheld the right of prison officials to restrict or deny such correspondence between prisoners as potentially disruptive of prison discipline. This action is not considered a violation of inmate free speech rights (*Vester v. Rogers,* 1986). However, sometimes prison officials may be asked to defend why and how they believed such communications threatened the security of their prisons and presented a "clear and present danger" to prison discipline (*Rowland v. Sigler,* 1971).

Fourth Amendment Violations. The Fourth Amendment provides that "the right of the people to be secure in their persons, houses, papers, and effects, against unreasonable searches and seizures, shall not be violated, and no Warrants shall issue, but upon probable cause, supported by Oath or affirmation, and particularly describing the place to be searched, and the persons or things to be seized." For all practical purposes, an inmate's right to privacy ends whenever he or she enters a prison or jail (Bronstein, 1980:35). Cell searches are necessary to discover contraband and dangerous materials, including weapons and other items. Some experts disagree and argue that interfering with a prisoner's right to privacy suppresses any possibility for rehabilitation (Schaar, 1985).

Inmates understand from the outset of their incarceration that they do not enjoy the same rights of privacy as do ordinary citizens (*United States v. Dawson,* 1975). Random shakedowns of cells are permitted in either jails or prisons, without prefacing such searches with a search warrant or probable cause (*Hudson v.*

Palmer, 1984; *United States v. Cohen,* 1986; *United States v. Mills,* 1983). However, prison officials and correctional officers are obliged to exercise due care when searching cells in order to avoid destroying or damaging inmates' personal effects not considered contraband. Probable cause and search warrants are not required to conduct searches of prisoner cells, however (*Clifton v. Robinson,* 1980; Gardner, 1985).

Eighth Amendment Violations. The Eighth Amendment says that "excessive bail shall not be required, nor excessive fines imposed, nor cruel and unusual punishments inflicted." The "cruel and unusual punishment" provision of this Amendment is most frequently cited by prisoners who challenge the conditions under which they are incarcerated and their treatment by prison staff. Prison overcrowding, double-bunking, strip searches, heat or temperature of cells, visitation rights, and adequacy of medical care are only a few of the many issues falling within the scope of cruel and unusual punishment under the Eighth Amendment.

Prisoners have exhausted practically every conceivable complaint under the Eighth Amendment. Relief has been sought in court because of a state prison's alleged failure to provide vocational or educational training for inmates, the alleged failure of the prison to provide Spanish-speaking prisoners with courses in Spanish, assignment by prison staff of inmates to work camp details, the alleged failure of prison officials to make it possible for inmates to hear their favorite television programs during the day, and the alleged failure of prison officials to allow inmates to exercise in any manner they see fit. Prisoners have also raised issues of prison hygiene and fire safety regulations, the presence of insects in dining areas, plumbing, lighting, and even the location of the prison in relation to the prisoner's family. Most of these complaints have been held by courts to be without merit and not in violation of the "cruel and unusual punishment" provisions of the Eighth Amendment. This does not mean that all prisoner complaints alleging such violations end in dismissals of these complaints. Deliberate indifference by prison officials to prisoner needs where prisoners are in need of medical treatment and the wanton infliction of pain violates a prisoner's Eighth Amendment rights (*Estelle v. Gamble,* 1976).

Highlighted previously as a major correctional issue, prison and jail overcrowding does contribute to inmate unrest and the potential for violence. There are limits reached by prison and jail populations where overcrowding becomes cruel and unusual within the provisions of the Eighth Amendment. Many prisons and jails are currently under court order to reduce their populations such that overcrowding will no longer be problematic and violate inmate rights. Some court decisions relating to prison and jail overcrowding have been favorable for prisoners. In the case of female pretrial detainees in a California women's detention facility, for example, it was determined that the degree of physical insecurity and psychological stress suffered by inmates as the result of noise, lack of privacy, and shortage of space constituted cruel and unusual punishment (*Fischer v. Winter,* 1983). In an Oklahoma prison, inmates were forced to sleep in garages, barbershops, libraries, and stairwells, and they were also placed in dormitories without any toilet or shower facilities. These conditions were determined by the Court to be in violation of the Eighth Amendment (*Battle v. Anderson,* 1977). The rated capacities of prisons and jails are usually used as standards for determining whether they are overcrowded.

Legal Setbacks for Inmates of Prisons and Jails: The Double-Bunking Issue. The landmark cases cited by correctional experts as "setbacks" for inmates relating to conditions of crowding in prisons and jails are *Bell v. Wolfish* (1979) and *Rhodes v. Chapman* (1981). The *Bell* case, involving short-term double-bunking, is considered a significant setback to the prisoners' rights movement (Singer, 1980:68; Coles, 1987:50). This case involved the minimum-security Metropolitan Correctional Center in New York City, a facility operated by the U.S. Bureau of Prisons and designed to accommodate 449 federal prisoners, including many pretrial detainees. It had been constructed in 1975 and was considered architecturally progressive and modern, generally a comfortable facility. Originally, the facility was designed to house inmates in individual cells. But soon, the capacity of the facility was exceeded by inmate overpopulation. Inmates soon were obligated to share their cells with other inmates. This "double-bunking" and other issues related to overcrowding eventually led to a class-action suit against the facility by several of the pretrial detainees and prisoners. A lower court ruled in favor of the prisoners, holding that "compelling necessity" had not been demonstrated by prison officials in their handling of the overcrowding situation. But the U.S. Supreme Court overturned the lower court and said that the "intent" of prison officials should decide whether double-bunking was intended as "punishment" or was a simple deprivation because of necessity. Since no "intent" to punish pretrial detainees could be demonstrated, there was no punishment. Hence, the Eighth Amendment was not violated. The lawsuit by the pretrial detainees and prisoners was subsequently lost.

The second case, involving long-term double-bunking, is *Rhodes v. Chapman,* an Ohio matter decided in 1981. In this instance, the single issue of double-bunking was raised and alleged to be "cruel and unusual" punishment prohibited by the Eighth and Fourteenth Amendments. Kelly Chapman and Richard Jaworski were two inmates of the Southern Ohio Correctional Facility and were housed in the same cell. They contended that double-celling violated their constitutional rights. Furthermore, in support of their claim, they cited the facts that their confinement was long-term and not short-term as was the case in the *Bell* case, that physical and mental injury will be sustained through such close contact and limited space for movement, and that the Ohio facility was housing 38 percent more inmates than its design capacity specified.

The U.S. Supreme Court held that double-celling in this long-term prison was neither cruel and unusual punishment nor unconstitutional per se. The Court used the standard of the "totality of circumstances" in making its ruling about Chapman's and Jaworski's confinement. The Court further noted that the "cruel and unusual" provisions of the Eighth Amendment must be construed in a "flexible and dynamic" manner. When we consider all factors, no evidence existed that Ohio authorities were wantonly inflicting pain on these or other inmates. These conditions, considered in their totality, did not constitute serious need deprivations. The long-term consequences of the *Bell* and *Chapman* decisions are the subjects of controversy among correctional experts and scholars (Herman, 1984; Singer, 1980; Coles, 1987; Palmer, 1985; Knight and Early, 1986; Davis and Leban, 1985). However, double-celling, made necessary by the unanticipated increase in prisoners in the facility, did not result in food deprivations, a decrease in the quality of medical care, or a decrease in sanitation standards (Palmer, 1985:441–443).

Fourteenth Amendment Violations. The portion of the Fourteenth Amendment most relevant for inmates is that "no state shall make or enforce any law which shall abridge the privileges or immunities of citizens of the United States; nor shall any State deprive any person of life, liberty, or property, without due process of law; nor deny to any person within its jurisdiction the equal protection of the laws." The "due process" and "equal protection" clauses have resulted in numerous legal challenges by inmates of jails and prisons. Anytime inmates perceive or feel that other inmates are receiving special treatment or privileges, the Fourteenth Amendment is cited as the basis for these grievances. Any discriminatory action by penal authorities against prisoners because of their gender, race, socioeconomic status, ethnicity, or religion would be grounds for Fourteenth Amendment action.

When inmates are classified according to minimum-security, medium-security, and maximum-security, these classifications usually result in widely disparate privileges for those in different security categories. Inmates have also alleged a denial of participation in various programs such as furloughs and work release, exercise and yard privileges, and conjugal visits with spouses. Many female prisoners do not receive the same sorts of benefits extended to male prisoners. Most prisons are designed for male inmates, with considerably less thought about provisions for female inmates. Services and vocational/educational programs are aimed primarily at male inmates, while female prisoners find these same programs totally unsuitable for their interests. It was held in 1979, however, that state prison authorities must provide women inmates with treatment and facilities that are "substantially equivalent" to those provided men inmates (*Glover v. Johnson*, 1979).

In the case of *Baraldini v. Thornburgh* (1989), two female inmates, Sylvia Baraldini and Susan Rosenberg, were in the custody of the Federal Bureau of Prisons and transferred to the Bureau's highest security facility for women. They alleged that their assignment to this high-security facility was motivated solely because of their previous "subversive" statements made in the presence of other inmates. According to these inmates, they had been model prisoners and had been incarcerated in their original facility for a lengthy period. However, the federal Circuit Court of Appeals upheld the constitutionality of their transfer, citing administrative concerns for institutional security as legitimate. Furthermore, the women were known to associate with groups that assisted in previous escapes or escape attempts, both women had access to dangerous weapons, and both had participated in violent and criminal activities prior to their federal confinement (*Corrections Compendium,* 1989b:2).

OVERCROWDING, INMATE VIOLENCE, AND MISCLASSIFICATION

Many of the problems involving prison operations and management are attributable to overcrowding. In 1987, only nine state prison systems had prisoner populations below their operating capacity. Overall, state prisons were operating between 105 and 120 percent of their capacities in 1987, while the federal prison capacity was exceeded by 37 to 73 percent (Greenfeld, 1988:4). Prison capacities are measured three ways: (1) rated capacity, (2) operational capacity, and (3) design capacity. Rated capacity refers to the number of beds or inmates assigned by a rating official to various state institutions. Operational capacity is the total number of inmates that can be accommodated based on the size of a facility's staff, programs, and other services. Design capacity is the optimum number of inmates that architects originally intended to be housed or accommodated by the facility (Greenfeld, 1988:4). Sometimes it is difficult to make valid comparisons among jurisdictions, because each prison system reports prison population excesses using different criteria. Most prisons report their inmate populations according to the system's operating capacity, however.

Violent deaths, suicides, psychiatric commitments, disciplinary infractions, and increased litigation by inmates have been linked closely with overcrowding (Paulus, McCain, and Cox, 1985; Maier and Miller, 1987; Champion, 1988; Palmer, 1985). AIDS in prisons and jails is increasing and poses a threat to the health and well-being of many unaffected prisoners. Therefore, overcrowding is a very important issue, since it represents a substantially greater risk of exposure for unaffected inmates (Williams, 1986). Many jurisdictions have new prison construction to accommodate growing numbers of convicts infected with the AIDS virus. But the risk of contracting AIDS persists as overcrowding persists. Existing prison construction in progress is insufficient to accommodate the numbers of new prisoners anticipated in most jurisdictions (Contact Center, Inc., 1987).

Overcrowding and Disciplinary Infractions

The problem of overcrowding intensifies the incidence of inmate disruption in every prison environment. Racial and ethnic differences bring all types of persons together in close interaction through chronic overcrowding, and often the result is greater prison violence (Braswell, Dillingham, and Montgomery, 1985; Leger and Barnes, 1986). While every prison screens new inmates and classifies them according to standard criteria, misclassifications frequently occur. Pathological offenders or those who are mentally retarded or ill often respond with aggression to their forced interaction with other inmates (Toch and Adams, 1986). In fact, several prisons have few, if any, provisions for segregating different classes of offenders, although corrections standards are improving annually and the courts are increasingly requiring such segregation for inmate safety (McGee, Warner, and Harlow, 1985).

Much prisoner violence escapes detection by prison correctional officers. And even when officers suspect or observe rule-breaking and certain forms of inmate violence, it is sometimes not reported. Some researchers say that correctional officers often do not report the misconduct they observe, since prisoner cooperation and compliance with prison rules are dependent upon the nonreporting behavior of officers (Hewitt, Poole, and Regoli, 1984). In some respects, this gives prisoners psychological power over the correctional officers who elect not to report the violence or infractions they may observe. Sexual assaults and psychological harassment are frequent in these high-risk settings (Cotton and Groth, 1984), although some researchers believe that our estimates about the incidence of sexual attacks in prisons are exaggerated. A study of sexual violence in the U.S. Penitentiary at Lewisburg, Pennsylvania, disclosed that only 9 percent of all inmates were actual victims of sexual attacks. Although 29 percent of the inmates reported sexual propositions from other inmates, a majority had not been involved with any kind of inmate sexual misconduct (Nacci and Kane, 1983).

Proposals and policies for reducing inmate violence are about as diverse as the many solutions for alleviating prison overcrowding. States such as South Carolina have implemented what appear to be sound classification systems and policies and then have acted aggressively to enforce these policies. Previously, we examined a program used by the South Carolina Department of Corrections called AIMS (Adult Inmate Management System) in 1984 (Leeke and Mohn, 1986). Briefly reviewing, this system divides prisoners into three basic aggressiveness levels, including alphas, betas, and gammas. Prison violence at at least one South Carolina prison has been reduced by 18 percent since using AIMS, where weaker prisoners are segregated from more violent and sexually aggressive prisoners during evening hours. Despite the fact that 70 percent of the prisoners in that South Carolina facility have violent offense records, AIMS has the lowest protective custody rate among its inmates in the entire state. This is largely attributable to greater prisoner participation in special programs and greater accessibility of prisoners to security and human services staffs (Leeke and Mohn, 1986).

Prison officials are in strategic positions to manipulate prisoners to some degree and control their violent conduct through staff reports and recommendations for an inmate's early release. Good-time credits may be earned by inmates who obey prison rules and do not engage in serious rule infractions. However, changes in sentencing policies such as the guidelines established by the U.S. Sentencing Commission in 1987 will eventually diminish the effectiveness of this type of staff control, since prisoners will have to serve all of their original sentences without parole. With an absence of incentives such as early release or recommendations for a prisoner's early release by correctional officers or officials based on a prisoner's good conduct, a powerful incentive for inmates to comply with prison rules is withdrawn (Stojkovic, 1986). Prisoners themselves in most state and federal facilities have evolved disciplinary councils as a productive alternative to administrative sanctioning mechanisms. These councils provide avenues whereby most inmate complaints against other inmates and prison staff can be resolved quickly and to almost everyone's satisfaction (Kane, 1987; Schafer, 1986). Interestingly, the corrections officer is added to provide the council with a degree of objectivity in processing inmate complaints. In some ways, these councils operate like alternative dispute resolution procedures, where matters are resolved informally rather than formally.

Inmate Allegations of Racism

Presently, nearly half the prison population is black, and a majority of that same population is nonwhite. Thus, there is considerable legal action prompted because of suspected or alleged racism. This is not particularly unique to corrections, however. Clayton (1983) and Petersilia and Turner (1987) observe that sentencing disparities, plea bargain arrangements, and arrests also seem closely connected with racial and ethnic factors. Successful legal action by inmates where racism is alleged is difficult to sustain in court. Many inmate petitions alleging discrimination or racism are categorically rejected as lacking merit or are dismissed out of hand by federal and state judges. For instance, many incarcerated Black Muslims deluged the courts with petitions alleging denial of racial and religious equality during the 1960s (Jacobs, 1980:434). According to Jacobs (1980:434), there were sixty-six reported federal court decisions pertaining to Black Muslims between 1961 and 1978. Despite the successes achieved by these actions, the Muslims experienced a fairly high failure or rejection rate in the suits they filed. But they emerged in the 1970s as the best organized prisoner aggregate that demonstrated for other prisoners the fruits of organized protest and the influence of solidarity in legal actions (Jacobs, 1980:435).

Intentional Neglect, Negligent Training

It is often difficult for judges to distinguish between actions of administrators of these facilities that are primarily the function of these conditions, and actions that are deliberately intended to cause prisoners physical or psychological harm. If inmates are sexually assaulted by other inmates, for instance, in a cell containing four inmates but designed to accommodate only two inmates, is this assault the result of prison staff or the result of overcrowding, something over which the administrator exerts little control? Ordinarily, negligence generally refers to the duty of one person to another, to act as a reasonable person might be expected to act, or the failure to act when action is appropriate. Legally, negligence is the failure to exercise reasonable care toward another (Black, 1979:930–932). There are different kinds of negligence as well as different degrees of negligence.

The prison officials and staff under various state and federal governments may be liable if their officers fail to follow procedures according to how they have been trained. Theories of negligent training (where an officer is simply improperly trained or untrained), negligent assignment (where an officer is assigned a position for which he is unqualified), negligent entrustment (where administrators fail to monitor those officers entrusted with items they are unfamiliar with using, such as giving firearms to prison correctional officers without first exposing them to firearms training), or negligent retention (where those officers determined to be unfit for their jobs are kept in those jobs anyway) may furnish inmates with the grounds to seek legal action against these officials (del Carmen, 1986:160–172).

Usually, negligence occurs by degree and includes slight, ordinary, and gross, although the courts regard as significant degrees of care rather than degrees of negligence (Black, 1979:931). However, gross negligence includes willful, wanton, and reckless negligence, where acts are performed that are totally unreasonable and without regard for the consequences. The standard for establishing negligence of officials or officers is a civil one, the "preponderance of evidence" standard. Thus, whether the plaintiff (usually the inmate) or defendant (usually administrators of a prison or jail or their agents—guards or other officers) prevails is contingent upon whether the preponderance of evidence is in the plaintiff's favor or the defendant's favor. These cases become "judgment calls" by either judges or juries, provided the cases reach trial. And, as we have seen, few inmate cases reach the trial stage because of motions to dismiss or summary judgments granted. Even when convicts win their cases, the monetary damages awarded, if any, are minimal and inconsequential.

If a government is found to be negligent, or if any agent or agency of the government is determined to be negligent in its inmate treatment, liability is incurred and damages may be sought by inmates for relief. However, it is difficult to establish negligence. Some examples are provided below. In one case, an inmate was placed in a District of Columbia prison in a cell with another inmate who had active tuberculosis (*Sypert v. United States*, 1983). The plaintiff sued the government and administrators alleging negligence, because he was placed in a cell with a tubercular inmate, and subsequent skin tests showed the presence of tubercle bacilli in his body. However, since he never developed active tuberculosis, the court ruled that he had suffered no physical injury and dismissed the case against the government. In another Oregon case, a prison inmate was stabbed with a knife by another inmate (*Walker v. United States*, 1977). The injured inmate sued Oregon officials, alleging they were negligent in the enforcement of prison rules regarding the search for contraband knives and other dangerous weapons potentially hazardous to other inmates. However, the preponderance of evidence presented in court by the injured inmate failed to show that either the guards or other correctional officials were negligent.

Sometimes an inmate's heirs may sue prison officials for negligence leading to the inmate's death. The District of Columbia Metropolitan Police Department (MPD) was sued by the family of Benny Washington, a potential suicide risk. Washington committed suicide by hanging himself in a cellblock of the MPD jail. Jail officers and administrators were sued because, as the lawsuit alleged, the jail officers had not been provided with adequate training to recognize potential suicide victims and prevent suicides. It was subsequently disclosed that the Police Academy and a local hospital conducted limited crisis training concerning suicide scenarios. Officers were taught about detecting abnormal behavior and suicidal tendencies. However, inmate Washington's behavior upon arrest and incarceration did not present any unusual problems for booking officers. No basis existed to alert the officers to Washington's suicidal propensities. Subsequently, the federal Circuit Court of Appeals sided with the jail officers, concluding that nothing had been unique to differentiate Washington from other inmates, and that the officers had removed dangerous objects from his cell and checked him every half hour during his confinement (*Dorman v. District of Columbia,* 1989).

Two additional cases involve administrative knowledge of gang warfare and violence and prisoner safety. In the first case, a prisoner alleged administrative negligence in the classification of the prisoner to a higher level of security and interaction with more dangerous prisoners. Later, the inmate was killed by other violent inmates and his relatives brought suit against the Administrator of Corrections (*Quinones v. Nettleship,* 1985). Affidavits were presented by inmates about general jail safety conditions, about where the correctional officers were or could have been positioned, and what steps were taken by administrators to protect other inmates from gang warfare. But administrative blame was not clearly established on the basis of the preponderance of the evidence. In another Texas case (*Hackett v. United States,* 1978), an inmate was being held in the Dallas County Jail. He testified against another inmate held in the same jail that the other inmate had told him he had possessed and transported another's stolen automobile. Through local newspapers distributed among other prisoners at the jail, all other inmates soon learned of the plaintiff's testimony. The inmate suffered a severe beating, and he sued the U.S. government and its jail employees, alleging that they had failed to foresee the tortious and criminal acts that would occur as the result of his court testimony. However, the court said that the government did not have a duty to foresee such acts, and it absolved jail officials of blame in the incident.

Authorities agree that inmates are at a disadvantage when they file lawsuits. Whenever they "win," it is difficult to determine the nature of their victory. Jail and prison officials may engage in subtle retaliation. This retaliation may involve civil rights violations or deliberate torts. But even flagrant tortious cases are difficult to prove, especially using the civil "preponderance of evidence" standard. Furthermore, whenever property claims are awarded prisoners, these amounts are often token damages and very small (Hunzeker and Conger, 1985).

SUMMARY

Measures of risk assessment are most often used in correctional facilities for the purpose of determining security and custody levels. Both prisons and jails use risk assessment devices to separate prisoners in various ways. For many decades, the short-term nature of jail confinement attracted little media interest or attention. Prisons were considered the sites most likely to exhibit inmate unrest and institutional disruption. However, chronic overcrowding throughout the United States has obligated many prisons to contract with local jail administrators to house a portion of their overflow. Such contracting has been in the context of court-mandated prison inmate population reductions. Reducing inmate overcrowding is also seen as a means of reducing the level of inmate violence, since it appears that these variables are closely correlated.

Currently every prison screens incoming inmates to determine their initial placement as well as particular needs which can be serviced by on-site facilities and programs. Primary considerations in these initial screenings are for institutional and public safety. Thus, those inmates considered more dangerous than others or more likely to pose escape risks are maintained in higher custody levels. Classification decisions are made by jail and prison administrators, usually in ports of entry to prisons or reception centers. Subsequently, inmate progress is charted with regularity, and periodic reclassification decisions are made to determine whether particular inmates should be retained at the same custody level or reclassified to a different custody level. Much weight is given to previous inmate behavior in order to forecast future behaviors of these inmates under different levels of custody. Criteria include an inmate's history of institutional violence, the severity of the present conviction offense, prior assaultive offense history, escape history, time to earliest release, alcohol or drug use/abuse, current detainer status, prior felony convictions, and stability factors (age, marital status, previous employment record, scholastic abilities). Major and minor infractions are cited as reasons for retaining or changing existing custody levels of inmates.

The primary purposes of reclassification are to either reward or punish inmates. Rewards are greater privileges that accompany lower custody levels. Punishments are withholding privileges that accompany higher custody levels. Good-time credits are awarded inmates as rewards for good conduct while incarcerated. Thus, inmates may earn substantial time off of their total sentences to be served if they behave well while in custody. Different state jurisdictions assign various numbers of days per month as good-time credit against the total time to be served.

Prison and jail administrators are subject to a wide variety of inmate lawsuits stemming from various potential constitutional rights violations. An inmate's assignment to a particular custody level or the location where time is to be served may be challenged under the equal protection clause of the Fourteenth Amendment. Many jails and prisons are old and ill-equipped to furnish inmates with adequate housing and medical care. Misclassifications of inmates occur, and many inmates rightly protest these decisions and housing placements. Yet, the U.S. Supreme Court says that states and the federal government have no duty to inmates to make them comfortable. Nevertheless, inmates may allege civil rights violations, initiate *habeas corpus* actions, or file various tort claims. The First, Fourth, Eighth, and Fourteenth Amendments are the bases for many of these lawsuits as well, as inmates seek to challenge the activities and procedures of correctional officials relating to mail censorship, cell searches, adequacy of medical care, overcrowded cell conditions, and other problems of incarceration. While inmates of prisons and jails have prevailed in a limited number of court actions against prison and jail officials, their victories are questionable in terms of their long-term tangible rewards. Currently, the courts are sympathetic with prison and jail administrators who attempt to do the best they can with limited resources.

Form 4.1
Colorado Actuarial Risk Assessment Scale

COLORADO ACTUARIAL RISK ASSESSMENT SCALE*

Shaded Area To Be Completed At Intake:

Date form completed ____________

Inmate Name ______________________________ DOC# ____________

Case Managers Name ______________________________ Facility ____________

For each item, enter the weight corresponding to the information in the offender's record.

1. Any prior adult or juvenile felony conviction for burglary, robbery, theft, or auto theft (Include deferred judgments):

   0 (No)
   7 (Yes) ___
   0 (Unknown)

2. Total number of original felony convictions on current prison sentence(s) (Do not count prior convictions):

   0 (1)
   3 (2-3)
   5 (4+) ___

3. Total number of prior adult and/or juvenile sentenced incarcerations to prison, jail or juvenile facility for felony offense: If UNKNOWN, substitute number of prior felony convictions.

   0 (None)
   3 (One)
   5 (Two or more) ___

4. Employed 50% or more of two consecutive years prior to original arrest date:

   0 (Yes)
   5 (No) ___
   0 (Unknown)

5. Convicted of a felony or adjudicated a delinquent before age 18:

   0 (No)
   4 (Yes) ___
   0 (Unknown)

VIOLENT AND GENERAL RISK SCALE

SCORE	RISK LEVEL
34 - 46	HIGH RISK
28 - 33	HIGH MEDIUM RISK
15 - 27	MEDIUM RISK
-3 - 14	LOW RISK

***Do not fill this form out on anyone who has a current sex offense conviction.**

6. Serious offender classification: Do one or more of the following apply? (check all that apply)

   ☐ - Current conviction for violent crime (use Table A on back);
   ☐ - Current court conviction for escape (include attempts/conspiracies);
   ☐ - Prior conviction for felony against a person in the last 5 years of street time;
   ☐ - Three or more prior adult or juvenile arrests for: robbery, rape, felony assault, kidnap, or aggravated burglary (weapon or injury);
   ☐ - Substance abuse history includes one of the following: PCP use, injections of speed, cocaine, or hallucinogens (not heroin), or sniffing volatile substances (glue, paint);

   0 (No)
   4 (Yes) ___
   0 (Unknown)

7. Ever legally married: (Do not include common law)

   0 (Yes)
   3 (No) ___

8. Present incarceration includes administrative action for an escape/walkaway or parole violation in the last 5 years : (technical violation or new crime)

   0 (No)
   1 (Escape) ___
   2 (Parole Violation)
   0 (Unknown)

To Be Completed by Case Manager:

9. Class I or Class IIA COPD disciplinary infractions during this incarceration:

   -3 (None)
   -1 (Yes, but none in last 6 months)
   3 (One last 6 months)
   5 (2+ last 6 months) ___

10. Code the most serious disciplinary infraction incurred during the past 6 months:

   0 (None)
   2 (Class IIA)
   3 (Class I) ___

11. Age at PED or next hearing for governing sentence (whichever applies):

   0 (35+)
   1 (25 - 34) ___
   3 (18 - 24)

TOTAL SCORE ☐

DC Form 205-1F (2/90)

Form 4.1 (continued)

INSTRUCTIONS FOR COMPLETING RISK SCALE FORM

DO NOT FILL THIS FORM OUT ON ANYONE WHO HAS A CURRENT SEX OFFENSE CONVICTION.

For Items 1 - 7: If offender is currently in on a TECHNICAL parole, probation or community corrections revocation, use information related to the original commitment offense.

1. File must specifically document adult conviction, juvenile adjudications or deferred judgments/sentences for burglary, robbery, theft, or auto theft. Do not include theft by fraud and deceit; include theft by receiving and attempts/conspiracies to commit burglary, robbery, theft, or auto theft.

2. Include total number of convictions for this sentence (i.e., two counts of burglary and two counts of robbery total four convictions). Include convictions from other states if the crime would have been a felony if committed in Colorado. If the inmate is currently serving time on a technical parole, probation or community corrections violation, do not count the revocation as a conviction; rather, consider only the original conviction(s).

3. "Incarcerations" include sentences to jail (not pretrial confinement); juvenile commitments to secure facilities, including any commitment to the Department of Institutions; commitments to prison as an adult. If you can't find incarceration information, substitute the number of prior felony convictions (do not count this one).

4. Consider the last 24 (consecutive) months the inmate was on the street before the original date of arrest. Time spent locked-up or in school is NOT employment. For technical parole, probation or community corrections violators, the 24 month period is the time BEFORE the original prison sentence.

   YES if file documents full-time or part-time employment which totals at least 12 of the last 24 street months (for example, if the inmate worked half-time for nine months, this totals 4.5 months of employment).

   NO if inmate was employed less than a total of 12 months.

   UNKNOWN if file contains inadequate employment information.

5. "Felony" refers to any crime that would be considered a felony if committed by an adult in Colorado.

6. If the offender is presently serving time on a technical parole/probation violation, code this item as if he was serving time on the original sentence.

   - Violent crime: See table A, this page.
   - Escape: Do not count escapes handled administratively.
   - Prior Conviction: Look for violent felony convictions during the last 60 months the inmate was free (on the street) to commit crimes.
   - Three or more violent arrests: Unlike the other items in the Risk Scale, this requires information on arrests, not convictions.
   - Substance Abuse: Note that these are substances that tend to make people behave unpredictably or violently.

7. Do not count common-law relationships.

8. Include county jail escapes and community corrections walk-aways. Do not include technical or community corrections violations.

9. Consider only DOC infractions which occurred during this term of incarceration (include time spent on technical violations).

10. Consider only DOC infractions which occurred anytime during this sentence.

11. Code according to the age the inmate will be at potential parole release date.

TABLE A
SERIOUS OFFENDER CLASSIFICATION: CURRENT CONVICTION FOR VIOLENT CRIME
Murder
Rape/Sex Assault
Kidnapping for Ransom
Aggravated Robbery
1st Degree Burglary
Arson of a Dwelling
Voluntary Manslaughter
Attempted Rape/Sex Assault
Sex Assault on a Child
Kidnapping
Robbery
Felony Assault
Terrorism
Arson
Involuntary Manslaughter
Extortion/Blackmail
Escape
Jailbreak
Aggravated Assault
Conspiracy/Attempt to Commit a Violent Felony

Form 4.2
Hawaii: Short-Term Inmate Security Designation

SECTION A: DEMOGRAPHICS

1. Name__________ 2. I.D. No.______ 3. Facility________ 4. Date ________
5. Sex M ( ) F ( ) 6. Race _____ 7. Date of Birth ______ 8. Primary Language ________
9. Hazard Codes:
   Substance/Drug Dependency__________
   Escape Risk__________
   Protective Custody (Separatee, Gay, etc.)__________
   Suicidal__________
   Violent__________
   Disruptive__________
   Other __________

   Comments:

SECTION B: SECURITY SCORING

1. AGE
   40 years and over 0
   30 - 39 years 1
   29 or less years 3
   ____

2. TYPE OF DETAINER OR PENDING CHARGE
   No detainer or pending charge 0
   Yes 3
   ____

3. TYPE OF PRIOR CONVICTIONS
   No previous convictions 0
   1 or 2 misdemeanor or petty misdemeanor convictions 1
   3 or 4 misdemeanor/petty misdemeanor or 1 felony conviction 3
   5 or more misdemeanor/petty misdemeanor, 2 or more felony convictions, or extended term 5
   ____

4. SEVERITY OF CURRENT CHARGE
   Misdemeanor, Petty Misdemeanor, Violation, Immigration 0
   Felony B and C 3
   Felony A, Probation/Parole Violations, Federal Charges 5
   ____

5. HISTORY OF ASSAULTIVE BEHAVIOR
   No history 0
   1 or 2 misdemeanor or petty misdemeanor convictions 1
   3 or 4 misdemeanor/petty misdemeanor or 1 felony conviction 3
   5 or more misdemeanor/petty misdemeanor or 2 or more felony convictions 5
   ____

6. HISTORY OF ESCAPES OR ESCAPE ATTEMPTS
   None 0
   Yes 5
   ____

7. SECURITY TOTAL (Total 1 - 6) .... ____

8. SECURITY LEVEL

Minimum	Medium	Maximum
0 - 8 points	9 - 17 points	18 - 26 points

9. EVALUATOR: __________ 10. Transfer Case ____ Exception Case ______

Reasons:__________

Security Level: ______ Facility/Housing: ______ REVIEWED BY: ________

Form 4.3
Hawaii: Mental Health Intake Screening

STATE OF HAWAII

DEPARTMENT OF PUBLIC SAFETY
FACILITY_______________

MENTAL HEALTH INTAKE SCREENING
(ALL questions must be asked of inmates)

A. (1) Name: (Last, First, Middle Initial)

____

(2) SSN:______________
(3) DOB:______________
(5) Day of the Week:________
(6) Month:______________
(7) Today's Date:__________
(8) Year:______________
(9) Sex:______M ______F

(4) Criminal charges:
Parv: Prbv:
Present/New Charges:______________
____
____

I give the following answers freely, and the results will be kept confidential in my medical record and will be used only by medical/mental health staff while I am in prison/jail.

(10) Have you ever seen a psychiatrist/psychologist/private therapist/ psych counselor? (Circle all that apply)

____
Date Location Doctor
____
Date Location Doctor

(11) Have you ever been hospitalized for mental health reasons?___Yes___No

______________________ ______________________
Date(s) Location Date(s) Location

(12) Have you ever been prescribed medication for mental health?__No__Yes

____
Date Name of drug(s)
____
Date Name of drug(s)

(13) What is the name of the place you are in now?______________

(14) What is the name of the city you are in now?______________

(15) Repeat these numbers: (a) 4736 (b) 5829
(Circle the letter if not accurately repeated)

	Yes	No
B. (1) Has drinking ever caused you to be arrested?	____	____
(a) If yes, how many times?______________		
(b) How long have you been drinking?__________		
How long have you been using drugs?__________		
(c) Have you ever been in treatment for drug problems?	____	____
(d) If yes, When______________ Where______________		

MENTAL HEALTH INTAKE SCREENING

C. (1) Have you ever used pot, uppers/downers, heroin, "ice" cocaine or any other drugs to make you feel good? (Circle all that apply)	____	____

Form 4.3 (continued)

D. (1) Have there been times when you have been unusually excited, irritible, or restless for no special reason? ____ ____
(a) If yes, did it occur after age 15? ____ ____
(b) Did you ever receive help for this? ____ ____

E. (1) Have there been times when you felt depressed, empty, sad, or hopeless for no special reason? ____ ____
(2) Have there been times when you felt very irritable or tired all the time for no special reason? ____ ____
(3) Have these feelings ever lasted more than a month? ____ ____
(4) Have you ever tried to end your life? ____ ____
(a) If yes, how long ago?____________________
Method:____________________________________

F. (1) Have you:
(a) Heard things that others around you could not hear? ____ ____
(b) Seen things that others around you could not see? ____ ____
(2) Have you ever felt your mind or body was secretly controlled? ____ ____
(3) Have you ever felt you have special powers? ____ ____
(4) Have you ever felt others were following you or out to get you? ____ ____
If yes to any of the above:
(5) Did it happen when not drinking or using drugs? ____ ____

G. (1) Do you have any physical problems that bother you frequently? ____ ____
(2) Do you see many doctors when you are sick who don't know why you are sick? ____ ____

H. (1) Have you had any homosexual experiences? ____ ____
(a) Before age 18? ____ ____
(b) After age 18? ____ ____
(2) Do you feel that you are a homosexual? ____ ____

Inmate's Signature______________________________

Intake worker's assessment of inmate's physical appearance: Hygiene, behavior, and inmate appears to need mental health services:

____
____

Completed by:__________________________ ____________________
ISC Worker's Name Date

Reviewed by:__________________________ ____________________
Mental Health Coordinator Date

Mental health observations:____________________________________
____
____
____
____

Form 4.4
Hawaii: Medical Admission Screening

STATE OF HAWAII
DEPARTMENT OF PUBLIC SAFETY

SID # ____________________

Facility____________________

Date Admitted____________________

MEDICAL ADMISSION SCREENING

Name:______________________________ DOB:________________ SSN:____________________ Sex:____

Observations:

1. Is the inmate sluggish or unconscious?....................Yes No
2. Does the inmate have obvious pain or bleeding?....................Yes No
3. Are there visible signs of injuries or illness?....................Yes No
4. Is there obvious fever or jaundice?....................Yes No
5. Are there signs of lice or crabs, rashes, bruises or needle marks?....................Yes No
6. Does the inmate appear to be under the influence of drugs or alcohol?....................Yes No
7. Are there any visible signs of alcohol/drug withdrawal (e.g., extreme perspiration, shakes, cramping, vomiting)? (Circle specific sign if yes)....................Yes No
8. Does the inmate's behavior suggest risk of suicide?....................Yes No
9. Does the inmate's behavior suggest risk of assault to staff or other inmates?....................Yes No
10. Are there any obvious physical handicaps?....................Yes No

Questions:

1. Are you presently taking medication?....................Yes No No Response
   If yes, what?____________________
2. Are you allergic to any medication?....................Yes No No Response
   If yes, what?____________________
3. Do you have any of the following? (Indicate with "X")

Diabetes	( )	Seizures	( )	Tuberculosis	( )
Heart Disease	( )	High Blood Pressure	( )	Venereal Disease	( )
Hepatitis	( )	Psychiatric Problems	( )	Painful Dental Condition	( )

4. Have you had a recent head injury?....................Yes No No Response
5. Do you wear eyeglasses/contact lenses, dentures, hearing aid, brace or artificial limb? If yes, describe____________________ Yes No No Response
6. Do you have any other medical problems we should know about?....................Yes No No Response
7. Have you ever thought of ending your life?....................Yes No No Response
   Do you feel that way now?....................Yes No No Response
8. Do you have any drug/alcohol use that could cause withdrawal problems?...Yes No No Response
   Type/amount used daily____________________
   Time of last dose or drink____________________
9. Do you inject drugs intravenously?....................Yes No No Response
10. Do you have any medical insurance coverage?....................Yes No No Response
    If yes, name of company____________________ #__________

Females:

11. Are you pregnant?....................Yes No No Response
12. Are you currently on birth control pills?....................Yes No No Response
13. Have you recently delivered?....................Yes No No Response
    When?____________________

Disposition:

Emergency room ( ) Nurse called ( ) General population, next sick call ( ) General Population ( )

______________________________ ______________________________
Completed By Date Reviewed By Date

I have been informed of sick call procedures of this facility.

Inmate's Signature:______________________________ Date:____________________

DOC 0416 (Rev. 1/90)
(doc #1449H)

Original - Institutional File
Canary - Health Care Unit

Form 4.5
Tennessee: Initial Classification Custody Assessment Form

OFFENDER LAST NAME | FIRST NAME | MI

OFFENDER NUMBER ______ INSTITUTION: ______ DATE: ______

COUNSELOR: ______

1. **HISTORY OF INSTITUTIONAL VIOLENCE** (jail or prison, rate most serious)
   - Assault. No weapon no serious injury (last 18 months).......... 3
   - Assault. With weapon, no serious injury (last 18 months)....... 5
   - Assault. With or without weapon with serious injury or death (last 42 months)........ 7
   - Assault. With or without weapon with serious injury or death (43 through 60 months)........ 5 ____ score

2. **SEVERITY OF CURRENT OFFENSE** (rate most serious)
   - Low........ 1
   - Moderate........ 2
   - High........ 4
   - Highest........ 6 ____ score

3. **PRIOR ASSAULTIVE OFFENSE HISTORY** (rate most serious)
   - Low........ 0
   - Moderate........ 2
   - High........ 4
   - Highest........ 6 ____ score

4. **ESCAPE HISTORY** (within last 3 years of incarceration)
   - Escape or attempt from minimum custody, no actual or threatened violence:
     - Over 1 year ago........ 1
     - Within the last year........ 3
   - Escape or attempt from medium or above custody, or from minimum custody with actual or threatened violence:
     - Over 1 year ago........ 5
     - Within the last year........ 7 ____ score

SCHEDULE A SCALE (add items 1 through 4)

☐ Close........... 10 or more. If score is 9 or less, complete items in Schedule B and score accordingly. [A]

---

5. **ALCOHOL/DRUG ABUSE**
   - Abuse causing occasional legal and social adjustment problems.. 1
   - Serious abuse, serious disruption of functioning.............. 3 ____ score

6. **CURRENT DETAINER/NOTIFICATION/CHARGE PENDING**
   - Felony detainer/notification/charges pending.................. 4
   - Extradition Initiated - felony........ 6 ____ score

7. **PRIOR FELONY CONVICTIONS**
   - One........ 2
   - Two........ 4 ____ score

8. **STABILITY FACTORS** (check box(es) and combine for score)
   - ☐ Age 26 or over........ -2
   - ☐ High school diploma or GED received........ -1
   - ☐ Employed or attending school (full or part-time) for 6 months or longer at time of arrest........ -1 ____ score

SCHEDULE B SCORE (combine items 5 through 8) [B]

CUSTODY LEVEL SCALE FOR TOTAL SCORE A + B:

TOTAL SCORE A + B	

☐ Medium............ 4-22

☐ Minimum........... 3or less

---

cc: Original - MIS Support Services - Inmate File
Institutional File
Correctional Classification Coordinator

Form 4.6
Idaho Department of Correction: Initial Classification Score Sheet

Facility ______

Inmate Name ______

Social Security Number ______

Inmate Number ______

Month Day Year
Date of Birth ______

SECTION I - SENTENCING INFORMATION

Category 1 - Crimes (If more than one, consider the most severe.)

Part A

☐
- ____ (13) Murder
- ____ (13) Rape
- ____ (13) Escape
- ____ (13) Hostage Taking/Riot/Strike in a Prison
- ____ (13) Battery on a Correctional Employee/Peace Officer
- ____ (04) Kidnapping
- ____ (04) Robbery/Burglary w/Weapons
- ____ (04) Arson
- ____ (04) Battery/Assault w/Intent to Commit Another Felony
- ____ (04) Voluntary Manslaughter
- ____ (04) L & L/Incest/Sexual Exploitation/High Risk for Institutional Management (See User Maual pp5)
- ____ (04) Mayhem
- ____ (04) Bombing/Weapons/Explosives
- ____ (04) Child Abuse
- ____ (04) Assault/Battery
- ____ (04) Racketeering
- ____ (04) Other High Risk Crime ______

- ____ (00) Involuntary Vehicular Manslaughter
- ____ (00) Controlled Substance
- ____ (00) Statutory Rape/L & L/Incest/Sexual Exploitation
- ____ (00) Burglary/Forgery/Theft
- ____ (00) DUI
- ____ (00) Other Low Risk Crime ______

Part B

☐ ____ 2) At least two or more crimes the inmate is incarcerated for are high risk crimes (See User Manual pp. 4 & 5)

Category 2 - Length of Sentence (See User Manual pp.9)

☐
- ____ (13) 20 or More
- ____ (04) More than 6 - Less than 20
- ____ (02) 6 Months - 6 Years
- ____ (00) Release from Custody with 6 Months

☐ **SECTION I TOTAL**

SECTION II - HISTORY / BEHAVIOR

Category 3 - Prior Record

☐
- ____ (13) 6 or More Prior Felony Convictions
- ____ (13) 3 or More Prior Felony Convictions for High Risk Crimes
- ____ (06) 2 or More Prior Felony Convictions
- ____ (06) 1 or More Prior Felony Convictions for High Risk Crimes

Category 4 - Escape History (See User Manual pp. 9-10)

Part A

☐
- ____ (08) From a Correctional Facility/Jail/Attempted within 10 Years
- ____ (03) From a Correctional Facility/Jail/Attempted not within 10 Years

Part B

☐
- ____ (05) Violence Involved (Against a Person)
- ____ (05) Two or More Escapes

Category 5 - Dangerous Behavior (See User Manual pp 10-11)

☐
- ____ (13) Aggressive/Predatory Behavior (Including Sex)
- ____ (13) Demonstrative Assaultive/Riotous/Coercive/Menacing Behavior

☐ **SECTION II TOTAL**

SECTION III - COMBINED SCORE

____ Section I

____ Section II

☐ **TOTAL**

SECTION IV - CUSTODY LEVEL

Close	13 or More
Medium	7 - 12
Minimum	2 - 6
Community	0 - 1

SECTION V - GENERAL CUSTODY LEVEL

☐

SECTION VI - SPECIAL CONSIDERATIONS N/A ❑ Not Applicable

- ❑ Inmate has detainer charges pending
- ❑ Inmate has retained 120/180 day jurisdiction
- ❑ Absconded probation/parole; fugitive from justice; AWOL; juvenile escape
- ❑ Parole date granted/release within 6 months
  (Eligible for minimum unless otherwise noted.)
- ❑ Required for personal protection
- ❑ Youthful offender

Other Considerations: Is there any other justification that should be considered in making custody assignment for this inmate? ❑ Yes ❑ No

If yes, indicate additional consideration(s). Be Specific.: ______________________

____

____

____

SECTION VII - CUSTODY LEVEL MODIFICATION:

As a result of having marked any of the exceptions noted above, is a modification of custody appropriate? ❑ Yes ❑ No

If yes, indicate modified custody level: ______________________

____

SECTION VIII - AUTHORIZATIONS

Recommended Housing Assignment: [ ]

Assigned Custody Level: [ ]

____
Report Prepared by — Date

____
Inmate verifies receipt of 48 hour notice — Date

____
Classification Chairman — Date

____
Inmate waives 48 hour notice — Date

____
Approved by Director or Designee — Date

DISTRIBUTION: WHITE – Central File; YELLOW – Central Office; PINK – Inmate

Revised July 1990

Form 4.7
Alabama: Initial Inmate Classification Security Level

Name____________________________________Number______________________

CLASSIFICATION SPECIALIST # ___________________________DATE ___/___/____

1. HISTORY OF INSTITUTIONAL VIOLENCE
   (Jail or prison, code most serious within last five years) _____ Score
   None..0
   Assault not involving use of a weapon or resulting in serious injury....................................3
   Assault either weapon or serious injury, but not both........5
   Assault involving use of a weapon and/or resulting in serious injury or death...............................7

2. SEVERITY OF CURRENT OFFENSE
   (Refer to Severity of Offense Scale. Score the most Serious offenses if there are multiple convictions.) _____ Score
   Low...0
   Low/Moderate..2
   Moderate..3
   High..4
   Highest...6

3. PRIOR ASSAULTIVE OFFENSE HISTORY
   (Score the most severe in inmate's history. Refer to the Severity of Offense Scale.) _____ Score
   None, Low, or Low/Moderate..................................0
   Moderate..2
   High..4
   Highest...6
   Deduct 1 point from "highest" level if more than 5 years ago of free world time.......................... -1

4. ESCAPE HISTORY (rate last 5 years of incarceration)
   No escapes or attempts (or no prior incarcerations)..........0 _____ Score
   Within the last year..3
   An escape or attempt from equivalent of level III or higher facility, or from minimum or community custody with actual or threatened violence:
   Over 1 year ago...5
   Within the last year..7
   2 or more within 5 years....................................8

TOTAL (add items 1-4) _____ TOTAL

If score is 10 or above, use schedule A. If score is under 10, complete items 5-9.

Form 4.7 (continued)

5. TIME TO EARLIEST RELEASE
   0-6 months..........0
   7-12 months..........1
   13-24 months..........3
   25-36 months..........4
   More than 36 months..........5

   ______ Score

6. ALCOHOL/DRUG ABUSE
   None..........0
   Abuse causing occasional legal and social adjustment problems..........1
   Serious abuse, serious disruption of functioning..........3

   ______ Score

7. CURRENT DETAINER
   None..........0
   Misdemeanor detainer..........1
   Extradition initiated--misdemeanor..........3
   Felony detainer..........4
   Extradition initiated-felony detainer..........6

   ______ Score

8. PRIOR FELONY CONVICTIONS
   None..........0
   One..........2
   Two or more..........4

   ______ Score

9. STABILITY FACTORS (check appropriate box(es) and combine score)
   Age 35 or over.......... -2
   High School Diploma or GED received.......... -1
   Verified employment or attending school (full or part time) for 6 months or longer at time of arrest.......... -1
   Age at first arrest 15 yrs. or less..........1

   ______ Score

   TOTAL (add items 1-9) Use Schedule B

   ______ TOTAL

Schedule A (Items 1-4

Level VII	**15 or more**
Level VI	**10 - 14**
Use Schedule B	

Schedule B (all items)

Level VII	**21 or more**
Level VI	**17 - 20**
Level V (Tutwiler or R & CC)	**Accepts all inmates**
Level IV	**11 - 16**
Level III	**10**
Level II	**7 - 9**
Level I	**6 or under**

Form 4.7 (continued)

I. **Institutional Recommendations:**

A. Point Security Level _____
B. Recommend Security Level _____

If A and B differ, list Special Security Level Considerations (SCI 01):

_____ ____________________ _____ ____________________________
Code Reason

_____ ____________________ _____ ____________________________

C. Recommend Institution(s):
1. _________________________ 2. ________________________________

If Security Level on recommended institutions differs with recommended security level, list Special Institutional Placement Consideration (SCI 02)

_____ ____________________ _____ ____________________________
Code Reason

D. Recommend Security Level Score_____ on SCI dated ________________

be changed to __________________.

Reasons: ____

____

II. **Central Review Board:**

Member 1: __________ _____ ____
Sec. Level Code and Reasons, if different from Inst. Rec. (SCI 01)

__________ _____ ____
Institution Code and Reasons, if inconsistent with security level

____
Signature

Member 2: __________ _____ ____
Sec. Level Code and Reasons, if different from Inst. Rec. (SCI 01)

__________ _____ ____
Institution Code and Reasons, if inconsistent with security level

____
Signature

Member 3: __________ _____ ____
Sec. Level Code and Reasons, if different from Inst. Rec. (SCI 01)

__________ _____ ____
Institution Code and Reasons, if inconsistent with security level

____
Signature

III. **Final Action:**

__________________________	________________________________
Security Level	**Institution**
SCI 01 (Codes only)	**SCI 02 (Codes only)**
_____ _____ _____	_____ _____ _____
_____ _____ _____	_____ _____ _____

Form 4.8
Community Correctional Center Classification System—Illinois: Female Classification Instrument

IDOC NUMBER □-□□□□□ NAME ______________________________________
(Last) (First)

CURRENT SECURITY LEVEL Maximum (2) Medium (4) Minimum (6) □ ADD BELOW

ITEMS

Current Age	
34 and Older	Enter 0□
24 to 33	Enter 1□
23 and Younger	Enter 3□
Age at Time of First Incarceration of 30 days or More	
28 and Older	Enter 0□
23-27	Enter 2□
22 and Younger	Enter 3□
Number of Prison Admissions (include Current Offense)	
2 or More	Enter 0□
Current in First Prison Stay	Enter 2□
Number of Prior Probation/Parole/Other (non-CCC) Supervision Terms Not Successfully Completed	
None	Enter 0□
1 or More	Enter 2□
Number of Prior CCC Supervision Terms Not Successfully Completed	
None	Enter 0□
1 or More	Enter 4□
Total Number of Tickets with a Guilty Outcome Received Within the Last 6 Months	
None	Enter 0□
One or More	Enter 1□
History of Alcohol Use	
No Alcohol Use Problems Indicated	Enter 1□
Alcohol Use Problems Indicated	Enter 2□
History of Drug Use	
No Cocaine or Heroin Use Indicated	Enter 0□
Cocaine or Heroin Use Indicated	Enter 4□
Vocational	
History Indicates Marketable Job Skills or has Completed Vocational Training Program at the Institution	Enter 0□
History Indicates a Need for Vocational Training and Inmate has Required Training Program but has not Completed or Allowed	Enter 3□
History Indicates a Need for Vocational Training, but Inmate Rejects or Refuses Training Program	Enter 4□
Academic	
Inmate has at least a High School Diploma or a G.E.D.	Enter 0□
Inmate does not have a High School Diploma or a G.E.D., but has Requested to Participate in Program to Complete G.E.D. OR Is Currently in a G.E.D. Program	Enter 1□
Inmate does not have a High School Diploma or a G.E.D. and Refuses and Rejects Placement in Program to Complete G.E.D.	Enter 2□

CLASSIFICATION LEVEL:

LOW	(0 - 7)	= 1	
LOW MEDIUM	(8 - 10)	= 2	□
HIGH MEDIUM	(11 - 12)	= 3	
HIGH	(13 - 26)	= 4	

Signature______________________________ Code □□□□ Date □□□□□□

Comment for Override, Administrative Concerns, Critical/Special Needs, Etc.

____

____

____

Form 4.9
Hawaii: Reclassification Instrument

SECTION I

SID:___ ___ ___ ___ ___ ___ ___ ___ LST NAME:______________________ FN:__________

DOB: ____-____-________ DATE: _____-______-_________ CLASSIFICATION TYPE: __________ SSN: _____-_______-______

SEX: M F FACILITY:____________ MIN SENTENCE (in months): ________ MIN EXP DATE:___-___-____

PAROLE ELIGIBILITY DATE: ___-___-______ DISCHARGE DATE: ___-____-_______ COMPLETED BY: ______________________

CHANGE IN SENTENCE STRUCTURE Yes No (if Yes list changes):

____

____

____

____

SECTION II

1. **SEVERITY OF INSTITUTIONAL VIOLENCE (Code the most serious)**

NONE	0	
High Category Misconduct (Past 18 Months).	3	______
Greatest Category (Past 24 Months)	7	SCORE
Extremely Violent Misconduct (Past 5 Years)	15	

2. **DID THE ABOVE VIOLENCE OCCUR WITHIN LAST 18 MONTHS ?**

Yes	3	
No	0	______
		SCORE

3. **SEVERITY OF CURRENT OFFENSE (Refer to Severity of Offense list in manual. Score most severe offense)**

Low Moderate	1	
Moderate	2	
High	3	______
Greatest	4	SCORE
Or Life with/without Parole		

4. **PRIOR OFFENSE HISTORY SEVERITY (Score most severe in inmate's history)**

None or Low Moderate	0	
Moderate	1	______
High	3	SCORE
Greatest, LWP	4	

5. **TIME LEFT TO SERVE ON MINIMUM SENTENCE**

21 Years or more	15	______
20 Years or less	0	SCORE

TOTAL ITEMS 1 THROUGH 5

If score is 15 or more assign to Close custody

If score is 10 to 14 assign to Medium custody (ALWAYS complete the remaining items, but do not total score if inmate is assigned to CLOSE or MEDIUM custody)

TOTAL (1-5)

6. **ESCAPE HISTORY**

Over 6 months in MINIMUM security, no escape or attempted escape.	-3	
No escapes or attempts	0	______
An escape or attempt from minimum/community security, without violence:		SCORE
Over 7 years	1	
Within the last 7 years.	5	
An escape or attempt from medium or above security, or escape from any custody with violence:		
Over 7 years	5	
Within the last 7 years.	7	

7. **FREQUENCY OF MISCONDUCT**

Past 13 months incarceration, no reports.	-3	
Past 07 months incarceration, no reports.	-1	
None in the last 06 months.	0	______
One in the last 06 months	1	SCORE
Two or more in last 06 months	4	

8. **SEVERITY OF MISCONDUCT (LAST 18 MONTHS)**

NONE, Minor, Low Moderate	0	______
Moderate	3	SCORE
High	5	
Greatest	7	

Form 4.9 (continued)

9. INVOLVEMENT WITH DRUG/ALCOHOL IN INSTITUTION

None	0	
One more than 18 months	1	
Two or more, more than 18 months	2	______
One within 18 months	3	SCORE
Two or more within 18 months	4	

10. RELEASE ELIGIBILITY (To parole eligibility or discharge whichever is sooner)

18 months or less	-3	
19 to 24 months	-2	(_____)
25 to 30 months	-1	
31 months or greater	0	

COMPREHENSIVE POINT TOTAL

SECTION III POINT SCALE SUMMARY

If point total is 10 or less complete Section IV
If point total is 11 to 16 then custody is MEDIUM
If point total is 17 or greater then custody is CLOSE

SECTION IV

NON-DISCRETIONARY EXCLUSIONS FOR MINIMUM CUSTODY

1. Less than one year from last violent episode yes no
2. Pending charges, felony hold or detainer yes no
3. Hawaii PSD escape/attempt within last 7 years yes no
4. 48 months or more to parole eligibility date yes no

If any factor is answered yes, then computed custody is **MEDIUM**
If all factors answered no, then go to Section V

SECTION V

1. Within 18 months of parole eligibility or discharge yes no

If yes then computed custody is <u>COMMUNITY</u>
If no then computed custody is Minimum

COMPUTED CUSTODY LEVEL ____________

SECTION VI

DISCRETIONARY CRITERIA FOR ANY CUSTODY OVER-RIDE

01 = Protective Custody	05 = Overcrowding
02 = Violent Offender	06 = Medical
03 = Youthful Offender	07 = Mental Health
04 = Sex Offender	08 = Management Problem
09 = Exemplary Adjustment	10 = Other

OVER-RIDE RECOMMENDED YES NO

PRIMARY OVER-RIDE REASON ______

RECOMMENDED CUSTODY LEVEL ______________

COMMENTS:____

____

CLASSIFICATION COMMITTEE ACTION SECTION:

Recommended Custody Level: __________ Recommended Facility ________________

Completion Date: __________________ Classification Office Code: _____

Special Reclassification Date: __________ Mandatory 6 Month Reclassification Date: ________

Comments:

____

____

Reviewed by: ____________________________ ______________
Facility Classification Coordinator Date

CLASSIFICATION OFFICE ACTION SECTION:

Assigned Custody Level: __________ Assigned Facility: ______________

Assignment Date: __________

COMMENTS:

Form 4.10
Alabama: Inmate Reclassification Security Level

Name______________________________ Number____________________

SPECIALIST______________________________ DATE _____/_____/_______

1. HISTORY OF INSTITUTIONAL VIOLENCE
   (Jail or prison, code most serious within last five years) ____ Score
   None..0
   Assault not involving use of a weapon or resulting in
   serious injury..3
   Assault either weapon or serious injury but not both....5
   Assault or fighting involving use of a weapon and/or
   resulting in serious injury or death..................7

2. Did above assault occur within last six months?
   Yes...3 ____ Score
   No..0

3. SEVERITY OF CURRENT OFFENSE
   (Refer to the severity of offense scale on back of form. ____ Score
   Score the most serious offense if there are multiple
   convictions.)
   Low...0
   Low/Moderate..2
   Moderate..3
   High..4
   Highest...6

4. PRIOR ASSAULTIVE OFFENSE HISTORY
   (Score the most severe in inmate's history. Refer to the ____ Score
   Severity of Offense Scale.)
   None, Low, or Low/Moderate............................0
   Moderate..3
   High..4
   Highest...5

TOTAL (add items 1 through 4)

____ TOTAL

If score is 10 or over, use Schedule A. If score is under 10, complete the remainder of the scale.

5. ESCAPE HISTORY (Rate last 5 years of incarceration)
   No escapes or attempts...............................-3 ____ Score
   An escape or attempt from equivalent of minimum
   or community based facility, no actual or threatened
   violence.
   Over 1 year ago.......................................0
   Within the last year..................................1
   An escape or attempt from equivalent of a level III or
   higher facility or an escape from minimum or community
   facility custody with actual or threatened violence:
   Over 1 year ago.......................................5
   Within the last year..................................7
   2 or more within 5 years..............................8

6. TIME TO EARLIEST RELEASE
   0-6 months..0 ____ Score
   7-12 months...1
   13-24 months..3
   25-36 months..4
   More than 36 months...................................5

7. NUMBER OF DISCIPLINARY REPORTS
   None in last 18 months.............................. -3 ____ Score
   None in last 12 months.............................. -2
   None in last 6 months............................... -1
   One in last 6 months..................................1
   Two or more major in last 6 months....................4

Form 4.10 (continued)

8. MOST SEVERE DISCIPLINARY REPORT RECEIVED (last 18 months)

None..	0	____ Score
Low/Moderate..................................	1	
Moderate......................................	2	
High..	5	
Highest.......................................	7	

9. CURRENT DETAINER

None, or prosecution/extradition not indicated..........	0	____ Score
Misdemeanor-extradition/prosecution indicated...........	3	
Felony-extradition/prosecution indicated................	5	

10. PRIOR FELONY CONVICTIONS

None..	0	____ Score
One...	2	
Two or more...................................	4	

TOTAL (Add items 1 - 10) Use Schedule B

____________ Total Score

Form 4.11
Tennessee: Reclassification-Custody Assessment Form

OFFENDER LAST NAME	FIRST NAME	MI

OFFENDER NUMBER ______ INSTITUTION: ______ DATE: ______

COUNSELOR: ______

1. **HISTORY OF INSTITUTIONAL VIOLENCE** (jail or prison, rate most serious)
   Assault. No weapon no serious injury (last 18 months)................. 3
   Assault. With weapon, no serious injury (last 18 months).............. 5
   Assault. With or without weapon with serious injury or death (last 42 months)... 7
   Assault. With or without weapon with serious injury or death (43 through 60 months).. 5 ____ score

2. Did above assault occur within the last six months?
   No.. 0
   Yes... 3 ____ score

3. **SEVERITY OF CURRENT OFFENSE** (rate most serious)
   Low... 0
   Moderate.. 1
   High.. 3
   Highest... 4 ____ score

4. **PRIOR ASSAULTIVE OFFENSE HISTORY** (rate most serious)
   Low... 0
   Moderate.. 1
   High.. 3
   Highest... 4 ____ score

SCHEDULE A SCALE (add items 1 through 4)

☐ Close......10-14.

☐ Maximum....15 or more.

If score is 9 or less, complete items in Schedule B and score accordingly. [A]

---

5. **ESCAPE HISTORY** (within last 3 years of incarceration)
   No escapes or attempts...-2
   Escape or attempt from minimum custody, no actual or threatened violence:
   Over 1 year ago... 0
   Within the last year.. 1
   Escape or attempt from medium or above custody, or from minimum custody with actual or threatened violence:
   Over 1 year ago... 5
   Within the last year.. 7 ____ score

6. **NUMBER OF DISCIPLINARY REPORTS WITH GUILTY DISPOSITIONS**
   None in last 13-18 months...-4
   None in last 7-12 months..-2
   None in last 6 months...-1
   One in last 6 months.. 1
   Two or more in last 6 months.. 4 ____ score

7. **MOST SEVERE DISCIPLINARY REPORT RECEIVED** (within last 18 months)
   Class C... 2
   Class B... 5
   Class A... 7 ____ score

8. **CURRENT DETAINER/NOTIFICATION/CHARGE PENDING**
   Misdemeanor... 3
   Felony.. 5 ____ score

9. **PRIOR FELONY CONVICTIONS**
   One... 2
   Two or more... 4 ____ score

SCHEDULE B SCORE (combine items 5 through 9) [B]

CUSTODY LEVEL SCALE FOR TOTAL SCORE A + B:

TOTAL SCORE A + B	

☐ Close...........17 or more.

☐ Medium..........7-16.

☐ Minimum.........6 or less.

---

cc: Original - MIS Support Services - Inmate File
Institutional File
Correctional Classification Coordinator

Form 4.12
Virginia: Department of Corrections–Adult Institutions Reclassification Custody Scoring Sheet

Name____ Number________
(Last Name) (First Name) (Middle Initial)

Institution__________

Last Date Received______________________________ Date__________
(DRC or RFP)

1. HISTORY OF VIOLENCE
(Jail or prison, code most serious within last five years)
None....................................0
Assault not involving use of a weapon or resulting in serious injury...3
Assault involving use of a weapon and/or resulting in serious injury or death...........7 ____ score

2. DID ABOVE ASSAULT OCCUR WITHIN LAST SIX MONTHS?
Yes..........3 No..........0 ____ score

3. SEVERITY OF CURRENT OFFENSE
(Refer to the Severity of Offense Scale. Score the most serious offense if there are multiple convictions.)
Low or Low Moderate..........0 High..........5
Moderate..........2 Highest..........7 ____ score

4. PRIOR FELONY ASSAULTIVE HISTORY
(Score the most severe in inmate's history. Refer to the Severity of Offense Score.)
None, Low, or Low Moderate......0 High..........4
Moderate..........1 Highest..........6 ____ score

5. LENGTH OF TIME TO PAROLE ELIGIBILITY DATE, IN YEARS.......... ____ score

6. LENGTH OF TIME SINCE LAST ASSIGNED B CUSTODY *(Number of years times minus 1.)* ____ score

7. ESCAPE HISTORY
(Rate last 5 years of incarceration.)
Now in C custody or less than one year since last assigned B custody...0
No escapes or attempts and in A or B custody one year or more........ -1
An escape or attempt from A custody, no actual or threatened violence
Over 1 year ago..........0 Within the last year..........1 ____ score
An escape or attempt from B or C custody, or an escape from A custody with actual or threatened violence:
Over 1 year ago..........5 Within the last year..........7

8. NUMBER DISCIPLINARY REPORTS
None in the last 13-18 months..........-3
None in the last 7-12 months..........-2
None in the last 6 months..........-1
One in the last 6 months..........0 ____ score
Two or more in the last 6 months..........4

9. MOST SEVERE DISCIPLINARY REPORT RECEIVED *(Last 18 months.)*
None..........0 High..........5
Low Moderate..........1 Highest..........7 ____ score

10. CURRENT DETAINER
None, or prosecution/extradition not indicated..........0
Misdemeanor extradition/prosecution indicated..........3
Felony extradition/prosecution indicated..........5 ____ score

11. PRIOR FELONY CONVICTIONS
None = 0 One = 2 Two or More = 4.......... ____ score

TOTAL SCORE = ____

Form 4.12 (continued)

SCORING GUIDE

INMATE CUSTODY RECLASSIFICATION

A. DATE RECEIVED
Enter date received into state corrections system on current sentence (DRC on Uniform Commitment Form) or date returned from parole to state corrections system (RFP).

B. LAST DATE ASSIGNED B CUSTODY
If currently in "A" or "B" custody enter last date on which custody was changed from "C" to "B". If currently in "C" custody enter N/A.

1. HISTORY OF INSTITUTIONAL VIOLENCE
Include inmate's entire history of incarceration for 5 years prior to present date. Consider only incidents in which there was finding of guilty by an institutional disciplinary committee or court.

(Jail or prison, code most serious within last five years). This means the last five years of incarceration regardless of whether or not they are consecutive years, not the last five chronological years.

EXAMPLE:
History Of Institutional Violence
(Jail or prison, code most serious within last five years)
None...0
Assault not involving use of a weapon or resulting in serious injury..............3
Assault involving use of a weapon and/or resulting in serious injury or death.....7

2. DID ABOVE ASSAULT OCCUR WITHIN SIX MONTHS PRIOR TO THIS DATE?
Consider incidents which occurred 6 months ago or less. If action is pending on an incident and a conviction would change the inmate's custody, temporarily maintain inmate in present custody and schedule an administrative review as soon as possible after the disciplinary committee takes action. Enter the date of the charge as shown in Item 1.

EXAMPLE:
Did above assault occur within last six months?
Yes...0
No.............................5/22/85.......................................0

3. SEVERITY OF CURRENT OFFENSE
The current offense as described in the Initial Classification Instrument unless the inmate has been convicted of a more severe offense after commitment.

EXAMPLE:
A person is committed to prison for Forgery. While serving this term, he kills another inmate and is convicted of Second Degree Murder (Highest Category). On subsequent reclassification, his current offense would be Second Degree Murder.

4. PRIOR ASSAULTIVE OFFENSE HISTORY (NON-INSTITUTIONAL)
An assaultive crime is defined as any incident in which bodily contact occurred or was attempted, regardless of the degree of actual injury; any offense in which a weapon was present; or any offense so defined by State statute. Consider only felony offenses for which the inmate was convicted by a Court of Law.

5

Parole and Other Options: Factors Influencing Early-Release Decisions

INTRODUCTION

This chapter describes parole and parole decision making in the United States. Parole or early release from prison under an indeterminate sentencing scheme results from the action of parole boards. Most states have parole as an early-release inmate option. First, a brief history of parole in the United States is provided. In a subsequent section, the importance of parole decision making is discussed. Parole board composition and functions are described.

Prospective parolees must convince parole boards that they are not only eligible for parole but also deserving of it. Parole boards differ greatly in the variety of criteria employed for making early-release decisions about parole-eligible inmates. Therefore, the early-release criteria used by different state jurisdictions will be identified and described. A common gauge of parole effectiveness is parolee recidivism. Some parolees are returned to prison or changed to a different parole program, depending upon whether they violate conditions of their parole or commit new crimes and are convicted of them. With the rapid growth of community corrections, a greater variety of parole programs exist to accommodate parolee needs. Thus, eligible parolees may be permitted to participate in work or educational release options. Other parolees may be allowed weekend visits with their families. Yet others may be placed in halfway houses where they can readjust to community living from the more highly regimented prison environment. This chapter examines these programs and their apparent effectiveness for participating parolees.

Crucial to the effectiveness of any parolee program is solid decision making from parole boards. These bodies depend upon and utilize the most pertinent and accurate information about future parolee behaviors. Thus, some of the risk assessment instrumentation used by parole boards will be presented here and evaluated. In recent years, the quality of parole board decision making has been questioned because of the conduct of particular parolees highlighted by the media. For better or worse, these isolated instances of parolee failures have triggered widespread criticism of parole boards generally and questions about termination of parole programs. Parole boards have the power to revoke the parole program of any parolee, provided there are grounds for doing so. Parolees themselves often question actions by parole boards and seek to challenge their decisions.

A BRIEF HISTORY OF PAROLE IN THE UNITED STATES

The United States did not invent parole. Parole has European origins, although we don't know who should be credited for inventing it. The early release of offenders from prison short of serving their full terms was known in sixteenth-century France and Spain, and Great Britain and Wales also used it during the same period. Most colonists in America came from England and Wales, however, and therefore, these countries have had the greatest impact on parole in the United States. When the Revolutionary War ended, Great Britain transported many of its prisoners to remote islands near Australia. These islands included Norfolk and Van Diemen's Land. The lieutenant governor of Van Diemen's Land appointed Alexander Maconochie (1787–1860), a former naval officer, as his private secretary in 1836. In 1840, Maconochie became superintendent of a penal colony on Norfolk Island. He saw firsthand the widespread use of corporal punishment. Maconochie was very critical of the existing penal system and sought to reform it. He sent his criticisms to the British Parliament and various prison officials. As a result, he became very unpopular with his administrators. They eventually relieved him.

Maconochie was subsequently appointed as the new governor of Birmingham Borough Prison. Again, he was dismissed from this job because of his excessive leniency with prison inmates. He consistently wanted more humane treatment for prisoners. He believed that they should be rehabilitated. He suggested an incentive system whereby prisoners could earn early release for good behavior. He established a system where prisoners could accumulate "marks of commendation," much like our present good-time provisions (see Chapter 4), for good work performed and for obedience to prison rules. These marks of commendation resulted in the early release of prisoners. Early release was earned according to the following principles:

1. Early release should not be computed on the amount of time served, but rather, upon the amount of work completed.
2. Prisoners can earn marks by hard work, better conduct, and industrious working habits. Prisoner release was determined on the basis of the number of marks accumulated.
3. Prisoners must earn everything they receive. Food and other indulgences were charged against the marks they had acquired.

4. Prisoners should work in small groups; the entire group would be held accountable for the conduct of individual members.
5. Prisoners would move through various stages of progressively less discipline; eventually, they would be given more rights in their own labor, in order to prepare them for release to society (Barnes and Teeters, 1959:419).

Maconochie approved releases for well-behaved prisoners. These administrative releases functioned well as incentives for prisoners to obey prison rules. Also, some degree of order was created within the prison system. Inmate misconduct operated against their early release, and most convicts were eager to be freed as early as possible.

Sir Walter Crofton, an Irish reformer and director of Ireland's prison system, was impressed with Maconochie's work. He gradually established the Irish system, which was very similar to what Maconochie had establislied. The Irish system was more elaborate, however, including a multi-stage process by which inmates could earn early release from prison. The Irish system consisted of solitary confinement and hard labor for two years, congregate labor (comparable to what was later used at the Auburn State Penitentiary in New York) for an "indeterminate period," limited work on outside jobs (comparable to our present version of work furloughs), and finally, early conditional release through tickets-of-leave. Tickets-of-leave were written authorizations for conditional early release from prison. If one or more conditions of the early release were violated, these leaves were revoked and inmates were returned to prison. Those granted tickets-of-leave were expected to submit regular reports of their progress while free. Tickets-of-leave are considered the first formal use of parole.

While these developments were occurring in England and Ireland, Gaylord Hubbell, the Sing Sing, New York, prison warden, traveled to Ireland in 1863 to discuss penal reforms and prisoner rehabilitation with Crofton. The National Prison Association (subsequently the American Correctional Association) convened for the first time in Cincinnati, Ohio, in 1870, and Hubbell, together with Crofton, explained the advantages of the Irish system to attendees. A Declaration of Principles was established, including both indeterminate sentencing and a relatively complex offender classification system. Crofton's influence is most apparent in the design of these principles and the classification system that was established.

New York was the first state to pass a good-time law in 1817 which made it possible for prison administrators to commute inmate sentences and practice early release (Levine, Musheno, and Palumbo, 1986). A major distinction is that in 1817, early release through good-time credits was the equivalent of a pardon from the governor. Thus, this did not amount to parole in a technical sense. Nevertheless, prisoners benefitted from their early releases. The Massachusetts State Legislature became the first to implement parole in 1884 (Shane-DuBow, Brown, and Olsen, 1985:6). By 1900, at least twenty states had passed parole statutes, and by 1944, all states practiced parole. The rehabilitative ideal had been promoted in the mid-1800s. However, it gradually fell into disfavor with the public for various reasons. For one thing, parolees had high rates of recidivism. As we have seen, however, there are no universal standards to determine what is high or low recidivism.

The gradual decline of rehabilitation was also attributable to political reasons, in that rehabilitation was not considered a sufficiently tough way of dealing with criminals. Many offenders were simply not being rehabilitated. Rather, they took advantage of the system and exploited it to their own ends. Maine was the first state to abolish parole in 1976. Subsequently, a few other states greatly modified or abolished parole. The Comprehensive Crime Control Act was passed in 1984 by Congress, and it prescribed that parole should be abolished for federal prisoners commencing November 1992. Furthermore, it authorized the establishment of a commission to study the existing sentencing system and implement new and more equitable guidelines for judges to follow. The U.S. Sentencing Commission was created and established a new sentencing guidelines which were officially instituted on November 1, 1987.

Many states continue to use indeterminate sentencing and parole board systems to effect inmate early releases. Even Maine and the other states that abolished parole earlier have acted to create ways through which prisoners can be released short of serving their full terms. Maine, for example, has greatly expanded good-time credits to reduce inmate sentences by as much as 20 percent. This is an important example of what might happen if states pass too much get-tough legislation. Getting tough by abolishing parole creates extensive prison overcrowding problems. Thus, Maine authorities have had to reassess their 1976 parole abolition. It is no coincidence that these more lenient good-time provisions were enacted by the Maine Legislature in 1983, only seven years after their original get-tough stance made prison overcrowding a major problem. If the original intent of Maine officials was to deter crime by eliminating the possibility of parole, then their action was ineffective. Despite this major penal reform, crime in Maine has increased steadily during the 1980s and early 1990s.

PAROLE BOARDS: THEIR FUNCTIONS AND DIVERSITY

The current philosophy of parole in most jurisdictions is a blend of accountability, punishment, reintegration, and rehabilitation. Parole boards wish to hold offenders accountable for their earlier crimes, but at the same time, parole is considered a reward for behaving well while confined. It is believed, rightly or wrongly, that behavior while incarcerated is indicative of future behavior if released conditionally within the community through a parole program. The requirements and conditions of parole programs are designed to continue a degree of supervision over parolees while furnishing them with opportunities to be successful in their communities. This is one reason why parole programs often have curfew provisions as well as employment, placement, and counseling services. Below are several general parole aims that reflect its philosophy:

1. Parole protects the public by controlling parolee conduct through supervised release. Parole officers visit parolee residences and workplaces and verify their whereabouts, attitude, and general conduct. The greater the supervision by parole officers, the less likelihood of committing new offenses.
2. Parole reduces sentencing disparities that are often attributable to race/ethnicity, gender, and socioeconomic status. Early-release decisions are calculated, in part, to remedy earlier sentencing disparities. This does not excuse parole board decisions that are not equitable, however.
3. Parole promotes rehabilitation. Few experts believe that inmates are rehabilitated by strict confinement. Inmates involved in prison vocational programs often fail to remain employed when released. At least, parole gives ex-convicts opportunities to support their families and participate in counseling.
4. Parole is a reintegrative mechanism for easing inmates back into their communities. The prison experience is highly regimented and far different from routine community life. Inmates who have served long prison terms frequently find it difficult to make the transition to community life.
5. Parole provides inmates with an incentive to obey prison rules. Failure to behave well while incarcerated will definitely jeopardize inmates' parole chances. As we have previously seen in at least one state, good-time credits may be earned and counted against extra time to be served which is added on to an incoming inmate's sentence. If inmates earn good-time credit by obeying prison rules, then they can reduce or even eliminate this extra time to be served. In most states with good-time provisions, however, inmates may shorten their original sentences by exhibiting good behavior or conforming behavior. This is a strong incentive to do well and does much to foster orderliness in prisons.
6. Prison overcrowding is eased through parole. It functions as an administrative safety valve to control overcrowding. However, some jurisdictions have restricted or eliminated entirely conditions under which parole may be granted (U.S. Sentencing Commission, 1987).
7. Parole is a deterrent to criminal conduct, because parolees require some amount of supervision by parole officers. Those programs with higher degrees of supervisory control over parolees tend to have lower rates of recidivism. Furthermore, electronic monitoring programs have enhanced parole officer abilities to monitor client whereabouts and verify their presence at home or work. Table 5.1 shows parole board sizes for all states, the District of Columbia, and the federal government, including the means whereby members are appointed.

The Ohio Parole Board has established the following mission statement: The Board is responsible for consideration of all available relevant information of an offender eligible for release or reduction of sentence and making a final decision on appropriateness of release; parole board decisions will be made with the use of guidelines to promote fairness, objectivity, and public safety; the parole board will maintain communication with victims, members of the community and components within the criminal justice system (Ohio Department of Rehabilitation and Correction, 1989:iv). The Michigan Parole Board has a similar statement.

Table 5.1
Parole Board Size and Nature of Parole Board Appointments in the United States

STATE	SIZE OF PAROLE BOARD	NATURE OF APPOINTMENT	FUNCTIONS
Alabama	3	Governor	Paroles adults, provides adult probation services
Alaska	5	Governor	Paroles adults
Arizona	7	Governor	Paroles adults, reviews executive clemency decisions
Arkansas	5	Governor	Paroles adults
California	10	Governor	Paroles adults, disparate sentence review, parole consideration for lifers
Colorado	5	Governor	Paroles adults
Connecticut	11	Governor	Paroles adults
Delaware	6	Governor	Paroles adults
Florida	9	Governor	Paroles adults
Georgia	5	Autonomous	Paroles adults, grants reprieves, pardons, commutations
Hawaii	3	Governor	Paroles adults
Idaho	5	Board of Corrections	Paroles adults
Illinois	10	Governor	Paroles adults
Indiana	5	Governor	Paroles adults, reviews clemency applications for those serving life
Iowa	5	Governor	Paroles adults
Kansas	3	Governor	Paroles

Table 5.1 (continued)

			adults, reviews clemency applications
Kentucky	7	Governor	Paroles adults
Louisiana	5	Governor	Paroles adults
Maine*	5	Governor	Paroles adults
Maryland	7	Secretary of Public Safety	Paroles adults, reviews clemency applications
Massachusetts	7	Governor	Paroles adults
Michigan	7	Department of Corrections	Paroles adults
Minnesota**		Commissioner of Corrections	Paroles adults
Mississippi	5	Governor	Paroles adults
Missouri	5	Governor	Paroles adults
Montana	***	Corrections Division	Paroles adults
Nebraska	5	Governor	Paroles adults
Nevada	3	Governor	Paroles adults
New Hampshire	5	Governor	Paroles adults
New Jersey	7	Governor	Paroles adults and juveniles
New Mexico	3	Governor	Paroles adults, reviews clemency applications
New York	15	Governor	Paroles adults
North Carolina	5	Governor	Paroles adults
North Dakota	3	Governor	Paroles adults
Ohio	7	Governor	Paroles adults
Oklahoma	5	Governor	Paroles adults, reviews pardons
Oregon	5	Governor	Paroles adults
Pennsylvania	5	Governor	Paroles adults
Rhode Island	5	Governor	Paroles adults
South Carolina	7	Governor	Paroles adults
South Dakota	3	Board of Charities and Corrections	Paroles adults

Table 5.1 (continued)

Tennessee............	5	Governor	Paroles adults
Texas................	6	Independent agency	Paroles adults
Utah.................	3	Board of Corrections	Paroles adults, reviews pardons
Vermont..............	5	Governor	Paroles adults
Virginia.............	5	Governor	Paroles adults
Washington...........	5	Independent agency	Paroles adults, fixes minimum terms
West Virginia........	3	Governor	Paroles adults
Wisconsin............	7	Secretary of Department of Health and Human Services	Paroles adults
Wyoming..............	5	Governor	Paroles adults
District of Columbia..	3	Mayor	Paroles adults
Federal Government....	****	U.S. Parole Commission	Paroles adults

*Maine has abolished parole; the Maine Parole Board meets only to hear parole requests from pre-1976 inmates.

**Minnesota abolished the Corrections Board in 1982; since then, the Office of Adult Release makes recommendations concerning parole for applicants, with the exception of those serving life sentences; a special advisory panel advises the Commissioner regarding life sentence inmates who apply for parole.

***Montana has a Board of Pardons which is attached administratively to the Division of Corrections but is autonomous in its authority to parole adults.

****U.S. Parole Commission uses services of regional staff for classification summaries, progress reports, and other materials concerning parole applicants.

Massachusetts probably has the most stringent criteria for parole board membership compared with other jurisdictions. Members of the Massachusetts Parole Board must possess a bachelor's degree and five or more years of experience in corrections, law enforcement, social work, or other related field. One parole board member must be an attorney, while another must be a physician. States such as Texas, Oregon, and North Dakota do not prescribe special qualifications. Governors make parole board appointments in most jurisdictions. Thus, membership on these boards is highly politicized.

Major functions of most parole boards include the following:

1. To evaluate prison inmates who are eligible for parole and act on their application to approve or deny parole;
2. To convene to determine whether a parolee's parole should be revoked on the basis of alleged parole violations;

3. To evaluate juveniles to determine their eligibility for release from detention;
4. To grant pardons or commutations of sentences to prisoners, where mitigating circumstances or new information is presented which was not considered at trial;
5. To make provisions for the supervision of adult offenders placed on parole; to establish supervisory agencies and select parole officers to monitor offender behavior;
6. To provide investigative and supervisory services to smaller jurisdictions within the state;
7. To grant reprieves in death sentence cases and to commute death penalties;
8. To restore full civil and political rights to parolees and others on conditional release including probationers;
9. To review disparate sentences and make recommendations to the governor for clemency; and
10. To review the pardons and executive clemency decisions made by the governor.

Most parole boards make parole decisions exclusively. In a limited number of jurisdictions, these additional functions are performed, either according to statute or at the pleasure of the governor. In a limited number of jurisdictions, the paroling authority is vested in agencies independent of the governor.

FACTORS INFLUENCING EARLY-RELEASE DECISIONS

The successfulness of parole board decision making is frequently measured by the degree of recidivism among parolees. Descriptive information about recidivist-parolees is abundant, although there is considerable inconsistency about which characteristics seem most associated with recidivism. Complicating the picture is the fact that many measures of recidivism are used, and each of these measures refers to a different conceptual phenomenon. For example, the Delaware Executive Department (1984) has shown that among parolees from Delaware prisons, those serving longer sentences have a greater likelihood of being rearrested and returned to prison than those serving shorter sentences. A study of parolees in fourteen states in the late 1970s showed that property offenders had higher rates of recidivism (return to prison) than violent offenders (Wallerstedt, 1984). But a study of North Carolina parolees conducted during the same period (1979–1980) showed that recidivism (return to prison) was higher for violent offenders than for property offenders (Clarke and Crum, 1985). With these sorts of contradictions, it is difficult for parole boards to formulate consistent policies about which prisoners should be granted parole and which prisoners should not be granted it.

These descriptions of parolees who are most likely to recidivate are interesting and insightful, but they don't tell us much about which inmates are going to recidivate when released. In a nonscientific sense, parole board members will often say that subjective impressions are their basic guides in making early-release decisions. The most fruitful predictors of parole success are age and prior record

(Wilson, 1985; Roundtree, Edwards, and Parker, 1984; Clarke and Crum, 1985; Boudouris, 1983). In Hoffman's Salient Factor Score Index (SFS 81) and other scales based upon it, the variable *age* is given considerable weight. But recidivism rates also depend upon the type of parole program. A trend toward establishing community-based corrections programs has been observed in recent years. Many of these programs include close supervision of offenders. Intensive supervised probation for probationers, house arrest or home incarceration, electronic monitoring, and other community-based programs are currently operating in many communities throughout the United States (McCarthy and McCarthy, 1984). Some of these programs will be discussed in a subsequent section.

Which factors and inmate characteristics seem most influential to parole board decision making? The Ohio Parole Board, for example, uses the following criteria primarily as guidelines:

1. Current offense and details of the crime
2. Prior record: felonies-misdemeanors-juvenile
3. Supervision experiences: parole-furlough-probation
4. Institution adjustment: job assignment-work evaluation-rule infractions
5. Substance abuse program participation
6. Vocational or academic training
7. Personality evaluation: I.Q.-highest grade completed
8. Psychological reports
9. Psychiatric reports
10. Personal history factors: marital status-employment history-work skills-special problems
11. Parole plan: living arrangements-employment plans
12. Community attitude: prosecutor's recommendation-judge's recommendation-police or sheriff's recommendation-victim's statement
13. Detainers
14. Type and number of prior hearings
15. Results of prehearing conference with Case Manager or Unit Manager (Ohio Department of Rehabilitation and Correction, 1989:4).

The Ohio Parole Board is careful to note, however, that these criteria are as indicated—guidelines. Thus, there may be departures—more or less punitive, considering the degree of aggravation or mitigation—accompanying any eligible inmate's early-release request. It is Ohio's experience that using these criteria in conjunction with several other measures will increase Parole Board effectiveness to about 75 percent. In short, Ohio authorities believe that 75 percent of their early-release decisions with these guidelines will result in successful decision making. Viewed another way, Ohio authorities expect no more than a 25 percent degree of recidivism among those paroled.

Actually, Ohio bases its guidelines system on five major components:

1. Risk Instrument: The risk instrument is critical to the guidelines system. It looks at several factors dealing with an inmate's prior criminal history including the number of probations, paroles, and revocations. Age at first felony conviction and substance abuse history are also related to risk assessed points. The risk level totals equal 1, 2, or 3. The higher the number, the higher the risk.
2. Offense Score: Included in the guideline system are several offenses designated as "Endangering Offenses." If an inmate has ever been convicted of an Endangering Offense, either as a juvenile or adult, one point is assessed towards the total score.
3. Institutional Score: The Parole Board will make a determination of the inmate's institutional adjustment at the time of the hearing. If the inmate is now serving or has recently served time in Disciplinary Control, Local Control or Administrative Control, one (1) point will be assessed towards the total score.
4. Aggregate Score: The sum total of the Risk Score, the Offense Score, and the Institution Score equals the Aggregate Score.
5. Matrix: The Matrix is a grid containing twenty-four (24) cell divisions. Each cell contains the guidelines procedure into which an inmate is placed and a continuance range if the decision is not to release. The horizontal axis of the grid is the "Aggregate Score" 1–5. The vertical axis is the felony level reflecting the inmate's sentence. Sentences range from fourth degree to Life (Ohio Department of Rehabilitation and Correction, 1989:6–7).

The Federal Bureau of Prisons uses the SFS 81 for determining parole eligibility or, more recently, supervised release, for its eligible inmates. The Salient Factor Score Index consists of six criteria, including (1) prior convictions/delinquency adjudications; (2) prior commitments of more than thirty days (either as an adult or as a juvenile); (3) age at current offense/prior commitments; (4) recent commitment-free period (three years); (5) probation/parole/confinement/escape status violator this time; and (6) heroin/opiate dependence. Eligible federal inmates receive up to three points for no prior convictions or delinquency adjudications, up to two points for no prior commitments of more than thirty days (as either an adult or a juvenile), up to two points for being twenty-six or older at the time of the current offense, and one point each for no prior commitment (in last three years), no probation/parole/confinement/escape status at time of current offense, and no history of opiate addiction. Thus, federal inmates can score a possible ten points and minimize their parole risk status. Scores of zero (0) or close to zero mean higher or highest parole risk.

Massachusetts has a similar parole risk instrument, with some interesting variations. For instance, the Massachusetts Parole Board uses a Release Risk Classification Instrument consisting of (1) number of returns to higher custody since Controlling Effective Date of Commitment; (2) custody standing prior to the Controlling Effective Date of Commitment; (3) total number of parole revocations; (4) number of adult convictions for property offenses; (5) number of charges for a person offense as a juvenile: (6) age at release hearing; and (7) evidence of heroin, opiate, or crack cocaine use. Both the number of returns to higher custody and age have maximum scores of "6" for four or more returns to higher custody and being twenty-three years of age or younger. Custody standing and evidence of drug use each contribute two points, while the other factors are weighted by one point each. A high score of nineteen points is possible. Such a person might be a twenty-two-year-old cocaine addict who has prior offenses of burglary as an adult and robbery as a juvenile, has been returned to a higher custody level on four previous occasions, has one previous parole revocation, and was incarcerated prior to the Controlling Effective Date. A three-part scale is used: 0–4 = low risk, 5–10 = moderate risk, and 11+ = high risk.

A fourth jurisdiction, Utah, uses the following factors to determine parole eligibility: (1) age at first arrest; (2) prior juvenile record; (3) prior adult arrests; (4) correctional supervision history; (5) supervision risk; (6) percentage of time employed in last twelve months, prior to incarceration; (7) alcohol usage problems; (8) drug usage problems; (9) attitude (motivation to change, willing to accept responsibility); (10) address changes during last twelve months (prior to incarceration); (11) family support; and (12) conviction or juvenile adjudication for assaultive offense in last five years.

It is clear that age, prior record, and drug/alcohol dependencies are significant risk scale components, at least for these instruments. In fact, these are critical components of most scales examined. Many jurisdictions believe that one's employment history and attitude (measured different ways) are also crucial to good parole decision making. The rationale for including these different components is grounded in considerable empirical research. We have already seen that many studies have focused upon recidivism and the characteristics of recidivists. Most of these studies have provided us with the bases for making actuarial predictions for various offender aggregates. Thus, younger offenders have higher recidivism rates than older offenders (Baird et al., 1987; Bonham, 1984; Decker and Salert, 1986). The age at which the onset of criminal behavior occurs is an important predictor. The earlier the onset of criminal conduct, the more likely recidivism will occur (Murphy, 1980:14). Those with poor previous employment histories have greater recidivism compared with those with good previous employment histories. Alcohol and/or drug dependencies seem highly correlated with program failure. Unstable community and family life (indicated, in part, by frequent changes of address and evidence of family instability) are also associated with higher recidivism rates. Likewise, poor attitudes toward accepting responsibility for one's actions seem indicative of higher recidivism than good attitudes in this regard. Independent investigations of each of these factors as predictors has confirmed their utility for accurate parole forecasting (Gottfredson and Gottfredson, 1990; Haapanen, 1988; Hiday, 1990; Hughes, 1985; Kalichman, 1988; Komala and Shepperd, 1990; Maier, 1989; McGrath, 1991; Rogers, Gillis, and Dickens, 1989; Towberman, 1992; Valenzuela, Vallaneuva, and Aguilera, 1991; Wright, 1988; Zimmerman and Cohen, 1990). Some investigators have also noted that gender is a distinguishing variable in some parole decision making. Therefore, gender may make a difference to one's parole chances (Erez, 1992).

Form 5.1 shows an inventory used by the Nevada Department of Corrections to assess inmate parole success (see forms at end of this chapter). This instrument contains Parole Success Likelihood Factors, including age, prior convictions, incarcerations since age seventeen, history of drug abuse, employment history, use of a weapon in the instant offense, and prison programming. On the basis of his or her score on this instrument, a prospective parolee will be placed into one severity level or another. These inmate placements significantly influence parole likelihood and subsequent parole board action. The Nevada Board of Parole Commissioners' recommendation and action are committed to writing and are illustrated by the form in Form 5.2.

Additional examples of instruments used by parole boards in various states are shown in Forms 5.3, 5.4, and 5.5. The North Dakota Parole Board uses an instrument as shown in Form 5.3. A simpler initial client assessment form is shown for North Carolina in Form 5.4. This form solicits and uses information about inmate financial situation, employment/student status, marital status, educational attainment, general attitude, and prior history of alcohol or drug dependencies. The instrument shown in Form 5.5 shows Parole Success Factors used by the Georgia Parole Board.

Similar to initial classifications conducted by prison officials and subsequent reassessments of inmates, parole boards also utilize reassessments of client risk after parolees have functioned for several months in their respective parole programs. Forms 5.6, 5.7, and 5.8 show different types of reassessment instruments used by North Carolina, Oregon, and Indiana. It should be noted that extensive explanatory commentaries accompany each of these instruments. It is beyond the scope of the present work to display all of this explanatory information. Rather, it is our intent to show the types of factors considered relevant by parole boards in determining whether an inmate's parole program should be continued or terminated.

Some jurisdictions have established rather specific prediction schemes based upon some or all of these criteria. For example, Michigan has created five risk groupings based primarily upon age, marital status, and previous institutional conduct. These are shown below:

RISK GROUP

Very High Risk: Instant offense of rape, robbery, or homicide and serious misconduct or security segregation and first arrest before 15th birthday.

High Risk: Instant offense of rape, robbery, or homicide and serious misconduct and age of first arrest was 15 or over.

Middle Risk: Instant offense (either rape, robbery, or homicide and no serious misconduct; or instant offense not rape, robbery, or homicide may be other assaultive crime) and no reported felony while juvenile and never been married at time of instant offense.

Very Low Risk: Instant offense not rape, robbery, or homicide and no reported felony while juvenile and not serving on other assaultive crime and has been married (Murphy, 1980:3).

Some criteria, such as a detainer, previous institutional misconduct, and one's personality profile, all seem to indicate whether would-be parolees would be successful if released short of serving their full sentences. A detainer warrant means that another jurisdiction wants the inmate on other charges. Thus, if detainer warrants are outstanding, a parolee might be more likely to flee the jurisdiction to escape prosecution from other jurisdictions. Institutional misconduct suggests an inability or unwillingness to comply with existing institutional rules. How will the offender react to a different set of rules if released on parole in the community? Does one type of behavior, nonconformist conduct, while incarcerated indicate similar behavior, nonconformist conduct, in a new situation? The chances are that if inmates are unruly while confined, they will be poor parole risks later. Finally, personality assessments are helpful to determine an inmate's potential for adjusting to community life. Personality disturbances or personal problems may interfere with normal functioning. If these problems can be detected in advance of parole, then affected inmates might benefit from specific treatment plans.

Ohio has one of the most comprehensive early-release schemes compared with other jurisdictions. The Ohio Parole Board incorporates all or most criteria used by other states. In addition, information is obtained relating to personality through psychiatric reports. Parolees must also file a parole plan, indicating their stability in the community if paroled. The Board also obtains input from victims, if any. Almost every salient dimension of an inmate's social and psychological life is profiled by the Board to render the most objective parole decisions. Despite this extensive personal and social information, however, the Board does not expect perfection in prediction. Again, the Board anticipates an accuracy factor of about 75 percent.

The National Council on Crime and Delinquency (1990a, 1990b) has examined risk prediction extensively and has constructed risk assessment devices for various states, including California, South Carolina, Oregon, Alaska, Illinois, Louisiana, and Tennessee (National Council on Crime and Delinquency, 1990b). The Council's survey of existing or currently used instruments indicates the following factors that most often appear as risk predictors:

1. Number of prior convictions
2. Number of prior incarcerations
3. Age at first commitment, conviction, or arrest
4. Drug abuse history
5. Convictions for burglary, forgery, theft
6. Alcohol abuse history
7. Employment history

8. School adjustment
9. Probation/parole history
10. Peer involvement (1990b:5).

Despite the predictive utility of these items, individually or collectively considered, the Council has incurred a failure rate in certain sample predictions of about 30 percent. The chief problem, according to the Council, is that accurate data concerning prospective parolees is often difficult to obtain. Therefore, predictions of success for different offender aggregates are always tainted by the unknown influence of extraneous variables (National Council on Crime and Delinquency, 1990b:6–7).

Another important factor is the extent to which offenders will be supervised when released. The closer the supervision, the greater the compliance with program requirements. Intensive supervised parole, with more face-to-face visits and drug/alcohol testing, seems to have a lower amount of recidivism compared with more standardized parole programs. Some programs for prospective parolees are most helpful in making the transition to community living, however. For instance, work and study release and furlough programs enable many program participants to gradually accept community responsibilities and prove themselves for full parole later. The rates of recidivism associated with these programs are considerably lower than rates of recidivism associated with standard parole.

WORK RELEASE

One type of temporary release program is work release. As we saw in an earlier chapter, work release (also called work furlough, day parole, day pass, and community work) refers to any program that provides for the labor of jail or prison inmates in the community under limited supervision, and that pays inmates the prevailing wage (McCarthy and McCarthy, 1984:159–160). From time to time, *work release* and *furlough* are used interchangeably, referring to activities such as participation in an educational program or work experience not immediately available to other incarcerated prison inmates. Work and study release programs seem directly connected with inmates' success chances when paroled. Inmates can acquire greater education and work skills to make them more employable.

In 1989, there were over 20,000 inmates on work release in the United States (Herrick, 1989:9). Herrick (1989:9) notes that most inmates who are likely to obtain work release are within a year of their parole or early release dates. One important component of these work release programs is that inmates are obligated to pay for their room and board. Most of these work releasees eventually complete their programs successfully. Besides the early-release date, other criteria for involvement in a work release program in most jurisdictions include the inmate's institutional record, physical and mental condition, proportion of sentence served and type of offense, classification status, criminal and escape history, and any pending detainers or warrants.

Besides exhibiting certain rehabilitative and reintegrative value, work release is also perceived by officials in at least nineteen jurisdictions as an alternative means of alleviating prison overcrowding (Herrick, 1989:9). But the low incidence of recidivism among work releasees suggests that the long-range benefit is enabling inmates to readjust to community living and providing them with the means to maintain or increase their employment potential. In fact, many of these work release programs have built-in arrangements where institutional counselors exist to provide job assistance and counseling. Working closely with various state employment agencies, these counselors are able to place many offenders in jobs. Other inmate placements may be in Job Training and Partnership Act programs that exist in at least sixteen states. Besides low recidivism rates, these work release programs also have low escape rates and a general lack of major incidents involving releasees.

EDUCATION RELEASE

Similar to work release is education release. In 1989, thirty-three states had educational release programs. Ohio had the largest number of educational releasees, with about 250 of them. No other system had more than 80 educational releasees (Davis, 1989:9). Educational release programs involve less than 5 percent of the number of inmates who participate in work release. Thus, in 1989 there were fewer than 900 inmates on educational release in the United States (Davis, 1989:9). The criteria for involvement in educational release programs are virtually identical for work release. Inmates must be within a set amount of time before regular discharge from prison or the parole date. Further, inmates must have clean institutional records, a low custody classification, no escape convictions, and no outstanding felony detainers. It is also important that inmates demonstrate an ability to pay for the educational costs associated with these programs.

Like their work releasee counterparts, eligible inmates who participate in educational release also exhibit low rates of recidivism, less than 10 percent. It should be noted, however, that some degree of "creaming" occurs, as authorities sift their inmate roles to determine only those most eligible. Inmates who have caused or participated in institutional disturbances, those with violent criminal histories, those with alcohol/drug dependencies, or those with outstanding felony detainers are among the least eligible for both work release and educational release program membership. Thus, program participation is a significant reward for those considered eligible.

FURLOUGHS

Furloughs or unescorted leaves from the prison granted to certain inmates are another early-release option for paroling authorities to consider. The typical furlough length is three days, where certain prisoners are granted leaves to attend funerals of family members or strengthen family ties (*Corrections Compendium,* 1992:19). In 1988, the number of furloughees in the United States was about 170,000 (Marlette, 1990:6). This figure represented a 30,000 decrease in the number of furloughees in 1987, or 200,000. One reason for the drastic drop in the number of furloughees was the media attention paid to the Massachusetts furlough program by the 1988 presidential candidates, George Bush and Michael Dukakis. An inmate serving a life sentence without parole was granted a furlough and escaped. The inmate, Willie Horton, subsequently raped a woman and stabbed her husband. His deeds while a furloughee sparked heated debate about the utility of furlough programs generally.

It is probably the case that Horton's involvement in the Massachusetts furlough program was atypical of most furloughees. For one thing, almost every furlough program bars such inmates with Horton's record from participating. Nevertheless, the damage was done, and furlough programs throughout the United States were drastically overhauled, even abandoned in some cases. Thus, in 1988 Nevada, New Hampshire, and three other states dropped their furlough programs entirely. Louisiana temporarily suspended its furlough program pending a major investigation and recommendation from experts (Marlette, 1990:6–7).

The manifest intent of furlough programs is to enable inmates to acquire experience with living on the outside (Tobin, 1983). Many furloughees can live with their families, make arrangements for long-term employment when released, participate in counseling, take educational courses or job training, and do many of the things routinely expected of work and educational releasees. However, furloughees do not appear to have the same types of program obligations. Furloughees must have sponsors, or responsible persons who will supervise them while free from prison regimentation and control. Sponsors may be family members, volunteers, or others approved by the corrections departments of different states (Marlette, 1990:6–7).

Eligibility requirements include minimum security status, within a certain time to parole or release date, and a good institutional record (Davis, 1991:10–12). Most states exclude sex offenders from involvement in furlough programs. Likewise, violent offenders may be excluded (Marlette, 1990:6). Further, victims may be contacted, may appear, and may offer testimony at hearings when an inmate's eligibility for furlough program involvement is to be determined. Interestingly, the recidivism rates of furloughees are most commendable. Some jurisdictions, such as Iowa, New Mexico, and Maryland, have reported a 100 percent success rate with their furloughees. Thus, recidivism among these persons is zero. Only two states had recidivism rates higher than 10 percent. These included Indiana (15 percent) and Oregon (25 percent). These low recidivism rates suggest that furlough programs are very instrumental in effective transitions from prison to community living for most inmate-participants. Institutional conduct is used as a significant predictor of subsequent program success. Thus, inmates who have no past history of institutional disruption and who are currently in minimum-security custody stand good chances of qualifying for furloughs.

Many of the instruments used for parole risk are also used to evaluate work release, educational release, and furlough candidacy.

HALFWAY HOUSES

An integral feature of community correction programs is the halfway house. These houses are either publicly or privately operated facilities staffed by professionals, paraprofessionals, and volunteers. Assisting parolees in making the transition from prison to the community, halfway houses provide food, clothing, temporary living quarters, employment assistance, and limited counseling. Again, if parolees have been confined for a long period, their transition to community living can be quite difficult (Donnelly and Forschner, 1984). Two-thirds of all states have halfway houses for parolees. The Prisoner Rehabilitation Act passed by Congress in 1965 authorized the creation of community-based residences for both adults and juveniles (Wilson, 1985). Typically, parolees assigned to halfway houses are generally in need of temporary housing to effect their full transition to community living. Halfway houses do not necessarily offer programs. Rather, they furnish ex-inmates a place to stay temporarily, counseling, and employment assistance. Many of these facilities are privately operated and staffed with volunteers. Estimates about the effectiveness of halfway houses are difficult to make, since little published information is available about halfway house success rates on a national scale. A general impression is that halfway houses assist many parolees during their transition periods, however. Recidivism rates of those who have used the services of halfway houses are relatively low (Donnelly and Forschner, 1984; McCarthy and McCarthy, 1984; Wilson, 1985).

DECISIONS BY PAROLE BOARDS TO GRANT OR DENY PAROLE

Parole boards do not have to automatically grant parole to anyone eligible to receive it. These boards have considerable discretionary power and almost absolute discretion over inmates' parole chances. Even when federal courts have been petitioned to intervene and challenge parole board actions, the decisions of parole boards have usually been upheld (*Tarlton v. Clark,* 1971). While we have already examined parole boards, their composition, and their functions, it is helpful to review briefly some of the more important factors influencing parole board decision making. In deciding whether to grant parole for given inmates or not grant parole, the following factors are considered:

1. The commission of serious disciplinary infractions while confined
2. The nature and pattern of previous convictions
3. The adjustment to previous probation, parole, and/or incarceration
4. The facts and circumstances of the offense
5. The aggravating and mitigating factors surrounding the offense

6. Participation in institutional programs that might have led to the improvement of problems diagnosed at admission or during incarceration
7. Documented changes in attitude toward self or others
8. Documentation of personal goals and strengths or motivation for law-abiding behavior
9. Parole plans
10. Inmate statements suggesting the likelihood that the inmate will not commit future offenses
11. Court statements about the reasons for the sentence (the presentence investigation report) (Dietz, 1985:32).

If parole boards grant certain inmates parole, then parole is usually conditional and subject to several rules and regulations. If parole board action is unfavorable and parole for certain inmates is denied, one or more reasons are given by these boards for their action. Parole boards in most jurisdictions must list the reasons for their actions or at least state their reasons for parole denials. These reasons provide inmates with opportunities to remedy past behaviors and to improve in those areas cited by the board as unsatisfactory or unfavorable. In most jurisdictions, rehearings are scheduled either annually or semiannually. In some jurisdictions, such as the District of Columbia, efforts are being made to extend parole release to older offenders and those suffering from various medical problems (*Corrections Compendium,* 1993:6). Medical and geriatric parolees would be those who fit the following qualification: "When confinement will greatly endanger or shorten the resident's life, and the resident's release poses no threat to society" (*Corrections Compendium,* 1993:6).

PAROLE REVOCATION ACTIONS

In 1987, about 21 percent of all parolees had their parole programs revoked (*Corrections Compendium,* 1989b:8). The primary reasons for parole revocations in the United States in 1987 included the following:

1. Failure to participate in stipulated treatment programs (44 percent)
2. Leaving assigned area without permission (44 percent)
3. Failure to report to parole officer (43 percent)
4. Alcohol or drug abuse (42 percent)
5. Failure to secure or hold employment (28 percent)
6. Possession of firearms
7. Failure to pay restitution or fines
8. Failure to comply with special conditions
9. Visiting or writing inmates without permission
10. Changing residence or employment without permission
11. Failure to report arrests, curfew violations (*Corrections Compendium,* 1989b:8).

Many of these 33,823 parole revocations in 1987 involved nonprison alternatives, such as a change in a parolee's program plan, assignment to a treatment center, assignment to a work release or other community center, electronic monitoring, house arrest, or intensive supervision (*Corrections Compendium,* 1989b:8).

Whenever parole has been granted and parolees are supervised by parole officers, parole may be revoked for several compelling reasons. Parole revocation is the decision to rescind parole and return parolees to prison, usually to serve the remainder of the originally imposed sentence, or to some other more intensified version of a parole program (e.g., home confinement with electronic monitoring). Before 1972, the right to due process for parolees was ignored by the courts. If certain technical violations were committed, including failing to submit a monthly report, submitting a falsified report, drinking alcoholic beverages, or violating curfew, parole officers could act to effect a parolee's return to prison. Parolees had little or no legal standing to challenge revocation decisions. Several landmark cases have vested all parolees and probationers with various due process rights, however. These landmark cases include (1) *Mempa v. Rhay* (1967), (2) *Morrissey v. Brewer* (1972), and (3) *Gagnon v. Scarpelli* (1973).

1. *Mempa v. Rhay* (1967). *Mempa* involved a probation revocation rather than a parole revocation, although the decision eventually influenced parole proceedings significantly. Jerry Mempa was convicted of "joyriding" in a stolen vehicle on June 17, 1959. He was placed on probation for two years by a Spokane, Washington, judge. Several months later, Mempa was involved in a burglary on September 15, 1959. The county prosecutor in Spokane moved to have Mempa's probation revoked. Mempa admitted participating in the burglary. At his probation revocation hearing, the sole testimony about his involvement in the burglary came from his probation officer. Mempa was not represented by counsel, was not asked if he wanted counsel, and was not given an opportunity to offer statements in his own behalf. Furthermore, there was no cross-examination of the probation officer about his statements. The court revoked Mempa's probation and sentenced him to ten years in the Washington State Penitentiary.

Six years later in 1965, Mempa filed a writ of *habeas corpus,* alleging that he had been denied a right to counsel at the revocation hearing. The Washington Supreme Court denied his petition, but the U.S. Supreme Court elected to hear it on appeal. The U.S. Supreme Court overturned the Washington decision and ruled in Mempa's favor. Specifically, the U.S. Supreme Court said Mempa was entitled to an attorney but was denied one. While the Court did not question Washington authority to defer sentencing in the probation matter, it said that any indigent (including Mempa) is entitled at every stage of a criminal proceeding to be represented by court-appointed counsel, where "substantial rights of a criminal accused may be affected." Thus, the U.S. Supreme Court considered a probation revocation hearing to be a "critical stage" that falls within the due process provisions of the Fourteenth Amendment. In subsequent years, several courts also applied this decision to parole revocation hearings.

2. *Morrissey v. Brewer* (1972). The first major case involving the constitu-

tional rights of parolees was *Morrissey v. Brewer* (1972). In 1967, John Morrissey was convicted by an Iowa court for "falsely drawing checks" and sentenced to not more than seven years in the Iowa State Prison. He was eventually paroled from prison in June 1968. However, seven months later, his parole officer learned that while on parole, Morrissey had bought a car under an assumed name and operated it without permission, obtained credit cards under a false name, and given false information to an insurance company when he was involved in a minor automobile accident. Also, Morrissey had given his parole officer a false address for his residence.

Morrissey's parole officer interviewed him and subsequently filed a report recommending that parole be revoked. Reasons for the revocation action given by the officer included the fact that Morrissey admitted buying the car and obtaining false I.D., obtaining credit under false pretenses, and being involved in the auto accident. Morrissey claimed he was ill, and that being ill prevented him from maintaining continuous contact with his parole officer. The parole officer claimed that Morrissey's parole should be revoked because Morrissey had a habit of continually violating the rules. The parole board revoked Morrissey's parole, and he was returned to the Iowa State Prison to serve the remainder of his sentence. Morrissey was not represented by counsel at the revocation proceeding. Furthermore, he was not given the opportunity to cross-examine witnesses against him, he was not advised in writing of the charges against him, no disclosure of the evidence against him was provided, and reasons for the revocation were not given. Morrissey also was not permitted to offer evidence in his own behalf or give personal testimony.

Morrissey's appeal to the Iowa Supreme Court was rejected, but the U.S. Supreme Court heard his appeal. While the Court did not address directly the question of whether Morrissey should have had court-appointed counsel, it did make a landmark decision in his case. It overturned the Iowa Parole Board action and established a two-stage proceeding for determining whether parole ought to be revoked. The first or preliminary hearing is held at the time of arrest and detention, where it is determined whether probable cause exists that the parolee actually committed the alleged parole violation. The second hearing is more involved and establishes the guilt of the parolee relating to the violations. This proceeding must extend to the parolee certain minimum due process rights. These rights are

1. the right to have written notice of the alleged violations of parole conditions;
2. the right to have disclosed to the parolee any evidence of the alleged violation;
3. the right of the parolee to be heard in person and to present exculpatory evidence as well as witnesses in his behalf;
4. the right to confront and cross-examine adverse witnesses, unless cause exists why they should not be cross-examined;
5. the right to a judgment by a neutral and detached body, such as the parole board itself; and
6. the right to a written statement of the reasons for the parole revocation.

Thus, the significance of the *Morrissey* case is that it set forth minimum due process rights for all parolees, creating a two-stage proceeding whereby the alleged infractions of parole conditions could be examined and a full hearing conducted to determine the most appropriate disposition of the offender. It is not mandatory that these are proceedings of record, however. In short, verbatim transcripts of parole revocation proceedings are not required. Minimum due process in such proceedings obligates authorities only to provide a written statement of evidence relied upon as well as the reasons for revoking the parole initially (*Glumb v. Honsted,* 1990).

3. *Gagnon v. Scarpelli* (1973). Since the matter of representation by counsel was not addressed directly in Morrissey's case, and since it had been the subject of previous U.S. Supreme Court action in the case of Jerry Mempa, it was only a matter of time before the U.S. Supreme Court made a decision about a parolee's right to court-appointed counsel in a parole revocation proceeding. This decision was rendered by the U.S. Supreme Court in the case of *Gagnon v. Scarpelli* (1973) a year following the *Morrissey* ruling.

Gerald Scarpelli pled guilty to a charge of robbery in July 1965 in a Wisconsin court. He was sentenced to fifteen years in prison. But the judge suspended this sentence on August 5, 1965, and placed Scarpelli on probation for a period of seven years. The next day, August 6, Scarpelli was arrested and charged with burglary. His probation was revoked without a hearing, and he was placed in the Wisconsin State Reformatory to serve his fifteen-year term. About three years later, Scarpelli was paroled. Shortly before his parole, he filed a *habeas corpus* petition, alleging that his probation revocation was invoked without a hearing and without benefit of counsel. Thus, this revocation constituted a denial of due process. Following his parole, the U.S. Supreme Court acted on his original *habeas corpus* petition and ruled in his favor. Specifically, the U.S. Supreme Court said that Scarpelli was denied his right to due process because no revocation hearing was held and he was not represented by court-appointed counsel within the indigent claim. In effect, the Court, referring to *Morrissey v. Brewer* (1972), said that "a probation revocation, like parole revocation, is not a stage of a criminal prosecution, but does result in loss of liberty. . . . We hold that a probationer, like a parolee, is entitled to a preliminary hearing and a final revocation hearing in the conditions specified in *Morrissey v. Brewer.*"

The significance of this case is that it equated probation with parole as well as the respective revocation proceedings. While the Court did not say that all parolees and probationers have a right to representation by counsel in all probation and parole revocation proceedings, it did say that counsel should be provided in cases where the probationer or parolee makes a timely claim contesting the allegations. While no constitutional basis exists for providing counsel in all probation or parole revocation proceedings, subsequent probation and parole revocation hearings usually involve defense counsel if legitimately requested. The U.S. Supreme Court declaration has been liberally interpreted in subsequent cases.

Two additional cases involving parolees and probationers and whether their probation or parole programs ought to be revoked are *Bearden v. Georgia* (1983) and *Black v. Romano* (1985) and are worth mentioning here. In the *Bearden* case, Bearden's probation was revoked by Georgia authorities because he failed to pay a fine and make restitution to his victim as required by the court. He claimed he was indigent, but the court rejected his claim as a valid explanation for his conduct. The U.S. Supreme Court disagreed. It ruled that probation may not be revoked in the case of indigent probationers who have failed to pay their fines or make restitution. They further suggested alternatives for restitution and punishments that were more compatible with the abilities and economic resources of indigent probationers such as community service. In short, probationers and parolees cannot be penalized where they have made a reasonable effort to pay their court-ordered fines and restitution.

In *Black v. Romano* (1985), a probationer's probation program was revoked because of alleged program violations. The defendant had left the scene of an automobile accident, a felony in the jurisdiction where the alleged offense occurred. The judge gave reasons for the revocation decision, but did not indicate that he had considered any option other than incarceration. The U.S. Supreme Court ruled that judges are not generally obligated to consider alternatives to incarceration before they revoke an offender's probation and place him in jail or prison. Clearly, probationers and parolees have obtained substantial rights in recent years. U.S. Supreme Court decisions have provided them with several important constitutional rights that invalidate the arbitrary and capricious revocation of their probation or parole programs by judges or parole boards. The two-stage hearing is extremely important to probationers and parolees, in that it permits ample airing of the allegations against the offender, cross-examinations by counsel, and testimony from individual offenders.

Parole revocation actions can be most penalizing for parolees, however. In a 1989 action, a parolee lost nearly three years of street time when he was convicted of a new offense while on parole for an earlier charge. Herbert Jessup, a federal parolee, had served three years on parole when he was convicted of a new offense. The U.S. Parole Commission revoked his parole and considered his three years on parole as "forfeit." Jessup sued, however, alleging that he was not given prior notice of the hearing nor an opportunity to defend against or mitigate the forfeiture of his street time. An appellate court ruled in his favor in this instance, since the U.S. Parole Commission acted prejudicially and deprived him of his due process rights (*Jessup v. U.S. Parole Commission,* 1989).

SUMMARY

Parole is early release from incarceration short of serving one's full term as prescribed at the time of sentencing. Parole originated in Europe, largely through the pioneering work of penal experts such as Alexander Maconochie and Sir Walter Crofton. Subsequently, the English and Irish parole systems were emulated by Gaylord Hubbell, the Sing Sing (New York) prison warden in the early 1860s.

The advantages and disadvantages of parole systems were discussed formally at the first meeting of the National Prison Association (subsequently the American Correctional Association) in 1870. Massachusetts was the first state to implement a parole system in 1884. Parole is granted on the basis of inmate eligibility. All departments of correction have guidelines governing institutional conduct and general inmate behavior. Depending upon the original sentence, the type of state sentencing system, and institutional behaviors, parole boards determine whether parole should be granted in individual cases.

While some jurisdictions, such as Maine, have discontinued the use of parole, all states convene parole boards presently to make early-release decisions about inmates. In Maine's case, the Maine Parole Board meets to make parole decisions for all inmates sentenced prior to 1976, the year parole was abolished in that state. Parole board membership is usually established through gubernatorial appointments. Diverse qualifying criteria exist for parole board membership. The general functions of parole include rehabilitation, reintegration, protection of the community, reduction of sentencing disparities, providing incentives for inmates to obey prison rules and regulations, deterring criminal conduct, and alleviating institutional overcrowding.

Parole boards utilize many types of instruments to forecast inmate risk if released. These risk assessments for prospective parolees include information about their current conviction offense, prior record, supervision experiences, institutional adjustment, substance abuse history, vocational or academic training, personality factors and psychiatric reports, personal history, their parole plan, and the possible existence of detainer warrants. Some eligible inmates may be granted admission to certain pre-release programs, including work and educational release and furloughs. When inmates are paroled, they may be placed initially in halfway houses to facilitate their adjustment from the highly regimented prison environment to the routine of life in their communities. Decisions by parole boards to grant or deny parole are governed largely by the inmate's prior record, behavioral history while incarcerated, present attitude, and the adequacy of parole plans.

All parole programs have behavioral conditions, including possible curfew, random drug/alcohol checks, and participation in individual or group therapy or vocational/educational programs. Parole revocation action is taken whenever parolees violate one or more parole conditions. Frequently cited reasons for parole revocations include the failure of parolees to participate in stipulated treatment programs, failure to report to their parole officers, possession of firearms, changing residences or employment without permission from parole officers, and failure to pay fines or make restitution to the state or to victims. Parole revocation actions are two-stage hearings where evidence is presented of an inculpatory or exculpatory nature. Parolees have the right to cross-examine witnesses and present evidence that their parole program should not be terminated. Parole revocation actions result in either return to prison or assignment to another parole program with more stringent supervisory conditions and behavioral requirements.

Form 5.1
Nevada: Parole Success Likelihood Factors

PAROLE SUCCESS LIKELIHOOD FACTORS

NAME	NUMBER	INSTITUTION	DATE
....	....	....	....

These guidelines indicate the customary range of time to be served for various combinations of offense and offender characteristics. It is emphasized that mitigating or aggravating factors may warrant decisions outside the guidelines and, in appropriate circumstances, the Board will exercise its discretion as provided by law. The basic guideline presupposes good institutional adjustment and program progress. Deviation from the normal conduct expected of all inmates could result in decisions outside the guidelines.

If the convicted person is serving sentences for multiple offenses, the most serious offense will determine the crime severity level. "Attempted" offenses will be rated one grade below the principal offense.

Convicted persons will appear for parole consideration when they have met the requirements of Nevada law.

As stated in NRS 213.10989, the establishment of these standards is not intended to create any right or interest in liberty, nor to create any reasonable expectation of parole, nor to establish any basis for a course of action against the State, its political subdivisions, agencies, boards, commissions, departments, officers or employees. The release or continuation on parole is an act of grace of the State.

Further, the Board's actions are also governed by NRS 213.1099, which delineates State policy on the granting of parole.

1. Age at first commitment:
   18 or older .... = 2
   17 or younger .... = 0
   ....

2. Prior convictions (F & M):
   None .... = 3
   One .... = 2
   Two/three .... = 1
   Four or more .... = 0
   ....

3. Incarcerations since age 17 prior to instant offense:
   None .... = 2
   One .... = 1
   Two or more .... = 0
   ....

4. Parole/probation failure:
   No failure .... = 1
   Otherwise .... = 0
   ....

5. No use, possession or attempt to obtain heroin, cocaine, opiates, amphetamines .... = 2
   History of drug abuse .... = 0
   ....

6. Current offense did not involve burglary or forgery, credit card or bad checks .... = 1
   Otherwise .... = 0
   ....

7. Fully-employed or full-time school for 6 months in year preceding offense .... = 1
   Otherwise .... = 0
   ....

8. Injury to/death of victim:
   Yes .... = 0
   Otherwise .... = 2
   ....

9. Use of weapon:
   Yes .... = 0
   Otherwise .... = 2
   ....

10. Not previously convicted of similar offense .... = 1
    Otherwise .... = 0
    ....

11. Prison programming:
    Has addressed educational/vocational deficiencies .... = 1
    Has sought and participated in counseling on substance abuse, alcohol or psychological programs .... = 1
    No history of prison problems ...... = 1
    All .... = 3
    ....

Parole Success Likelihood Score ....

Form 5.1 (continued)

GUIDELINES-RECOMMENDED MONTHS TO SERVE

Read across from your Crime Severity Level and down from your Parole Success Likelihood Score to find your guidelines-recommended months to serve. For Crime Severity Levels I through V, the grid reflects a shift in months to serve based on the court-imposed sentence length. If your sentence is less than 25 percent of the statutory maximum penalty, the lesser figure is used. If your sentence exceeds 75 percent of the statutory maximum penalty, the greater figure is used. For all other sentence lengths, the median figure is used. For Crime Severity Levels VI or VII, the guidelines recommendation will be one-third of the court imposed sentence length or the grid recommendation, whichever is greater. The Board, using its discretion in your case, may depart from guidelines recommendation.

PAROLE SUCCESS LIKELIHOOD SCORE

Crime Severity Level	*Excellent 15–20*	*Good 10–14*	*Average 6–9*	*Poor 0–5*
I	4	6	8	14–16–18
II	12	14	16–18–20	18–20–22
III	20–22–24	22–24–26	24–26–28	26–28–30
IV	28–30–32	30–32–34	32–34–36	34–36–38
V	36–38–40	38–40–42	40–42–44	42–44–46
VI	48	54	60	66
VII	60	66	72	78
VIII	90	102	114	126
IX	138	150	162	174

Crime Severity Level: ....

Parole Success Likelihood Score: ....

Guideline-Recommended Months: ....

WHITE—Prison "C" File; CANARY—Inmate; PINK—Board File; BLUE—Prison "I" File

(Rev. 10/91)

Form 5.2

Nevada: Recommendation—Certification of Board of Parole Commissioners Action

NEVADA CERTIFICATION OF BOARD OF PAROLE COMMISSIONERS ACTION

CC No. ______

Count No.______

____________ ____________ ____________ ____________

NAME NUMBER INSTITUTION DATE

Only the paragraph checked applies to you: ☐ **Personal hearing** ☐ **In absentia**

☐ The Board has decided to parole you effective: ____________

____

Special Conditions: ____________

____

____

____

____

☐ **Parole has been denied to:** ____________

☐ **Because your guideline-recommended parole month is later than your projected expiration date, parole is denied to expiration.**

☐ **The Board has determined that the crime severity level and/or parole success factors do not adequately reflect the true nature of your case. Therefore, the Board has departed from the guideline recommendation. The reasons for the departure are listed below:**

____

____

____

____

☐ **COMMENT:**____________

____

☐ **No action has been taken in your case due to the following:** ____________

____

If you believe your crime-severity level or parole likelihood success score is miscalculated, requests for recomputation should be sent within 30 days following the hearing to the Chairman, Nevada Board of Parole Commissioners, 5500 Snyder Avenue, Capitol Complex, Carson City, Nevada, 89710.

Crime Severity Level: ____________

Parole Success Likelihood Score:____________

Guideline-Recommended Months:____________

____________ ____________

Prison Staff Representative For the Nevada Parole Commissioners

Panel Recommendation:____________

Form 5.2 (continued)

Final Action:

Commissioner Armstrong: ☐ Grant ☐ Deny **Commissioner Wright: ☐ Grant ☐ Deny**

Commissioner Chickory: ☐ Grant ☐ Deny **Commissioner Wyett: ☐ Grant ☐ Deny**

Commissioner Franklin: ☐ Grant ☐ Deny **Hearing Rep____________: ☐ Grant ☐ Deny**

Commissioner Kinsley: ☐ Grant ☐ Deny **______________________: ☐ Grant ☐ Deny**

Recommendation: ☐ Ratified ☐ Overturned ☐ Amended ☐ By Board majority

Form 5.3
North Dakota: Admission to Caseload

ADMISSION TO CASELOAD
NORTH DAKOTA PAROLE AND PROBATION DEPARTMENT
SFN 13374 Page 1 (7-88)

Client's Name: Last	First	MI	Client's SID Number	Client's Soc. Sec. No.	Agent's No./Radio No.

The following information must be forwarded to the central office to open up a case:

(1) Admission to Caseload
(2) Criminal Judgment / Court Order
(3) Appendix A (If not included in Criminal Judgment)
(4) Criminal Information or Criminal Complaint (Class A Misdemeanors)
(5) Copy of North Dakota B. C. I. Criminal Rap Sheet

___ A - RACE / ETHNICITY
1 White
2 Black
3 American Indian
4 Asian
5 Hispanic

___ B - SEX
1 Male
2 Female

___ C - MARITAL STATUS
1 Single
2 Married
3 Divorced or Separated
4 Widowed

___ D - NUMBER OF DEPENDENTS
(Enter 99 if not reported)

___ E - LIVING ARRANGEMENTS
1 Alone
2 With Spouse Only
3 With Child(ren) and Spouse
4 With Child(ren) Only
5 With Parent(s)
6 With Sibling(s)
7 With Friend(s)
8 Non-legal Alliance
9 Correctional Facility
10 Other ______________

___ F - VETERAN
1 Yes
2 No

___ G - GROSS MONTHLY INCOME
1 None
2 $1 - $499
3 $500 - $999
4 $1,000 - $1,499
5 $1,500 - $1,999
6 $2,000 or more

H - EMPLOYMENT ___ H
1 Unemployed and Not Looking
2 Unemployed and Looking
3 Full-time (35 hrs/week and over)
4 Full-time but Seasonal
5 Part-time
6 Not Employable
7 Student
8 Homemaker
9 Retired

I - JOB CLASSIFICATION ___ I
1 Professional, Technical, Managerial
2 Clerical, Sales or Service
3 Farming
4 Skilled Trade
5 Unskilled Labor
6 Student / Homemaker
7 Not Employable

J - LAST GRADE COMPLETED: ___ J
1 -12 (Enter Specific Number)
13 High School Graduate
14 Some College
15 College Graduate
16 Some Graduate Work
17 Graduate Degree
18 GED or HED
19 Technical or Vocational School

K. CURRENTLY ON PUBLIC ASSISTANCE ___ K
1 Yes
2 No

L - Number of Prior Adult Misdemeanor Convictions (Enter 99 if not reported) ___ L

M - Number of Prior Adult Felony Convictions (Enter 99 if not reported) ___ M

N - Number of Previous Adult Probations (Enter 99 if not reported) ___ N

O - Number of Times Previously Released on Parole (Enter 99 if not reported) ___ O

P. Number of Prior Incarcerations in a Federal or State Institution (Enter 99 if not reported) ___ P

Form 5.3 (continued)

ADMISSION TO CASELOAD

NORTH DAKOTA PAROLE AND PROBATION DEPARTMENT
SFN 13374 Page 2 (7-88)

Client's Name: Last First MI	Client's SID Number	Client's Soc. Sec. No.	Agent's No./Radio No.

RA - Number of Address Changes in Last 12 Months (Prior to incarceration for parolees)	0 None 2 One 3 Two or More	RA
RB Percentage of Time Employed in Last 12 Months (Prior to incarceration for parolees)	0 60% or more 1 40% - 59% 2 Under 40% 0 Not Applicable	RB
RC - Alcohol Usage Problems (Prior to incarceration for parolees)	0 No interference with functioning 2 Occasional abuse; some disruption of functioning 4 Frequent abse, serious disruption; needs treatment	RC
RD - Other Drug Problems (Prior to incarceration for parolees)	0 No interference with functioning 1 Occasional abuse, some disruption of functioning 2 Frequent abuse, serious disruption, needs treatment	RD
RE - Attitude	0 Motivated to change; receptive to assistance 3 Dependent or unwilling to accept responsibility 5 Rationalizes behavior; negative, not motivated to change	RE
RF - Age at First Conviction	0 24 or older 2 20-23 4 19 or younger	RF
RG - Number of Prior Periods of Probation/Parole Supervision (Adult or Juvenile)	0 None 4 One or More	RG
RH - Number of Prior Probation / Parole Revocations	0 None 4 One or More	RH
RI - Number of Prior Felony Convictions	0 None 2 One 4 Two or More	RI
RJ - Convictions or Juvenile Adjudications for: (Select applicable and add for score. Do not exceed total of 5. Include current offense.)	2 Burglary, theft, auto theft or robbery 3 Worthless checks or forgery	RJ
RK - Conviction or Juvenile Adjudication for Assaultive Offense within Last Five Years: (An offense which involves the use of a weapon, physical force or threat of force.)	15 Yes 0 No	RK
	RL-TOTAL	RL

Form 5.3 (continued)

ADMISSION TO CASELOAD

NORTH DAKOTA PAROLE AND PROBATION DEPARTMENT

SFN 13374 Page 3 (7-88)

Client's Name: Last	First	MI	Client's SID Number	Client's Soc. Sec. No.	Agent's No./Radio No.

NA - ACADEMIC / VOCATIONAL SKILLS
- -1 High school or above skill level
- 0 Adequate skills; able to handle everyday requirements
- +2 Low skill level causing minor adjustment problems
- +4 Minimal skill level causing serious adjustment problems

NB - EMPLOYMENT
- -1 Satisfactory employment for one year or longer
- 0 Secure employment; no difficulties reported; or homemaker, student, or retired
- +3 Unsatisfactory employment; or unemployed but has adequate job skills
- +6 Unemployed and virtually unemployable; needs training

NC - FINANCIAL MANAGEMENT
- -1 Long standing pattern of self-sufficiency; e.g.: good credit rating
- 0 No current difficulties
- +3 Situational or minor difficulties
- +5 Severe difficulties; may include garnishment, bad checks or bankruptcy

ND - MARITAL / FAMILY RELATIONSHIPS
- -1 Relationships and support exceptionally strong
- 0 Relatively stable relationships
- +3 Some disorganization or stress but potential for improvement
- +5 Major disorganization or stress

NE - COMPANIONS
- -1 Good support and influence
- 0 No adverse relationships
- +2 Associations with occasional negative results
- +4 Associations almost completely negative

NF - EMOTIONAL STABILITY
- -2 Exceptionally well adjusted; accepts responsibility for actions
- 0 No symptoms of emotional instability; appropriate emotional responses
- +4 Symptoms limit but do not prohibit adequate functioning, e.g.: excessive anxiety
- +7 Symptoms prohibit adequate functioning, e.g.: lashes out or retreats into self

NA	NG
NB	NH
NC	NI
ND	NJ
NE	NK
NF	NL
	NM

NG - ALCOHOL USAGE
- 0 No interference with functioning
- +3 Occasional abuse; some disruption of functioning
- +6 Frequent abuse; serious disruption; needs treatment

NH - OTHER DRUG USAGE
- 0 No interference with functioning
- +3 Occasional substance abuse; some disruption of functioning
- +5 Frequent substance abuse, serious disruption; needs treatment

NI - MENTAL ABILITY
- 0 Able to function independently
- +3 Some need for assistance; potential for adequate adjustment; mild retardation
- +6 Deficiencies severely limit independent functioning; moderate retardation

NJ - HEALTH
- 0 Sound physical health; seldom ill
- +1 Handicap or illness interferes with functioning on a recurring basis
- +2 Serious handicap or chronic illness needs frequent medical care

NK - SEXUAL BEHAVIOR
- 0 No apparent dysfunction
- +3 Real or perceived situational or minor problems
- +5 Real or perceived chronic or severe problems

NL - AGENT'S IMPRESSION OF CLIENT'S NEEDS
- -1 Minimum
- 0 Low
- +3 Medium
- +5 Maximum

NM - TOTAL

Form 5.3 (continued)

ADMISSION TO CASELOAD ☐ Admission ☐ Reclassification ☐ Change

NORTH DAKOTA PAROLE AND PROBATION DEPARTMENT

SFN 13374 Page 4 (7-88)

Client's Name: Last First MI	Client's SID Number	Client's Soc. Sec. No.	Agent's No./Radio No.

Address

Telephone No. | Date of Birth | P.O.B.

SENTENCE ☐ Parole ☐ Deferred ☐ Suspended ☐ Other | YRS | MOS | Parole/Probation From | Parole/Probation To

Current Offense	Offense Level F/M/U	NCIC Code	Counts
①			
②			
③			
④			

County(ies) /State(s) of Offense ① ② ③ ④

Judge's Name

PSI - By Agent No. | PSI - Date

Driver's License State: ___ ☐Current ☐Suspended ☐ None

COURT ORDERED	Yes	No	Amount
Costs			
Fines			
Fees			
Restitution			

Ht | Wt | Hair | Eyes

Marks, Scars, Health Disabilities, Etc.

Family (Name, Age & Address)

Spouse

Children

Parents

Presently Living With

EMERGENCY CONTACT: Name/Address/Phone

Employer (Present / Immediate Past)

Address

Job Type

Earnings | Dates To

PSYCHOLOGICAL EVALUATION / TREATMENT (Court Ordered / Parole Board Order)

	Yes	No
Emotional / Psychological		
Chemical Addiction		
Sex Offender Program		

SPECIFIC CONDITIONS (Court Ordered / Parole Board Order)

	Yes	No
Urinalysis Ordered		
Search Ordered		
No Alcohol Ordered		

Special Conditions

States Attorney

Defense Attorney

Accomplices

A B C D E F G

NA NB NC ND NE NF

NG NH NI NJ NK NL NM

RA RB RC RD RE RF RG RH RI RJ RK RL

H I J K L M N O P

DATE OF THIS RECORD

SUPERVISION LEVEL
☐ 1 Minimum
☐ 2 Medium
☐ 3 Maximum
☐ 4 Intensive
☐ 5 Not Classified
☐ 6 Administrative

STATUS OF SUPERVISION
☐1 ND Client, Supervised in ND
☐2 ND Client Supervised by Other State: #________
☐3 Other State (#________)Client Supervised in ND
☐4 Paroled to Consecutive Sentence in Institution
☐5 Paroled to Detainer
☐6 Other ________

Form 5.4
North Carolina: Initial Client Assessment

42
(16-17)

Client Name: LAST, FIRST M. I.	DOC# (1-15)

Select the appropriate answer and enter the associated code in the adjacent blank(s)

ASSESSMENT ITEM — SCORE

NUMBER OF ADDRESS CHANGES IN LAST 12 MONTHS:
- 0 Less than two, or N/A (Institutionalized)
- 4 Two or more

_____ (18)

* AGE AT FIRST CONVICTION (INCLUDE JUVENILE CONVICTIONS):
- 0 24 or older
- 3 17 - 23
- 6 16 or younger

_____ (19)

* FELONY CONVICTION (EITHER CURRENT OR PAST):
- 0 None
- 2 One or more

_____ (20)

* CURRENT AND/OR PAST CONVICTIONS FOR (SELECT ALL APPLICABLE AND ADD FOR SCORE):
- 1 DUI
- 2 Housebreaking, B&E, Burglary, Stolen property
- 2 Vechicle theft, all other Larceny/thefts
- 2 Robbery
- 3 Forgery, Worthless checks, Fraud
- 0 Other

_____ (21-22)

* OFFENSE INVOLVING THE USE OF A WEAPON, PHYSICAL FORCE OR THE THREAT OF FORCE. (SCORE FOR A CURRENT OR PAST OFFENSE OCCURRING WITHIN 24 MONTHS) (SCORE FOR A CURRENT OR PAST OFFENSE OCCURRING WITHIN 5 YEARS IF MURDER, MANSLAUGHTER, RAPE, ROBBERY, OR OTHER OFFENSE IN WHICH A DEADLY WEAPON WAS USED):
- 4 Yes
- 0 No

_____ (23)

ALCOHOL USAGE/PROBLEMS:
- 0 No apparent problems
- 2 Moderate problems
- 4 Serious problems

_____ (24)

HAS PAST HISTORY OF DRUG ADDICTION:
- 8 Yes
- 0 No

_____ (25)

TIME EMPLOYED IN LAST 12 MONTHS:
- 0 7 months or more or N/A
- 3 Under 7 months

_____ (26)

ATTITUDE:
- 0 Motivated to change, receptive to assistance
- 4 Dependent or unwilling to accept responsibility
- 5 Rationalizes behavior, negative, not motivated to change

_____ (27)

PRIOR PERIODS OF ADULT PROBATION/PAROLE SUPERVISION:
- 0 None
- 2 One or more

_____ (28)

ASSESSMENT ITEM — SCORE

EMPLOYMENT/STUDENT (CIRCLE IF STUDENT):
- 0 Stable employment/Satisfactory employment/Student/Study Release
- 4 Unemployed/Unstable employment/Problem student

_____ (29)

FINANCIAL SITUATION:
- 0 Self-sufficient, capable of handling finances
- 2 No known difficulty
- 4 Some or severe difficulty in meeting court and other obligations

_____ (30)

FRIENDS/ASSOCIATES:
- 0 Easily influenced (basically positive friends) or has little or no interaction with others
- 1 Assertive - not easily influenced (basically positive friends)
- 2 Easily influenced (basically negative friends)
- 5 Assertive - not easily influenced (basically negative friends)

_____ (31)

EDUCATIONAL ATTAINMENT:
- 0 High school graduate or above or a student
- 3 High school dropout
- 4 Less than high school

_____ (32)

MARITAL STATUS:
- 0 Married/Widowed
- 2 Separated or Divorced
- 5 Single

_____ (33)

TOTAL SCORE _____ (34-35)

ALL ITEMS MARKED (*) VERIFIED:
- 1 Yes
- 0 No

_____ (36)

SUPERVISION LEVEL ASSIGNED:
- 5 High Risk
- 7 Intermediate
- 8 Special

_____ (53)

SUPERVISION LEVEL ESTABLISHED BY:
- 0 Assessment score
- 1 Supervisor's approved override
- 2 Parole Commission order
- 3 Court order

_____ (54)

OVER 24: High Risk
14-24: Intermediate
UNDER 14: Special

PPO NAME

US #	DATE (65-70)	DIST # (74-76)

Form 5.5
Georgia: Parole Success Factors

```
ITEM A.  AGE AT FIRST COMMITMENT                                    ____
         (26 or over      = 5)
         (22 - 25         = 3)
         (18 - 21         = 2)
         (17 or less      = 0)

ITEM B.  PRIOR CONVICTIONS (JUVENILE AND ADULT)                     ____
         (None            = 3)
         (1               = 2)
         (2 - 3           = 1)
         (4 or more       = 0)

ITEM C.  PRIOR INCARCERATION SINCE AGE 17                           ____
         (None            = 2)
         (1               = 1)
         (2 or more       = 0)

ITEM D.  PAROLE AND PROBATION FAILURE                               ____
         (No Failures     = 4)
         (Probation Only  = 2)
         (Parole Only     = 1)
         (Both            = 0)

ITEM E.  NO USE, POSSESSION OR ATTEMPT TO OBTAIN HEROIN OR OPIATE
         DRUGS = 1
         OTHERWISE = 0                                              ____

ITEM F.  COMMITMENT OFFENSE DID NOT INVOLVE BURGLARY OR FORGERY = 2
         OTHERWISE = 0                                              ____

ITEM G.  FULLY EMPLOYED DURING 6 MONTHS PRECEDING CURRENT OFFENSE = 1
         OTHERWISE = 0                                              ____

ITEM H.  HAD WRAT SCORE OF 8 OR HIGHER AT TIME OF DIAGNOSTIC TESTING = 2
         OTHERWISE = 0                                              ____

         TOTAL                                                      ____
```

Form 5.6
North Carolina: Client Reassessment

CLIENT REASSESSMENT

43
(16-17)

Client Name: LAST, FIRST M. I.	DOC# (1-15)

Select the appropriate answer and enter the associated code in the adjacent blank(s)

REASSESSMENT ITEM	SCORE
* AGE OF 16 OR YOUNGER AT FIRST CONVICTION (INCLUDE JUVENILE): 3 Yes 0 No	(18)
* PRIOR ADULT PROBATION/PAROLE REVOCATION: 4 Yes 0 No	(19)
* CURRENT AND/OR PAST CONVICTIONS FOR (SELECT ALL APPLICABLE AND ADD FOR SCORE): 2 DUI 2 Housebreaking, B&E, Burglary, Stolen property 2 Vechicle theft, all other Larceny/thefts 2 Robbery 4 Forgery, Worthless checks, Fraud 0 Other	(20-21)
* OFFENSE INVOLVING THE USE OF A WEAPON, PHYSICAL FORCE OR THE THREAT OF FORCE. (SCORE FOR A CURRENT OR PAST OFFENSE OCCURRING WITHIN 24 MONTHS) (SCORE FOR A CURRENT OR PAST OFFENSE OCCURRING WITHIN 5 YEARS IF MURDER, MANSLAUGHTER, RAPE, ROBBERY, OR OTHER OFFENSE IN WHICH A DEADLY WEAPON WAS USED): 6 Yes 0 No	(22)
* CURRENT OR PAST CONVICTION FOR A NON-VIOLENT FELONY: 5 Yes 0 No	(23)
HAS HISTORY OF DRUG ADDICTION: 9 Yes 0 No	(24)
HAS HISTORY OF ALCOHOLISM: 5 Yes 0 No	(25)
SOCIAL IDENTIFICATION: 0 Primarily with positive individuals 8 Primarily or totally with negative or delinquent or criminal individuals	(26)

REASSESSMENT ITEM	SCORE
RESPONSE TO COURT OR COMMISSION CONDITIONS: 0 No problems of consequence 10 Moderate compliance problems 19 Unwilling to comply	(27-28)
UNEMPLOYED (STUDENTS, HOUSEWIVES, RETIREES, MILITARY AND DISABLED PERSONS ARE CONSIDERED EMPLOYED): 3 Yes 0 No	(29)
MOTIVATION AND SKILLS FOR WORK: 0 Adequate skills (Motivated or not motivated) 3 Motivated with poor skills 5 Not motivated with poor skills	(30)
MARITAL STATUS: 0 Married or Widowed 4 Single or Separated or Divorced	(31)
TOTAL SCORE	(32-33)
ALL ITEMS MARKED (*) VERIFIED: 1 Yes 0 No	(34)
SUPERVISION LEVEL ASSIGNED: 5 High Risk 7 Intermediate 8 Special	(53)
SUPERVISION LEVEL ESTABLISHED BY: 0 Assessment score 1 Supervisor's approved override 2 Parole Commission order 3 Court order	(54)

OVER 26: High Risk
11-26: Intermediate
UNDER 11: Special

PPO NAME

US #	DATE (65-70)	DIST # (74-76)

Form 5.7
Oregon: Risk Assessment

OREGON DEPARTMENT OF CORRECTIONS
Community Services

___ISP Case

RISK REASSESSMENT

Final Supervision Level
___High ___Medium
___Low ___Limited

NAME: **SID #:** **COUNTY:**

Data

A. How many prior felony convictions?
0-1 conviction ______ 2
2-3 convictions ______ 1
4 or more convictions ______ 0
#Priors: ____

B. How many prior incarcerations (executed sentences of 90 days or more, felony or misdemeanor, adult or juvenile)?
No incarcerations ______ 2
1-2 incarcerations ______ 1
3 or more incarcerations ______ 0
#Priors: ____

C. Does present supervision include parole, probation, failure to appear, release agreement, escape or custody violation?
No ______ 1
Yes ______ 0
Y / N

RATE THE FOLLOWING BASED UPON THE OFFENDER'S PERFORMANCE SINCE THE LAST ASSESSMENT

D. Substance abuse problems:
No use/possession of illegal substances or alcohol abuse ______ 2
Occasional abuse; some disruption of functioning ______ 1
Frequent abuse; serious disruption of functioning; failure to comply with treatment ______ 0

E. Response to conditions of supervision:
No problems of consequence ______ 2
Some problems of consequence ______ 1
Has been unwilling to comply ______ 0

F. Verified employment:
60-100% ______ 2
40-59% ______ 1
0-39% ______ 0
(If N/A, enter 101% into Data Box)
%____

G. Number of address changes:
0-1 ______ 1
2 or more ______ 0
#____

TOTAL SCORE: ______

Override Request

Categories	***Information Source(s)***
Level Increase	
___Assault Offender	___Official Documents
___Sex Offender	___Offender Statements
___Offender Needs	___Law Enforcement
___Extreme Criminal Conduct	___Clinical Testing
___New Criminal Activity	___Needs Assessment
___Major Non-Conformance	___Collateral Sources
___Associations	
Level Increase/Decrease	
___Officer Discretion	
Level Decrease	
___Conformance to Conditions	
___In Custody	
___Unavailable	

Justification

____

Scored Level: ___**High** ___**Medium** ___**Low** ___**Limited**

☐**Override/**☐**Policy Level:** ___**High** ___**Medium** ___**Low** ___**Limited**

REMOVE OVERRIDE ☐

OFFICER:______________________ DATE:__________

SUPERVISOR:______________________

DATE:______________ ☐Accept ☐Reject

White: File Canary: Data Entry CD1140aF (9/90)

Form 5.8
Indiana: Proposed Adult Risk Reassessment Instrument

Indiana Judicial Center
101 West Ohio Street, Suite 1110
Indianapolis, Indiana 46204-1989

Probationer's Name ______________________ **Cause No.** ______________

Probation Officer's Name ______________________ **Date Completed** ____________

1.	AGE AT FIRST CONVICTION OR ADJUDICATION	
	24 or Greater	0
	20 - 23	2
	19 or Less	3
2.	NUMBER OF PRIOR CONVICTIONS	
	0	0
	One	2
	Two or More	3
3.	NUMBER OF PRIOR COMMUNITY SUPERVISIONS	
	0	0
	One or More	2
4.	NUMBER OF PRIOR VIOLATIONS OF COMMUNITY SUPERVISIONS	
	0	0
	One or More	2
5.	NUMBER OF PRIOR COMMITMENTS	
	None	0
	One or More	2

RATE THE FOLLOWING SINCE THE LAST CLASSIFICATION:

6.	SUBSTANCE USE	
	No Known Interference	0
	Some Disruption	1
	Serious Disruption	2
7.	VIOLATIONS OF PROBATION	
	None	0
	One or More	6
8.	REPORTING PERFORMANCE	
	Acceptable or N/A	0
	Improvement Needed	2
	Unacceptable	4
9.	SPECIAL CONDITIONS COMPLIANCE	
	Acceptable or N/A	0
	Improvement Needed	2
	Unacceptable	4
10.	EMPLOYMENT RECORD	
	Acceptable or N/A	0
	Improvement Needed	2
	Unacceptable	4
11.	PAYMENT RECORD	
	Acceptable	0
	Improvement Needed	2
	Unacceptable	4
	TOTAL	____

OVERRIDE/UNDERRIDE

Must explain: ____

____

____.

Supervision level needed: ______________________________.

Supervisor's signature: ______________________________.

CUT OFF SCORES

0 - 10	LOW
11 - 19	MEDIUM
20 OR MORE	HIGH

6

Risk Assessment in Retrospect: Current Trends

INTRODUCTION

This chapter reviews briefly the use of risk and needs assessment instrumentation used in both the criminal and juvenile justice systems. Much work has been completed by numerous researchers and clinicians in an attempt to construct valid and reliable predictive tools for use by adult and juvenile probation departments, corrections officials, and parole boards. Not all states utilize risk assessment instruments for offender program placements. Many jurisdictions are in the process of either establishing original devices or revising previously constructed tools designed for classification purposes. Therefore, we will first review those points where risk assessment is most crucial for effective decision making.

Decision making about offender risk and needs is imperfect presently, and it is unlikely that perfect assessment instruments will be constructed in the near future. Nevertheless, there are acceptable levels of error in behavioral prediction. Broadly applied to offender aggregates, actuarial instruments have achieved prediction levels of 90 percent or higher. However, prediction levels of 65 or 70 percent or higher are regarded in many jurisdictions as functional for decision-making purposes. Thus, it might be anticipated that for any given offender aggregate, accurate behavioral forecasts might be made for between 65 and 90 percent of that aggregate, depending upon the initial aggregate characteristics and the type of behavior predicted. Another way of viewing the accuracy of predictive devices is to consider that from 10 to 35 percent of any aggregate may not behave in predictable ways. We have previously examined some of the problems that arise from these different circumstances. These are the problems of false positives and false negatives. Therefore, for any offender aggregate (e.g., all parole-eligible Nevada inmates, all new Kansas probationers, or all entering Georgia inmates), we would expect some placement inaccuracies in our client or prisoner assessments and behavioral predictions. The nature of this prediction error will be re-examined in a subsequent chapter section.

Finally, several important trends relating to risk assessment will be described. As we become increasingly knowledgeable about recidivists and their characteristics, the sophistication of our risk assessment devices is enhanced accordingly. These selected trends are grouped according to salient decision-making points in the criminal justice process, including the probation stage, the initial and subsequent classifications of inmates in prisons and jails, and the parole or early-release process.

PREDICTING RISK IN RETROSPECT

Risk assessment measures have been established to determine probabilities that particular clients or inmates will engage in either dangerous or maladjusted behaviors. These probabilities will be used subsequently for placement, program, and security decision making (Joyce, 1985). Some of the early efforts at predicting risk and propensities toward deviant, dangerous conduct focused upon visible physical deformities and irregularities, such as unusual skull shapes, physiognomic features, and body types. Subsequent risk assessment devices increasingly utilized and relied upon diverse personal, social, psychological, socioeconomic, and demographic criteria for dangerousness forecasts.

Assessing both juvenile and adult offender risk is an important enterprise. Assessing offender level of risk is an important factor, perhaps the most important factor, in maximizing offender placement. In the general case, risk assessment gauges whether particular programs or placements will work best for certain offenders. For judges, it would make no sense to make uninformed probation decisions for convicted offenders without considering their potential for reoffending or harming themselves or members of the community. Prison wardens and superintendents would create social disasters in their facilities if they made no effort to assess whether any inmate would pose a high escape risk or prove dangerous to other inmates by exhibiting assaultive propensities or behavior. The rehabilitative value and effectiveness of various prison programs would be seriously undermined if no effort were made to screen the inmate applicants to determine their eligibility, background, and personal/social qualifications.

Parole boards would be remiss in their responsibilities if they failed to make critical distinctions between eligible parole candidates. Both prospective probationers and prospective parolees are suspect regarding their likelihood of reoffending, since they all have a record and history of prior offending. We have seen that it is impossible to incarcerate everyone who commits a crime. Furthermore, it is unrealistic to expect that those who are incarcerated will be incarcerated indefinitely, except in sentencing circumstances such as life-without-parole.

Those engaged in the business of risk forecasting, including judges, correctional administrators and staff, and parole boards, are continuously confronted with the problem of deciding which convicted offenders, probationers, parolees, and/or clients should be supervised more or less closely, and under which types of circumstances. All of these decision makers try to make the best of available, but limited, information. This information comes in various forms, and may include statements, conclusions, and observations from presentence investigation reports, personality inventory summaries, risk scale scores, and accounts of versions of events from candidates themselves in self-appraisals.

Accurate risk prediction is dependent upon the effectiveness of classification, or the process of differentiating between persons according to certain possessed properties. Crude classifications applied to offenders might be misdemeanants and felons, although few, if any, experts would conclude that all felons are alike except in the respect that they have been convicted of crimes carrying potential incarcerative penalties of one or more years. Further developing our felon category into several subcategories so that a distinction may be made between property offenders and violent offenders is a slight improvement. But again, few experts, if any, would agree that all property offenders are alike or that all violent offenders are alike. Focusing upon the violent offender subcategory, for instance, we may continue refining our subdivisions to distinguish between murderers, robbers, rapists, assaultists, and arsonists. Also, property offenders might be subdivided into burglars and thieves. Again, the value of such categorizations and classifications is questionable, since there are great differences among all murderers. Some of them are serial or mass killers, while others have conviction offenses of vehicular homicide. Some offenders convicted of murder may only be incidentally involved in the homicide act itself, as in the case of drivers of automobiles during which one or more murders occurs resulting from an armed robbery perpetrated by one of the automobile passengers. Yet others convicted of homicide may be once-in-a-lifetime white-collar business persons who killed their spouses in the heat of the moment during an argument.

Effective classification schemes are important, therefore, because they enable authorities at different stages of the criminal justice process to channel certain offenders in particular directions where they can be most effectively managed and/or treated. Managing offenders means to situate them in positions which are most advantageous to their supervisors. Supervisors may be probation officers, correctional officers, parole officers, or community corrections program directors. Offender management suggests variable control over client or inmate behavior. Thus, some probationer-clients are placed in probation programs requiring minimal supervision by probation officers, while other probationer-clients are placed in intensive supervision programs where their actions are frequently and closely monitored.

A general re-examination of the functions of classification systems includes the fact that classification schemes serve to identify offender needs and provide for effective services or treatments designed to meet those needs. Other functions include optimum program placements with designated levels of behavioral control. Some clients are mentally abnormal, while others are troublemakers or vulnerable. Attempts are made to identify the client's educational level, vocational skills, and psychological needs, and to separate more predatory clients from more nonviolent ones. Custody and security level assignments and reassignments are facilitated through classification and reclassification at regular intervals. Reclassifications may be used as rewards for good inmate conduct, if custody level is decreased from a higher level to a lower one. Accordingly, reclassifications might be regarded as punishments through security level upgrades over time. Classification level is considered relevant for early release or parole consideration, where good behavior in a minimum-security custody level over time is evidence of subsequent good conduct in the community if paroled. Classification systems enable program coordinators in communities to screen parolees for inclusion or exclusion, depending upon their assessed risk or presumed dangerousness.

Useful as screening tools are risk assessment devices that are intended to distinguish between different types of offenders to determine their initial institutional classification, their security placement and subsequent management, their early-release eligibility and success potential, and the particular level of supervision they might require if placed in conditional probation or parole programs. Also useful for treatment purposes are needs assessment devices. These tools measure the offender's personal and social skills, general health well-being and emotional stability, educational level, employment potential, and stability. They are intended to highlight problem areas which might be addressed by channeling certain offenders into programs or services with remedial, and/or rehabilitative, and/or reintegrative value.

From an organizational perspective, risk and needs assessment inventories have value relative to program planning, budgeting, and resource deployment. Simultaneously, prisons and community corrections programs are also service organizations complete with a division of labor, specialized staffs, specific clientele, and assorted services delivery systems. Risk instruments enhance organizational accountability by creating a degree of standardization relative to offender processing. Management and processing criteria may be established to assist in fulfilling or promoting various bureaucratic aims, including maximizing efficiency, reducing duplication of function, and creating spheres of competence where specialists can excel in the services they provide. A key feature of bureaucratization is the predictability of rewards and behavioral incentives. Consistent with this feature is an objective classification system designed to recognize and reward particular inmate achievements and to provide safe, secure, and humane institutional conditions.

In both the criminal and juvenile justice systems, the relevance of effective classification tools is apparent. Fairly crude classifications are made for adults and juveniles when police officers make arrests and take suspects into custody. When their age is known, juveniles are separated from adults while confined temporarily in jail quarters awaiting an initial appearance. The jail removal initiative implemented during the 1980s has sought to remove all known juveniles from adult jail facilities, even if the intent of law enforcement officers and jail personnel is to hold suspects for only a few hours. This jail removal initiative has successfully diverted most juveniles from jails to various community agencies where they can be held temporarily and subsequently released to parents or guardians. However, many of the nation's smaller communities do not have the same array of community services as might be found in larger urban areas. Thus, confining juveniles in lockups or local city or county jails, even on a temporary basis, continues because of necessity, since alternative facilities and temporary placement centers or shelters are nonexistent.

For adults who are arrested and taken to jail for initial processing, some separation while confined is evident. For instance, those charged with driving under the influence of alcohol or drugs are frequently detained in separate areas compared with those arrested for felonies or more serious misdemeanors. Thus, jails often establish long-term and short-term areas to accommodate different types of offenders.

As we have seen in previous chapters, different types of screening processes are utilized to separate both adult and youthful offenders at later processing stages. Magistrates may release certain adults on their own recognizance, while others are placed in pretrial detention. Youths are screened by intake officers, and decisions are made regarding which juveniles should be released to parents or guardians and which ones ought to be held pending further action in juvenile court. In both the criminal and juvenile justice systems, prosecutors make decisions about cases to be prosecuted or pursued formally. Subsequently, both adult and juvenile offenders are processed by their respective criminal and juvenile courts.

Both juvenile and criminal court judges have a vested interest in the accuracy of risk and needs assessment instruments. This is because the sentences they impose are designed, in part, to reflect the seriousness of the offenses committed and to prescribe appropriate therapeutic or rehabilitative measures that will assist offenders in dealing with some of their problems. Offenders who have limited reading ability or whose skills are insufficient to find and retain decent employment will be inclined to recidivate, since their future personal and social circumstances will be quite similar to their present circumstances. Therefore, certain types of interventions may be necessary to enable offenders to cultivate better self-concepts and acquire educational, vocational, social, and/or psychological skills such that they can cope more effectively with community living.

Judges must determine which treatment programs are most appropriate for particular offenders. Should certain offenders be placed on probation? Which offenders should receive more intensive supervision? Which offenders are most likely to recidivate if sentenced to a nonincarcerative option? Presentence investigation reports or predispositional reports prepared by probation officers in both criminal and juvenile courts furnish judges with considerable information about an offender's background and present circumstances. Often, these documents contain assessments of offender behaviors and recommendations for particular punishments and/or treatment programs.

When adult and youthful offenders are incarcerated for short or long terms, corrections officials must decide where to place these inmates in their institutions. Because many adult and juvenile correctional facilities offer various services and have different security levels, risk and needs assessments are crucial in determining inmate eligibility for certain types of program participation and whether particular inmates can get along with others if situated in common areas. The higher the custody or security level in any prison, the more costly it is to accommodate inmates placed in those levels. Thus, prison officials seek to maximize the number of inmates to be confined in the lowest security levels. Not all prisoners are equally able or inclined to comply with institutional rules and respect the rights of other inmates. Some inmates are more inclined to attempt escape from confinement than others. Some inmates deserve to be trustees and to be granted a greater range of prison privileges. All of these decisions must be made by corrections officials vested with classification responsibilities, usually at times when incoming inmates are processed in intake screening and reception centers or at regular reclassification or reassessment hearings at regular intervals later.

As we have also seen, it is in an inmate's best interests to be placed in the lowest custody levels, particularly in advance of parole board hearings for the purpose of determining early-release eligibility. Parole boards rely heavily on documented evidence of an inmate's institutional behavior over time. Further, documents are consulted, such as presentence investigation reports. These may be used as benchmarks for the purpose of determining how much progress has been made from the point of conviction to the point of possible parole. Victim impact statements, which may or may not be appended to such PSI documents, are also read and used to guide parole board action. But more often than not, risk and needs assessment devices and scale scores are consulted by parole board members as gauges to determine (1) an inmate's parole eligibility, (2) the nature of supervision to be maintained over the prospective parolee if released into the community, and (3) the nature and scope of any treatments or programs that may enhance a parolee's success potential if granted early release.

Parole is seen both as a reward for good behavior while institutionalized and as an opportunity for offenders to become reintegrated into their communities and work productively to lead law-abiding lives. Because parolees may be serious ex-offenders, parole boards are especially sensitive about releasing the wrong inmates, or those who will commit new and serious offenses while on parole. The Massachusetts Parole Board does not like to recall the case of Willie Horton. One unfortunate fact is that virtually every parole board has released a Willie Horton at one time or another and must pay the price for that decision. No parole board wants to commit similar errors of judgment in the future. Therefore, parole board decision making is somewhat conservative. Many decisions by parole boards denying early release to particular inmates are errors on the side of caution. That is, parole board actions tend to overpenalize eligible inmates because of suspected high future-offending potential. At the same time, parole boards are encouraged to release any offender who exhibits a fairly good chance of successfully adapting to life within the community. Much parole board action, then, has the consequence of alleviating prison overcrowding by eliminating the least serious offenders from these prison populations.

The Connecticut Parole Board parole eligibility criteria were examined in Chapter 2. Besides institutional conduct variables, these eligibility criteria also included the nature and circumstances of the inmate's conviction offense; the inmate's attitude about that offense; the inmate's attitude toward family, victims, and authority in general; the inmate's employment history and level of educational and vocational training; and the adequacy of the parole plan. Any one or more of these criteria could reasonably be cited by the Connecticut Parole Board for either approving or denying an early-release request. The inherently subjective nature of most of these eligibility criteria (e.g., the inmate's insight into the causes of the past criminal behavior, the adequacy of the inmate's parole plan and planned place of residence, the inmate's attitude toward the conviction offense) permit widely different interpretations to be made of the inmate's parole eligibility. The same is true of psychiatric reports prepared for any inmate. Different interpretations may be made of them to justify virtually any decision about the examined inmate in question.

In an effort to safeguard individual inmate rights and promote equal protection of them at parole board hearings and other critical processing stages, recommendations have been made by some authorities about the characteristics good risk assessment measures and classification instruments should manifest. For instance, Rans (1984) has advised that any developed classification model should be valid, reflect reality, be designed for changing personal and social conditions, serve practical interests, should not be substituted for responsible judgment, and should blend both qualitative and quantitative characteristics. The latter characteristic suggests that sometimes, numerical indicators of dangerousness propensities are misleading and should be overridden. Therefore, many instruments have provisions allowing for administrative overrides, if independent evidence exists to suggest serious measurement errors.

FALSE POSITIVES AND FALSE NEGATIVES REVISITED

False positives are those offenders who suffer the most as the result of measurement errors at different processing stages of both the juvenile and criminal justice process. These are persons designated by various instruments to pose the greatest risk for reoffending or the greatest danger to others if released. We will not revive arguments made in earlier chapters about the moral, ethical, and legal implications of selective incapacitation, or incarcerating those most likely to reoffend on the basis of certain criteria contained in prediction instruments. It is sufficient to note that all instruments exhibit some failure relative to predicting future behaviors, particularly offending behaviors.

At the same time, some offenders, such as Willie Horton, are released on furloughs or various parole programs and are considered "safe" by criminal justice system actors. However, some of these persons commit new and serious crimes. Some of these criminal acts cause serious victim injuries or even death. These false negatives slip through the cracks as well, since no instrument can predict their future behaviors perfectly. Of course, the ultimate objective of any prediction instrument is to minimize the incidence of both false positives and false negatives, while maximizing instances of decision making where community safety and offender reintegration and rehabilitation are ensured and enhanced.

Risk assessment instruments and decision making are either anamnestic, actuarial, or clinical. Although different scholars express preferences for one type of instrument over the others, no particular instrument has been found to be absolutely foolproof for predicting future behavior patterns. Both underpredictions and overpredictions are anticipated, therefore, and we have ultimately settled for acceptable margins of error in either direction. Unofficial error margins of 30 percent or less are considered acceptable by authorities in most jurisdictions. However, some instruments and assessment tools boast much lower error margins resulting from their applications to certain classes of offenders under heavily controlled conditions.

Evaluating a risk instrument's effectiveness is a more or less objective enterprise. We might agree, for instance, to consider an instrument effective if it results in a low amount of recidivism (e.g., less than 30 percent) for particular offender aggregates (e.g., property offenders, convicted DUI offenders, or embezzlers). But recidivism is measured many different ways. Common meanings of recidivism include rearrests, reconvictions, probation or parole program revocations, and reincarcerations. Reconvictions for new crimes are perhaps the best indicators of an instrument's successfulness or unsuccessfulness. However we choose to define recidivism, artificial criteria can be established to verify an instrument's worth in practical situations. But regardless of the way we choose to define recidivism, there will always be a proportion of offenders that fits the false positive or false negative appellation.

Accepting various imperfections of risk instruments, then, is a necessary first step in utilizing these measures for decision making at crucial points, such as initially classifying incoming inmates or deciding who should or should not be paroled. Numerical indicators are frequently equated with objectivity of judgment, but all too often, numerical scores fail to reflect critical factors that may be more important determinants of an inmate's future conduct. For example, Colorado officials have found that unemployment history and employment potential are highly correlated with program successes or failures. If this factor is equally important in affecting program success in other jurisdictions, then all risk assessment instruments should contain one or more items related to employment potential and unemployment history. But many instruments do not make use of this factor. We might argue that if Colorado finds this factor to be an important predictor for parolee success or failure, then other jurisdictions probably would also. Even if other jurisdictions include such items on their risk assessment instruments, these items may not be weighted in such a way to properly acknowledge their important effects. This is one reason why so many jurisdictions are in the process of revising or revamping their existing instrumentation. Each jurisdiction is seeking to improve existing scaling procedures so that decision making at critical stages or points can be optimized. Hopefully, the compendium of instruments in the Appendixes of this book will assist various jurisdictions in their instrument development through the sharing process.

SELECTED TRENDS IN RISK ASSESSMENT

We will conclude this chapter by listing several trends relating to risk and needs assessment. It should be noted that these trends are largely impressionistic and are gleaned from the relevant research literature. It is convenient to group these trends according to specific areas where risk and needs assessment instruments are employed most frequently: (1) probation; (2) institutional classification; and (3) parole board decision making.

Probation and Risk Assessment

In the area of probation, risk assessment instruments will continue to play an important role in evaluating a probationer's success chances and probation eligibility. Probation officers complete presentence investigation reports for convicted offenders, usually in response to judicial requests. In turn, judges rely on such PSIs, in part, for determining the nature and length of an offender's sentence. As one type of sentence judges may impose, probation is warranted in cases where there is the likelihood that eligible offenders will not reoffend or pose risks to their communities. Probation is also an indication of the court's trust that designated probationers will be law-abiding and comply with their probation conditions.

First offenders who have been convicted of minor crimes are typically those most deserving of probation from the court. However, in states with unusually large prison and jail populations and serious overcrowding problems, probation is being increasingly extended to more serious offenders. For example, California places approximately 70 percent of its convicted felons on probation annually, primarily because there is no room to accommodate these offenders if they are sentenced to hard time in jail or prison. The ideal scenario of incarcerating all offenders who deserve to be incarcerated is a luxury enjoyed by only a few jurisdictions with few offenders and greater prison space. For the great majority of jurisdictions, however, probation is a necessity precisely because of precious prison and jail space limitations. Unfortunately, the recidivism figures for convicted felons who are placed in probation programs are quite high. Petersilia (1985a) reports that approximately 65 percent of these felony probationers will recidivate within a year or so after being placed on probation. Thus, a turnstile or revolving door phenomenon occurs, as convicted offenders are released on probation but continue to reoffend.

Therefore, it is not difficult to understand and appreciate the need for proven instruments and assessment tools in order for judges and others to make the best probation decisions. Judges must usually decide which levels of supervised probation should be imposed, rather than the less frequent decision about which offenders should be incarcerated. The following trends are projected relative to probation decision making.

1. There will be increased attention given to validation studies of probationers to determine the effectiveness and reliability of scales used in probation decision making. In virtually all cases involving instrument development, both the reliability and validity of such instrumentation is enhanced by empirical research. Actual applications of instruments in practical situations involving large numbers of probationers will assist scale developers in focusing upon only the most salient criteria useful in behavioral forecasting. Many of the studies that have been conducted are actuarial in nature, where large numbers of offenders are described initially and tracked over time to determine their degree of reoffending. Lower rates of reoffending among certain offender aggregates will highlight variables that might be useful in reducing recidivism rates among subsequent offender aggregates.

2. Risk/needs devices will continue to be created and revised, although they will be increasingly offense-specific. Some departments of correction have devised risk instruments that assess one's potential for assaultive behavior or theft behavior. Other instruments have been devised to determine psychopathic or sociopathic propensities. Sex offenders are assessed with selected instruments that focus upon aspects of their lives and thoughts that appear closely linked with sex-offending behavior. Currently, many established instruments only superficially assess specific problem areas that might interfere with adjustment and reintegration while on probation. As the sophistication of assessment centers increases, it is likely that the instruments used by these centers or agencies will be more specialized to target specific types of problems. Thus, more appropriate treatments or interventions might be used to enable probationers to complete their programs successfully.

3. There will be greater attention given to devising risk and needs measures for female probationer-clients as well as for male probationer-clients. Most risk and needs devices devised presently are geared toward male offenders. Only a handful of states have devised risk measures for female offenders. The growing female offender population is desperately in need of more specialized instruments to target female problem areas not commonly associated with male offenders. Many female offenders are mothers with children. Thus, their particular circumstances must be addressed by specific items in scales to enable authorities to help them adjust and attempt to deal with family needs. Furthermore, many probation programs have been designed almost exclusively for males. More gender-specific instrumentation may help agencies to establish more services oriented toward female clients.

4. Risk and needs assessment instrumentation will be increasingly geared toward increasing offender accountability by indicating more restrictive conditions

of probation to be imposed. Probation is a punishment, despite public sentiment suggesting that it is no punishment compared with offender incarceration. Risk instrumentation can be geared in the future toward prescribing higher supervision levels for those offenders most deserving of closer management by probation officers. Offender accountability may also be heightened by incorporating certain punitive elements into risk/needs schemes. Such elements might include items related to victim compensation, restitution, or community service.

5. Instrumentation will be more specific at targeting appropriate services and treatments for a greater number of offender categories. According to the *Uniform Crime Reports,* there are dozens of crime designations. These are also listed in state and federal documents pertaining to offender classification and risk assessment. Thus, risk instruments might become increasingly offense-specific as a means of identifying more accurately the amount of risk different offender-clients might pose.

6. Risk instrumentation will be increasingly supplemented by clinical-type input from probation officers and others who monitor offender-clients through their program duration. Probation officers are involved in clients' lives prior to sentencing through the preparation of presentence investigation reports. These officers have direct contact with most persons involved in the offender's life. It is likely that they will assume more important roles and provide much valuable input regarding sentencing decisions and probation program selection beyond the recommendations they state in their PSI documentation. Oral evaluations of offenders will be increasingly required and relied upon for more effective probation placement. Thus, probation officers can offer some clinical information based upon their impressions and observations. PSIs are not always this inclusive, since it is difficult to commit to writing all one observes or encounters in the preparation of these documents.

7. Instrumentation will become increasingly individualized and encompass subscales to assess potentially emergent behaviors that might interfere with the successful completion of the offender's probation program. A key problem that must be settled at the time of sentencing is whether there are any debilitating factors that might interfere with an offender's probation program successfulness. These factors may be social or psychological, or a combination of both. Some problems relate to educational level and amount of vocational training and preparation. Becoming employed and remaining employed are often crucial determinants of successful probation program completion. Psychological problems may have been evident in earlier clinical assessments conducted by court-appointed psychiatrists. Risk and needs instruments will likely focus increasingly on adjustment factors, such as previous drug or alcohol dependencies. Appropriate services and support groups may be designated for particular offenders as a part of their treatment and recovery.

8. More sophisticated instrument development will necessitate more effective training of those administering and interpreting the results of assessment devices of any kind. Officers who are vested with the responsibility of administering and interpreting test results will require greater amounts of training, since the instru-

ments themselves will become increasingly sophisticated in their construction. Complicated scoring procedures and weighting arrangements must be performed by an increasingly competent officer contingent.

Institutional Classification and Risk Assessment

1. Instruments used for security determination, custody-level decision making, and inmate needs assessments will become more specialized and lead to more elaborate security designation schemes. Institutions that house juvenile and adult offenders rely heavily upon risk assessment scores to determine proper security level placements for incoming inmates. Further, these instruments are also relied upon to direct particular inmates to receive certain services and/or treatments. Depending upon the range of services and treatment programs available in any given institution, risk/needs tools will increasingly be devised to reflect a broader range of suggested or recommended services and treatments. Present security-level designations are rather simplified in many jurisdictions. Over time, these security-level classification schemes will become more elaborate, and the instruments used for effective inmate security placements will reflect these changes.

2. More attention will be given to developing both male and female classification and initial security placement criteria. Both male and female inmates must be accommodated by prison services. However, many prison systems are geared primarily to cater to the needs of male offenders. Women's institutions and incarcerative facilities tend to be smaller than men's institutions. Further, fewer services are provided to women in these smaller institutions. More refined risk and needs instruments will include valuable information about women's needs as well as those of men. In turn, existing services may be expanded to provide a broader range of treatment programs and accommodations for women than exist presently. Initial security placement instruments can also be constructed along gender-specific lines. Some states already have such instruments in place, and other states are in the process of developing them. In future years, it is likely that all jurisdictions will have appropriate breakdowns and distinctions among both male and female inmates.

3. Instrumentation will be increasingly supplemented by correctional officer input, where officers who interact with inmates closely and regularly can provide valuable feedback about classification effectiveness which otherwise would be undetected by relying upon purely numerical scores. Correctional officers who supervise inmates on a regular basis are in the best positions to evaluate their institutional behavior. Paper-pencil instrumentation doesn't always target behavioral problems or identify those most disruptive inmates who would not be particularly successful at adapting to different, less secure, custody levels. Thus, reclassifications of inmates over time will be increasingly supplemented by both oral and written testimony provided by corrections officers who are strategically placed in the inmate environment. Many states currently have override provisions incorporated into their initial classification and reclassification instruments. More effective override decision making can be made through greater correc-

tional officer involvement and participation in the risk and custody-level classification process.

4. Instruments will feature subscales that will minimize overclassifications of inmates and lead to more minimum-security placements. Minimum-security space is the most economical space in prison and jail facilities. Inmates in these lower custody levels require less direct monitoring and supervision and cause correctional officers fewer disruptive problems. However, a common classification problem is that many inmates are overclassified and assigned to higher custody levels. These classifications and placements are not particularly cost-effective. Furthermore, the parole eligibility chances of inmates assigned to higher custody levels are jeopardized to some extent. At the same time, prison officials do not want to place more dangerous offenders in low-security areas where they might harm or seek to dominate other inmates. Thus, more instruments will be devised that incorporate subscales that assess offenders' behavioral propensities and potential for causing disruption or interpersonal problems. Presently, several states have scales that assess an inmate's potential assaultive risk relative to other inmates. But many other jurisdictions are not specialized to that degree. Future instrument development will likely use such risk measures to make more effective minimum-security placements.

5. More evaluative studies will be conducted concerning the "fit" between scale scores and predicted institutional behaviors. These reliability and validity checks will furnish corrections officials with more accurate information about inmate placements while institutionalized. As is the case with probation risk instrument development, continuing efforts will be made by prison institutions and departments of corrections to construct more effective classification tools. The adequacy of instrumentation is often assessed by paying attention to studies of instrument applications for particular offender populations. The more we learn about the "fit" between inmate adjustment to prison life and scale scores on classification instruments, the better the instrument that can be devised to enable authorities to make more effective inmate placements. Reliability and validity checks of existing instruments on diverse prisoner populations can do much to improve an instrument's predictive utility. Ultimately, offender management is enhanced to reduce institutional operating costs and maximize inmate rehabilitative potential.

Parole Board Decision Making and Risk Assessment

1. Existing instrumentation will be further refined to reflect parolee adjustment criteria. Parole boards currently use risk assessment instruments, together with other input from various sources, to make their early-release decisions. Greater concern for a parolee's adjustment to community living will be evident in future instrument development. More community adjustment–specific criteria will be incorporated into these risk and needs instruments for more appropriate parole program placements.

2. More comparative research and information exchange will occur between

departments of correction and parole boards for the purpose of sharing the most useful predictive criteria and parole decision-making information. It is important for different jurisdictions to share their information about offender decision making. An inspection of the parole risk and needs assessment instruments presented in this book will disclose significant differences among the topics assessed. Obviously, not all risk/needs measures are alike. Certain benefits may accrue to jurisdictions that examine instrumentation developed in other jurisdictions for essentially the same decision-making purposes. This book represents one effort to disseminate such instrument information in the hope that inter-jurisdictional sharing will occur. Through such sharing, risk and needs instrumentation can be improved over time. The long-range result is more effective and informed early-release decision making by parole boards.

3. More appropriate statistical models will be devised to strengthen the predictive utility of existing parole risk and needs instruments, and to determine which types of program involvement and supervision levels are most appropriate for different parolees. In the process of developing and testing different types of instrumentation, researchers are continually experimenting with a variety of statistical models and tools to yield the best and soundest predictive results. Different types of analytical problems can isolate those factors most important in decision making and long-range behavioral forecasting. It is not so much the case that more sophisticated statistical models will necessarily be more effective than more simplified models. We have already discussed these differences and reported that researcher reactions are mixed. Rather, more experimentation will likely yield more productive ways of designing and administering instruments, taking into account the most relevant parole-success criteria. An inspection of existing risk/needs parole decision-making instruments suggests that although many of the same factors are used in different scales, there are often great differences in how these common factors are weighted. Thus, certain offenders in some states may be rejected as parolees because of a one- or two-point fluctuation in their risk scale score, whereas offenders in other states may be granted parole because of a similar, minor point fluctuation in the opposite direction. Essentially the same item weighted differently will cause dramatic differences in parole outcomes when such differences are not truly warranted. This type of weighting problem can be addressed and certain effective solutions may be proposed.

4. Instrumentation used by parole boards for assessing an inmate's potential risk will be increasingly supplemented with direct probation officer and victim input. Parole boards currently rely on risk instrument scores and oral information provided by inmates themselves in order to decide whether to grant an inmate's parole request. Also relied upon are presentence investigation reports that contain early background information compiled by probation officers prior to sentencing. It would be valuable if probation officers themselves could offer direct input relating to the PSI documents they originally prepared. Victim testimony is also solicited, although this option is not mandatory in most jurisdictions. Raw risk scores may not reveal aspects of the original conviction offense that may

contain mitigating or aggravating circumstances inadvertently overlooked. Probation officers might clarify scale scores and lend oral testimony for the purpose of a more informed parole board decision.

5. Greater monitoring of instrument applications will be undertaken to assess whether predicted behaviors/observed behaviors of parolees coincide and whether recommended actions, treatments, and programs are having desirable impacts or effects. The true test of any instrument is whether the predicted behavior actually occurs in the future. Increasingly, risk assessment devices as well as needs instruments will be examined in terms of offender-client behavioral outcomes. If certain treatments or program involvements were required or recommended, were these treatments and program involvements effective in changing client behaviors and law-abiding conduct? Increasingly, the correspondence between scale scores and parole board recommendations and early-release decisions will be compared and evaluated. In time, these instruments will be revised and refined to reflect more stable predictive criteria.

SUMMARY

Risk and needs assessments conducted currently among various state and federal corrections departments and bureaus are an imperfect enterprise. Nevertheless, acceptable levels of error result in general offender classifications and program placements. Judges assess offender risk and success potential for probationary sentences, while correctional officers assess incoming inmates for security and custody-level placements. Parole boards make early-release decisions, in part, by consulting risk assessment devices and needs inventories. All of this decision making necessarily generates proportions of offenders known as false positives and false negatives. The intent of all decision making at all points in both the criminal and juvenile justice system is to reduce both types of prediction error. Prediction errors are minimized by continuous instrument refinement, validation studies, and reliability checks of risk and needs devices on diverse offender samples.

Areas where risk and needs assessment are most crucial include probation decision making, classification decision making in prison and jail institutions, and parole board decision making. Several trends are noted regarding instrument development in each of these crucial decision making areas. More offense-specific instruments will be created in probation decision making, together with the inclusion of items intended to increase offender accountability. More specific scale items will be included that indicate particular services or treatment programs for clients. In all areas, more studies will be conducted to determine test reliability and validity for more accurate inmate and offender-client assessments. Prison institutions will increasingly utilize gender-specific instruments to differentiate between male and female inmates and their respective needs. More emphasis will be placed upon identifying inmates most eligible for minimum-security placements, and diagnostic commentaries will be increasingly solicited from correctional officers themselves about particular inmate classification decisions and placements. Parole boards will devise more effective statistical prediction models for the purpose of making more informed early-release decisions. Greater comparative research and information exchange will occur among jurisdictions, as different departments of corrections seek to share their scale developments with other jurisdictions. Greater attempts will be made to assess both the short- and long-range predictive utility of measures that seek to match prospective parolees with particular post-prison programs in communities. More effective monitoring will occur that will help to modify and improve existing instrumentation to reflect program changes and community corrections developments over time.

Appendix A

Forms: Adult

Form A-1
Federal Bureau of Prisons Worksheet and Salient Factor Index

U.S. Department of Justice
United States Parole Commission

Preliminary Assessment/Retroactivity/Statutory Interim/ Rescission Worksheet

Institution: ______________

Name: ______________ **Reg. No.:** ______________ **Hearing Date:** ______________

Reasons: *(Circle and complete each applicable reason)*

1. Your *(offense) (parole violation)* behavior is rated as Category ______ severity because ______________ ______________.

Your salient factor score *(SFS-81)* is ______ *(See below)*. You have been in *(federal) (state) (state and federal)* confinement as a result of your behavior for a total of ______ months *(as of:* [date] ______________*)*. Guidelines established by the Commission indicate a range of ______ months to be served for cases with a good institutional adjustment and program achievement.

2. At a statutory interim hearing, if either the revised severity rating or revised salient factor score category is more favorable, complete reasons will be provided *(whether or not the actual decision is modified)* — use item (B) below. If neither is more favorable, complete reasons need not be given — use item (A) below.

(A) Retroactivity does not apply: Neither your recalculated severity rating *(old Category* ______________ *; new Category* ______________ *)* nor your recalculated salient factor risk category *(old Category* ______________ *; old score* ______ *; new Category* ______ *, new score* ______ *— see attached sheet)* is more favorable.

(B) Your guidelines are recalculated as follows. Your offense severity *(is recalculated as) (remains as)* ______________ . Your offense behavior involved ______________ ______________.

Your salient factor score risk category *(is recalculated as) (remains as)* ______ . *(Old score* ______ *; new score* ______ *— see attached sheet.)* Continue with full reasons from 1. above.

3. The above decision includes a ______ month credit for superior program achievement; specifically ______________ ______________

4. *(Furthermore)* you have committed behavior that constitutes new criminal conduct *(that extends into)* in the community while on *(pass from a community treatment center) (furlough) (work release) (escape)* which is rated as Category ______________ severity because ______________ ______________.

Your new salient factor score *(SFS-81)* is ______________ . Guidelines established by the Commission which consider the above factors indicate a range of ______________ months to be added to your original *(guideline range) (presumptive) (effective) (parole date)*.

5. *(In addition,)* you have committed behavior that constitutes new criminal conduct in a prison facility or in a community treatment center which is rated as Category ______ severity because ______________ ______________ which indicates ______ months to be added to your original *(guideline range) (presumptive) (effective) (parole date)*.

6. *(Also,)* you *(failed to appear) (escaped or attempted to escape) (from) (secure) (non-secure) (custody) (with voluntary return in 6 days or less)* which requires *(0-6) (6-12) (8-16)* months to be added to your original guideline range.

7. *(In addition,)* you have committed recission behavior classified as administrative. Guidelines established by the Commission indicate a range of *(up to 8 months per drug-related infractions) (and) (up to 2 months for non-drug related infractions.)* You have committed (______ *drug-related infraction(s) (and)* (______ *non-drug related infraction(s).*

8. Your *(aggregate)* guideline range is ______ months *(to be served) (to be added to your original [presumptive] [parole] [effective] [date] [guideline range] [* ______________ *]). (Plus the time in escape status.)*

Form A-1 (continued)

Salient Factors (Old) (New)

A. PRIOR CONVICTIONS/ADJUDICATIONS *(ADULT OR JUVENILE)*.............................. ☐ ☐
None = 3; One = 2; Two or three = 1; Four or more = 0

B. PRIOR COMMITMENT(S) OF MORE THAN THIRTY DAYS *(ADULT OR JUVENILE)*.............. ☐ ☐
None = 2; One or two = 1; Three or more = 0

C. AGE AT CURRENT OFFENSE/PRIOR COMMITMENTS.. ☐ ☐
Age at commencement of current offense:
26 years of age or more = 2★; 20-25 years of age = 1★; 19 years of age or less = 0
★**Exception:** If five or more prior commitments of more than thirty days *(adult or juvenile)*, place an "x" here ______ and score this Item = 0

D. RECENT COMMITMENT FREE PERIOD *(THREE YEARS)*.. ☐ ☐
No prior commitment of more than thirty days (adult or juvenile) or released to the community from last such commitment at least three years prior to the commencement of the current offense = 1; Otherwise = 0

E. PROBATION/PAROLE/CONFINEMENT/ESCAPE STATUS VIOLATOR THIS TIME............... ☐ ☐
Neither on probation, parole, confinement, or escape status at the time of the current offense; nor committed as a probation, parole, confinement, or escape status violator this time = 1; Otherwise = 0

F. HEROIN/OPIATE DEPENDENCE.. ☐ ☐
No history of heroin/opiate dependence = 1; Otherwise = 0

Total Score.. ☐ ☐

9. After review of all relevant factors and information presented,

(a) A decision outside the guidelines at this consideration is not found warranted.

(b) A decision *(above) (below)* the guidelines appears warranted because:

- ☐ **Your offense behavior involved the following *(aggravating) (mitigating)* factors:**
- ☐ **You are a *(poorer) (better)* risk that indicated by your salient factor score in that:**
- ☐ **You are a more serious risk than indicated by your salient factor score in that:**
- ☐ **You have a record of *(institutional misconduct) (superior institution program achievement)*, specifically:**
- ☐ **A decision above the guidelines is mandated in that you have a minimum sentence which exceeds the guideline range.**
- ☐ **The following *(exceptional) (circumstances)* are present:**

____
____
____
____
____

For Category Eight, no upper limits are specified due to the extreme variability of the cases within this category. For decisions exceeding the lower limit of the applicable guideline category BY MORE THAN 48 MONTHS, the pertinent aggravating case factors considered are to be specified in the reasons given *(e.g., that a homicide was premeditated or committed during the course of another felony; or that extreme cruelty or brutality was demonstrated).*

***Note:* When using more than one reason in 9(b), number each and draw a line from the colon to each applicable continuation.**

10. As required by law, you have also been scheduled for a statutory interim hearing *(during* ______________ *)* *(during the docket immediately preceding completion of the minimum term).*

Examiner's Initials:
______________ **(Primary)**
______________ **(Secondary)**

Form A.2
Florida: Control Release Action and Salient Factor Scoring System

FLORIDA PAROLE COMMISSION
CONTROL RELEASE AUTHORITY
1309 WINEWOOD BOULEVARD
TALLAHASSEE, FLORIDA 32399-2450

CONTROL RELEASE ACTION

Inmate Name: ______________________ Date Reviewed ____________

Inmate Number: ______________________ Institution: ____________

I. MATRIX GRID RESULTS – EXAMINER'S SCORING

A. Salient Factor Points

1=___ 2=___ 3=___ 4=___ 5=___ 6=___ 7=___ 8=___ TOTAL:____ GRID:____
Case #:__________ Offense Type:__________ Offense Severity:__________

1. Immediate Release
2. Eligible for Early or Advanceable CRD
3. Maximum Sentence Length - Non Advanceable A
4. Maximum Sentence Length - Non Advanceable B

II. PAROLE EXAMINER'S RECOMMENDATION

A. Control Release Status
1. Immediate Release
2. Eligible for Early or Advanceable CRD
3. Maximum Sentence Length - Non Advanceable A
4. Maximum Sentence Length - Non Advanceable B

Reason (If departure from grid):______________________

B. CRD Setting
1. Immediate Release
2. TRD - Advanceable
3. Maximum Sentence Length - Non Advanceable B
4. Fixed Date Certain:______________________
5. Advanceable CRD (Other than set at TRD):______________________
6. Maximum Sentence Length - Non Advanceable A

C. Post-Release Supervision
1. No Supervision
2. No longer used (Three-Month Supervision deleted 5/25/92)
3. 6 Months Supervision
4. 12 Months Supervision
5. Other:______________________

Reason (If departure from grid):______________________

D. Special Condition(s) of Supervision:______________________
Examiner recommends Administrative Caseload (D-22) Yes___ No___

Form A.2 (continued)

CONTROL RELEASE SALIENT FACTOR SCORING SYSTEM

ITEM 1
TOTAL NUMBER OF ALL PRIOR CONVICTIONS:

Four or more	=	3 Points
Three	=	2 Points
One or two	=	1 Point
None	=	0 Points

ITEM 2
NUMBER OF PRIOR VIOLENT CONVICTIONS:
(felony, misd., juv. adjudications)

Four	=	4 Points
Three	=	3 Points
Two	=	2 Points
One	=	1 Point
None	=	0 Points

ITEM 3
NUMBER OF PRIOR INCARCERATIONS:
(sentenced to 60 days or more in jail, prison or juv. commitments)

Three or more	=	2 Points
One or Two	=	1 Points
None	=	0 Points

ITEM 4
TOTAL PRIOR SENTENCES IN YEARS:

Two or more years	=	2 Points
Less than Two years but more than 59 days	=	1 Point
All prior sentences of 59 days or less	=	0 Points

ITEM 5
AGE AT OFFENSE WHICH LED TO THE FIRST INCARCERATION: (Juvenile or Adult)

17 years or younger	=	2 Points
18 - 25	=	1 Point
26 years or older	=	0 Points

ITEM 6
NUMBER OF REVOCATIONS:

Three or more	=	2 Points
One or Two	=	1 Point
None	=	0 Points

ITEM 7
NUMBER OF PRIOR ESCAPE CONVICTIONS:

One or More Prior Escapes	=	1 Point
No Prior Escapes	=	0 Points

ITEM 8
BURGLARY OR BREAKING & ENTERING AS THE PRESENT OFFENSE OF CONVICTION:

Burglary Conviction	=	1 Point
No Burglary Conviction	=	0 Points

I VIOLENT OFFENSE* — **C.R. SALIENT FACTOR SCORE**

OFFENSE SEVERITY	0	1	2	3	4	5	6	7	8	9	10+
3rd Degree Felony	A	A	A	A	A	A	A	A	NA	NA	NB
2nd Degree Felony	A	A	A	A	A6	NA	NA	NA	NB	NB	NB
1st Degree Felony	A	A6	NB	NB	NB	NB	NB	NB	NB	NB	NB
Life Felony	A12	A12	NB	NB	NB	NB	NB	NB	NB	NB	NB
Capital Felony	NB	NB	NB	NB	NB	NB	NB	NB	NB	NB	NB

II PROPERTY OFFENSE* — **C.R. SALIENT FACTOR SCORE**

OFFENSE SEVERITY	0	1	2	3	4	5	6	7	8	9	10+
3rd Degree Felony	M	M	A	A	A	A	A	A	A	A6	A12
2nd Degree Felony	A	A	A	A	A	A6	A6	A6	A12	A12	NA
1st Degree Felony	A	A	A6	A6	A12	A12	NA	NA	NA	NA	NA
Life Felony	A6	A12	A12	NB	NB	NB	NB	NB	NB	NB	NB
Capital Felony	NB	NB	NB	NB	NB	NB	NB	NB	NB	NB	NB

III DRUG OFFENSE* — **C.R. SALIENT FACTOR SCORE**

OFFENSE SEVERITY	0	1	2	3	4	5	6	7	8	9	10+
3rd Degree Felony	M	M	A	A	A	A	A	A	A	A	A
2nd Degree Felony	A	A	A	A	A	A	A	A6	A6	A12	A12
1st Degree Felony	A	A	A	A	A12	A12	A12	NA	NA	NA	NA
Life Felony	A6	A6	A12	A12	NB	NB	NB	NB	NB	NB	NB
Capital Felony	NB	NB	NB	NB	NB	NB	NB	NB	NB	NB	NB

M	=	Eligible for Immediate Release
A	=	Eligible for Early Release (before maximum release date) and/or Advanceable C.R. Date)
NA	=	Maximum non-advanceable Category A. May be transferred to advanceable category in the event of critical depletion of advanceable category (less than 4000).
NB	=	Not Eligible for Early Release or Advanceable C.R. Date (Maximum non-advanceable Category B)
A6	=	Post Release Supervision of 6 Months
A12	=	Post Release Supervision of 12 Months

*Primary Offense of Conviction

I	Violent	=	Primary Offense contained in Guidelines categories 1-4 (9-Kidnapping, Child Abuse)
II	Property	=	Primary Offense contained in Guidelines categories 5,6,8 (9-Other than Kidnapping and Child Abuse)
III	Drugs	=	Primary Offense in Guidelines category 7

Form A.3
Hawaii: Initial Classification Instrument

INITIAL CLASSIFICATION INSTRUMENT

SECTION I

SID: __ __ __ __ __ __ __ __ LST NAME:______________ FN:________

DOB: ____-____-____ DATE: ____-____-____ HEARING TYPE: ____

SEX: M F FACILITY:__________ COMMITTMENT DATE:____-____-____

MAX SENTENCE (in months): __________ COMPLETED BY: ______________

SENTENCE STRUCTURE (List Offenses and sentences):

____

____

____

____

____

SECTION II CUSTODY EVALUATION

1. **SEVERITY OF INSTITUTIONAL VIOLENCE (Jail or Prison, score most serious)**

None	0	
High Category Misconduct (18 months)	3	
Greatest Category Misconduct (24 months)	7	____ SCORE
Extremely Violent Misconduct (5 years)	9	

2. **SEVERITY OF CURRENT OFFENSE (Refer to Severity of Offense list in manual. Score the most serious offense).**

Low Moderate	1	
Moderate	2	
High	4	____ SCORE
Greatest	6	
Life With or Without Parole	10	

3. **PRIOR OFFENSE HISTORY SEVERITY (Score the most serious offense)**

None , Low Moderate	0	
Moderate	2	
High	4	
Greatest, LWP	6	____ SCORE

4. **ESCAPE HISTORY**

No escapes or attempts, no prior incarcerations	0	
An escape or attempt from minimum/community security, without violence:		
Over 7 years	1	
Within the last 7 years.	5	
An escape or attempt from medium or above security or an escape from minimum or community security with violence:		____ SCORE
Over 7 years	5	
Within the last 7 years	9	

TOTAL ITEMS 1 through 4, if score is 10 or more assign to close custody (ALWAYS complete the remaining items, but do not total score if inmate is assigned to CLOSE custody). ________

____

5. **HISTORY OF ASSAULTIVE BEHAVIOR**

None	0	
Misdemeanor (Past 3 years)	1	
Felony C (Past 5 years)	2	
Felony A or B (Past 15 years)	3	____ SCORE

6. **INVOLVEMENT IN SUBSTANCE ABUSE**

None	0	
Abuse causing occasional legal problems, some disruption of functioning	2	____ SCORE
Abuse causing serious legal problems	3	

7. **PRIOR FELONY CONVICTIONS**

None	0	
One	1	
Two or More	2	____ SCORE

8. **STABILITY FACTORS (Check appropriate factors and combine score)**

Age 30 or older	-2 __	
High School Diploma or GED	-1 __	(______)
Employed or attending school (full or part-time for 12 months or longer at time of arrest	-1 __	
None	0 __	

COMPREHENSIVE POINT TOTAL [ ]

Form A.3 (continued)

SECTION III POINT SCALE SUMMARY
If point total is 6 or less complete Section IV
If point total is 7 to 16 then custody is MEDIUM
If point total is 17 or greater then custody is CLOSE

SECTION IV
NON-DISCRETIONARY EXCLUSIONS FOR MINIMUM CUSTODY

1.	Less than one year from last violent episode	yes	no
2.	Pending charges, felony hold or detainer	yes	no
3.	Hawaii PSD escape/attempt escape within last 7 years	yes	no
4.	Maximum sentence greater than 60 months	yes	no

If any factor answered <u>yes</u>, then computed custody is **MEDIUM**
If all factors answered <u>no</u>, then computed custody is MINIMUM

COMPUTED CUSTODY LEVEL ________________

SECTION V
DISCRETIONARY CRITERIA FOR ANY CUSTODY EXEMPTION

01 = Protective Custody	05 = Overcrowding
02 = Violent Offender	06 = Medical
03 = Youthful Offender	07 = Mental Health
04 = Sex Offender	08 = Management Problem
09 = Exemplary Adjustment	10 = Other

OVER-RIDE RECOMMENDED YES NO

PRIMARY OVER- RIDE REASON ____

RECOMMENDED CUSTODY LEVEL __________

COMMENTS:

SECTION VI RAD CLASSIFICATION ACTION

Recommended Custody Level ____________ **Recommended Facilty Placement** ______________

Completion Date ______________________ **CO Action Code** __________

Comments :

Special Classification Date: ___________ Mandatory 6 Month Reclassification Date: ________

Reviewed by: ______________________________ _______________
RAD Classification Coordinator Date

SECTION VII CENTRAL CLASSIFCATION

Assigned Custody Level ________________ Assigned Facility ______________

Assignment Date ______________________

Comments:

_________________________________ __________
Classification Officer Date

Form A.4
Illinois: Male Classification Instrument

COMMUNITY CORRECTIONAL CENTER CLASSIFICATION SYSTEM
MALE CLASSIFICATION INSTRUMENT

INSTITUTION CODE ☐☐

IDOC NUMBER ☐ - ☐☐☐☐☐ NAME ______________________________
Last First MI

ITEMS

Current Age

28 and Older	Enter 0	☐
23 to 27	Enter 2	
22 and Younger	Enter 4	

Number of Prison Admissions (Include Current Offense)

First Incarceration	Enter 0	☐
2 or More Incarcerations over 30 Days	Enter 2	

Number of Prior Supervision Terms Not Successfully Completed
(Include Probation/Parole/MSR/CCC/Other Supervision Terms)

None	Enter 0	☐
1 or More	Enter 1	

History of Alcohol Use

No Alcohol Use Problems Indicated	Enter 0	☐
Alcohol Use Problems Indicated	Enter 2	

History of Drug Use

No Drug Use Problems Indicated	Enter 0	☐
Drug Use Problems Indicated	Enter 3	

Vocational

History Indicates Marketable Job Skills or has Completed Vocational Training Program at the Institution	Enter 0	☐
History Indicates a Need for Vocational Training	Enter 3	

Academic

Inmate has at least a High School Diploma or a G.E.D.	Enter 0	☐
Inmate does not have a High School Diploma or a G.E.D.	Enter 3	

Total Score ☐☐

CURRENT SECURITY LEVEL Maximum (1) Medium (2) Minimum (3) ☐

CLASSIFICATION LEVEL:
(0 - 4) = 1
(5 - 7) = 2
(8 - 9) = 3
(10 - 11) = 4
(12 - 15) = 5
(16 - 18) = 6
☐

Signature ______________________ Code ☐☐☐☐ Date ☐☐-☐☐-☐☐

Comment for Override, Administrative Concerns, Critical/Special Needs, Etc.

____

____

____

Form A.5
Illinois: Assessment of Adult Probationer Risk

STATE OF ILLINOIS

ILLINOIS ADULT PROBATION CLASSIFICATION SYSTEM

Circuit Court of Cook County

ASSESSMENT OF ADULT PROBATIONER RISK

Probationer's Name ______________________ Case # __________
Last First Middle

Sentencing Date __________ Officer's Name __________
Mo. Day Year

Assessment Date __________ Expiration Date __________
Mo. Day Year Mo. Day Yr.

			SCORE
Number of Address Changes in Last 12 Months:	0 2 3	None One Two or more	______
Percentage of Time Employed in Last 12 Months:	0 1 2 0	60% or more 40%-59% Under 40% Not applicable	______
Alcohol Usage Problems:	0 2 4	No interference with functioning Occasional abuse; some disruption of functioning Frequent abuse, serious disruption; needs treatment	______
Other Drug Usage Problems:	0 1 2	No interference with functioning Occasional abuse; some disruption of functioning Frequent abuse; serious disruption; needs treatment	______
Attitude:	0 3 5	Motivated to change; receptive to assistance Dependent or unwilling to accept responsibility Rationalizes behavior; negative; not motivated to change	______
Age at First Conviction: (or Juvenile Adjudication)	0 2 4	24 or older 20-23 19 or younger	______
Number of Prior Periods of Probation/Parole Supervision: (Adult or Juvenile)	0 4	None One or more	______
Number of Prior Probation/Parole Revocations: (Adult or Juvenile)	0 4	None One or more	______
Number of Prior Felony Convictions: (or Juvenile Adjudications)	0 2 4	None One Two or more	______
Convictions or Juvenile Adjudications for: (Select applicable and add for score.) (Include current offense.)	0 2 3	None Burglary, theft, auto theft, or robbery Worthless checks or forgery	______
Conviction or Juvenile Adjudication for Assaultive Offense within Last Two Years: (An offense which involves the use of a weapon, physical force or the threat of force)	15 0	Yes No	______
		TOTAL	______

Form A.5 (continued)

COOK COUNTY ADULT PROBATION DEPARTMENT

OVERRIDE FORM

TO: ______________________ FROM: ______________________

DIVISION: ______________________ DATE: ______________________

PROBATIONER'S NAME: ______________________

CASE NUMBER: ______________________

REQUESTED OVERRIDE LEVEL CHANGE (CHECK APPROPRIATE BOXES)

FROM:	☐ MAXIMUM	☐ MEDIUM	☐ MINIMUM
TO:	☐ MAXIMUM	☐ MEDIUM	☐ MINIMUM

REASON FOR OVERRIDE: ______________________

____

____

____

____

____

☐ APPROVED ☐ DENIED

SUPERVISOR'S COMMENTS: ______________________

____

____

____

RESULTING SUPERVISION LEVEL: ☐ MAXIMUM ☐ MEDIUM ☐ MINIMUM

______________________ Probation Officer's Signature

______________________ Supervisor's Signature

______________________ Date

Form A.6
Illinois: Reassessment of Adult Probationer Risk

ILLINOIS ADULT PROBATION CLASSIFICATION SYSTEM
Circuit Court of Cook County
REASSESSMENT OF ADULT PROBATIONER RISK

STATE OF ILLINOIS
Check One: Routine ______ Special ______ Transfer ______

Probationer's Name ______________ (Last) ______________ (First) ______________ (Middle) Case # ______________
Reassessment Date ______ (Mo) ______ (Day) ______ (Year) Officer's Name ______________
Previous Reassessment ______ (Mo) ______ (Day) ______ (Year) Expiration Date ______ (Mo) ______ (Day) ______ (Yr.)

			SCORE
Number of Address Changes in Last 12 Months:	0 2 3	None One Two or more	______
Age at First Conviction: (or Juvenile Adjudication)	0 1 2	24 or older 20-23 19 or younger	______
Number of Probation/Parole Revocations: (Adult or Juvenile)	0 2	None One or more	______
Number of Prior Felony Convictions: (or Juvenile Adjudications) (Exclude Current Probation Case)	0 1 3	None One Two or more	______
Convictions or Juvenile Adjudications for: (Select Applicable and Add for Score.) (Include Current Probation Case)	0 1 2	None Burglary, Theft, Auto Theft, or Robbery Worthless checks or Forgery	______
RATE THE FOLLOWING BASED ON PERIOD SINCE LAST CLASSIFICATION			
Percentage of Time Employed:	0 1 2 0	60% or More 40%-59% Under 40% Not applicable	______
Alcohol Usage/Problems:	0 2 5	No Apparent Problems Moderate Problems Serious Problems	______
Other Drug Usage/Problems:	0 1 3	No Apparent Problems Moderate Problems Serious Problems	______
Problems in Interpersonal Relationships: (Living/Working Situation)	0 1 3 5	None Few Moderate Severe	______
Social Identification:	0 3	Mainly with Positive Individuals Mainly with Delinquent Individuals	______
Response to Court Imposed Conditions:	0 3 5	No Problems of Consequence Moderate Compliance Problems Has Been Unwilling to Comply	______
Use of Community Resources:	0 0 2 3 4	Not Needed Productively Utilized Needed but Not Available Utilized but Not Beneficial Available but Rejected	______
		TOTAL	______

Form A.6 (continued)

COOK COUNTY ADULT PROBATION DEPARTMENT

OVERRIDE FORM

TO: ______________________ FROM: ______________________

DIVISION: ______________________ DATE: ______________________

PROBATIONER'S NAME: ______________________

CASE NUMBER: ______________________

REQUESTED OVERRIDE LEVEL CHANGE (CHECK APPROPRIATE BOXES)

FROM:	☐ MAXIMUM	☐ MEDIUM	☐ MINIMUM
TO:	☐ MAXIMUM	☐ MEDIUM	☐ MINIMUM

REASON FOR OVERRIDE: ______________________

____

____

____

____

____

☐ APPROVED ☐ DENIED

SUPERVISOR'S COMMENTS: ______________________

____

____

____

RESULTING SUPERVISION LEVEL: ☐ MAXIMUM ☐ MEDIUM ☐ MINIMUM

______________________ Probation Officer's Signature

______________________ Supervisor's Signature

______________________ Date

Form A.7
Kansas: Department of Corrections—Offender Risk/Needs Initial Assessment Coding Form

OFFENDER NAME: |__|__|__|__|__|__|__|__|__|__|__|__|__|__|__|__|__|__|__|__|__|__|__|__|__|

NUMBER: |__|__|__|__|__|__|__|__|__| **ASSESSMENT DATE:** |__|__| |__|__| |__|__|

ACTION CODE: |__| **PAROLE REGION:** |___| **OFFICER #:** |_______|

			SCORE
1	**Prior Parole/Probation** ____ Actual Number Reported	None = 0 One or More = 3	_____
2	**Attitude:**	Motivated to Change = 0 Dependent or Unwilling = 2 Not Motivated = 5	_____
3	**Age of First Felony:** ____ Actual Age	24 or older = 0 18 to 23 = 2 17 or younger = 4	_____
4	**Prior Felony Convictions:** ____ Actual Number Reported	None = 0 One = 1 Two or More = 3	_____
5	**Convictions or Juvenile Adjudications:** Category A/Burglary, Auto Theft & Robbery Category B/Worthless Checks & Forgery Actual Number Reported: _____ Burglaries _____ Robberies _____ Auto Theft _____ Worthless Checks _____ Forgery	None for A or B = 0 One prior for A or B = 1 Two priors for A or B = 3	_____
6	**Number of Prior Parole/Probation Terminated by Revocation:** ____ Actual Number Reported	None, no prior = 0 One or more = 3	_____
7	**Alcohol Usage Problems:**	No interference = 0 Occasional or frequent abuse = 3	_____
8	**Other Drug Usage Problems:**	No interference = 0 Occasional abuse = 1 Frequent abuse, needs treatment = 3	_____
9	**Officer Impressions**	Min. Risk Level = 0 Medium Risk = 1 Maximum Risk = 3	_____
10	**Percentage of Time employed in last 12 months:**	N/A or 40% or more = 0 Less than 40% = 2	_____
11	**Companions:**	Good support and influence; No adverse relationships = 0 Occasional negative association = 1 Almost complete negative associations = 3	_____
		RISK TOTAL	_____
16	**Exception** Director's Signature:______________________________	Y = Yes N = No	_____

Risk Levels:(4)0-12 Reduced (3)13-19 Intermediate (2)20-25 Close (1)26-35 High **ASSIGNED RISK** _____

Form A.8
Kansas: Department of Corrections—Offender Risk Reassessment Coding Form

Name: |_|_|_|_|_|_|_|_|_|_|_|_|_|_|_|_|_|_|_|_|_|_|_|

No. |_|_|_|_|_|_|_| Date: |_|_|_|_|_|_| Re-assessemnt |___| (S or U)

CODE: |_| Region |_| Officer#: |_______| RISK LEVEL ASSIGNED: |___|

RISK ASSESSMENT		Score
1 Prior Parole/Probation	None = 0 One or more = 3	____
3 Age at First Felony	24 or older = 0 18 - 23 = 1 17 or younger = 2	____
4 Prior Felony Convictions	None = 0 One = 1 Two or More = 3	____
5 Convictions or Juvenile Adjud. Category <u>A</u>/Burg,Auto Theft,Robb. Category <u>B</u>/Checks and Forgery	None (A or B) = 0 One (A or B) = 1 Two (A or B) = 3	____
6 Prior Parole/Probation Revocations	No Apparent Problem = 0 One or more = 3	____
<u>Rate the following based on behavior since last assessment</u>		
7 Alcohol Usage	No Apparent Problem = 0 Moderate or Serious Problem = 2	____
8 Drug Usage	No Apparent Problem = 0 Moderate Problem = 1 Serious Problem = 3	____
10 Percent of time employed in last 12 months	N/A or 40% or More = 0 Less than 40% = 2	____
12 Social Identity	Positive = 0 Delinquent = 3	____
13 Problems in Interpersonal Relationships	None = 0 Few = 1 Moderate = 3 Severe = 4	____
14 Use of Community Resources	Not needed/or used well = 0 Needed or unavailable = 2 Used but not beneficial = 3 Available <u>but</u> rejected = 4	____
15 Response to Supervision	No Problem = 0 Moderate Compliance = 1 Unwilling to comply = 3	____
16 EXCEPTION	YES = Y NO = N	
	RISK LEVEL ASSSIGNED:	____
	TOTAL RISK[1]:	____

[1] (4) 0-12 = REDUCED (3) 13-19 = INTERMEDIATE
(2) 20-25 = CLOSE (1) 26-35 = HIGH

Form A.9
Kansas: Department of Corrections—Needs Assessment

NEEDS ASSESSMENT

		SCORE
1 Academic/Vocational skills	None = 0 Adequate = 1 Minimal = 3 Low = 4	___
2 Employment	Secure = 0 Unsatisfactory = 1 Unemployed or unemployable = 3	___
3 Financial Management	No Difficulties = 0 Situational or Minor Difficulties = 1 Severe Difficulties = 2	___
4 Marital/Family Relations	Relatively Stable = 0 Some Stress and/or Disorganization = 1 Major Stress and Disorganization = 3	___
5 Companions	Good Support and Influence = 0 Occasional Negative Associations = 1 Almost Completely Negative Associates = 3	___
6 Emotional Stability	Well Adjusted = 0 No Symptoms of Instability = 1 Serious Handicap or Chronic Illness = 3	___
7 Alcohol Use	No Interference = 0 Occasional or Frequent Abuse = 3	___
8 Other Drug Abuse	No Interference = 0 Occasional Abuse = 1 Frequent abuse, Needs Treatment = 3	___
9 Mental Ability	Socially Adept = 0 Some Difficulties = 1 Inept Socially. Difficulties = 3	___
10 Health	No Current Health Problems = 0 No Disabilities. History of Minor Problems = 1 History of acute, chronic and/or disabling injuries and/or illnesses = 2	___
11 Sexual Behavior	No Known Disfunction = 0 Minor Difficulties = 1 Chronic or Severe Problems or Difficulties = 3	___
12 Officer Impressions of Need level	Minimum = 0 Medium = 1 Maximum = 3	___

Next Assessment Date: |___|___|___|___|
Month Year

NEEDS TOTAL |_____|

Data Entry by ______________________ Date_________________

Form A.10
Minnesota: Psychopathic Personality Screening Tool

Name: ________________________

Sex Offender History This category includes any offense in the individual's criminal history which appears to be related to sexual deviance, including kidnapping, burglary, and assault.

SCORE

Number of Convictions (including current) for sex/sex-related offenses, both felony/gross misdemeanors (adult and juvenile.)
(0) one conviction
(4) two convictions
(8) three or more convictions ______

Age of First Conviction for Sex/Sex-Related Offense
(0) 24 years and above
(2) 20-23 years
(4) 19 years and under ______

Weapon (use of weapon in past/present sex/sex-related offenses)
(0) none present
(4) displayed during offense
(6) used to inflict injury during offense ______

Age of Victims (This is a cumulative score. Check all age ranges that apply for victims. If there was only one victim, please check one age range.)
(1) 0-6 years
(1) 7-12 years
(1) 13-16 years
(1) 17 plus years ______

Total Number of Victims of All Sex Offenses
(0) one
(4) two - three
(8) four or more ______

Violence (Check most severe category only. Include prior and current offense)
(0) offense (s) involved-no bodily harm to victim
(2) offense (s) involved-bodily harm to victim
(4) offense (s) involved-substantial bodily harm
(8) offense (s) involved-great bodily harm to victim
(12) offense (s) resulted in victim's death ______

Escalation
(0) current offense is first conviction or does not reflect an escalation in level of violence
(4) current offense reflects increased level of violence as compared to prior offenses ______

Form A.10 (continued)

Other Characteristics of Current Offense (rate all that apply)

(4) victim was tied up
(4) duration of the crime was more than 3 hours
(4) victim was transported forcefully to another location
(4) victim was mutilated/tortured during offense ______

Alcohol/Drug Usage Problems

(0) no interference with functioning
(2) occasional abuse; some disruption of functioning
(4) frequent abuse; serious disruption ______

Prior Sex Offender Treatment

(6) involvement in sex offender treatment prior to committing current offense ______

Discipline History While Incarcerated

(0) no major discipline reports
(4) history of major discipline report that does not involve violence
(8) history of major discipline report that does involve assaultiveness ______

Sex Offender Treatment While Incarcerated

(2) sex offender treatment during incarceration recommended: recommendation not followed
(6) involved in sex offender programming during incarceration with failure to complete ______

Age at Release From Institution

(0) 30 years plus
(2) 24-29 years old
(4) 23 years and under ______

Felony Committed Upon Previous Release From Institution

(4) 7-12 months following release
(6) 4-6 months following release
(8) 0-3 months following release ______

Form Preparer: ______________________________ TOTAL SCORE ______

Screening agent may aggravate/mitigate and recommend further review for commitment if there is reason to believe the score does not accurately reflect the level of risk that this offender poses. Rationale for aggravation/mitigation must be documented below.

Screening Agent Override: ______________________________

Caution: The factors included in this screening tool are not based upon current empirical research. The weighting scale of the individual items are being tested for reliability and validity.

Date Form Prepared:__________

Form A.11
Minnesota: Assessment of Client Risk

State of Minnesota
Department of Corrections
300 Bigelow Bldg.
450 No. Syndicate St.
St. Paul, Minnesota 55104
(612) 642-0200

Client Name	Last	First	Middle	OID Number

'e of Review (Month, Day, Year)	Agent Last Name	Agent Number	Convicted Offense(s)

Select the appropriate answer and enter the associated weight in the score column. Total all scores to arrive at the risk assessment score.

			SCORE
Number of address changes during last 12 months client was in community	0	None	
	2	One	
	3	Two or more	______
Age of first conviction (or juvenile adjudication)	0	24 or older	
	2	20 - 23	
	4	19 or younger	______
Number of prior probation/parole adjudicated violations (adult or juvenile)	0	None	
	4	One or more	______
Number of prior felony convictions (or juvenile adjudications)	0	None	
	2	One	
	4	Two or more	______
Convictions or juvenile adjudications for: (select applicable and add for score — do not exceed a total of 5 — include current offense)			
Burglary, theft, auto theft or robbery	2		
Worthless checks or forgery	3		
	0	N/A	______
Percentage of time employed during last 12 months client was in community	0	60%	
	1	40% - 59%	
	2	Under 40%	
	0	N/A	______
Alcohol usage problems (last 12 months in community):			
No interference with functioning	0		
Some interference with functioning	2		
Serious interference with functioning	4		______
Other drug usage problems (last 12 months in community):			
No interference with functioning	0		
Some interference with functioning	1		
Serious interference with functioning	2		______
Attitude:			
Motivated to change; receptive to assistance	0		
Dependent or unwilling to accept responsibility	3		
Negative; rationalizes/justifies behavior or not motivated to change	5		______
Number of prior supervised periods of probation/parole (adult or juvenile)	0	None	
	4	One or more	______
Conviction or juvenile adjudication of any crime against a person (felony, gross misdemeanor or misdemeanor) within the last five years	15	Yes	
	0	No	______
		TOTAL	______

Form A.11 (continued)

Client Name	Last	First	Middle	OID Number

Date of Review (Month, Day, Year)	Agent Last Name	Agent Number	Convicted Offense(s)

SCORE

Clients are assigned to the highest level of supervision that is indicated on the following scale:

Risk	**Level of Supervision**
15 and above	Maximum
8 to 14	Medium
7 and below	Minimum

Risk Scale SCORE ________

LEVEL OF SUPERVISION ________

If the agent feels that the level of supervision should be higher, supervisory approval is required. State the reasons for higher classification:

____

____

____

____

In light of the above, the client shall be classified:

____

Approved: ________

If the agent feels that the classification should be lower, supervisory approval is required. State the reasons for changing the classification:

____

____

____

____

In light of the above, the client shall be classified:

____

Approved: ________

TOTAL ____

Form A.12
Nevada: Initial Assessment of Client Risk

INITIAL ASSESSMENT OF CLIENT RISK

STATE OF NEVADA
PAROLE AND PROBATION FORM

Case Name *(Last, first, middle)*	File No. *(One only)*	Social Security No. *(First on PSI)*

Assessment Date *(Month, day, year)*	Officer Name	P.O. CID No.	CC No. *(One only)*	Dist.	Unit

Select appropriate answer and enter associated weight in score column. Total all item scores to get total risk score.

Number of address changes in last 12 months..........0—None
2—One
3—Two or more
____ (0,2,3)

Percentage of time employed in last 12 months..........0—60% or more
1—40%-59%
2—Under 40%
0—Not applicable (acceptable program)
____ (0,1,2,0)

Alcohol usage problems..........0—No interference with functioning
2—Occasional abuse; some disruption of functioning
4—Frequent abuse; serious disruption; needs treatment
____ (0,2,4)

Other drug usage problems (prior to incarceration for parolees)..........0—No use
1—Occasional use; no disruption of functioning
2—Occasional abuse; some disruption of functioning
4—Frequent abuse; serious disruption; needs treatment
____ (0,1,2,4)

Attitude..........0—Motivated to change; receptive to assistance
3—Dependent or unwilling to accept responsibility
5—Rationalized behavior; negative; not motivated to change
____ (0,3,5)

Age at first arrest (adult or juvenile)..........0—24 or older
2—20-23
4—19 or younger
____ (0,2,4)

Number of prior periods of probation/parole supervision (adult or juvenile)..........0—None
4—One or more
____ (0,4)

Number of prior probation/parole revocations (adult or juvenile)..........0—None
4—One or more
____ (0,4)

Number of prior gross misdemeanor/felony convictions..........0—None
2—One
4—Two or more
____ (0,2,4)

Convictions or juvenile adjudications for (if 2 and 3 both apply, enter total of 5)..........0—None
2—Burglary, theft, auto theft or robbery
3—Worthless checks or forgery
5—Both (add 2 and 3)
____ (0,2,3,5)

____ **TOTAL**

Conviction or juvenile adjudication for offense involving assaultive behavior within last five years (an offense which involves the use of a weapon, physical force or the threat of force)..........1—Yes
0—No
☐ *(Do not add to total)*

NOTE: A "Yes" answer denotes maximum supervision level. If scores do not indicate max, then override box on pink copy must be checked and supervisor's initials added.

Form A.12 (continued)

INITIAL ASSESSMENT OF CLIENT RISK

STATE OF NEVADA
PAROLE AND PROBATION FORM

Case Name *(Last, first, middle)*	File No. *(One only)*	Social Security No. *(First on PSI)*

Assessment Date *(Month, day, year)*	Officer Name	P.O. CID No.	CC No. *(One only)*	Dist.	Unit

Circle appropriate number.

RISK NEEDS

***PRIOR SUPERVISION HISTORY**
1—Nevada probation
2—NV probation revocation
3—Nevada parole
4—NV parole revocation
5—Out-of-state probation
6—Out-of-state probation revocation
7—Out-of-state parole
8—Out-of-state parole revocation
9—N/A

GROSS INCOME LAST SIX MONTHS
0—None
1—Under $2,500
2—$2,500 to $5,000
3—$5,000 to $7,500
4—$7,500 to $10,000
5—Over $10,000

JOB SKILL CLASSIFICATION
1—Professional/management
2—Skilled
3—Semi-skilled
4—Unskilled
5—N/A

***CASE TYPE**
1—Normal
2—120 day
3—Street readiness
4—Waived PSI (Nevada only)

S.C.S. APPROACH
1—Limit setting
2—Casework/control
3—Environmental structuring
4—Selective intervention situation
5—Selective intervention treatment
6—N/A

CURRENT EMPLOYMENT STATUS
1—Employed full-time
2—Employed part-time
3—Unemployed
4—N/A

EDUCATION STATUS
Enter highest grade **completed** or circle the following choices:..........
13—High school graduate
14—Some college
15—College graduate
16—Some graduate school
17—Graduate degree
18—Special education
19—Technical/vocational
20—G.E.D.
99—Not reported

SUPERVISION LEVEL
1—I.S.U.
2—Maximum
3—Medium
4—Minimum

OVERRIDE
Yes ☐ ....
(Supervisor's initials)

SUPERVISOR:
Please sign if all categories completed and correct on all 3 pages

....

RISK:
____ (0,2,3)
____ (0,1,2,0)
____ (0,2,4)
____ (0,1,2,4)
____ (0,3,5)
____ (0,2,4)
____ (0,4)
____ (0,4)
____ (0,2,4)
____ (0,2,3,5)
____ **TOTAL**

Assaultive Behavior? ☐

NEEDS:
____ (−1,0,2,4)
____ (−1,0,3,6)
____ (−1,0,3,5)
____ (−1,0,3,5)
____ (−1,0,2,4)
____ (−2,0,4,7)
____ (0,3,6)
____ (0,3,6)
____ (0,3,6)
____ (0,1,2)
____ (0,3,5)
____ (−1,0,3,5)
____ **TOTAL**

*Circle one or more applicable choices.

Form A.12 (continued)

INITIAL ASSESSMENT OF CLIENT RISK

STATE OF NEVADA
PAROLE AND PROBATION FORM

Case Name *(Last, first, middle)*		File No. *(One only)*	Social Security No. *(First on PSI)*		
Assessment Date *(Month, day, year)*	Officer Name	P.O. CID No.	CC No. *(One only)*	Dist.	Unit

Select appropriate answer and enter associated weight in score column. Total all item scores to get total needs score.

				Score
ACADEMIC/VOCATIONAL SKILLS				
−1—High school or above level	0—Adequate skill able to handle requirements	+2—Low skill level causing minor adjustment problems	+4—Minimal skill level causing serious adjustment problems	____ (−1.0.2.4)
EMPLOYMENT				
−1—Satisfactory employment for one year or longer	0—Secure employment; no difficulties reported; or homemaker/student or retired	+3—Unsatisfactory employment or unemployed but has adequate job skills	+6—Unemployed and virtually unemployable, needs training	____ (−1.0.3.6)
FINANCIAL MANAGEMENT				
−1—Long standing pattern of self-sufficiency, e.g. good credit rating	0—No current difficulties	+3—Situational or minor difficulties	+5—Severe difficulties; may include garnishment, bad checks or bankruptcy	____ (−1.0.3.5)
MARITAL/FAMILY RELATIONSHIPS				
−1—Relationships and support exceptionally strong	0—Relatively stable relationships	+3—Some disorganization or stress but potential for improvement	+5—Major disorganization or stress	____ (−1.0.3.5)
COMPANIONS				
−1—Good support and influence	0—No adverse relationships	+2—Associations with occasional negative results	+4—Associations almost completely negative	____ (−1.0.2.4)
EMOTIONAL STABILITY				
−2—Exceptionally well adjusted, accepts responsibility for actions	0—No symptoms of emotional instability; appropriate emotional responsibility	+4—Symptoms limit but do not prohibit adequate functioning; e.g. excessive anxiety	+7—Symptoms prohibit adequate functioning, e.g. lashes out or retreats into self	____ (−2.0.4.7)
ALCOHOL USAGE				
	0—No interference with functioning	+3—Occasional substance abuse; some disruption of functioning	+6—Frequent substance abuse; serious disruption; needs treatment	____ (0.3.6)
OTHER DRUG USAGE				
	0—No interference with functioning	+3—Occasional substance abuse; some disruption of functioning	+6—Frequent substance abuse; needs treatment	____ (0.3.6)
MENTAL ABILITY				
	0—Able to function independently	+3—Some need for assistance, potential for adequate adjustment; mild retardation	+6—Deficiencies severely limit independent functioning; moderate retardation	____ (0.3.6)
HEALTH				
	0—Sound physical health; seldom ill	+1—Handicap or illness interferes with functioning on a recurring basis	+2—Serious handicap or chronic illness needs frequent medical care	____ (0.1.2)
SEXUAL BEHAVIOR				
	0—No apparent dysfunction	+3—Real or perceived situational or minor problems	+5—Real or perceived chronic or severe problems	____ (0.3.5)
AGENT'S IMPRESSION OF CLIENT'S NEEDS				
−1—Minimum	0—Low	+3—Medium	+5—Maximum	____ (−1.0.3.5)
				____ **TOTAL**

Form A.13
Nevada: Probation Success Probability

PROBATION SUCCESS PROBABILITY

Name.................................District.................................SCORE.................

Writer.................................Date.................................FY No.................

CC No. ....

OFFENSE DATA: (60%)

PRIOR CRIMINAL HISTORY (Excluding Minor Traffic Violations):

Felony Convictions:	None (1)	One (0)	2 or more (-1)	[ ]
Misdemeanor Convictions (Including Gross Misdemeanor):	None (2)	1-3 (1)	4 or more (0)	[ ]
Pending, Unrelated Cases:	None (2)	Misd. (1)	Felony (0)	[ ]
Subsequent Criminal History:	None (2)	Arrest/Pending (1)	Convictions (0)	[ ]
Prior Incarcerations, Times in Prison:	None (3)	One (1)	2 or more (0)	[ ]
Times in Jail (Actual Sentences):	None (2)	2 or less (1)	3 or more (0)	[ ]
Juvenile Commitments (If defendant under 24).	None/or Over 24 (2)	One (1)	Two (0)	[ ]
Years in the Community Free of Convictions (Juvenile or Adult):	Over 5 (4)	3-5 (2)	Less than 3 (0)	[ ]
Prior Formal Supervision (Include Juvenile if under 24):	None (2)	One (1)	More than 1 (0)	[ ]
Criminal Patterns:	None/ No Record (2)	Random/ Decreased Severity (1) History of Violence (-2)	Same Type or Increased Severity (0)	[ ]

PRESENT OFFENSE:

Circumstances of Arrest:	Voluntary (3)	Non-prob. (2) Violent (-2)	Resistive (0)	[ ]
Type of Offense:	Victimless (Excluding Sales) (3)	Property (2) Person (0) Multiple Person 3 or More (-2)	Sales (1) Mult. Pers.—2 (-1)	[ ]
Psychological or Medical Crime Impact:	N/A (3)	Minor/No Treatment (2) Disability (0) Death (-10)	Required Medical Treatment/Psych. (1)	[ ]
Financial Crime Impact:	N/A (3)	Minimal or no loss (2) Excessive (0)	Moderate (1)	[ ]
Controlled Substances:	N/A (3)	Simple Possession (2) Sales/Smuggling/Manufacturing (-2)	Possession for Sale/ Minor Sales (0)	[ ]
Sophistication/Premeditation:	None (2)	Moderate (1)	High (0)	[ ]
Plea Bargaining Benefits to Applicant:	N/A (2)	Somewhat (1)	Significant (0)	[ ]
Weapon:	N/A (3)	Implied/ Concealed (0) Used (-4)	Brandished (-2)	[ ]
Co-Offender:	Follower (2)	Equal Responsibility (1)	Leader/Coerced Others or None (0)	[ ]
Motive:	Unintentional (3)	Situational (2) Deliberate (0)	Under Influence/ Alcohol or Drugs (1)	[ ]

TOTAL OFFENSE SCORE..................POINTS x 1.2 = ... [ ]

Form A.14
New York: Initial Security Classification Guideline–Adult

STATE OF NEW YORK - DEPARTMENT OF CORRECTIONAL SERVICES

INITIAL SECURITY CLASSIFICATION GUIDELINE – ADULT

INMATE NAME/__/__/__/__/__/__/__/__/__/__/__/ (Last Name)   /__/__/__/__/__/__/__/__/ (First Name)

/__/__/__/__/__/__/__/ (DIN)

1. PUBLIC RISK SCORE

A. Criminal Behavior
Instant Offense = Weapon (0 = No, 1 = Yes) + Forcible Contact (0 = None, 1 = Threat, 2 = Force/Injury, 3 = Serious Injury, 4 = Death) ☐
+
Other Offense = Weapon (0 = No, 1 = Yes) + Forcible Contact (0 = None, 1 = Threat, 2 = Force/Injury, 3 = Serious Injury, 4 = Death) ☐
Crime/Year Committed __________
+
B. Time to Earliest Release
1 = 0-12 Months   3 = 25-36 Months   5 = 49-60 Months
2 = 13-24 Months   4 = 37-48 Months   6 = Over 60 Months
Score for Possible Additional Time ______ ☐
+
C. Escape, Abscondance, Bail Jump, AWOL
– 1 = Successful Pre-trial Release   2 = Two   12 = Escape
0 = None/No Incarceration   3 = Two-More serious
1 = One/Never on Supervision   4 = Temp. Rel. Abscond. ☐
+
D. Street Stability
0 = High   1 = Average   2 = Low ☐ = ☐

II. INSTITUTIONAL RISK SCORE

A. Prior DOCS Institutional Adjustment
0 = Good-Average/No Incarcerations   2 = Below Average   6 = SHU
1 = No Prior DOCS Record   4 = Poor ☐
+ = ☐
B. Street Stability
0 = High   1 = Average   2 = Low ☐

Guideline Decision

INSTITUTIONAL RISK \ PUBLIC RISK	1 - 5	6	7 - 9	10 - 11	12 - 30
0 - 2	Minimum	Medium B	Medium A	Maximum B	Maximum A
3 - 4	Minimum	Medium B	Medium A	Maximum B	Maximum A
5 - 8	Maximum B	Maximum B	Maximum B	Maximum B	Maximum A

Guideline Override

☐ (Specify) __________

COUNSELOR'S FINAL SECURITY CLASSIFICATION DECISION

☐ MINIMUM ☐ MEDIUM B ☐ MEDIUM A ☐ MAXIMUM B ☐ MAXIMUM A

OTHER CHARACTERISTICS

1 ☐ Notoriety of Crime(s) or Criminal
2 ☐ Sophistication of Crime(s) or Criminal
3 ☐ Involvement in Crime(s) was minimal
4 ☐ Pattern of Callous Violence
5 ☐ Vicious Violence
6 ☐ Pattern of Impulsive Violence
9 ☐ Sex Crime(s)
10 ☐ Arson (not for money)
11 ☐ Violence Against Authorities
22 ☐ Nomad
7 ☐ Inmate Negative Attitude
8 ☐ Family/Other Street Circumstances
12 ☐ Riot Leader
13 ☐ Aggressive Homosexual
14 ☐ Overt Homosexual
15 ☐ INS Detainer
16 ☐ Family Court Protection Warrent
17 ☐ Group Membership
18 ☐ Sentence Structure
19 ☐ Suicidal
20 ☐ Psychological Instability
21 ☐ Vulnerability
23 ☐ Enemies
24 ☐ Other

CLASSIFICATION COUNSELOR __________ (Signature)   __________ (Date)

Form A.15
New York: Female Initial Security Classification Guideline

INMATE NAME/__/__/__/__/__/__/__/__/__/__/__/__/__ /__/__/__/__/__/__/__/__/__/__
(Last Name) (First Name)

FACILITY/__/__/__/__/__/__/__/__/__/__/__/__/__/ /__/__/__/__/__/
(DIN)

1. PUBLIC RISK SCORE:

A. Criminal Behavior

Instant Offense = Weapon + Forcible Contact [ ]
0 = No; 1 = Yes
0 = None; 1 = Threat; 3 = Serious Injury; 4 = Death
+

Other Offense = Weapon + Forcible Contact [ ]
0 = No; 1 = Yes
0 = None; 1 = Threat; 3 = Serious Injury; 4 = Death

Crime/Year Committed ______________________
+

Isolated Personal Violence [ ]
-2 = Yes
0 = No
+

B. Time to Earliest Release [ ]
1 = 0-12 Months
2 = 13-24 Months
3 = 25-36 Months
4 = 37-48 Months
5 = 49-60 Months
6 = Over 60 Months

Score for Possible Additional Time ________
+

C. Escape, Abscondence, Bail Jump, AWOL [ ]
0 = None/No Incarceration
1 = One/Never on Supervision
2 = Two
3 = Two More Serious
4 = Temp. Rel. Abscond.
12 = Escape

Successful Pre-Trial Release __________ Total = [ ]
-1 = Yes
0 = No

Guideline Decision

-1 - 4	5 - 6	7 - 8	9 - 32
Minimum	Medium B	Medium A	Maximum

Guideline Override

[ ] (Specify)______________________________

COUNSELOR'S FINAL SECURITY CLASSIFICATION DECISION

[ ] MINIMUM [ ] MEDIUM B [ ] MEDIUM A [ ] MAXIMUM

OTHER CHARACTERISTICS

1 ☐ Notoriety of Crime(s) or Criminal
2 ☐ Sophistication of Crime(s) or Criminal
3 ☐ Involvement in Crime(s) Was Minimal
4 ☐ Pattern of Callous Violence
5 ☐ Vicious Violence
6 ☐ Pattern of Impulsive Violence
9 ☐ Sex Crime(s)
10 ☐ Arson (not for money)
11 ☐ Violence Against Authorities
22 ☐ Nomad
7 ☐ Inmate Negative Attitude
8 ☐ Family/Other Street Circumstances
12 ☐ Riot Leader
13 ☐ Aggressive Homosexual
14 ☐ Overt Homosexual
15 ☐ INS Detainer
16 ☐ Family Court Protection Warrant
17 ☐ Group Membership
18 ☐ Sentence Structure
19 ☐ Suicidal
20 ☐ Psychological Instability
21 ☐ Vulnerability
23 ☐ Enemies
24 ☐ Other

CLASSIFICATION COUNSELOR ______________________ ______________
(Signature) (Date)

Form A.16
Pennsylvania: Parole Decision Making Guidelines

PENNSYLVANIA BOARD OF PROBATION AND PAROLE

CLIENT NAME ______________________ PAROLE NUMBER ______________

DATE OF INTERVIEW ______________________ INSTITUTION ______________

PAROLE DECISION MAKING GUIDELINES

I PAROLE PROGNOSIS ASSESSMENT

INSTRUCTIONS: Information on age-at-minimum-sentence, prior convictions, PPA offense code and prior probation or parole revocations should be provided in column 1. The appropriate risk classification score in column 2 should be placed in column 3 and subsequently added together in the total PPA score box. Based upon the total score number, the client may then be classified into a risk category according to the range of scores shown at the bottom of the instrument. Clients with multiple offenses should have each offense ranked in ascending score order according to the offense ranking at the bottom of the page. This process results in a risk assessment which is sensitive to potential future crime. Column 4 may be used to reassess a case if the interview suggests that the assessment information was incorrect.

COLUMN 1 Variable	COLUMN 2 Score Allocation for Risk Assessment	COLUMN 3 Classification Score	COLUMN 4 Reassessment
Age at Minimum: ____ yr. Minimum Sentence Date ___/___/___	0 if 40 years or older 21 if 26-39 years 38 if 25 years or younger	______	______
Prior Convictions: Number: ______________	0 if no prior convictions 9 if 1 or 2 convictions 26 if 3 or more convictions	______	______
PPA Offense (Ranked According to Index) 1. ______________ 2. ______________ 3. ______________ 4. ______________ 5. ______________	0 if not elsewhere classified 20 if theft, fraud, burglary or robbery	______	______
Probation Revocations ______ Parole Revocations ______ Total: ______	0 if none 16 if 1 or more	______	______
TOTAL P.P.A. SCORE			

Parole Prognosis Assessment Score Category **CHECK ONE:** 71-100 High Risk ☐ 45-70 Medium Risk ☐ 0-44 Low Risk ☐

Instant Offense in descending recidivism rank order: 1) Theft/Fraud, 2) Burglary, 3) Robbery, 4) Aggravated Assault, 5) Drug Law Violation, 6) Arson & Miscellaneous, 7) Simple Assault & Kidnapping; 8) Sex Offenses, 9) Manslaughter, 10) Murder.

II POTENTIAL ASSAULTIVENESS/DANGEROUSNESS SCREEN

Assaultivness is a course of conduct that presents, or is calculated to present, a danger or perceived danger to any person. An assaultive instant offense is defined as any single conviction offense for the current sentence of the following type: murder, manslaughter, rape, and other assaultive sex offenses, robbery, kidnapping, aggravated or simple assault, arson against persons, weapon law violations, or homicide by vehicle.

Official versions or facts of crime are required for all offenses in the definition above prior to a final Board action.

1. Does the client have an assaultive instant offense based upon the definition above, or based upon the official version of the offense in the case of a plea bargain? ☐ YES ☐ NO
   If the answer to the above question is "yes", mark a score of (1) on p. 2, III(7), and answer the following question.
   If the answer to the above question is "no", stop here.
2. Does the client have a mental health problem which requires treatment in the form of either individual or group therapy/counseling and/or psychotropic medication? (Rape and all other assaultive sex offenses require a "yes" answer). ☐ YES ☐ NO
   If the answer to the above question is "yes", mark the client as having a very high assault potential with a score of (3) on p. 2, III(8) and stop here.
   If the answer to #2 is "no", answer the following question:
3. Did the client have any institutional problems/misconducts which were assaultive in nature within the last 12 months or the last one-half of the minimum sentence, whichever is longer? ☐ YES ☐ NO
   If the answer to the above question is "yes", mark the client as having a high assault potential with a score of (2) on p. 2, III(9).

Form A.16 (continued)

III PAROLE CONSIDERATION FACTORS

Each unfavorable factor listed below is a possible reason for refusing parole as a matter of policy. Select the appropriate column from the PPA on p. 1. If the response to a specific unfavorable factor is in the affirmative, the appropriate score of 2 or 1 must be entered. If the response is in the negative, a 0 goes in the blank space provided. Enter the total score of unfavorable factors at the bottom of the appropriate column.

REASONS FOR PAROLE REFUSAL	SCORE	PAROLE PROGNOSIS ASSESSMENT High Risk	Medium Risk	Low Risk
Unfavorable Factors from Institutional Performance:				
1) Three or more Class II misconducts, or two Class II and one Class I misconducts, during the last twelve (12) months or the last one-half of the minimum sentence, whichever is longer.	1	____	____	____
2) Two or more Class I misconducts during the last twelve (12) months, or the last one-half of the minimum sentence, whichever is longer.	1	____	____	____
3) Open charges* for new crimes, or new convictions, while serving this prison sentence.	2	____	____	____
4) Removed from CSC, work release or prerelease for cause. *(prima facie case was established.)	2	____	____	____
Unfavorable Factors from Prior Record:				
5) Substance Abuse	2	____	____	____
6) Habitual Offender	1	____	____	____
Unfavorable Factors from Instant Offense:				
7) Assaultive Instant Offense (from page 1, II (i)	1	____	____	____
8) Very high assaultive behavior potential (from page 1, II (2))	3	____	____	____
9) High assaultive behavior potential (from page 1, II (3))	2	____	____	____
10) Victim Injury	1	____	____	____
11) Client had weapon in the commission of offense. ☐ Firearm ☐ Knife ☐ Other	1	____	____	____
TOTAL UNFAVORABLE FACTOR SCORE				
Parole Policy Guideline Recommends Refuse if Total Score is:		**5 or more**	**6 or more**	**7 or more**

Guideline Policy Recommendation: Parole ☐ Refuse ☐

DEFINITIONS:

a) **Open Charges** - This refers to new criminal charges being filed while on pre-release or as a result of criminal conduct at a correctional facility. If open charges are to be accepted as a basis for parole refusal, a prima facie case must have been established.

b) **Substance Abuse** - There is a record of substance abuse which lead to police arrests and/or clinical determinations.

c) **Habitual Offender** - This refers to a person who has a total of three or more prior convictions for similar types of offenses in his criminal history. For example, they may be convictions for burglary and robbery, or for drug law violations. Also, a person is included who simply appears to have developed a criminal life style based upon four or more convictions which may be dissimilar. A corollary concept refers to a person in syndicated or organized crime.

d) **Victim Injury** - The official version of the offense must indicate physical injury to the victim of the crime, however slight. In cases of sexually assaultive behavior, psychological injury to the victim is also frequently the case; therefore, in all cases of sexual assault an unfavorable factor score of 1 is to be entered.

e) **Weapon** - The official version of the offense must place the client in actual or constructive possession of a weapon. The definition of weapon contained in Board regulations states: "Anything readily capable of causing harm to **or intimidating** another, possessed under circumstances not manifestly appropriate for any lawful use that the object may have". In a crime such as "homocide by vehicle", the vehicle would not be a weapon under the above definition unless: 1) there was a DUI involved, or; 2) there was a clear intent to harm the victim by using the vehicle as a weapon. Under both exceptions, the circumstances were not manifestly appropriate for any lawful use according to our definition.

Form A.16 (continued)

IV COUNTERVAILING FACTORS TO EXPLICIT POLICY OF PAROLE DECISION MAKING GUIDELINES

A. Factors Countervailing a Guideline Recommendation to Refuse Parole:

GENERAL POLICY: Where factors of risk have been reduced by participation in available institutional programming, the quantity and quality of program participation should correspond to the level of risk involved to be a meaningful countervailance to a parole guideline recommendation to refuse. Where available prison programming could reduce the risk of parole failure, it will be prescribed by the Board as a necessary program to assure release.

YES NO

1. Inventory of Institutional Programming ☐ ☐
   a. Was there positive response to prescriptive or other prison program plans?

Program 1) ____________ Benefit 1) ____________

Program 2) ____________ Benefit 2) ____________

Program 3) ____________ Benefit 3) ____________

YES NO

2. Do other factors support a parole action? (For example, recommendations by the Department of Corrections, Board staff, strength of parole plan) ____________ ☐ ☐

B. Factors Countervailing a Guideline Recommendation to Parole:

GENERAL POLICY: The parole guidelines provide a uniform method for assessing parole suitability and risk. In some instances, guideline assessments may indicate medium or low risk; however, other risk factors may contravene and suggest that the likelihood of successful reintegration is low while the threat to the safety of the community is high. The factors listed represent risks outside of the parole guideline for which a parole refusal may be justified.

	YES	NO
1. The client displayed psychotic or clearly dangerous behavioral characteristics during the parole interview.	☐	☐
2. The client had a recent psychiatric/psychological report which causes concern.	☐	☐
3. There were strong objections from the sentencing judge, the district attorney, or the victim of the crime.	☐	☐
4. The client is a habitual offender for assaultive crimes.	☐	☐
5. There is an unfavorable recommendation from the Department of Corrections or Board Staff.	☐	☐
6. There are other factors supporting a parole refusal:	☐	☐

Instructions: The countervailing factors to a guideline recommendation to refuse parole (A) or to parole (B) are for information to the decision makers only. Countervailing factors checked in (B) are **not** to be communicated in the Board action as such. The Board Member/Hearing Examiner will supply the appropriate reasons for refusal in his/her decisions in section VII of this guideline document.

Form A.16 (continued)

V FINAL DECISION MAKING ANALYSIS

Decision Outcome and Guideline Consistency: Use the appropriate guideline recommendation column to check off the interviewer decision.

Instructions: **Inmates refused parole may be eligible for the Special Early Release Program.** If eligible, indicate a parole action in item 2 below and check the box titled SERP. The initial and date space on this page is to be completed for a "continue" decision only. Final decisions are initialed on page 6 of this document when there is no "continue" action preceeding it. If the case has been continued, for whatever reason, the final decision can be initialed on this page with the appropriate completion of section VI or VII, whichever is appropriate to the decision.

Initial & Date

____

____

____

BOARD DECISION	Guideline Recommendation Parole	Guideline Recommendation Refuse
1) Continue:		
a) to approved plan	☐	☐
b) pending receipt of information (Specify) ________ ________	☐	☐
c) pending successful adjustment to C.S.C., review in ________	☐	☐
d) pending disposition of criminal charges	☐	☐
2) Parole to Approved Plan ☐ SERP	☐	☐
3) Parole to in-patient program; approved home to be available	☐	☐
4) Parole to Detainers:		
☐ To Board/backtime detainer sentence only; ☐ to State Sentence; approved home to be available prior to release to the community. ☐ while confined must participate in ________	☐	☐
☐ To other detainer sentence; approved home to be available. Check one: ☐ County ☐ Sentence ☐ Untried Case; ☐ Other State (approved home necessary if untried case); ☐ Federal ☐ Sentence ☐ Untried Case; ☐ Violation of Probation Parole; ☐ Immigration and Naturalization; ☐ When released to the community, special conditions as prescribed imposed.; ☐ Other: ________	☐	☐
5) Refuse Parole	☐	☐

NOTES:

____

____

____

____

____

____

____

Form A.16 (continued)

VI SPECIAL CONDITIONS OF PAROLE

	YES	NO
1. Are special conditions of parole necessary?	☐	☐
2. Did the inmate raise objections to any special condition?	☐	☐

3. What is the presenting problem to adjustment, or danger to the community? ____________

____

4. **Complete if special conditions of parole are necessary:**

___ Prior to release to an in-patient program, you will be required to sign the appropriate release form for confidential information.

___ Removal or termination from the in-patient program for any reason other than successful completion is a violation of your parole.

WHEN PAROLED OR AFTER SUCCESSFUL COMPLETION OF THE IN-PATIENT PROGRAM, YOU MUST COMPLY WITH THE FOLLOWING SPECIAL CONDITIONS OF PAROLE:

___ ___ You must abide by all of the supervision requirements in the Special Early Release Program

___ ___ Out-patient (drug/alcohol/sex offender/mental health/other: ____________) treatment [circle] is a special condition of your parole supervision until the treatment source and/or parole supervision staff determine it is no longer necessary. You will be required to sign the appropriate release form for confidential information.

___ ___ You must cooperate with TASC-SCI and follow all treatment recommendations.

___ ___ Upon your release on parole, you will be evaluated to determine your need for (drug/alcohol/mental health/other: ____________) treatment [circle]. Prior to the evaluation being conducted, you will be required to sign the appropriate release form for confidential information. If the evaluation reveals that treatment is indicated, this special condition of parole will be amended to include other appropriate special conditions imposed by your parole agent.

___ ___ You must submit to (urinalysis testing/mandatory urinalysis testing) [circle]

___ ___ You must achieve negative results in screening tests ramdomly applied for the detection of the presence of controlled substances or designer drugs and you must pay for the costs of the tests. (Act 97 - ______)

___ ___ You must not consume alcohol under any conditions or for any reason

___ ___ You must not enter establishments that sell or dispense alcohol

___ ___ You must not contact or associate with persons who sell drugs, or with drug users, outside of a treatment setting.

___ ___ You must take psychotropic medication if prescribed by your doctor

___ ___ You must support your dependents

___ ___ You must not contact or associate with ____________ for any reason

___ ___ You must maintain (employment/vocational training/educational training/other/ ____________) [circle] as approved by parole supervision staff.

___ ___ You must engage in an active job search during any period of unemployment, and provide verification as directed by parole supervision staff.

___ ___ Other: ____________

SPECIAL INSTRUCTIONS TO PAROLE SUPERVISION STAFF

____

____

Form A.16 (continued)

VII REASON FOR PAROLE REFUSAL AND REVIEW DATE

1) Reasons for refusal:

_________ a) factors cited in guidelines section(s) ______/______/______/______/______/______

_________ b) negative interest in parole

_________ c) your need for: (check the appropriate need)

☐ counseling
☐ treatment
☐ education
☐ vocational training

_________ d) failure to participate in and benefit from a treatment program for:

☐ sex offenders
☐ substance abuse
☐ mental health problems
☐ other: ______________________

_________ e) unfavorable recommendation from the:

☐ district attorney
☐ sentencing judge
☐ warden of county prison
☐ Department of Corrections

_________ f) other: ______________________

2) Review date and conditions for release consideration:

_________ a) review in ______________ (Mo./Yr.) for tentative ______________ (Mo./Yr.) release

_________ b) must participate in ______________________

_________ c) you must maintain a clear conduct record and earn an institutional recommendation for parole.

_________ d) review in ______________, or earlier, if recommended by the Department of Corrections because of demonstrable benefit from participation in an appropriate treatment program for:

☐ sex offenders
☐ substance abuse
☐ mental health problems
☐ other: ______________

_________ e) serve your unexpired maximum sentence ______/______/______

_________ f) parole to an approved plan upon condition that there are no misconducts, effective ______________ and subject to the following special conditions (see page 5)

VIII PANEL MEMBER CONCURRENCE

1) Interviewing Panel Member ______________________ Date ______/______/______

	Agree	Disagree
2) Board/Panel Member ______________________ Date ______/______/______	☐	☐
Explain Disagreement: ______________________		
3) Board/Panel Member ______________________ Date ______/______/______	☐	☐
Explain Disagreement: ______________________		

Instruction: Agreement or Disagreement references position relative to the preceding response.

Form A.16 (continued)

IX SPECIAL CONDITIONS OF PAROLE AND THE PAROLE PLAN

GENERAL POLICY: The parole plan is a contract which provides the public some assurance that their community will be protected while the means to reintegrate the offender are implemented. The plan is judged therefore in context of the client's P.P.A. and unfavorable factors which suggest risk to the community. The higher risk client requires more stringent criteria when the plan is viewed as a countervailance to risk. Discretion for approval of a parole plan is a field staff prerogative unless the Board has specific cause to intervene. Where an approved plan is not available, specific approval criteria commensurate with assessed risk will be set by the Board as special conditions of parole.

A. PAROLE PLAN CHECK LIST	**YES**	**NO**
1. Does the client have a detainer sentence?	☐	☐
Type: ☐ State ☐ Board ☐ County ☐ Federal ☐ Untried Case ☐ Immigration and Naturalization ☐ Violation of Probation or Parole ☐ Other		
2. The client made some effort to prepare a parole plan.	☐	☐
3. The client submitted a completed parole plan to the IPR: Date _____/_____/_____	☐	☐
4. The IPR sent the parole plan for a field investigation: Date _____/_____/_____	☐	☐
5. There were field investigation responses received for:		
a) Residence	☐	☐
b) Employment/Education/Training	☐	☐
6. Was a parole plan accepted as adequate by field staff: Date _____/_____/_____	☐	☐

Appendix B

Forms and Figure: Juvenile

Form B.1
Alabama: Risk Assessment Instrument

RISK ASSESSMENT INSTRUMENT

Youth ____________________ Date ____________________

Instant Offense ____________________ County ____________________

Most Serious Prior Offense ____________________

SCORING SHEET

Circle the appropriate number in each column:

	POINT VALUE	
	Most Serious Instant Adjudication	Most Serious Prior Adjudication
Class A Felony	10	7
Class B Felony	7	5
Class C Felony (involving violence to people)	5	3
All Other Class C Felonies	4	2
Class A Misdemeanors (involving violence to people)	3	2
All Other Misdemeanors	2	1
Technical Violations of Probation/Parole	1	0
Status Offenders who non-criminally violate a Court Order (e.g., don't go to school, run from foster care, etc.)	1	0

Other Scoring Factors		POINT VALUE	
Three Adjudications for a Felony Within prior 2 Years (or two felonies and an adjudication for a misdemeanor involving violence to people)		5	
First Delinquency Adjudication at 12 Years Old or Younger		1	
Prior Out-Of-Home Placement as a Result of a Delinquency Adjudication		1	
	None	Some	High
Gang Involvement with Instant Offense	0	1	2
Substance Abuse Involvement with Instant Offense:			
a) Alcohol, Marijuana, Inhalants	0	1	2
OR			
b) Crack, Cocaine, Heroin	0	2	3

Scorer ____________________ Total ____________________

Note: The development of the Alabama Risk Assessment Instrument was made possible, in part, through a grant from the McConnell-Clark Foundation.

Form B.2
Alabama: Needs Assessment Instrument

NEEDS ASSESSMENT INSTRUMENT

Youth's Name ____________________ DOB __________ Probation Officer/ DYS Staff ____________________

From your knowledge of this youth, list at least one strength, talent or positive interest of this youth. (You may include more than one.) Examples might include sports, music, cooking, hobbies, church, a **special friend, a special** relationship with a relative, etc. Be as specific as you can be.

____

____

____

____

____

Needs Score: Low (0-12) __________; Medium (13-23) __________; High (24-36) __________

Are there other service needs that are not identified by the needs assessment form? Or is there one service need that is so pressing that it needs immediate, "emergent" attention? Please specify.

____

____

____

____

Did you share the results of the needs assessment with the youth? His parents? Yes ______; No ______
If not, why not?

____

____

____

Does the youth generally agree with the results of the needs assessment? Yes ______; No ______

If the youth disagrees with the needs assessment, what are the major areas of disagreement?

____

____

____

____

____

Form B.2 (continued)

NEEDS ASSESSMENT INSTRUMENT

For each item below, select the single appropriate answer and enter the associated number in the adjacent blank. Where appropriate, concretely describe the present situation/need.

DRUG/CHEMICAL ABUSE

0		1		2		
0	No interference with functioning	1	Occasional abuse, some disruption of functioning, unwilling to participate in treatment program	2	Frequent abuse, serious disruption, needs immediate treatment	___

SPECIFY:

ALCOHOL ABUSE

0	No known use	1	Occasional abuse, some disruption of functioning, unwilling to participate in treatment program	2	Frequent abuse, serious disruption, needs immediate treatment	___

SPECIFY:

PRIMARY FAMILY RELATIONSHIPS

0	Relatively stable relationships or not applicable	1	Some disorganization or stress but potential for improvement	2	Major disorganization or stress	___

SPECIFY:

ALTERNATIVE FAMILY RELATIONSHIPS ("Significant" adult relationships)

0	Relatively stable relationships or not applicable	1	Some disorganization or stress but potential for improvement	2	Major disorganization	___

SPECIFY:

EMOTIONAL STABILITY

0	Appropriate adolescent responses	1	Exaggerated periodic or sporadic responses, e.g., aggressive acting out or depressive withdrawal	2	Excessive responses; prohibits or limits adequate functioning	___

SPECIFY:

INTELLECTUAL ABILITY

0	Able to function independently	1	Some need for assistance, potential for adequate adjustment; mild retardation	2	Deficiencies severely limit independent functioning, moderate retardation	___

SPECIFY:

LEARNING DISABILITY

0	None	1	Mild disability, able to function in a classroom	2	Serious disability, interferes with social functioning	___

SPECIFY:

EMPLOYMENT (Where applicable)

0	Not needed or currently employed	1	Currently employed but poor work habits	2	Needs employment	___

SPECIFY:

VOCATIONAL/TECHNICAL SKILLS

0	Currently developing marketable skill	1	Needs to develop marketable skill	___

SPECIFY:

Form B.2 (continued)

NEEDS ASSESSMENT INSTRUMENT

If appropriate, enter the value 1 for each characteristic which applies to this case.

Educational Adjustment	Not working to potential	____	
	Poor attendance	____	
	Program not appropriate for needs, age and/or ability	____	
	Disruptive school behavior	____	TOTAL ____
Peer Relationships	Socially inept	____	
	Loner behavior	____	
	Receives basically negative influence from peers	____	
	Dependent upon others	____	
	Exploits and/or victimizes others (especially in placement)	____	TOTAL ____
Health, Mental Health and Hygiene	Medical or dental referral needed	____	
	Needs health or hygiene education	____	
	Handicap or illness limits functioning	____	
	Need for mental health intervention (Specify)	____	TOTAL ____
Sexual Adjustment	Lacks knowledge (sex education)	____	
	Avoidance of the opposite sex	____	
	Promiscuity (not prostitution)	____	
	Sexual deviant (not prostitution)	____	
	Unwed parent	____	
	Prostitution	____	TOTAL ____

Range: Low (0-12); Medium (13-23); High (24-36) **TOTAL NEEDS SCORE ____**

Note: The development of the Alabama Needs Assessment Instrument was made possible, in part, through a grant from the McConnell-Clark Foundation.

Figure B.1
Georgia: Risk and Needs Matrix

RISK AND NEEDS MATRIX

RISK SCORES →

NEEDS SCORE ↓

	19-32	11-18	0-10
19+	HIGH SUPERVISION	HIGH SUPERVISION	REGULAR SUPERVISION
16-18	HIGH SUPERVISION	REGULAR SUPERVISION	LOW SUPERVISION
0-15	REGULAR SUPERVISION	LOW SUPERVISION	LOW SUPERVISION

Form B.3
Georgia: Reassessment of Risk

REASSESSMENT OF RISK

Select the highest point total applicable for each category.

		1st	2nd	3rd
1. Age at First Adjudication (with any court)		____	____	____
15 or over	0			
12-14	1			
11 or under	2			

Age when child was first referred to a court and found guilty of an offense. The date the court order was entered is the date of adjudication. Do not include informal adjustments.

2. Number of Prior Delinquent Adjudications (with any court)		____	____	____
One or two	0			
Three or more	1			

A delinquent act is one which would be considered a crime if committed by an adult. **Examples:** burglary, theft, criminal trespass, any drug violation, any traffic violation which is petitioned into juvenile court.

3. Number of prior Unruly Adjudications (with any court)		____	____	____
One or two	0			
Three or more	1			

Unruly acts are those which can only be considered a violation of the law because they are committed by a juvenile. **Examples:** runaway, turancy, minor in possession of alcohol, violation of curfew, ungovernable.

4. Number of prior Informal Adjustments		____	____	____
One or two	0			
Three or more	1			

An informal adjustment is a complaint which has been diverted from formal adjudication and disposition. The period of supervision is from 30-90 days.

Form B.3 (continued)

5. Number of Prior Out-of-Home Placements ___ ___ ___
   One 0
   Two or more 1

   Out-of-home placements include, but are not limited to, the following: blood relatives, non-relatives, DFCS placements, self-supporting/emancipated youths, psychiatric hospitals, residential treatment, group/contract/attention homes, substance abuse treatment facility or boarding/military schools.

6. Number of Runaways from Prior Placements ___ ___ ___
   One or more 1

   Runaway will include those occasions within the past three years when, without permission or authorization, a youth leaves his/her placement.

7. Alcohol or Drug Abuse ___ ___ ___
   Suspected but unsubstantiated 0
   Low/situational 1
   Medium/abuse 2
   High dependency 3

   Consider youth's involvement with drugs for the past twelve (12) months. Suspected but unsubstantiated use is substance use which is suspected by reliable sources such as parents, teachers, the interviewer, etc. Low/situational use include experimentation or sporadic usage. Medium/abuse is continued use despite knowledge of negative consequences. Recreational or leisure time activities consistently involve the use of drugs or alcohol. Youth at this level have no more than one adjudication for a substance related offense. High/dependency involves the lack of control over use, i.e., daily use, increased tolerance or withdrawal symptoms. Youth at this level may have two or more drug related offenses.

8. School Disciplinary Problems ___ ___ ___
   Attending, graduated, GED equivalence 0
   Recent truancy or behavioral problems 1
   Chronic truancy or behavioral problems 2
   Not attending/expelled 3

   Recent is defined as the last twelve (12) months. Chronic is considered anything in excess of 12 months.

Form B.3 (continued)

9. Level of Parental/Caretaker Control ___ ___ ___
   - Generally effective 0
   - Inconsistent and/or ineffective 1
   - Little or no supervision provided 2

   Consider the last twelve (12) months. Generally effective parental control is demonstrated when parents are concerned and expect youth to attend school, obey the law, etc. Parental expectations for the youth are clear and they sanction misbehavior. Inconsistent or ineffective control is evidenced when parents expect good behavior but are either inconsistent or don't sanction misbehavior. Youth frequently ignore their parents. Little or no supervision is when parents have given up on youth. Youth sets his own rules and completely ignores his/her parents. Parents may minimize or deny youth's responsibility. Intervention by the CSW or other agencies is resisted. Parents may contribute to the delinquency of youth by their own antisocial conduct.

10. Peer Relationships ___ ___ ___
    - Not mentioned 0
    - Inappropriate relationships 1
    - Significant/documented negative peer involvement .. 2
    - Gang/Occult 3

    Inappropriate relationships include parental disapproval of some peers or no significant friends. Significant/ documented negative peer involvement involves co-defenddants as friends, peers with juvenile/criminal records, significant age difference in peers or boy/girlfriend over-involvement resulting in negative consequences. Gang/Occult is any involvement with gang members or occult practices.

11. Documented Criminal Activity by Child's Family ___ ___ ___
    - None 0
    - One member 1
    - Two or more members 2

    Child's family includes any natural family member either on probation/parole or incarcerated in jail/prison. If it is a stepfamily member or one who is currently involved with the family and who has been on probation/parole or incarcerated at any time during the last twenty-four (24) months, they also will be considered the child's family.

12. Use or Possession of Firearms ___ ___ ___
    - No 0
    - Yes 1

    This is to include the current charges and any charges incurred during the past two (2) years.

Form B.3 (continued)

13. Current Living Situation ___ ___ ___
    Natural mother and natural father 0
    Natural mother and other 1
    Natural father and other 1
    Relative 2
    Non-relative 3

14. Extracurricular/Community Activities ___ ___ ___
    Yes 0
    No 1

    Examples: Volunteer organizations, athletics, clubs, church, bands, girls/boys clubs, etc.

15. Employment ___ ___ ___
    N/A (under 16 years of age) 0
    16 years of age/has maintained employment for 2 months ... 0
    16 years of age/has been employed 1
    16 years of age/no employment history 2

16. Response to supervision requirements ___ ___ ___
    No problems of consequence 0
    Moderate compliance problems 1
    Major compliance problems, totally uncooperative .. 2

    Consider the parents' response to requirements as well as the minor's response. **No problems of consequence** indicates good cooperation and motivation to comply with conditions. **Moderate compliance** is evidenced by such things as missed appointments and resistance to authorty. **Major compliance** is when the clients/family is totally uncooperative.

17. Use of Community Resources/Treatment Programs ___ ___ ___
    Not needed 0
    Productively utilized 0
    Needed but not available 1
    Utilized but not beneficial 2
    Available but rejected 3

    From your knowledge of the minor and/or the case record, select the responses which most closely represents your view of the minor's utilization of community resources to deal with identifed problems.

TOTAL SCORE: ___ ___ ___

Form B.4
Georgia: Division of Youth Services Treatment Plan

Division of Youth Services Treatment Plan

A. Child ______________________ County____________ Sex _______ DOB _____

Case Status: Commitment Date _______________ Probation Date ____________

Permanency Goal: Return / Remain Home ____ Independent Living _____
(16 years or older)

Risk/ Needs: Risk Score ______ Needs Score _______

Level of Supervision: High ____ Medium ____ Low ____

B. Special Early Release Conditions: ____

____

____

____

____

C. The attached plan/ plan revision has been explained to us and we understand it. By our signatures below we acknowledge receipt of a copy of this plan and pledge our cooperation in reaching the stated goals.

Youth ______________________ Date _______________

Parent/Guardian ________________________________ Date _______________

Case Manager __________________________________ Date _______________

Other ______________________ Date ________________

D. Initial Plan _____ Review/Revision ________

Effective Term: From _______________ to ________________

Form B.4 (continued)

TREATMENT PLAN

Assessment Category_______________________________ Level ___________

Goal: ____

____

Objective: Youth agrees to ____

____

Parent/ Guardian Responsibilities ____

____

Case Managers Responsibilties ____

____

Objective: Youth agrees to ____

____

Parent/Guardian Responsibilities ____

____

Case Managers Responsibilities ____

____

Objective: Youth agrees to ____

____

Parent/Guardian Responsibilities ____

____

Case Managers Responsibilities ____

____

Objective: Youth agrees to ____

____

Parent/Guardian Responsibilities ____

____

Case Managers Responsibilities ____

Form B.5
Minnesota: Initial Risk Assessment

Ramsey Co. Community Corrections Dept.
Juvenile Probation/Parole

CLIENT NAME (Last) (First) (M.I.) (INCLUDE ALIASES)			LEVEL OF SUPERVISION	SUPERVISION START DATE
DATE OF ASSESSMENT	CLIENT'S DOB	PO'S LAST NAME	PO'S CODE NO.	BRANCH OFFICE CODE NO.

Select the answer and enter the point value in the adjacent blank.

SCORE

AGE AT WHICH FIRST PETITION WAS SUSTAINED:
- **0** 16 or older
- **3** 14 or 15
- **5** 13 or younger

____

PRIOR CRIMINAL BEHAVIOR: (Does not include present offense)
- **0** No prior arrests
- **2** Prior arrest record; no court action
- **3** Prior petitions sustained but no assaultive offenses
- **5** Prior felony petitions sustained or at least one assaultive offense on record

____

INSTITUTIONAL COMMITMENTS OR PLACEMENTS OF 30 DAYS OR MORE:
(Do not include commitments or placements for current offense)
- **0** None
- **2** One
- **4** Two or more

____

DRUG/CHEMICAL ABUSE:
- **0** No known use or interferance with functioning
- **1** Some disruption of functioning
- **3** Chronic use or dependency; serious disruption of functioning

____

ALCOHOL ABUSE:
- **0** No known use or no interference with functioning
- **2** Occasional use; some disruption of functioning
- **5** Chronic use; serious disruption of functioning

____

PARENTAL CONTROL:
- **0** Generally effective
- **2** Concerned, but inconsistent and/or ineffective
- **4** Little or none

____

SCHOOL DISCIPLINARY PROBLEMS:
- **0** Attending; graduated; GED
- **1** Problems handled at school level
- **3** Severe truancy or behavioral problems
- **5** Not attending

____

PEER RELATIONSHIPS:
- **0** Good support and influence
- **2** Negative influence; companions involved in delinquent behavior
- **4** Gang member

____

TOTAL RISK SCORE ____

Form B.6
Minnesota: Initial Needs Assessment

Ramsey Co. Community Corrections Dept.
Juvenile Probation/Parole

CLIENT NAME (Last) (First) (M.I.) (INCLUDE ALIASES)				LEVEL OF SUPERVISION	SUPERVISION START DATE
DATE OF ASSESSMENT	CLIENT'S DOB	PO'S LAST NAME	PO'S CODE NO.		BRANCH OFFICE CODE NO.

Select the answer and enter the point value in the adjacent blank.

			SCORE
FAMILY RELATIONSHIPS:			
0 Relatively stable relationship; not applicable	**3** Some disorganization or stress but potential for improvement	**6** Major disorganization or stress	____
ALCOHOL ABUSE:			
0 No known use; no interference with functioning	**4** Occasional abuse; some disruption of functioning; unwilling to participate in treatment program	**6** Frequent abuse; serious disruption; needs immediate treatment	____
DRUG/CHEMICAL ABUSE:			
0 No known use; no interference with functioning	**3** Occasional abuse; some disruption of functioning; unwilling to participate in treatment program	**5** Frequent abuse; serious disruption; needs immediate treatment	____
EMOTIONAL STABILITY:			
0 Appropriate adolescent responses	**3** Exaggerated periodic or sporadic responses; e.g., aggressive acting out or depressive withdrawal	**5** Excessive responses; prohibits or limits adequate functioning	____
EMPLOYMENT:			
0 Not needed	**3** Needs employment		
0 Currently employed			____
LIVING ARRANGEMENTS:			
0 Suitable living arrangements	**1** Unacceptable living situtation or nomadic lifestyle		____
INTELLECTUAL ABILITY:			
0 Able to function independently	**2** Some need for assistance; potential for adjustment; mild retardation	**4** Deficiencies severely limit independent functioning; moderate retardation	____
EXTRACURRICULAR ACTIVITIES:			
-2 Involved in regular systematic leisure time activity	**0** Not involved in regular systematic leisure time activity		____
HEALTH:			
0 Sound physical health	**2** Handicap or illness does not interfere with functioning	**3** Handicap or illness does interfere with functioning	____

For each of the following items, score the points indicated for each characteristic which applies to the case and enter the total on the Score line.

PHYSICAL/SEXUAL ABUSE AND ADJUSTMENT:

1 Sexual deviant	____	**1** Unwed parent	____	
1 Prostitution	____	**1** Child has been sexually abused	____	
1 Child has been physically abused	____	**1** Child has sexually abused others	____	Score ____
1 Child has physically abused others	____			

EDUCATIONAL ADJUSTMENT:

1 Poor school performance	____	**1** Poor attendance record	____	
1 Refusal to participate in any educational program	____	**1** Program not appropriate for needs, age, and/or ability	____	Score ____
1 Disruptive school behavior	____			

PEER RELATIONSHIPS:

1 Socially inept	____	**1** Dependent upon others	____	
2 Receives basically negative influence from peers	____	**2** Exploits and/or manipulates others	____	
				Score ____

TOTAL NEEDS SCORE ____

Form B.7
Minnesota: Reassessment of Risk

Ramsey Co. Community Corrections Dept.
Juvenile Probation/Parole

CLIENT NAME (Last) (INCLUDE ALIASES)		(First)	(M.I.)	LEVEL OF SUPERVISION
DATE OF REASSESSMENT	CLIENT'S DOB	PO'S LAST NAME	PO'S CODE NO.	BRANCH OFFICE CODE NO.

Select the answer and enter the point value in the adjacent blank.

				SCORE
AGE AT WHICH FIRST PETITION WAS SUSTAINED:				
0 16 or older	**2** 14 or 15	**3** 13 or younger		____
PRIOR CRIMINAL BEHAVIOR: (Do not include current offense unless there has been a new offense since intake.)				
0 No prior arrests	**1** Prior arrest record; no court action	**2** Prior petitions sustained but no assaultive offenses	**4** Prior felony petitions sustained or at least one assaultive offense on record	____
INSTITUTIONAL COMMITMENTS OR PLACEMENTS OF 30 DAYS OR MORE:				
0 None	**1** One	**3** Two or more		____

Rate the following based on experience since the last assessment.

DRUG/CHEMICAL ABUSE:				
0 No known use or interferance with functioning	**1** Some disruption of functioning	**3** Chronic use or dependency; serious disruption of functioning		____
ALCOHOL ABUSE				
0 No known use or no interference with functioning	**2** Occasional use; some disruption of functioning	**5** Chronic abuse; serious disruption of functioning		____
PARENTAL CONTROL:				
0 Generally effective	**2** Concerned, but inconsistent and/or ineffective	**4** Little or none		____
SCHOOL DISCIPLINARY PROBLEMS:				
0 Attending; graduated; GED	**1** Problems handled at school level	**3** Severe truancy or behavioral problems	**5** Not attending	____
RESPONSE TO SUPERVISION REQUIREMENTS:				
0 No problems of consequence	**2** Moderate compliance problems	**5** Major compliance problems; generally uncooperative		____
USE OF COMMUNITY RESOURCES/TREATMENT PROGRAMS:				
0 Not needed **0** Productively utilized	2 Needed but not available	**3** Utilized but not beneficial	**5** Available, but rejected	____

TOTAL RISK SCORE ____

Form B.8
Minnesota: Reassessment of Needs

Ramsey Co. Community Corrections Dept.
Juvenile Probation/Parole

CLIENT NAME (Last) (INCLUDE ALIASES)		(First)	(M.I.)	LEVEL OF SUPERVISION
DATE OF REASSESSMENT	CLIENT'S DOB	PO'S LAST NAME	PO'S CODE NO.	BRANCH OFFICE CODE NO.

Select the answer and enter the point value in the adjacent blank.

			SCORE
FAMILY RELATIONSHIPS:			
0 Relatively stable relationship; not applicable	3 Some disorganization or stress but potential for improvement	6 Major disorganization or stress	____
ALCOHOL ABUSE:			
0 No known use; no interference with functioning	4 Occasional abuse; some disruption of functioning; unwilling to participate in treatment program	6 Frequent abuse; serious disruption; needs immediate treatment	____
DRUG/CHEMICAL ABUSE:			
0 No known use; no interference with functioning	3 Occasional abuse; some disruption of functioning; unwilling to participate in treatment program	5 Frequent abuse; serious disruption; needs treatment	____
EMOTIONAL STABILITY:			
0 Appropriate adolescent responses	3 Exaggerated periodic or sporadic responses; e.g., aggressive acting out or depressive withdrawal	5 Excessive responses; prohibits or limits adequate functioning	____
EMPLOYMENT:			
0 Not needed 0 Currently employed	3 Needs employment		____
LIVING ARRANGEMENTS:			
0 Suitable living arrangements	1 Unacceptable living situtation or nomadic lifestyle		____
INTELLECTUAL ABILITY:			
0 Able to function independently	2 Some need for assistance; potential for adjustment; mild retardation	4 Deficiencies severely limit independent functioning; moderate retardation	____
EXTRACURRICULAR ACTIVITIES:			
-2 Involved in regular systematic leisure time activity	0 Not involved in regular systematic leisure time activity		____
HEALTH:			
0 Sound physical health	2 Handicap or illness does not interfere with functioning	3 Handicap or illness does interfere with functioning	____

For each of the following items, score the points indicated for each characteristic which applies to the case and enter the total on the Score line.

PHYSICAL/SEXUAL ABUSE AND ADJUSTMENT:
- 1 Sexual deviant ____
- 1 Prostitution ____
- 1 Child has been physically abused ____
- 2 Child has physically abused others ____
- 1 Unwed parent ____
- 1 Child has been sexually abused ____
- 2 Child has sexually abused others ____

Score____

EDUCATIONAL ADJUSTMENT:
- 1 Poor school performance ____
- 2 Refusal to participate in any educational program ____
- 2 Disruptive school behavior ____
- 2 Poor attendance record ____
- 1 Program not appropriate for needs, age, and/or ability ____

Score____

PEER RELATIONSHIPS:
- 1 Socially inept
- 2 Receives basically negative influence from peers ____ ____
- 1 Dependent upon others ____
- 2 Exploits and/or manipulates others ____

Score____

TOTAL NEEDS SCORE____

Form B.9
Minnesota: Assessment of Needs at Termination

Ramsey Co. Community Corrections Dept.
Juvenile Probation/Parole

CLIENT NAME (Last) (First) (INCLUDE ALIASES)			LEVEL OF SUPERVISION	DISMISSAL DATE
DATE OF TERMINATION	CLIENT'S DOB	PO'S LAST NAME	PO'S CODE NO.	BRANCH OFFICE CODE NO.

Select the answer and enter the point value in the adjacent blank.

			SCORE
FAMILY RELATIONSHIPS:			
0 Relatively stable relationship; not applicable	**3** Some disorganization or stress but potential for improvement	**6** Major disorganization or stress	____
ALCOHOL ABUSE:			
0 No known use; no interference with functioning	**4** Occasional abuse; some disruption of functioning; unwilling to participate in treatment program	**6** Frequent abuse; serious disruption; needs immediate treatment	____
DRUG/CHEMICAL ABUSE:			
0 No known use; no interference with functioning	**3** Occasional abuse; some disruption of functioning; unwilling to participate in treatment program	**5** Frequent abuse; serious disruption; needs treatment	____
EMOTIONAL STABILITY:			
0 Appropriate adolescent responses	**3** Exaggerated periodic or sporadic responses; e.g., aggressive acting out or depressive withdrawal	**5** Excessive responses; prohibits or limits adequate functioning	____
EMPLOYMENT:			
0 Not needed **0** Currently employed	**3** Needs employment		____
LIVING ARRANGEMENTS:			
0 Suitable living arrangements	**1** Unacceptable living situation or nomadic lifestyle		____
INTELLECTUAL ABILITY:			
0 Able to function independently	**2** Some need for assistance; potential for adjustment; mild retardation	**4** Deficiencies severely limit independent functioning; moderate retardation	____
EXTRACURRICULAR ACTIVITIES:			
-2 Involved in regular systematic leisure time activity	**0** Not involved in regular systematic leisure time activity		____
HEALTH:			
0 Sound physical health	**2** Handicap or illness does not interfere with functioning	**3** Handicap or illness does interfere with functioning	____

For each of the following items, score the points indicated for each characteristic which applies to the case and enter the total on the Score line.

PHYSICAL/SEXUAL ABUSE AND ADJUSTMENT:

1	Sexual deviant	____	**1**	Unwed parent	____	
1	Prostitution	____	**1**	Child has been sexually abused	____	
1	Child has been physically abused	____	**2**	Child has sexually abused others	____	Score ____
2	Child has physically abused others	____				

EDUCATIONAL ADJUSTMENT:

1	Poor school performance	____	**2**	Poor attendance record	____	
2	Refusal to participate in any educational program	____	**1**	Program not appropriate for needs, age, and/or ability	____	Score ____
2	Disruptive school behavior	____				

PEER RELATIONSHIPS:

1	Socially inept	____	**1**	Dependent upon others	____	
2	Receives basically negative influence from peers	____	**2**	Exploits and/or manipulates others	____	Score ____

TOTAL NEEDS SCORE ____

Form B.10
Missouri Division of Youth Services Risk Assessment Form

Name: ____________________ **No:** __________ **Region:** ____ **Date:** _______

1.	Age at first juvenile court referral (excluding CA/N) (consider both sustained and unsustained)		_______
	12 and under	5	
	13-14	3	
	15	2	
	16 and over	0	
2.	Most serious juvenile court referral (consider only sustained referrals)		_______
	Highest	6	
	High	5	
	Moderate	3	
	Low	1	
3.	No. of juv. court referrals (excluding CA/N) (consider both sustained and unsustained)		_______
	8 or more	6	
	5-7	4	
	3-4	2	
	2 or fewer	0	
4.	Most serious assaultive behavior		_______
	Assault leading to sust . court referral	6	
	Assault on authority figure, no conviction	5	
	Fighting resulting in injury or school susp	4	
	None	0	
5.	Most serious escapes/runaways (within past 12 mos)		_______
	Escape from detention/institution/custody	6	
	Run from group care/foster care	4	
	Run or attempt from home	2	
	None	0	

Form B.10 (continued)

6. Drug/Chemical/Alcohol abuse ______

Chronic abuse	5
Abuse resulting in some disruption	3
No known use/use with no interference	0

7. Most recent public school adjustment (prior to commitment) ______

Not attending/expelled	5
Severe truancy, behavior problems	3
Problems handled at school level	1
Attending/graduated/GED	0

8. Peer relationships at time of commitment ______

Gang member	4
Negatively influenced, companions involved in delinquency	2
Good support, positively influenced	0

TOTAL SCORE ______

*See document titled "Risk Assessment Offense Codes" adopted 5-17-90.

"Highest" means those offenses which involve aggressiveness and are crimes against people. Examples are: homicide, rape, assault, armed robbery, sodomy.

"High" means those offenses which are serious property offenses. Examples are: burglary, stealing, arson, property damage, fraud.

"Moderate" means those offenses which do not involve aggressive behavior. These crimes may be either felonies or misdemeanors. Examples are: peace disturbance, weapon possession, possession of drugs, public drunkenness, trespass, petty theft.

"Low" means status offenses or very minor law violations. In violation of court order commitments are included in this category.

Form B.11
North Dakota: Risk Assessment and Offense Codes

Division of Juvenile Services

CLASSIFICATION/RISK ASSESSMENT

NAME: ______________________________ DOB: __________
Last First MI

Score

1. Severity of Current Offense (adjudications/informals) ________

See offense list (10)
See offense list (5)
See offense list (1)
See offense list (0)

2. Severity of Prior Adjudications (adjudications/informals) ________

See offense list (5)
See offense list (3)
See offense list (1)
See offense list (0)

3. Number of Prior Adjudications and/or Informals ________

2 or more felonies (5)
Less than 2 (0)

4. Age at First Adjudication ________

12-13 years old (2)
14+ years old (0)

5. Prior Runaway Behavior While Under Supervision ________

Secure facility (2)
Community placement (1)
Parents' home (0)

Placement Scale:

10 and above:	Consider for Secure Placement
5-9	Short-term placement
0-4	Community placement/services

Mitigating/Aggravating Factors--Review for Placement: Yes ___ No ___

Form B.11 (continued)

OFFENSE CODES

F = Felony; M = Misdemeanor

TYPE	CURRENT OFFENSE	OFFENSE	F/M	PRIOR OFFENSE
PERSON	10	Murder, Homicide	F	5
	5	Manslaughter	F	3
	3	Negligent Manslaughter	F	1
	10	Gross Sexual Imposition	F	5
	5	Sexual Imposition	F	3
	3	Sexual Assault	M	2
	5	Robbery	F	3
	10	Armed Robberty	F	5
	10	Aggravated Assault	F	5
	3	Assault	M	2
	1	Simple Assault	M	1
	10	Kidnapping	F	5
	5	Terrorizing, Reckless Endangerment	F	3
	3	Menacing	F	2
	5	Vehicular Manslaughter (alcohol related)	F	3
PROPERTY	5	Arson	F	3
	5	Burglary	F	3
	3	Theft	F	2
	1	Theft	M	1
	3	Criminal Trespass	F	2
	1	Trespassing, Tampering, and Mischief	M	1
	3	Forgery	F	2
	1	Forgery	M	1
	3	Fraud	F	2
	1	Fraud	M	1
PUBLIC ORDER	1	Obscenity	F/M	1
	1	Prostitution	M	1
	1	Public Indecency	M	1
	1	Obstruction	F/M	1
	1	Contraband	M	1

Form B.11 (continued)

OFFENSE CODES

F = Felony; M = Misdemeanor

TYPE	CURRENT OFFENSE	OFFENSE	F/M	PRIOR OFFENSE
PUBLIC ORDER (CONT.)	1	Public Peace and Order, Disorderly Conduct, Loitering	M	1
	1	Cruelty to Animals	M	1
	1	Gambling	F/M	1
	3	Firearms and Weapons	F	2
	1	Firearms and Weapons	M	1
DRUG & ALCOHOL	5	(Sales) Controlled Substances and Marijuana	F	3
	1	(Sales) Controlled Substances and Marijuana	M	1
	1	Drug Paraphenalia	M	1
		Criminal Attempt 1 pt. less than offense attempted (1 pt. minimum)	F/M	
		Criminal Conspiracy 1 pt. less than offense attempting (1 pt. minimum)	F/M	

POINTS FOR OFFENSES NOT LISTED ABOVE

Class A Felony	10
Class B Felony	5
Class C Felony	3
Misdemeanor	1
Status Offenses	0

Form B.12
Texas: Juvenile Probation and Aftercare Assessment of Risk

Select the <u>highest</u> point total applicable for each category

AGE AT FIRST REFERRAL
- 0 = 16 or older
- 3 = 14 or 15
- 5 = 13 or younger ______

AGE AT FIRST ADJUDICATION
- 0 = 16 or older
- 3 = 14 or 15
- 5 = 13 or younger ______

PRIOR CRIMINAL BEHAVIOR
- 0 = No prior arrests
- 2 = Prior arrest record, no formal sanctions
- 3 = Informal Adjustment/Continuance
- 4 = Prior delinquency petition sustained; no assaultive offenses on petition
- 5 = Prior delinquency petitions sustained; at least one assaultive offense on petition ______

INSTITUTIONAL COMMITMENTS OF PLACEMENTS OF 30 DAYS OR MORE
- 0 = None
- 2 = One
- 4 = Two or more ______

DRUG/CHEMICAL ABUSE
- 0 = No known use or no interference with functioning
- 2 = Some disruption of functioning
- 5 = Chronic abuse or dependency ______

ALCOHOL ABUSE
- 0 = No known use or no interference with functioning
- 1 = Occasional abuse, some disruption of functioning
- 3 = Chronic abuse, serious disruption of functioning ______

PARENTAL CONTROL
- 0 = Generally effective
- 2 = Inconsistent and/or ineffective
- 4 = Little or none ______

SCHOOL DISCIPLINARY PROBLEMS
- 0 = Attending, graduated, GED equivalence
- 1 = Problems handled at school level
- 3 = Severe truancy or severe behavioral problems
- 5 = Not attending/expelled ______

PEER RELATIONSHIPS
- 0 = Good support and influence
- 2 = Negative Influence
- 3 = Several friends involved in delinquent type behavior
- 4 = Gang member ______

TOTAL ______

Form B.13
Texas: Initial Placement

TEXAS YOUTH COMMISSION
CHILD CARE FORM

Placement Committee Review Date: ____________ (MM-DD-YY)

Case Number: ____________ Youth's Name: ____________ Last First MI

Age at Placement Review: ________

Home Region: ____________ Caseworker: ____________

Committing Offense: ____________ (name and code)

Classifying Offense: ____________ (name and code if different than committing offense)

High Risk Offense: ☐ Yes ☐ No

Offense: ☐ Sentenced ☐ Type A Violent ☐ Type B Violent ☐ Chronic Serious ☐ Nonviolent Felonious Drug Sale ☐ Nonviolent Firearms Violation ☐ Nonviolent Other ☐ VCP

A. RISK ASSESSMENT INDEX

	Count	Question Score		Index Total
Delinquency Index				
1. Number of Felony Adjudications		______		
2. Number of Felony Referrals	______	______	(max. 4)	
Delinquency Index Score				______
Behavior Index				
1. Number of Prior Placements	______	______	(max. 2)	
2. Ever Referred for Runaway				
A. No	0			
B. Yes	1	______		
3. Number of Escapes from Facilities	______	______	(max. 2)	
4. Reception Center Observed Behavior (select highest)				
A. Acceptable	0			
B. Moderate or Multiple Minor Disruptions	1			
C. Serious Disruption(s)	2	______		
Behavior Index Score				______
TOTAL RISK SCORE				______

Risk Criteria		Risk Level	Presumptive Restriction Level
High Risk Offense or Risk Score of:	7 or more	☐ High	☐ Maximum ☐ High
Not High Risk Offense and Risk Score of:	1 - 6	☐ Medium	☐ Medium
Not High Risk Offense and Risk Score of:	0	☐ Low	☐ Minimum

Risk Assessment Comments: ____________

Form B.13 (continued)

B. NEEDS ASSESSMENT

	Needs Level
1. Medical:	
A. Requires daily medication or frequent monitoring by a physician for chronic physical illness.	☐ High
B. Possesses physical disability or physical handicap which requires a specialized program.	☐ High
C. Possesses a physical disability or physical handicap prohibiting active participation in some specialized programs only.	☐ Medium
D. None of the above.	☐ Low
2. Mental Health:	
A. Requires emergency treatment in state hospital for psychosis, danger to self, or danger to others.	☐ High
B. Requires treatment in residential treatment center for psychological disorder.	☐ High
C. Requires mental health outpatient services.	☐ Medium
D. None of the above.	☐ Low
DSM III Diagnosis Axis I ___ __ Axis II ___ __	
3. Substance Abuse:	
A. Diagnosis of alcohol or drug dependence.	☐ High
B. Diagnosis of alcohol or drug abuse.	☐ Medium
C. Evidence of regular alcohol or drug use, but not part of diagnosis.	☐ Medium
D. No evidence of regular alcohol or drug abuse, and no diagnosis for alcohol or drug abuse or dependence.	☐ Low
4. English Proficiency:	
A. Little or no use of English	☐ High
B. Marginal use of English.	☐ Medium
C. Adequate English proficiency.	☐ Low
5. Education:	
A. Needs self-contained special education.	☐ High
B. Needs full-time vocational curriculum.	☐ Medium
C. Needs academic curriculum supplemented by vocational education.	☐ Medium
D. Needs academic curriculum only.	☐ Low

Needs Assessment Comments: ____

____

____

____

____

____

____

____

____

Form B.13 (continued)

C. **RISK/NEEDS PROFILE**
For each area, circle the corresponding level in the profile.

Risk	Medical	Mental Health	Substance Abuse	English Proficiency	Education
High	High	High	High	High	High
Medium	Medium	Medium	Medium	Medium	Medium
Low	Low	Low	Low	Low	Low

D. **APPLICABLE POLICIES**

Policy Category or Exception	Policy Level of Restriction	Comply	Policy Exception	Waive
☐ Sentenced Offender	Maximum	☐	☐	☐
☐ Violent Offender - A	Maximum	☐	☐	☐
☐ Violent Offender - B	Maximum or High	☐	☐	☐
☐ Chronic Serious Offender	High	☐	☐	☐
☐ Under 13 Years of Age	Medium or Minimum	☐	☐	☐
☐ Pregnancy	Appropriate to Need	☐	☐	☐
☐ Physical or Mental Handicap	Specialized for Handicap	☐	☐	☐
☐ Other ________	________	☐	☐	☐
☐ None of the Above				

E. **PLACEMENT RECOMMENDATIONS/ACTUAL PLACEMENT**

	Caseworker Recommendation	Committee Recommendation	Actual Placement
1. Training School			
A. For Violent Offenders	☐	☐	☐
B. Other	☐	☐	☐
2. Other			
A. Residential Treatment Center - High	☐	☐	☐
B. Residential Treatment Center - Medium	☐	☐	☐
C. Halfway House	☐	☐	☐
D. Group Care	☐	☐	☐
E. Foster Care	☐	☐	☐
F. Special Needs Program			
1. Psychiatric Hospital	☐	☐	☐
2. Substance Abuse Program	☐	☐	☐
3. Vocational Program	☐	☐	☐
4. Wilderness Camping Program	☐	☐	☐
G. Other ________	☐	☐	☐

Form B.13 (continued)

F. PLACEMENT TEAM

	Concurred with Committee Yes	No	Recommendation
______ Chairperson Signature	☐	☐	______
______ Caseworker Signature	☐	☐	______
______ Committee Member Signature	☐	☐	______
______ Committee Member Signature	☐	☐	______
______ Committee Member Signature	☐	☐	______
______ Committee Member Signature	☐	☐	______

G. PLACEMENT SUMMARY

____
____
____
____
____
____
____
____
____
____
____
____
____
____

Form B.14
Texas: Parole Initial Assessment

Date: ____________________
mm-dd-yy

CASE NUMBER: ____________ YOUTH'S NAME: ____________

REGION: ____________ PAROLE OFFICER: ____________

Risk Index	Count	Index Score	Index Total
1. Number of felony adjudications	______		______
2. Number of felony referrals	______	Maximum 7	______
3. Number of placements prior to TYC	______	Maximum 4	______
4. Number of placements in TYC maximum or high restriction facilities	______		
0		0	
1		3	
2 or more		6	______
5. Major incidents at TYC	______		
0		0	
1		2	
2-4		4	
5-8		6	
9 or more		8	______
		Total Risk Score	______

6. High Risk Offense ______ Yes ______ No

If Yes, check offense:

_____ Murder (19.02)
_____ Capital Murder (19.03)
_____ Attempted Capital Murder (A19.03)
_____ Voluntary Manslaughter (19.04)
_____ Aggravated Kidnapping (20.04)
_____ Sexual Assault (22.11 or 22.011)
_____ Aggravated Sexual Assault (22.21 or 22.021)
_____ Deadly Assault (22.03)

Place on maximum supervision if the answer to item 6 is Yes

	TOTAL	______
RISK SCORE OF 21 OR MORE	**HIGH**	______
RISK SCORE OF 13 - 20	**MEDIUM**	______
RISK SCORE OF 0 - 12	**LOW**	______

Form B.14 (continued)

Need Index

I. For each item below, select the single appropriate answer and enter the associated number in the adjacent blank.

	0	1	2	
DRUG CHEMICAL ABUSE	0 No interference with functioning.	1. Occasional abuse, some disruption of functioning, unwilling to participate in treatment program.	2. Frequent abuse, serious disruption, needs immediate treatment.	______
ALCOHOL ABUSE	0 No known use.	1. Occasional abuse, some disruption of functioning, unwilling to participate in treatment program.	2. Frequent abuse, serious disruption, needs immediate treatment.	______
FAMILY RELATIONSHIPS	0 Relatively stable relationship.	1. Some disorganization or stress but potential for improvement.	2. Major disorganization or stress, unwilling to comply with family rules.	______
EMOTIONAL STABILITY	0 Appropriate adolescent responses.	1. Exaggerated periodic or sporadic responses e.g., aggressive acting out or depressive withdrawal.	2. Excessive responses; prohibits or limits adequate functioning.	______
INTELLECTUAL ABILITY	0 Able to function independently.	1. Some need for assistance, potential for adequate adjustment; mild retardation.	2. Deficiencies severely limit independent functioning, moderate retardation.	______
LEARNING DISABILITY	0 None.	1. Mild disability, able to function in classroom.	2. Serious disability, interferes with social functioning.	______
EMPLOYMENT	0 Not needed or currently employed.	1. Currently employed but poor work habits.	2. Needs employment.	______
VOCATIONAL/TECHNICAL SKILLS	0 Currently developing marketable skill.	1. Needs to develop marketable skill.		______

II. Enter the value 1 for each characteristic which applies to the case.

EDUCATIONAL ADJUSTMENT	Not working to potential	______		
	Poor attendance record	______		
	Refusal to participate in any educational program	______	0 = 0	
	Program not appropriate for needs, age and/or ability	______	1-2 = 1	
	Disruptive school behavior	______	3-5 = 2	______
PEER RELATIONSHIPS	Socially inept	______		
	Loner behavior	______	0 = 0	
	Receives basically negative influence from peers	______	1-2 = 1	
	Dependent upon others	______	3-5 = 2	______
	Exploits and/or manipulates others	______		

TOTAL		______
NEED SCORE OF 12 OR MORE	**HIGH**	______
NEED SCORE OF 8-11	**MEDIUM**	______
NEED SCORE OF 0-7	**LOW**	______

Form B.14 (continued)

Composite

CASE NUMBER: ______________________ YOUTH'S NAME: ______________________

RISK: ______________________

NEED: ______________________

LEVEL OF SUPERVISION
(circle level indicated)

Need Level

		HIGH	***MEDIUM***	***LOW***
Risk Level	***HIGH***	Maximum	Maximum	Moderate
	MEDIUM	Moderate	Moderate	Moderate
	LOW	Moderate	Minimum	Minimum

RECOMMENDED SUPERVISION LEVEL: ______________________

Reasons for supervision level that is higher than scores indicate:

____

____

____

____

____
Parole Officer Signature

Approved: ______________________

Disapproved: ______________________

______________________ Date: ______________________
Parole Supervisor's Signature mm-dd-yy

Form B.15
Texas: Parole Reassessment

TEXAS YOUTH COMMISSION
CHILD CARE FORM

Date: ______________ mm-dd-yy

CASE NUMBER: ______________ YOUTH'S NAME: ______________

REGION: ______________ PAROLE OFFICER: ______________

I. **NEEDS**: For each item below, select the single appropriate answer and enter the associated number in the adjacent blank.

	0	1	2	
DRUG CHEMICAL ABUSE	0 No interference with functioning.	1. Occasional abuse, some disruption of functioning, unwilling to participate in treatment program.	2. Frequent abuse, serious disruption, needs immediate treatment.	______
ALCOHOL ABUSE	0 No known use.	1. Occasional abuse, some disruption of functioning, unwilling to participate in treatment program.	2. Frequent abuse, serious disruption, needs immediate treatment.	______
FAMILY RELATIONSHIPS	0 Relatively stable relationship.	1. Some disorganization or stress but potential for improvement. Inconsistent parental control.	2. Major disorganization or stress, unwilling to comply with family rules. Little or no parental control.	______
PEER RELATIONSHIPS	0 Relatively normal peer relationships.	1. Dependent upon others, influenced negatively by peers, loner.	2. Socially inept, exploits or manipulates others.	______
EMOTIONAL STABILITY	0 Appropriate adolescent responses.	1. Exaggerated periodic or sporadic responses e.g., aggressive acting out or depressive withdrawal.	2. Excessive responses: prohibits or limits adequate functioning.	______
SCHOOL	0 Attending, Graduated or has GED, employed full-time.	1. Attendance or behavior problems handled at school.	2. Severe truancy or behavior problems, expelled, not attending without good reason.	______
EMPLOYMENT	0 Employed, actively seeking employment, in school full-time.	1. Problems handled at employee's level, poor work habits.	2. Severe attendance or problems at work, fired, refuses to seek employment.	______
VOCATIONAL/TECHNICAL SKILLS	0 None needed or actively participating in training.	1. Currently developing vocational skills and problems handled at program level.	2. Needs vocational skills but refuses to participate in training.	______
COMMUNITY RESOURCES/ TREATMENT PROGRAMS	0 None needed or productivity utilized.	1. Inconsistently utilized.	2. Available but not utilized.	______
RESPONSE TO SUPERVISION REQUIREMENTS	0 No problems of consequence.	1. Moderate compliance problems.	2. Major compliance problems, totally uncooperative.	______

TOTAL NEEDS SCORE ______

NEED SCORE OF 12 OR MORE ______ HIGH

NEED SCORE OF 8-11 ______ MEDIUM

NEED SCORE OF 0-7 ______ LOW

Form B.15 (continued)

II. **RISK**:

1. Major incident since last risk assessment or reassessment?
   _______ YES: Recalculate risk level using the Initial Risk Assessment Index. Enter the result in item 4 - Revised Risk Score. If the original offense was a high risk offense enter 30 or the recalculated risk score, whichever is higher. (skip items 2 and 3.)
   _______ NO: Enter the Total Risk Score from the most recent risk assessment or reassessment. _______

2. Was the original offense a High Risk Offense?
   _______ YES: a. If this is the first reassessment enter 30 or the Total Risk Score from the Initial Risk Assessment, whichever is higher.
   b. Otherwise enter the Total Risk Score from item 1.
   _______ NO: Enter the Total Risk Score from item 1.
   ADJUSTED TOTAL RISK SCORE _______

3. Subtract 5 from the Adjusted Total Risk Score (if no major incidents since the last risk assessment). __5__

4. Revised Risk Score _______

5. Risk Level

RISK SCORE OF 21 OR MORE _______ HIGH
RISK SCORE OF 13-20 _______ MEDIUM
RISK SCORE OF 0-12 _______ LOW

COMPOSITE

RISK LEVEL: ______________________ NEED LEVEL: ______________________

LEVEL OF SUPERVISION
(circle level indicated)

Need Level

		HIGH	***MEDIUM***	***LOW***
Risk Level	***HIGH***	Maximum	Maximum	Moderate
	MEDIUM	Moderate	Moderate	Moderate
	LOW	Moderate	Minimum	Minimum

RECOMMENDED SUPERVISION LEVEL: ______________________

Reasons for supervision level that is higher than scores indicate:

____

____

____

____

Approved: ______________________

____
Parole Officer's Signature

Disapproved: ______________________

______________________ Date: ______________________
Parole Supervisor's Signature mm-dd-yy

Cases Cited

Baraldini v. Thornburgh, 45 CrL 2471 (CADC 1989)

Barefoot v. Estelle, 103 S.Ct. 3383 (1983)

Battle v. Anderson, 447 F.Supp. 516 (1977)

Bearden v. Georgia, 461 U.S. 660 (1983)

Bell v. Wolfish, 441 U.S. 520 (1979)

Black v. Romano, 471 U.S. 606 (1985)

Childs v. United States Board of Parole, 371 F.Supp. 1246 (1973)

Clifton v. Robinson, 494 F.Supp. 364 (1980)

Coffin v. Reichard, 143 F.2d 443 (1944)

Dorman v. District of Columbia, 46 CrL 1171 (DC Cir. 1989)

Estelle v. Gamble, 429 U.S. 97 (1976)

Ex parte Hull, 312 U.S. 546 (1941)

Fischer v. Winter, 564 F.Supp. 281 (1983)

Furman v. Georgia, 408 U.S. 238 (1972)

Gagnon v. Scarpelli, 411 U.S. 788 (1973)

Glover v. Johnson, 478 F.Supp. 1075 (1979)

Glumb v. Honsted, 891 F.2d 872 (1990)

Gregg v. Georgia, 428 U.S. 153 (1976)

Hackett v. United States, 606 F.2d 319 (1978)

Hudson v. Palmer, 468 U.S. 517 (1984)

In re Green, 669 F.2d 779 (1981)

Jessup v. U.S. Parole Commission, 889 F.2d 831 (1989)

Jones v. United States, 103 S.Ct. 3043 (1983)
Lynch v. U.S. Parole Commission, 768 F.2d 491 (1985)
Mempa v. Rhay, 389 U.S. 129 (1967)
Morrissey v. Brewer, 400 U.S. 471 (1972)
Myrick v. Gunnell, 563 F.Supp. 51 (1983)
Preiser v. Rodriguez, 429 U.S. 475 (1973)
Procunier v. Martinez, 416 U.S. 396 (1974)
Quinones v. Nettleship, 773 F.2d 10 (1985)
Rhodes v. Chapman, 452 U.S. 337 (1981)
Robinson v. Hadden, 723 F.2d 59 (1983)
Rowland v. Sigler, 452 U.S. 337 (1971)
Ruffin v. Commonwealth, 62 Va. (21 Gratt) 790 (1871)
Stroud v. U.S. Parole Commission, 668 F.2d 843 (1982)
Sypert v. United States, 559 F.Supp. 546 (1983)
Tarlton v. Clark, 441 F.2d 384 (1971)
United States v. Cohen, 796 F.2d 20 (1986)
United States v. Dawson, 423 U.S. 855 (1975)
United States v. Mills, 704 F.2d 1553 (1983)
United States v. Muniz, 374 U.S. 150 (1963)
Vester v. Rogers, 795 F.Supp. 1179 (1986)
Walker v. United States, 437 F.Supp. 1081 (1977)
Wolff v. McDonnell, 428 U.S. 280 (1974)
Yamamoto v. U.S. Parole Commission, 794 F.2d 1295 (1986)

Bibliography

Abel, Gene G., Judith V. Becker, and Linda J. Skinner. 1987. "Behavioral Approaches to Treatment of the Violent Sex Offender." In *Clinical Treatment of the Violent Person,* Loren H. Roth (ed.). New York: Guilford Press.

Abrahamse, Allan F. et al. 1991. "An Experimental Evaluation of the Phoenix Repeat Offender Program." *Justice Quarterly* 8:141–168.

Abt Associates, Inc. 1987. *Sentencing and Time Served.* Washington, DC: Bureau of Justice Statistics.

Alabama Department of Corrections.1987. *Security Classification Manual and Forms.* Montgomery, AL: Alabama Department of Corrections.

Alaska Department of Corrections. 1986. *Department Policy and Procedure Review.* Anchorage, AK: Alaska Department of Corrections, Office of Technical Services.

Albonetti, Celesta A. 1991. "An Integration of Theories to Explain Judicial Discretion." *Social Problems* 38:247–266.

Alexander, Jack. 1980. *Security Classification Guideline Project—Working Paper VIII: A Proposed Guideline for Initial Security Classification of Adult Males.* Albany, NY: Department of Correctional Services, Program Planning, Evaluation and Research, Classification and Movement.

Allen, G. Frederick. 1985. "The Probationers Speak: Analysis of the Probationers' Experiences and Attitudes." *Federal Probation* 49:67–75.

Allen, Harry E. et al. 1985. *Probation and Parole in America.* New York: Macmillan.

American Correctional Association. 1983. *The American Prison: From the Beginning . . . A Pictorial History.* College Park, MD: American Correctional Association.

American Correctional Association. 1987. *Juvenile and Adult Correctional Departments, Institutions, Agencies and Paroling Authorities: United States and Canada.* College Park, MD: American Correctional Association.

American Correctional Association. 1992. *1991 Directory.* College Park, MD: American Correctional Association.

Anderson, Debra J. 1986. *Curbing the Abuses of Inmate Litigation.* College Park, MD: American Correctional Association.

Apao, William K., Larry D. Haugh, and Elizabeth Meyer. 1988. "Improving Prison Classification Procedures: Application of an Interaction Model." Washington, DC: U.S. National Institute of Justice. (Unpublished)

Araza, Jack. 1990. "Antisocial Children and Adolescents: A Risk Assessment Inventory and Diagnostic Manual." *Juvenile & Family Court Journal* 42:11–36.

Arizona Department of Corrections. 1991. *Offender Classification System (OCS): Classification Operating Manual.* Phoenix, AZ: Arizona Department of Corrections.

Armor, Jerry C. et al. 1989. "Amenability to Rehabilitation among Prison Inmates." *Journal of Offender Counseling, Services, & Rehabilitation* 14:137–142.

Atkinson, Donald. 1986. "Parole Can Work!" *Corrections Today* 48:54–56.

Austin, James. 1983. "Assessing the New Generation of Prison Classification Models." *Crime & Delinquency* 29:561–576.

Austin, James. 1986. *National Survey of Automated Correctional Information Systems for the Illinois Department of Corrections.* San Francisco: National Council on Crime and Delinquency.

Austin, James. 1987. "An Overview of a Model Jail Classification System: Design and Structure." Unpublished paper presented at the annual meeting of the American Society of Criminology. Montreal. (November).

Austin, James, and William Pannell. 1986. *The Growing Imprisonment of California.* San Francisco: National Council on Crime and Delinquency.

Baird, S. Christopher. 1974. *Parole Prediction Report No. 3.* Joliette, IL: Illinois Department of Corrections.

Baird S. Christopher. 1985. "Classifying Juveniles: Making the Most of an Important Management Tool." *Corrections Today* 47:32–38.

Baird, S. Christopher. 1987. *A Model Management System for Juvenile Corrections.* Madison, WI: Isthmus Associates.

Baird, S. Christopher et al. 1987. *Oregon Risk Assessment Project: Final Report.* Madison, WI: National Council on Crime and Delinquency.

Baird, S. Christopher, and James Austin. 1986. *Current State of the Art in Prison Classification Models: A Literature Review for the California Department of Corrections.* Sacramento, CA: California Department of Corrections.

Baird, S. Christopher, and Richard Heinz. 1978. "Risk Assessment in Juvenile Probation and Aftercare." Madison, WI: Wisconsin Division of Corrections. (Unpublished)

Baird, S. Christopher, Gregory M. Storrs, and Helen Connelly. 1984. *Classification of Juveniles in Corrections: A Model Systems Report.* Washington, DC: Arthur D. Little, Inc.

Bakal, Yitzhak, and Barry Krisberg. 1987. *Placement Needs Assessment for Youth Committed to Oregon Training Schools.* San Francisco, CA: National Council on Crime and Delinquency.

Banks, Jerry. 1984. *Validation of Risk and Needs Assessment Instruments: Final Report.* Atlanta, GA: Georgia Department of Offender Rehabilitation.

Barnes, Allan R. 1987. "Distribution of Megargee MMPI-Based Inmate Classification Types in a Sample of Alaska Native and Non-Native Inmates." Unpublished paper presented at the annual meetings of the American Society of Criminology. Montreal. (November).

Barnes, Harry E., and Negley D. Teeters. 1959. *New Horizons in Criminology.* Englewood Cliffs, NJ: Prentice-Hall.

Barnett, A., and A. J. Lofaso. 1985. "Selective Incapacitation and the Philadelphia Cohort Data." *Journal of Quantitative Criminology* 1:3–36.

Beck, Allen J., and Bernard E. Shipley. 1983. *Recidivism of Young Parolees.* Washington, DC: U.S. Department of Justice, Bureau of Justice Statistics.

Beck, Allen J., and Bernard E. Shipley. 1987. *Recidivism of Young Parolees.* Washington, DC: U.S. Department of Justice, Bureau of Justice Statistics.

Beck, Allen J., and Bernard E. Shipley. 1989. *Recidivism of Prisoners Released in 1983.* Washington, DC: U.S. Department of Justice, Bureau of Justice Statistics.

Beck, James L., and Peter B. Hoffman. 1985. "Reliability in Guideline Application: Initial Hearings – 1982." *Federal Probation* 49:33–41.

Bench, Larry L. 1990. "Validating the National Institute of Corrections Objective Prison Classification Model." Unpublished paper presented at the annual meeting of the American Society of Criminology. Baltimore, MD (November).

Benekos, Peter J. 1990. "Beyond Reintegration: Community Corrections in a Retributive Era." *Federal Probation* 54:52–56.

Berk, Richard A. 1987. "Causal Inference as a Prediction Problem." In *Prediction and Classification: Criminal Justice Decision Making,* Don M. Gottfredson and Michael Tonry (eds.). Chicago: University of Chicago Press.

Black, Henry Campbell. 1979. *Black's Law Dictionary.* St. Paul, MN: West.

Blackmore, John, and Jane Welsh. 1983. "Selective Incapacitation: Sentencing According to Risk." *Crime and Delinquency* 29:504–528.

Blumstein, Alfred. 1983a. "Comment: Research on Deterrent and Incapacitative Effects of Criminal Sanctions." *Journal of Criminal Justice* 6:1.

Blumstein, Alfred. 1983b. "Prisons: Population, Capacity, and Alternatives." In *Crime and Public Policy,* James Q. Wilson (ed.). San Francisco: ICS Press.

Blumstein, Alfred, 1983c, "Selective Incapacitation as a Means of Crime Control." *American Behavioral Scientist* 27:87–108.

Blumstein, Alfred, Jose Canela-Cacho, and Jacqueline Cohen. 1990. "Selective Incapacitation Revisited: Issues Raised by Heterogeneity in Offenders Criminality." Unpublished paper presented at the annual meeting of the American Society of Criminology. Baltimore, MD (November).

Blumstein, Alfred, and D. Nagin. 1978. "On the Optimum Use of Incarceration for Crime Control." *Operations Research* 26:381–405.

Bodapati, Madhava, and James Marquart. 1992. "Analyzing Parole Decision Making in Texas: 1980–1990." Unpublished paper presented at the annual meetings of the American Society of Criminology. New Orleans, LA (November).

Boland, B., and J. Q. Wilson. 1978. "Age, Crime, and Punishment." *Public Interest* 51:24-34.

Bonham, G., Jr. 1984. "Predicting Parole Outcomes via Discriminant Analysis." *Justice Quarterly* 1:329-341.

Boudouris, James. 1983. *The Recidivism of Releasees from the Iowa State Penitentiary at Fort Madison.* Des Moines, IA: Iowa Department of Corrections, Bureau of Data, Research, and Planning.

Brannon, James M. et al. 1989. "Applied Behavioral Typologies: Implications for the Residential Treatment and Community Reintegration of Juvenile Offenders." *Journal of Offender Counseling, Services, & Rehabilitation* 14:77–87.

Brannon, Marilyn E. et al. 1990. "Toward the Nonpathological Assessment of Behavioral and Conduct Disordered Adolescents." *Journal of Addictions & Offender Counseling* 11:20-30.

Braswell, Michael C., Steven D. Dillingham, and Reid H. Montgomery. 1985. *Prison Violence in America.* Cincinnati, OH: Anderson.

Brennan, Tim. 1987a. "Classfication: An Overview of Selected Methodological Issues." In *Prediction and Classification: Criminal Justice Decision Making,* Don M. Gottfredson and Michael Tonry (eds.). Chicago: University of Chicago Press.

Brennan, Tim. 1987b. "Classification for Control in Jails and Prisons." In *Prediction and Classification: Criminal Justice Decision Making,* Don M. Gottfredson and Michael Tonry (eds.). Chicago: University of Chicago Press.

Brennan, Tim, and David Wells. 1992. "The Importance of Inmate Classification in Small Jails." *American Jails* 6:49–52.

Bronstein, Alvin J. 1980. "Prisoners' Rights: A History." In *Legal Rights of Prisoners,* Geoffrey Alpert (ed.). Beverly Hills, CA: Sage.

Bronstein, Alvin J. 1987. "15 Years of Prison Litigation: What Has It Accomplished?" *Journal of the National Prison Project* 11:6–9.

Brown, Marjorie E., and Donald Cochran. 1984. *Executive Summary of Research Findings from the Massachusetts Risk/Need Classification System, Report #5*. Boston: Office of the Commissioner of Probation.

Buchanan, R. A. 1986. *Evaluation of Objective Prison Classification Systems.* Kansas City, MO: Correctional Services Group.

Bunch, Barbara J. et al. 1983. "The Psychology of Violent Female Offenders: A Sex Role Perspective." *Prison Journal* 63:66–79.

Burke, Peggy. 1987. "Empirical Tools for Parole Decision-Making: Implementation Issues." Unpublished paper presented at the annual meeting of the American Society of Criminology. Montreal. (November).

Bush, Robert A. Baruch. 1991. *Mediation Involving Juveniles: Ethical Dilemmas and Policy Questions.* Ann Arbor, MI: Center for the Study of Youth Policy, University of Michigan.

Busher, Walter. 1973. *Ordering Time to Serve Prisoners.* Washington, DC: U.S. Government Printing Office.

Byrd, John. 1987. "Risk Assessment for Parole Decision." Unpublished paper presented at the annual meeting of the American Society of Criminology. Montreal. (November).

Callanan, Thomas J. 1986. "Pointers for Probation and Parole Leadership." *Corrections Today* 48:76–81.

Campbell, Curtis, Candace McCoy, and Chimezie A. B. Osigweh. 1990. "The Influence of Probation Recommendations on Sentencing Decisions and Their Predictive Accuracy." *Federal Probation* 54:13–21.

Capune, W. Garrett. 1988. "Selective Incapacitation: A Review of the Law and the Literature." *Criminal Justice Journal* 10:187–196.

Carney, Francis L. 1989. *Criminality and Its Treatment: The Patuxent Experience.* Malabar, FL: Robert E. Krieger Publishing.

Chaiken, Marcia R., and Jan M. Chaiken. 1987. "Selecting 'Career Criminals' for Priority Prosecution." Unpublished paper presented at the annual meeting of the American Society of Criminology. Montreal. (November).

Champion, Dean J. 1988. *Felony Probation: Problems and Prospects.* New York: Praeger.

Champion, Dean J. 1990a. *Criminal Justice in the United States.* Columbus, OH: Merrill (A Macmillan Publisher).

Champion, Dean J. 1990b. " 'Just-Deserts' and Selective Incapacitation: Some Judicial and Prosecutorial Consideration and Priorities." Unpublished paper presented at the annual meeting of the American Society of Criminology. Baltimore, MD (November).

Champion, Dean J. 1990c. *Probation and Parole in the United States.* Columbus, OH: Merrill Publishing Company (A Macmillan Publisher).

Champion, Dean J. 1992. *The Juvenile Justice System: Delinquency, Processing, and the Law.* New York: Macmillan.

Champion, Dean J. 1993. *Research Methods for Criminal Justice and Criminology.* Englewood Cliffs, NJ: Regents/Prentice-Hall.

Chown, Bill, and Steven Davis. 1986. *Recidivism Among Offenders Incarcerated by the Oklahoma Department of Corrections: A Survival Data Analysis.* Oklahoma City, OK: Oklahoma Department of Corrections.

Clark, Patrick M., David Canales-Portalatin, and Jo Ellen Weth. 1992. "Inmate Classification in the United States: A Survey of Policy and Procedures." Unpublished paper presented at the annual meetings of the American Society of Criminology. New Orleans, LA (November).

Clarke, Stevens H., and Larry Crum. 1985. *Returns to Prison in North Carolina.* Chapel Hill: Institute of Government, University of North Carolina, Chapel Hill.

Clarke, Stevens H., W. LeAnn Wallace, and Yuan-Huei Lin. 1987. "Probationer Recidivism and Alternative Classification Strategies." Unpublished paper presented at the annual meeting of the American Society of Criminology. Montreal. (November).

Clayton, Obie, Jr. 1983. "Reconsideration of the Effects of Race in Criminal Sentencing." *Criminal Justice Review* 8:15–20.

Clear, Todd R., and Donald M. Barry. 1983. "Some Conceptual Issues in Incapacitating Offenders." *Crime & Delinquency* 29:529–545.

Clear, Todd R., Val B. Clear, and William D. Burrell. 1989. *Offender Assessment and Evaluation: The Presentence Investigation Report.* Cincinnati, OH: Anderson.

Clear, Todd R., and Vincent O'Leary. 1983. *Controlling the Offender in the Community.* Lexington, MA: Lexington Books.

Cohen, Jacqueline. 1983. "Incapacitation as a Strategy for Crime Control: Possibilities and Pitfalls." In *Crime and Justice: An Annual Review of Research, Vol. 5,* Michael Tonry and Norval Morris (eds.). Chicago: University of Chicago Press.

Cohen, Jacqueline, and Sherwood Zimmerman. 1990. "Assessing the Accuracy of Criminal Justice Prediction Scales." Unpublished paper presented at the annual meeting of the American Society of Criminology. Baltimore, MD (November).

Cohen, Morris R., and Ernest Nagel. 1934. *An Introduction to Logic and the Scientific Method.* New York: Harcourt, Brace.

Cohen, Robyn L. 1991. *Prisoners in 1990.* Washington, DC: U.S. Department of Justice, Bureau of Justice Statistics.

Cohn, Alvin W., and Michael M. Ferriter. 1990. "The Presentence Investigation: An Old Saw with New Teeth." *Federal Probation* 54:15–25.

Coles, Frances S. 1987. "The Impact of *Bell v. Wolfish* Upon Prisoners' Rights." *Journal of Crime and Justice* 10:47–70.

Colley, Lori, Robert G. Culbertson, and Edward J. Latessa. 1987. "Juvenile Probation Officers: A Job Analysis." *Juvenile and Family Court Journal* 38:1–12.

Colorado Division of Criminal Justice. 1986. *Custody Needs and Public Risk of Colorado's Prisoners: An Assessment.* Denver, CO: Colorado Division of Criminal Justice.

Colorado Parole Guidelines Commission. 1988. *Report to the Legislature.* Denver, CO:

Colorado Parole Guidelines Commission.

Commonwealth of Pennsylvania Department of Corrections. 1992. *Pennsylvania Additive Classification Tool (PACT): Managing Pennsylvania's Correctional Population Through Effective Classification.* Philadelphia, PA: Commonwealth of Pennsylvania Department of Corrections.

Connecticut Board of Parole. 1974. *Statement of Organization and Procedures.* Hartford, CT: Connecticut Board of Parole.

Conrad, John P. 1985. *The Dangerous and the Endangered.* Lexington, MA: Lexington Books.

Contact Center, Inc. 1987. "Correctional Officers." *Corrections Compendium* 11:9–12.

Cook, Phillip J. 1986. "Criminal Incapacitation Effects Considered in an Adaptive Choice Framework." In *The Reasoning Criminal: Rational Choice Perspectives on Offending,* Derek B. Cornish and Ronald V. Clarke (eds.). New York: Springer-Verlag.

Cormack, R. M.1971. "A Review of Classification." *Journal of the Royal Statistical Society* 3:321–367.

Corrections Compendium. 1989a. "Legal Issues." *Corrections Compendium* 14:2–4.

Corrections Compendium. 1989b. "Survey." *Corrections Compendium* 14:8.

Corrections Compendium. 1992. "State to State." *Corrections Compendium* 17:19.

Corrections Compendium. 1993. "District of Columbia's 'Medical Parole and Geriatric Release.' " *Corrections Compendium* 18:6.

Cortes, Joan B., and Florence M. Gatti. 1972. *Delinquency and Crime: A Biopsychological Approach.* New York: Seminar.

Cotton, Donald J., and Nicholas A. Groth. 1984. "Sexual Assault in Correctional Institutions: Prevention and Intervention." In *Victims of Sexual Aggression,* Irving R. Stuart and J. Greer (eds.). New York: Van Nostrand Reinhold.

Craddock, Amy. 1987. "Classification and Correctional Policies: An Empirical Assessment." Unpublished paper presented at the annual meeting of the American Society of Criminology. Montreal. (November).

Criminal Justice Newsletter. 1988. "Juvenile Justice." *Criminal Justice Newsletter* 19:1–8.

Crimmins, Susan, and Michael Foley. 1990. "The Diagnosis Is Violence." Unpublished paper presented at the annual meeting of the Academy of Criminal Justice Sciences. Denver, CO (March).

Culliver, Concetta C., and Robert T. Sigler. 1990. "Characteristics of Inmates Sentenced to LWOP under Habitual Offender Statutes." Unpublished paper presented at the annual meetings of the American Society of Criminology. Baltimore, MD (November).

Dale, Michael J. 1988. "Detaining Juveniles in Adult Jails and Lockups: An Analysis of Rights and Liabilities." *American Jails* 2:46–50.

Danto, Bruce. 1985. *Identification and Control of Dangerous and Mentally Disordered Offenders.* Laguna Hills, CA: Eagle Books.

Davis, James. 1990. "New Issues in the Concept of Dangerousness." Unpublished paper presented at the annual meeting of the Academy of Criminal Justice Sciences. Denver, CO (March).

Davis, Rendell A., and Janet A. Leban (eds.). 1985. "The Role of Litigation in Changing Prison Conditions." *Prison Journal* 65:3–118.

Davis, Su Perk. 1989. "Survey." *Corrections Compendium* 14:9.

Davis, Su Perk. 1990. "Good Time." *Corrections Compendium* 15:1, 4–11.

Davis, Su Perk. 1991. "Survey." *Corrections Compendium* 16:10–21.

Decker, Scott H., and Barbara Salert. 1986. "Predicting the Career Criminal: An Empirical Test of the Greenwood Scale." *Journal of Criminal Law and Criminology* 77:215–236.

Delaware Bureau of Prisons. 1992. *Delaware Bureau of Prisons Procedures Manual.* Smyrna, DE: State of Delaware Department of Corrections, Bureau of Adult Correction.

Delaware Executive Department. 1984. *Recidivism in Delaware: A Study of Rearrest after Release from Incarceration.* Dover, DE: Delaware Executive Department Statistical Analysis Center.

del Carmen, Rolando V. 1986. *Potential Liabilities of Probation and Parole Officers.* Cincinnati, OH: Anderson.

Dembo, Richard et al. 1990. *Urine Testing of Detained Juveniles to Identify High-Risk Youth.* Washington, DC: U.S. National Institute of Justice.

DiChiara, Albert, and John F. Galliher. 1984. "Thirty Years of Deterrence Research: Characteristics, Causes, and Consequences." *Contemporary Crises* 8:243–263.

Dietz, Park Elliott. 1985. "Hypothetical Criteria for the Prediction of Individual Criminality." In *Dangerousness: Probability and Prediction, Psychiatry, and Public Policy,* Christopher D. Webster, Mark H. Ben-Aron, and Stephen J. Hucker (eds.). Cambridge, UK: Cambridge University Press.

DiIulio, John J., Jr. 1987. *Governing Prisons: A Comparative Study of Correctional Management.* New York: Free Press.

Di Vito, Robert J. 1991. "Survey of Mandatory Education Policies in State Penal Institutions." *Journal of Correctional Education* 42:126–132.

Donnelly, Patrick G., and Brian Forschner. 1984. "Client Success or Failure in a Halfway House." *Federal Probation* 48:38–44.

Dowell, David, Cecelia Klein, and Cheryl Krichmar. 1985. "Evaluation of a Halfway House for Women." *Journal of Criminal Justice* 13:217–226.

Drass, Kriss A., and J. William Spencer. 1987. "Accounting for Pre-Sentencing Recommendations: Typologies and Probation Officers' Theory of Office." *Social Problems* 34:277–293.

Dutton Donald. 1985. "A Systems Approach to the Prediction of Wife Assault: Relevance to Criminal Justice System Policy." In *Dangerousness: Probability and Prediction, Psychiatry, and Public Policy,* Christopher D. Webster, Mark H. Ben-Aron, and Stephen J. Hucker (eds.). Cambridge, UK: Cambridge University Press.

Eisenberg, Michael. 1985a. *Release Outcome Study: Early Mandatory Release.* Austin, TX: Texas Board of Pardons and Paroles.

Eisenberg, Michael. 1985b. *Factors Associated with Recidivism.* Austin, TX: Texas Board of Pardons and Paroles.

Eisenberg, Michael. 1986. *Case Classification: Two-Year Outcome Study.* Austin, TX: Texas Board of Pardons and Paroles.

Eisenberg, Michael. 1990. *Special Release and Supervision Programs: Two-Year Outcome Study: Halfway House/PPT Placements.* Austin, TX: Texas Department of Criminal Justice.

Epps, P., and R. W. Parnell. 1952. "Physique and Temperament of Women Delinquents Compared with Women Undergraduates." *British Journal of Medical Psychology* 25:249–255.

Erez, Edna. 1992. "Dangerous Men, Evil Women: Gender and Parole Decision-Making." *Justice Quarterly* 9:105–126.

Fagan, Jeffrey, and Martin Guggenheim. 1990. "Preventive Detention and the Prediction of Dangerousness for Juveniles." Unpublished paper presented at the annual meeting of the American Society of Criminology. Baltimore, MD (November).

Farmer, J. Forbes. 1988. "A Case Study in Regaining Control of a Violent State Prison." *Federal Probation* 52:41–47.

Farrell, Ronald A. 1990. "The Normal Primitive Revisited: Reconstructing an Institutionalized Stereotype of Violent Criminality." Unpublished paper presented at the annual meeting of the American Society of Criminology. Baltimore, MD (November).

Farrington, David P. 1987. "Predicting Individual Crime Rates." In *Prediction and Classification: Criminal Justice Decision Making,* Don M. Gottfredson and Michael Tonry (eds.). Chicago: University of Chicago Press.

Farrington, David P., and Roger Tarling. 1983. *Criminological Prediction.* London, UK: Home Office Research and Planning Unit.

Farrington, David P., and Roger Tarling. 1985. "Criminological Prediction: An Introduction." In *Prediction in Criminology,* David P. Farrington and Roger Tarling (eds.). Albany, NY: State University of New York Press.

Feazell, David M., Herbert C. Quay, and Edward J. Murray. 1991. "The Validity and Utility of Lanyon's Psychological Screening Inventory in a Youth Services Agency Sample." *Criminal Justice and Behavior* 18:166–179.

Federal Bureau of Prisons. 1992. *Program Statement: Security Designation and Custody Classification Manual.* Washington, DC: U.S. Department of Justice, Federal Bureau of Prisons.

Feeney, Floyd. 1987. "Defense Counsel for Delinquents: Does Quality Matter?" Unpublished paper presented at the American Society of Criminology meetings, Montreal. (November).

Feld, Barry C. 1988. "The Juvenile Court Meets the Principle of Offense: Punishment, Treatment, and the Difference It Makes." *Boston University Law Review* 68:393–424.

Feld, Barry C. 1989. "The Right to Counsel in Juvenile Court: An Empirical Study of When Lawyers Appear and the Differences They Make." Unpublished paper presented at the American Society of Criminology meetings, Chicago, IL (November).

Fillmore, Ann, and Coralie Jewell. 1987. "The Sex Offender Treatment Program: An Evaluative Overview." In *Sex, Gender and Care Work,* Gordon Horobin (ed.). Aberdeen, UK: Department of Social Work, University of Aberdeen.

Fink, Ann. 1992. "Inmate Subcultures: Typological Synthesis." Unpublished paper presented at the annual meeting of the American Society of Criminology. New Orleans, LA (November).

Flanagan, Timothy J., and Katherine M. Jamieson. 1991. *Sourcebook of Criminal Justice Statistics, 1990.* Albany, NY: Hindelang Criminal Justice Research Center.

Flint, Gail A. 1987. "Inmates Diagnosed as Antisocial: Demographic Correlates and Clinical Criteria." Unpublished paper presented at the annual meeting of the American Society of Criminology. Montreal. (November).

Florida Department of Corrections. 1986. *Implementation Manual for Community Control: A New Concept.* Tallahassee, FL: Florida Department of Corrections, Probation and Parole Services Program Office.

Floud, Jean, and Warren Young. 1981. *Dangerouness and Criminal Justice.* London, UK: Heinemann Educational Books.

Fogel, David, and Joe Hudson (eds.). 1981. *Justice as Fairness: Perspectives on the Justice Model.* Cincinnati, OH: Anderson Publishing Company.

Forst, Brian. 1983. "Selective Incapacitation: An Idea Whose Time Has Come?" *Federal Probation* 47:19–23.

Forst, Brian. 1984. "Selective Incapacitation: A Sheep in Wolf's Clothing." *Judicature* 68:153–160.

Frishtik, Mordechai. 1988. "The Probation Officer's Recommendation in His 'Investigative Report.' " *Journal of Offender Counseling, Services & Rehabilitation* 13:101–132.

Gabor, Thomas. 1986. *The Prediction of Criminal Behavior: Statistical Approaches.* Toronto: University of Toronto Press.

Gardner, Martin R. 1985. *"Hudson v. Palmer:* 'Bright Lines' But Dark Directions for Prisoner Privacy Rights." *Journal of Criminal Law and Criminology* 76:75–115.

Garner, Joel H. 1991. "The Feasibility of Predictive Classification for Inmates Held Pretrial in Federal BOP Facilities." Unpublished paper presented at the annual meeting of the American Society of Criminology meetings. Baltimore, MD (November).

Gendreau, Paul, and Robert R. Ross. 1987. "Revivification of Rehabilitation: Evidence from the 1980s." *Justice Quarterly* 4:349–408.

Gitchoff, G. Thomas, and George E. Rush. 1989. The Criminological Case Evaluation and Sentencing Recommendation: An Idea Whose Time Has Come." *International Journal of Offender Therapy and Comparative Criminology* 33:77–83.

Glaser, Daniel. 1987. "Classification for Risk." In *Prediction and Classification. Criminal Justice Decision Making,* Don M. Gottfredson and Michael Tonry (eds.). Chicago: University of Chicago Press.

Goetting, Ann, and R. M. Howsen. 1986. "Correlates of Prisoner Misconduct." *Journal of Quantitative Criminology* 2:49–67.

Goldkamp, John S. 1987. "Prediction in Criminal Justice Policy Development." In *Prediction and Classification: Criminal Justice Decision Making,* Don M. Gottfredson and Michael Tonry (eds.). Chicago: University of Chicago Press.

Gordon, Arthur, and Frank J. Porporino. 1991. "Canada Targets Sex Offenders According to Treatment Needs." *Corrections Today* 53:162–168.

Gottfredson, Don M. 1984. "Selective Incapacitation." *Corrections Today* 46:82–84.

Gottfredson, Don M. 1987. "Prediction and Classification in Criminal Justice Decision Making." In *Prediction and Classification: Criminal Justice Decision Making,* Don M. Gottfredson and Michael Tonry (eds.). Chicago: University of Chicago Press.

Gottfredson, Don M., P. B. Hoffman, M. Sigler, and L. Wilkins. 1973. "Making Parole Policy Explicit." *Crime and Delinquency* 52:52–58.

Gottfredson, Don M., and Michael Tonry (eds.). 1987. *Prediction and Classification: Criminal Justice Decision Making.* Chicago: University of Chicago Press.

Gottfredson, Don M., Leslie T. Wilkins, and Peter B. Hoffman. 1978. *Guidelines for Parole and Sentencing.* Lexington, MA: D. C. Heath.

Gottfredson, Michael R., and Don M. Gottfredson. 1988. *Decision Making in Criminal Justice: Toward the Rational Exercise of Discretion.* 2nd ed. New York: Plenum Press.

Gottfredson, Stephen D. 1986. "Statistical and Actuarial Considerations." In *The Prediction of Criminal Violence,* Fernand Dutile and Cleon Foust (eds.). Springfield, IL: Charles C Thomas.

Gottfredson, Stephen D. 1987. "Prediction: An Overview of Selected Methodological Issues." In *Prediction and Classification: Criminal Justice Decision Making,* Don M. Gottfredson and Michael Tonry (eds.). Chicago: University of Chicago Press.

Gottfredson, Stephen D., and Don M. Gottfredson. 1982. "Risk Assessment: An Evaluation of Statistical Classification Methods." In *Classification as a Management Tool.* College Park, MD: American Correctional Association.

Gottfredson, Stephen D., and Don M. Gottfredson. 1985. "Screening for Risk Among Parolees: Policy, Practice, and Method." In *Prediction in Criminology,* David P. Farrington and Roger Tarling (eds.). Albany, NY: State University of New York Press.

Gottfredson, Stephen D., and Don M. Gottfredson. 1990. *Classification, Prediction, and Criminal Justice Policy: Final Report to the National Institute of Justice.* Washington, DC: U.S. National Institute of Justice.

Gottlieb, Barbara. 1984. *The Pretrial Processing of "Dangerous" Defendants: A Comparative Analysis of State Laws.* Washington, DC: Toborg Associates, prepared for the U.S. National Institute of Justice.

Gottlieb, Barbara, and Phillip Rosen. 1984. *Public Danger as a Factor in Pretrial Release: Summaries of State Danger Laws.* Washington, DC: Toborg Associates.

Greenfeld, Lawrence A. 1985. *Examining Recidivism.* Washington, DC: U.S. Department of Justice, Bureau of Justice Statistics.

Greenfeld, Lawrence A. 1988. *Prisoners in 1987.* Washington, DC: U.S. Department of Justice.

Greenwood, Peter, and A. Abrahamse. 1982. *Selective Incapacitation.* Santa Monica, CA: Rand Corporation.

Haapanen, Rudy A. 1988. *Selective Incapacitation and the Serious Offender: A Longitudinal Study of Criminal Career Patterns.* Sacramento, CA: California Department of the Youth Authority.

Haas, Kenneth C., and Geoffrey P. Alpert. 1986. *The Dilemmas of Punishment: Readings in Contemporary Corrections.* Prospect Heights, IL: Waveland Press.

Hall, Andy. 1987. *Systemwide Strategies to Alleviate Jail Overcrowding.* Washington, DC: National Institute of Justice.

Hall, Julia. 1992. "Parole Agents: Casemakers for Elderly Clients: A New Role." Unpublished paper presented at the annual meeting of the American Society of Criminology. New Orleans, LA (November).

Hanson, Richard W. et al. 1983. "Predicting Inmate Penitentiary Adjustment: An Assessment of Four Classificatory Methods." *Criminal Justice and Behavior* 10:293–309.

Harding, T. W., and H. Adserballe. 1983. "Assessments of Dangerousness: Observations in Six Countries. A Summary of Results from a WHO Coordinated Study." *International Journal of Law and Psychiatry* 6:391–398.

Hart, Cynthia Baroody. 1990. "The Social Readjustment Rating Scale Adapted for an Institutionalized Population." Unpublished paper presented at the annual meeting of the American Society of Criminology. Baltimore, MD (November).

Hatalyn, Thomas V., and E. A. Wenk. 1974. "An Analysis of Classification for Young Adult Offenders." *NCCD Research,* Vol. 6. San Francisco: National Council on Crime and Delinquency.

Henman, Gary. 1988. "Inside Marion: Warden Gary Henman Talks about BOP's Most Secure Prison." *Corrections Today* 50:92–101, 155.

Herman, Susan N. 1984. "Institutional Litigation in the Post-Chapman World." *New York University Review of Law and Social Change* 12:299–321.

Herrick, Emily. 1989. "Survey." *Corrections Compendium* 14:9.

Herzberger, Sharon D., and Noreen L. Channels. 1990. "The Predictors and Consequences of Bail Decision-Making." Unpublished paper presented at the annual meeting of the American Society of Criminology. Baltimore, MD (November).

Hewitt, John D., Eric D. Poole, and Robert M. Regoli. 1984. "Self-Reported and Observed Rule-Breaking in Prison: A Look at Disciplinary Response." *Justice Quarterly* 1:437–447.

Hiday, Virginia Aldige. 1990. "Dangerousness of Civil Commitment Candidates: A Six-Month Follow-up." *Law and Human Behavior* 14:551–567.

Hill, Gillian. 1985. "Predicting Recidivism using Institutional Measures." In *Prediction in Criminology,* David P. Farrington and Roger Tarling (eds.). Albany, NY: State University of New York Press.

Hoffman, Peter B. 1983. "Screening for Risk: A Revised Salient Factor Score (SFS 81)." *Journal of Criminal Justice* 11:539–547.

Hoffman, Peter B., and Sheldon Adelberg. 1980. "The Salient Factor Score: A Nontechnical Overview." *Federal Probation* 44:44–52.

Hoge, Steven K. et al. 1989. "Dangerousness and the Civil Commitment Process." *American Journal of Psychiatry* 146:170–193.

Holman, John E., and James F. Quinn. 1992. "Dysphoria and Electronically Monitored Home Confinement." *Deviant Behavior* 13:21–32.

Holt, Norman, Gary Ducat, and H. Gene Eakles. 1981. "California's New Inmate Classification System." *Corrections Today* 42:24–30.

Howard, John B., Jr. 1989. "The Trial of Pretrial Dangerousness: Preventive Detention after *United States v. Salerno.*" *Virginia Law Review* 75:639–679.

Hughes, Graham. 1985. "Legal Aspects of Predicting Dangerousness." In *Critical Issues in American Psychiatry and the Law,* Richard Rosner (ed.). New York: Plenum.

Hunzeker, Donna, and Cindy Conger (eds.). 1985. *Inmate Lawsuits: A Report on Inmate Lawsuits against State and Federal Correctional Systems Resulting in Monetary Damages and Settlements.* Lincoln, NE: Contact Center, Inc.

Hurwitz, Jeffrey N. 1987. "House Arrest: A Critical Analysis of an Intermediate-Level Penal Sanction." *University of Pennsylvania Law Review* 135:711–811.

Huskey, Bobbie L. 1990. "In Illinois: Law Forces Change in Juvenile Lockups." *Corrections Today* 52:122–123.

Illinois Department of Corrections. 1988. *Female Classification, Report 5, Assessment Instrument.* Springfield, IL: Illinois Department of Corrections.

Iowa Department of Correctional Services. 1992. *Iowa Classification System: Assessment & Reassessment of Client Risk Instructions & Scoring Guide.* Davenport, IA: Iowa Department of Correctional Services.

Iowa Office for Criminal Justice and Juvenile Justice Planning. 1983. *Impact of Objective Parole Criteria on Parole Release.* Des Moines, IA: Iowa Office for Criminal Justice and Juvenile Justice Planning.

Iowa Statistical Analysis Center. 1985. *Prison Population, Parole, and Offender Risk Assessment in Iowa: An Overview.* Des Moines, IA: Office for Planning and Programming.

Israel, Michael. 1983. "Jack Henry Abbott, American Prison Writing, and the Experience of Punishment." *Criminal Justice and Behavior* 10:441–460.

Jackson, Margaret A. 1989. "The Clinical Assessment and Prediction of Violent Behavior: Toward a Scientific Analysis." *Criminal Justice and Behavior* 16:114–131.

Jacobs, James B. 1980. "The Prisoners' Rights Movement and Its Impact: 1960–1980." In *Crime and Justice, Vol. 2,* Norval Morris and Michael Tonry (eds.). Chicago: University of Chicago Press.

Jamieson, Katherine M., and Timothy J. Flanagan. 1989. *Sourcebook of Criminal Justice Statistics.* Albany, NY: The Hindelang Criminal Justice Research Center.

Jankowski, Louis. 1991. *Probation and Parole 1990.* Washington, DC: U.S. Department of Justice, Bureau of Justice Statistics.

Jefferson, Terry W., and James H. Johnson. 1991. "The Relationship of Hyperactivity and Sensation Seeking to Delinquency Subtypes." *Criminal Justice and Behavior* 18:195–201.

Jemelka, Ron, Elizabeth Von Cleve, and Eric Trupin. 1987. "Validation of a Computerized Screening Battery for Predicting Institutional Adjustment of Adult Offenders." Unpublished paper presented at the annual meeting of the American Society of Criminology. Montreal. (November).

Jengeleski, James L., LeeAnn S. Labecki, and Andrew D. Kayser. 1992. "Community Placement Instrument Validation: An Effort to Balance Behavioral Predictability with Public Safety and Sensitivity." Unpublished paper presented at the annual meeting of the American Society of Criminology. New Orleans, LA (November).

Jenson, Jeff. 1984. *The Impact of Proposed Standards for Montana County Jails.* Helena, MT: Montana Board of Crime Control.

Jesness, Carl F., M. Bohnstedt, and M. Molof. 1973. *Sequential I-Level Classification.* Sacramento, CA: American Justice Institute.

Johnson, Dennis L., James G. Simmons, and B. Carl Gordon. 1983. "Temporal Consistency of the Meyer-Megargee Inmate Typology." *Criminal Justice and Behavior* 10:263–268.

Johnson, Jan. 1987. *The Context for Crisis: Background Report for the Kansas Corrections System.* Topeka, KS: Division of the Budget, Kansas Department of Administration.

Jones, Michael. 1982. *A Report on the Virginia Work Release Program.* Roanoke, VA: Research and Reporting Unit, Division of Program Development and Evaluation, Virginia Department of Corrections.

Joyce, Nola M. 1985. "Classification Research: Facing the Challenge." *Corrections Today* 47:78–86.

Kalichman, Seth C. 1988. "Empirically Derived MMPI Profile Subgroups of Incarcerated Homicide Offenders." *Journal of Clinical Psychology* 44:733–738.

Kalinich, David B., and John Klofas (eds.). 1986. *Sneaking Inmates Down the Alley: Problems and Prospects in Jail Management.* Springfield, IL: Charles C Thomas.

Kane, Thomas R. 1987. "Inmates' Perceptions of Justice in Prison Disciplinary Sanctions." Unpublished paper presented at the American Society of Criminology meetings, Montreal. (November).

Klein, Stephen P., and Michael N. Caggiano. 1986. *The Prevalence, Predictability, and Policy Implications of Recidivism.* Santa Monica, CA: The Rand Corporation.

Knepper, Paul. 1989. "Selective Participation, Effectiveness, and Prison College Programs." *Journal of Offender Counseling, Services, & Rehabilitation* 14:109–135.

Knight, Barbara B., and Stephen T. Early, Jr. 1986. *Prisoners' Rights in America.* Chicago: Nelson-Hall.

Kochis, Donna. 1992. "Utilization of the Experimental Design in a Correctional Setting: A Study of the Partial Hospitalization Program at Saint Gabriel's Hall." Unpublished paper presented at the annual meeting of the American Society of Criminology. New Orleans, LA (November).

Komala, Merly, and Val Shepperd. 1990. "The Development of Texas Felony Offender Risk Assessment." Unpublished paper presented at the annual meeting of the American Society of Criminology. Baltimore, MD (November).

Kosinski, R. Douglas, Randy J. Knapp, and June Daman. 1989. *Validation of the Michigan Security Classification System.* Lansing, MI: Special Studies Unit, Research Division, Program Bureau, Michigan Department of Corrections.

Krisberg, Barry. 1988. *The Juvenile Court: Reclaiming the Vision.* San Francisco, CA: National Council on Crime and Delinquency.

Krisberg, Barry et al. 1986. *The Incarceration of Minority Youth.* Minneapolis: Hubert H. Humphrey Institute of Public Affairs, University of Minnesota.

Kuplinski, John R. 1990. *Electronic Offender Monitoring in Virginia: Evaluation Report.* Richmond, VA: Virginia Department of Criminal Justice Services.

Langan, Patrick A., and Mark A. Cunniff. 1992. *Recidivism of Felons on Probation, 1986–1989.* Washington, DC: U.S. Department of Justice, Bureau of Justice Statistics.

Latessa Edward J.. 1986. "The Cost Effectiveness of Probation." *Federal Probation* 50:70–74.

Latessa, Edward J., and Harry E. Allen. 1982. "Halfway Houses and Parole: A National Assessment." *Journal of Criminal Justice* 10:153–163.

Lawson, Robert H. 1984. *Join Federal State Administration of Prisons: An Exploration of Options.* Washington, DC: Office of Legal Policy, Federal Justice Research Program, U.S. Department of Justice.

LeClair, Daniel P. 1985. *The Effect of Community Reintegration on Rates of Recidivism: A Statistical Overview of Data for the Years 1971–1982.* Boston: Massachusetts Department of Corrections.

LeClair, Daniel P., and Susan Guarino-Ghezzi. 1991. "Does Incapacitation Guarantee Public Safety? Lessons from the Massachusetts Furlough and Prerelease Programs." *Justice Quarterly* 8:9–36.

Leeke, William D., and Heidi Mohn. 1986. "Violent Offenders: AIMS and Unit Management Maintain Control." *Corrections Today* 48:22–24.

Leger, Robert G., and Harvey Gray Barnes. 1986. "Black Attitudes in Prison: A Sociological Analysis." *Journal of Criminal Justice* 14:105–122.

Levine, James P., Michael C. Musheno, and Dennis J. Palumbo. 1986. *Criminal Justice in America: Law in Action.* New York: Wiley.

Levinson, Robert B. 1984. "Developments in the Classification Process: Quay's AIMS Approach." *Criminal Justice and Behavior* 15:24–38.

Levinson, Robert B., and R. E. Gerard. 1973. "Functional Units: A Different Correctional Approach." *Federal Probation* 37:14–18.

Loeber, Rolf, David P. Farrington, and Welmoet B. Van Kammen. 1987. "Developmental Factors in High-Rate Offending." Unpublished paper presented at the annual meeting of the American Society of Criminology. Montreal. (November).

Lombardi, John H. 1981. "Florida's Objective Parole Guidelines: Analysis of the First Year's Implementation." Ph.D. Dissertation, Florida State University, Tallahassee, FL.

Lombardi, John H., and Donna M. Lombardi. 1986. "Objective Parole Criteria: More Harm than Good?" *Corrections Today* 48:86–87.

Lombroso, Cesare. 1911. *Crime: Its Causes and Remedies.* Boston: Little, Brown (originally published in 1876).

Louscher, P. Kent, Ray E. Hosford, and C. Scott Moss. 1983. "Predicting Dangerous Behavior in a Penitentiary Using the Megargee Typology." *Criminal Justice and Behavior* 10:269–284.

Lovegrove, Austin. 1989. *Judicial Decision Making, Sentencing Policy, and Numerical Guidance.* New York & Berlin: Springer-Verlag. [Research in Criminology Series]

Lowrence, William. 1976. *Of Acceptable Risk: Science and the Determination of Safety.* Los Altos, CA: William Kaufman.

MacDonald, Donald, and Gerald Bala. 1983. *Follow-up Study Sample of Rochester Work Release Participants.* Albany, NY: Division of Program Planning, Research, and Evaluation, New York Department of Correctional Services.

MacKenzie, Doris Layton. 1987. "Prison Classification in a Rapidly Changing System." Unpublished paper presented at the annual meeting of the American Society of Criminology. Montreal. (November).

Maier, Gary J., and Robert D. Miller. 1987. "Models of Mental Health Service Delivery to Corrections Institutions." *Journal of Forensic Sciences* 32:225–232.

Maier, George (ed.). 1989. *Risk Prediction and Probation: Papers from a Research and Planning Unit Workshop.* London, UK: U.K. Home Office.

Maltz, Michael D. 1984. *Recidivism.* Orlando, FL: Academic Press.

Mande, M., and H. C. Covey. 1982. "Perceived Criteria Used by Criminal Justice and Mental Health Professionals to Predict Dangerous Behavior of Mentally Ill Persons." *Justice Quarterly* 1:343–356.

Marlette, Marjorie. 1990. "Furloughs Tightened—Success Rates High." *Corrections Compendium* 15:1, 6–8.

Marley, C. W. 1973. "Furlough Programs and Conjugal Visiting in Adult Correctional Institutions." *Federal Probation* 37:19–25.

Martin, Susan E. 1983. "Commutation of Prison Sentences." *Crime and Delinquency* 29:593–612.

Mason, John H. 1992. "Inmate Classification in a Southern Correctional System." Unpublished paper presented at the annual meeting of the American Society of Criminology. New Orleans, LA (November).

Massachusetts House of Representatives. 1988. *Department of Correction: Furlough Program.* Boston, MA: Massachusetts House of Representatives, Committee on Post Audit and Oversight.

Mays, G. Larry, and Joel Thompson (eds.). 1991. *American Jails: Public Policy Issues.* Chicago, IL: Waveland Press.

McCarthy, Belinda R. 1987. *Intermediate Punishments: Intensive Probation, Home Confinement, and Electronic Surveillance.* Monsey, NY: Willow Tree Press.

McCarthy, Belinda R., and Bernard J. McCarthy. 1984. *Community-Based Corrections.* Monterey, CA: Brooks/Cole Publishing Company.

McDonald, Douglas et al. 1990. *Study to Evaluate Patuxent Institution—Volume I (Executive Summary).* Cambridge, MA: Abt Associates; prepared for the Maryland Department of Public Safety and Correctional Services.

McGee, Richard A., George Warner, and Nora Harlow. 1985. *The Special Management Inmate.* Washington, DC: U.S. National Institute of Justice.

McGrath, Robert J. 1991. "Sex-Offender Risk Assessment and Disposition Planning: A Review of Empirical and Clinical Findings." *International Journal of Offender Therapy and Comparative Criminology* 35:328–350.

McGriff, M. David. 1985. *A Test of Incapacitation Theory on Burglars.* Ann Arbor, MI: University Microfilms International.

McMurray, Harvey L., and George P. Wilson. 1991. "A Cooperative Venture in Alleviating Jail Overcrowding in Durham, North Carolina." *American Jails* 5:36–37.

Megargee, Edwin I., and Martin J. Bohn. 1979. *Classifying Criminal Offenders: A New System Based on the MMPI.* Beverly Hills, CA: Sage Publishing Company.

Megargee, Edwin I., and Joyce Carbonell. 1985. "Predicting Prison Adjustment with MMPI Correctional Scales." *Journal of Consulting and Clinical Psychology* 53:874–883.

Megargee, E. I., J. L. Carbonell, and M. J. Bohn, Jr. 1988. *Cross-Validation and Test of the Generality of the MMPI-Based Offender Clasification System.* Washington, DC: U.S. National Institute of Justice.

Menzies, Robert, Christopher D. Webster, and Diana Sepejak. 1985. "Hitting the Forensic Sound Barrier: Predictions of Dangerousness in a Pre-Trial Psychiatry Clinic." In *Dangerousness: Probability and Prediction, Psychiatry, and Public Policy,* Christopher D. Webster, Mark H. Ben-Aron and Stephen J. Hucker (eds.). Cambridge, UK: Cambridge University Press.

Metckik, Eric. 1992. "Legal Views of Parole Decision Making: A Social Science Perspective." Unpublished paper presented at the annual meeting of the American Society of Criminology. New Orleans, LA (November).

Metzner, Jeffrey L. 1992. "A Survey of University-Prison Collaboration and Computerized Tracking Systems in Prisons." *Hospital & Community Psychiatry* 43:713–715.

Michaels, David et al. 1992. "Homelessness and Indicators of Mental Illness among Inmates in New York City's Correctional System." *Hospital & Community Psychiatry* 43:150–154.

Michigan Department of Management and Budget. 1986. *Developing a Model for Predicting Probation Outcome.* Lansing, MI: Michigan Department of Corrections, Department of Management and Budget, Office of Management and Information Systems.

Miller, Debra T. 1984. *Profile of Inmates in the Texas Department of Corrections 60 Years of Age and Older as of May 31, 1984.* Huntsville, TX: Texas Department of Corrections.

Miller, Frank W. et al. 1985. *The Juvenile Justice Process.* Mineola, NY: Foundation Press.

Miller, Marc, and Norval Morris. 1986. "Predictions of Dangerousness: Ethical Concerns and Proposed Limits." *Notre Dame Journal of Law, Ethics, & Social Policy* 2:2.

Minor, Kevin I., Sharon K. Karr, and Swaran K. Jain. 1987. "An Examination of the Utility of the MMPI in Predicting Male Prison Inmates' Abusive Parenting Attitudes." *Psychological Record* 37:429–436.

Miranne, Alfred C., and Michael R. Geerken. 1991. "The New Orleans Inmate Survey: A Test of Greenwood's Predictive Scale." *Criminology* 29:497–518.

Monahan, John. 1981. *The Clinical Prediction of Violent Behavior.* Rockville, MD: U.S. Department of Health and Human Services.

Monahan, John. 1984. "The Prediction of Violent Behavior: Toward a Second Generation of Theory and Public Policy." *American Journal of Psychiatry* 141:10–15.

Moore, Mark H., Susan Estrich, and Daniel McGillis (with William Spelman). 1984. *Dangerous Offenders.* Cambridge, MA: Harvard University Press.

Moriarty, Laura J. 1987. "Ethical Issues of Selective Incapacitation." *Criminal Justice Research Bulletin* 3:1–4.

Morris, Norval. 1984. "On Dangerousness in the Judicial Process." *The Record of the Association of the Bar of the City of New York* 39:102–128.

Morris, Norval, and Marc Miller. 1985. "Predictions of Dangerousness." In *Crime and Justice: An Annual Review of Research, Vol. 6,* Michael Tonry and Norval Morris (eds.). Chicago: University of Chicago Press.

Morris, Norval, and Marc Miller. 1987. *Predictions of Dangerousness in the Criminal Law.* Washington, DC: National Institute of Justice.

Motiuk, Michelė S., Laurence L. Motiuk, and James Bonta. 1992. "A Comparison between Self-Report and Interview-Based Inventories in Offender Classification." *Criminal Justice and Behavior* 19:143–159.

Murphy, Terrence H. 1980. *Final Report (#AP-O) Michigan Risk Prediction: A Replication Study.* Lansing, MI: Program Bureau, Michigan Department of Corrections.

Nacci, Peter, and Thomas R. Kane. 1983. "Incidence of Sex and Sexual Aggression in Federal Prisons." *Federal Probation* 47:31–36.

Napolitano, Susan, and Lillian G. Brown. 1991. "Strategic Approach to Group Anger Management with Incarcerated Murderers." *Journal of Offender Rehabilitation* 16:93–101.

National Alliance of Business. 1983. *Employment Training of Ex-Offenders: A Community Program Approach.* Washington, DC: National Alliance of Business.

National Conference of State Legislatures. 1988. *Legal Dispositions and Confinement Policies for Delinquent Youth.* Denver, CO: National Conference of State Legislatures.

National Council on Crime and Delinquency. 1990a. *Development of Risk Prediction Scales for the California Youthful Offender Parole Board Based on Assessment of 1981–1982 Releases.* San Francisco: National Council on Crime and Delinquency.

National Council on Crime and Delinquency. 1990b. *Tennessee Board of Paroles Risk Assessment Report.* San Francisco, CA: National Council on Crime and Delinquency.

National Institute of Corrections. 1981. *The Model Probation and Parole Management Program.* Washington, DC: National Institute of Corrections.

Nelson. Paul L. 1985. "Marketable Skills." *Corrections Today* 47:70.

New Jersey Juvenile Delinquency Commission. 1991. *The Chronic Juvenile Offender: A Challenge to New Jersey's Juvenile Justice System.* Trenton, NJ: New Jersey Juvenile Delinquency Commission.

New York Department of Corrections. 1988. *Initial Security Classification Guideline for Young Males.* Albany, NY: New York Department of Corrections.

New York State Unified Court System. 1985. *The Community Dispute Resolution Centers Program: A Progress Report: January 1, 1984 to March 31, 1985.* Albany, NY: New York State Unified Court System.

Norman, Michael D. 1986. "Discretionary Justice: Decision-making in a State Juvenile Parole Board." *Juvenile and Family Court Journal* 37:19–25.

Oberst, Margaret. 1988. *Inmate Literacy Programs: Virginia's 'No Read, No Release' Program.* Lexington, KY: Council of State Governments.

Ohio Department of Rehabilitation and Correction. 1989. *The Ohio Parole Board.* Columbus, OH: Ohio Department of Rehabilitation and Correction.

Ohio Parole Board. 1992. *The Parole Board Guidelines.* Columbus, OH: Ohio Parole Board.

O'Leary, Vincent, and J. Hall. 1976. *Frames of Reference in Parole.* Hackensack, NJ:

National Council on Crime and Delinquency Training Center, National Parole Institute Training Document.

O'Leary, Vincent, and K. J. Hanrahan. 1976. *Parole Systems in the United States.* Hackensack, NJ: National Council on Crime and Delinquency.

Oregon Crime Analysis Center. 1984. *Recidivism of Releasees from Oregon Corrections Institutions.* Salem, OR: Oregon Crime Analysis Center.

Orrick, David. 1989. "New Construction as a Solution to Jail Overcrowding: Some Policy and Funding Considerations." *American Journal of Criminal Justice* 14:71–86.

Palmer, John W. 1985. *Constitutional Rights of Prisoners.* Cincinnati, OH: Anderson.

Parsonage, William H. 1992. "The Impact of Victim Testimony on Parole Decision Making." Unpublished paper presented at the annual meeting of the American Society of Criminology. New Orleans, LA (November).

Paulus, Paul, Garvin McCain, and Verne Cox. 1985. "The Effects of Crowding in Prisons and Jails." In *Reaction to Crime: The Public, the Police, and Prisons,* David Farrington and J. Gunn (eds.). New York: Wiley.

Pennsylvania Department of Corrections. 1992. *Pennsylvania Additive Correction Tool.* Philadelphia, PA: Pennsylvania Department of Corrections.

Perras, Tom. 1987. "The Use of Prediction in Treatment." Unpublished paper presented at the annual meeting of the American Society of Criminology. Montreal. (November).

Petersilia, Joan M. 1985a. *Probation and Felony Offenders.* Washington, DC: U.S. Department of Justice, Bureau of Justice Statistics.

Petersilia, Joan M. 1985b. "Rand's Research: A Closer Look." *Corrections Today* 47:37–40.

Petersilia, Joan M. 1987. *Expanding Options for Criminal Sentencing.* Santa Monica, CA: Rand.

Petersilia, Joan, and Susan Turner. 1987. "Guideline-Based Justice: Prediction and Racial Minorities." In *Prediction and Classification: Criminal Justice Decision Making,* Don M. Gottfredson and Michael Tonry (eds.). Chicago: University of Chicago Press.

Petersilia, Joan M., Susan Turner, James Kahan, and Joyce Peterson. 1985. *Granting Felons Probation: Public Risks and Alternatives.* Santa Monica, CA: The Rand Corporation.

Petersilia, Joan M., Susan Turner, and Joyce Peterson. 1986. *Prison v. Probation in California: Implications for Crime and Offender Recidivism.* Santa Monica, CA: Rand.

Posey, C. Dale (ed.). 1988. "Special Issue: Correctional Classification Based upon Psychological Characteristics." *Criminal Justice and Behavior* 15:3–136.

Powers, Kevin. 1992. *Intensive Supervision in the Northern District of Ohio.* Washington, DC: U.S. Parole Commission.

Prentky, Robert. 1990. "Development of a Risk Assessment Scale for Child Molesters." Unpublished paper presented at the annual meeting of the Academy of Criminal Justice Sciences. Denver, CO (March).

Prentky, Robert, Austin Lee, Raymond Knight, and David Cerce. 1990. "Validating a Taxonomic Construct for Rapists Using Survival Analysis." Unpublished paper presented at the annual meeting of the Academy of Criminal Justice Sciences. Denver, CO (March).

Quay, Herbert C. 1984. *Managing Adult Inmates.* College Park, MD: American Correctional Association.

Quay, Herbert C., and L. B. Parsons. 1971. *The Differential Behavioral Classification of the Adult Male Offender.* Philadelphia, PA: Temple University [Technical report prepared for the U.S. Department of Justice Bureau of Prisons, Contract J–1C–22, 253].

Rans, Laurel L. 1984. "The Validity of Models to Predict Violence in Community and Prison Settings." *Corrections Today* 46:50–63.

Reboussin, Roland, Robert Hazelwood, and Janet Warren. 1990. "Prediction of Rapist Type and Violence in Serial Rape from Offender and Victim Statements." Unpublished paper presented at the annual meeting of the Academy of Criminal Justice Sciences. Denver, CO (March).

Richards, Ann W. 1992. "Do We Need More Prisons?" *State Government News* 35:12–13.

Robins, Arthur J. et al. 1986. "The Missouri Classification System Applied to Female Offenders: Reliability and Validity." *Corrective and Social Psychiatry and Journal of Behavior Technology Methods and Therapy* 32:21–30.

Rocheleau, Ann Marie. 1986. *Inmates in the Departmental Segregation Unit.* Boston: Massachusetts Department of Corrections.

Rogers, Joseph W., and G. Larry Mays. 1987. *Juvenile Delinquency and Juvenile Justice.* New York: Wiley.

Rogers, Richard, J. Roy Gillis, and Susan E. Dickens. 1989. "A Research Note on the MMPI Pd Scale and Sociopathy." *International Journal of Offender Therapy and Comparative Criminology* 33:21–25.

Rosecrance, John. 1986. "Probation Supervision: Mission Impossible," *Federal Probation* 50:25–34.

Rosecrance, John. 1988. "The Presentence Probation Report: No Longer Relevant?" Unpublished paper presented at the Academy of Criminal Justice Sciences meetings. San Francisco, CA (March).

Rossum, Ralph A., Benedict J. Koller, and Christopher Manfredi. 1987. *Juvenile Justice Reform: A Model for the States.* Claremont, CA: Rose Institute of State and Local Government and the American Legislative Council.

Roundtree, George A., Dan W. Edwards, and Jack B. Parker. 1984. "A Study of the Personal Characteristics of Probationers as Related to Recidivism." *Journal of Offender Counseling* 8:53–61.

Royse, David, and Steven A. Buck. 1991. "Evaluating a Diversion Program for First-Time Shoplifters." *Journal of Offender Rehabilitation* 17:147–158.

Schaar, Jill A. 1985. "Prisoners' Fourth Amendment Right to Privacy: Expanding a Constructed View." *Houston Law Review* 22:1065–1091.

Schafer, N. E. 1986. "Discretion, Due Process, and the Prison Discipline Committee." *Criminal Justice Review* 11:37–46.

Schumacker, Randall E., Dennis B. Anderson, and Sara L. Anderson. 1990. "Vocational and Academic Indicators of Parole Success." *Journal of Correctional Education* 41:8–13.

Sechrest, Dale K. 1989. "Population Density and Assaults in Jails for Men and Women." *American Journal of Criminal Justice* 14:87–103.

Sechrest, Lee. 1987. "Classification for Treatment." In *Prediction and Classification: Criminal Justice Decision Making,* Don M. Gottfredson and Michael Tonry (eds.). Chicago: University of Chicago Press.

Sepejak, Diana S., Christopher D. Webster, and R. J. Menzies. 1984. "The Clinical Prediction of Dangerousness: Getting Beyond the Basic Questions." In *Psychology and Law: Topics from an International Conference,* Dave J. Muller, Derek E. Blackman, and Antony J. Chapman (eds.). Chichester, UK: John Wiley and Sons.

Shaffer, C. Edward, David Bluoin, and Gary C. Pettigrew. 1985. "Assessment of Prison Escape Risk." *Journal of Police and Criminal Psychology* 1:42–48.

Shah, Saleena. 1981. "Dangerousness: Conceptual, Prediction, and Public Policy Issues." In *Violence and the Violent Individual,* J. Hays, T. Roberts, and K. Solway (eds.). New York: Medical and Scientific Books.

Shane-Dubow, Sandra, Alice P. Brown, and Eric Olsen. 1985. *Sentencing Reform in the United States: History, Content, and Effect.* Washington, DC: U.S. Department of Justice.

Siddiqi, Qudsia. 1991. "Alternative Models of Pretrial Failure to Appear: A Comparison in New York City." Unpublished paper presented at the annual meetings of the American Society of Criminology. Baltimore, MD (November).

Sigler, Robert T., and Leslie Johnson. 1989. "Judicial Influence in Changing Attitudes toward Use of Work Release." *International Journal of Comparative and Applied Criminal Justice* 13:109–122.

Singer, Richard G. 1980. "Desert Sentencing and Prison Overcrowding: Some Doubts and Tentative Answers." *New York University Review of Law and Social Change* 12:85–110.

Skelton, Paul. 1984. *Comprehensive Statewide Study to Determine the Current and Future Needs for All Types of Correctional Facilities in the State and Development of a Siting Criteria to Be Used in Evaluating Sites for Location of Correctional Facilities.* Tallahassee, FL: Florida Department of Corrections.

Slack, William R., and Frank A. Dixon. 1990. "Behavior Alert Classification Identification System." *American Jails* 3:45–47.

Smith, Robert R., and David A. Sabatino. 1990. "American Prisoner Home Furloughs." *Journal of Offender Counseling* 10:18–25.

South Carolina Department of Corrections. 1992. *Manual for Initial Classification and Institutional Assignment.* Columbia, SC: South Carolina Department of Corrections.

South Carolina Department of Youth Services. 1989. *South Carolina Delinquent Males: A Follow-up into Adult Corrections.* Columbia, SC: South Carolina Department of Youth Services.

Sperbeck, David J., and Richard R. Parlour. 1986. "Screening and Managing Suicidal Prisoners." *Corrective and Social Psychiatry and Journal of Behavior Technology Methods and Therapy* 32:95–98.

Spieker, Diane J., and Timothy A. Pierson. 1989. *Adult Internal Management System (AIMS): Implementation Manual.* Washington, DC: U.S. Department of Justice, National Institute of Corrections (National Institute of Corrections Grant #87–N081).

Springer, Charles E. 1987. *Justice for Juveniles.* Rockville, MD: U.S. National Institute for Juvenile Justice and Delinquency Prevention.

Steadman, Henry J. 1985. "Prediction at the System Level: Measuring the Presumed Changes in the Clientele of the Criminal Justice and Mental Health Systems." In *Dangerousness: Probability and Prediction, Psychiatry, and Public Policy,* Christopher D. Webster, Mark H. Ben-Aron, and Stephen J. Hucker (eds.). Cambridge,

UK: Cambridge University Press.

Stephan, James J., and Louis W. Jankowski. 1991. *Jail Inmates, 1990.* Washington, DC: U.S. Department of Justice, Bureau of Justice Statistics.

Stephens, Robert T. 1992. "To What Extent and Why Do Inmates Attend School in Prison?" *Journal of Correctional Education* 43:52–56.

Steury, Ellen Hochstedler. 1991. "Specifying 'Criminalization' of the Mentally Disordered Misdemeanant." *Journal of Criminal Law and Criminology* 82:334–359.

Stevens, S. S. 1951. "Mathematics, Measurement, and Psychophysics." In *Handbook of Experimental Psychology,* S. S. Stevens (ed.). New York: Wiley.

Stojkovic, Stan. 1986. "Social Bases of Power and Control Mechanisms among Correctional Administrators in a Prison Organization." *Journal of Criminal Justice* 14:157–166.

Stone, Alan A. 1985. "The New Legal Standard of Dangerousness: Fair in Theory, Unfair in Practice." In *Dangerousness: Probability and Prediction, Psychiatry, and Public Policy,* Christopher D. Webster, Mark H. Ben-Aron, and Stephen J. Hucker (eds.). Cambridge, UK: Cambridge University Press.

Struckhoff, David R. 1987. "Selective Incapacitation: Good Theory, Bad Practice." *Corrections Today* 49:30–34.

Stuebing, William K. 1984. *Victims and Witnesses: Experiences, Needs, and Community/Criminal Justice Response.* Ottawa: Research and Statistics Section, Policy Planning and Development Branch, Canada Department of Justice.

Sullivan, C., M. Q. Grant, and J. D. Grant. 1957. "The Development of Interpersonal Maturity: Applications to Delinquency." *Psychiatry* 23:373–385.

Talty, Richard B. 1985. *Intensive Supervision Program: Report to the Advisory Committee.* Trenton, NJ: New Jersey Administrative Office of the Courts.

Tiberia, Thomas. 1992. "Helping Correction Officers Recognize and Interact with Handicapped Offenders." *American Jails* 6:31–34.

Tobin, Patricia. 1983. *1982 Yearly Statistical Report of the Furlough Program.* Boston, MA: Massachusetts Department of Corrections.

Toborg, Mary A. 1984. *Pretrial Release Assessment of Danger and Flight: Method Makes a Difference.* McLean, VA: Lazar Management Group, Inc.

Toch, Hans, and Kenneth Adams. 1986. "Pathology and Disruptiveness among Prison Inmates." *Journal of Research in Crime and Delinquency* 23:7–21.

Tonry, Michael. 1987. "Prediction and Classification: Legal and Ethical Issues." In *Prediction and Classification: Criminal Justice Decision Making,* Don M. Gottfredson and Michael Tonry (eds.). Chicago: University of Chicago Press.

Towberman, Donna B. 1992. "A National Survey of Juvenile Risk Assessment." *Juvenile & Family Court Journal* 43:61–67.

U.S. Bureau of Justice Statistics. 1989. *National Corrections Reporting Program, 1985.* Washington, DC: Bureau of Justice Statistics.

U.S. Department of Justice. 1988. *Report to the Nation on Crime and Justice.* Washington, DC: U.S. Department of Justice, Bureau of Justice Statistics.

U.S. Sentencing Commission. 1987. *United States Sentencing Commission Guidelines Manual.* Washington, DC: U.S. Sentencing Commission.

University of Hawaii–Manoa. 1984. *Recidivism of 1979 Adult Probation, Third Circuit Court.* Honolulu: Youth Development and Research Center.

Uriell, Patricia. 1984. *The Furlough Program: An Evaluation.* Manoa, HI: Youth Development and Research Center, School of Social Work, University of Hawaii–Manoa.

Valenzuela, Aurora, Enrique Vallaneuva, and Jose Aguilera. 1991. "Importance of Criminal Behavior Related Variables in Criminal Prognosis." *American Journal of Forensic Psychology* 9:31–42.

Van Vleet, Russell, and Jeffrey A. Butts. 1990. *Risk Assessment of Committed Delinquents: Nebraska Youth Development Centers.* Ann Arbor, MI: Center for the Study of Youth Policy, University of Michigan.

Van Voorhis, Patricia. 1990. "A Comparison of Five Psychological Classification Systems among Adult, Male, Prison Inmates." Unpublished paper presented at the annual meeting of the American Society of Criminology. Baltimore, MD (November).

Visher, Christy. 1987. "Incapacitation and Crime Control: Does a 'Lock 'Em Up' Strategy Reduce Crime?" *Justice Quarterly* 4:513–543.

Vito, Gennaro F. 1986. "Felony Probation and Recidivism: Replication and Response." *Federal Probation* 50:17–25.

von Hirsch, Andrew. 1984. "The Ethics of Selective Incapacitation: Observations on the Contemporary Debate." *Crime and Delinquency* 30:175–194.

von Hirsch, Andrew. 1985. *Past or Future Crimes: Deservedness and Dangerousness in the Sentencing of Criminals.* New Brunswick, NJ: Rutgers University Press.

von Hirsch, Andrew, and Don Gottfredson. 1983. "Selective Incapacitation: Some Queries about Research Designs and Equity." *New York University Review of Law and Social Change* 12:1–30.

Walker, Samuel, 1985. *Sense and Nonsense about Crime: A Policy Guide.* Monterey, CA: Brooks/Cole Publishing Company.

Wallerstedt, John F. 1984. *Returning to Prison.* Washington, DC: Bureau of Justice Statistics.

Warren, M. Q. 1973. "Applications of Interpersonal-Maturity Theory to Offender Populations." In *Personality Theory, Moral Development, and Criminal Behavior,* W. S. Laufer and J. M. Day (eds.). Lexington, MA: Lexington Books.

Webster, Christopher D., Mark H. Ben-Aron, and Stephen J. Hucker (eds.). 1985. *Dangerousness: Probability and Prediction, Psychiatry, and Public Policy.* Cambridge, UK: Cambridge University Press.

Webster, Christopher D., Bernard Dickens, and Susan Addario. 1985. *Constructing Dangerousness: Scientific, Legal, and Policy Implications.* Toronto, Canada: Centre of Criminology, University of Toronto.

Weiner, Neil Alan. 1987. "Violent Juvenile and Adult Offenders in the 1958 Philadelphia Birth Cohort." Unpublished paper presented at the annual meeting of the American Society of Criminology. Montreal. (November).

Weintraub, Benson B. 1987. "The Role of Defense Counsel at Sentencing." *Federal Probation,* 51:25–29.

Wells, Dave, and Tim Brennan. 1992. "Jail Inmate Classification System: The Michigan Classification Project." *American Jails* 6:59–62.

Welsh, Wayne N. et al. 1990. "Jail Overcrowding: An Analysis of Policy Makers' Perceptions." *Justice Quarterly* 7:341–370.

Wenck, Ernst A., and R. L. Emerick. 1976. "Assaultive Youth: An Exploratory Study of the Assaultive Experience and the Assaultive Potential of CYA Wards." *Journal of Research of Crime and Delinquency* 9:1–20.

Wenck, Ernst A., James O. Robison, and Gerald W. Smith. 1972. "Can Violence Be Predicted?" *Crime and Delinquency* 18:393–402.

Wheaton, David. 1990. "Adult Intensive Probation Client Selection Scale." Unpublished paper presented at the annual meeting of the Academy of Criminal Justice Sciences. Denver, CO (March).

Wieczorek, W. F., J. W. Welte, and A. L. Mirand. 1991. "Preliminary Development of a Screening Instrument for Delinquency." Unpublished paper presented at the annual meetings of the American Society of Criminology. Baltimore, MD (November).

Wilbanks, William L. 1985. "Predicting Failure on Parole." In *Prediction in Criminology,* David P. Farrington and Roger Tarling (eds.). Albany, NY: State University of New York Press.

Wilkins, Leslie T. 1985. "The Politics of Prediction." In *Prediction in Criminology,* David P. Farrington and Roger Tarling (eds.). Albany, NY: State University of New York Press.

Williams, Susan Darst. 1986. "AIDS in Prison: Coping with a Strange New Death Penalty." *Corrections Compendium* 10:1–9.

Wilson, Deborah G. 1985. *Persistent Felony Offenders in Kentucky: A Profile of the Institutional Population.* Louisville, KY: Kentucky Criminal Justice Statistical Analysis Center.

Wolfgang, Marvin, Robert M. Figlio, and Thorsten Sellin. 1972. *Delinquency in a Birth Cohort.* Chicago: University of Chicago Press.

Wood, Doyle A., and James W. Brown. 1989. *Juvenile Electronic Monitoring: Assessment Report.* Champaign, IL: Community Research Associates; prepared for the U.S. Office of Juvenile Justice and Delinquency Prevention.

Wood, Frank W. 1991. *Risk Assessment and Release Procedures for Violent Offenders/Sexual Psychopaths.* St. Paul, MN: Minnesota Department of Corrections.

Wooldredge, John D. 1989. "Correlates of Jail Crowding in the United States." *American Journal of Criminal Justice* 14:16–25.

Wright, Kevin N. 1986a. "An Exploratory Study of Transactional Classification." *Journal of Research in Crime and Delinquency* 23:326–348.

Wright, Kevin N. 1986b. *Improving Correctional Classification through a Study of the Placement of Inmates in Environmental Settings.* Binghampton, NY: Center for Social Analysis, State University of New York at Binghampton.

Wright, Kevin N. 1988. "The Relationship of Risk, Needs, and Personality Classification Systems and Prison Adjustment." *Criminal Justice and Behavior* 15:454–471.

Wright, Kevin N., Todd R. Clear, and Paul Dickson. 1984. "Universal Applicability of Probation Risk Assessment Instruments: A Critique." *Criminology* 22:113–134.

Zenoff, Elyce H. 1985. "Controlling the Dangers of Dangerousness: The ABA Standards and Beyond." *George Washington Law Review* 53:562–607.

Zevitz, Richard G. 1988. "Penal Reform in Retreat: A Legal History of Jail Parole in California, 1950–1974." In *Criminal Justice History: An International Annual, Volume VIII: 1987.* Westport, CT: Meckler.

Zimmerman, Sherwood E., and Jacqueline Cohen. 1990. "Criminal Justice Prediction Instruments." Unpublished paper presented at the annual meetings of the American Society of Criminology. Baltimore, MD (November).

Zwetchkenbaum-Segal, Rebecca. 1984. *Case Preparation and Follow-up Study: Major Findings.* Boston, MA: Planning, Research, and Program Development Unit, Massachusetts Parole Board.

Acknowledgments

I would like to gratefully acknowledge and thank the following persons who provided me with much valuable information concerning their state classification schemes at both adult and juvenile levels:

ALABAMA

Mr. Patrick J. Pendergast
Alabama Department of Youth Services

Mr. George M. Phyfer, Director
Alabama Department of Youth Services

Mr.. Thomas A. Gilkeson, Director
Research, Monitoring & Evaluation
Alabama Department of Corrections

ALASKA

Mr. Randall G. Hines, Associate Coordinator
Youth Corrections Section
Division of Family and Youth Services
Alaska Department of Health and Social Services

Mr. Leonard G. Jones, Department Policy Coordinator
Alaska Department of Corrections, Southcentral Region Office

ARIZONA

Dr. Daryl Fischer, Research Unit Supervisor
Planning Bureau
Arizona Department of Corrections

Ms. Trisha Polmear Lemon, Acting Administrator
Planning Bureau
Arizona Department of Corrections

Mr. Samuel A. Lewis, Director
Arizona Department of Corrections

ARKANSAS

Ms. Donna L. Gay, Coordinator of Juvenile Courts
Administrative Office of the Courts
Supreme Court of Arkansas

Mr. J. D. Gingerich, Director
Administrative Office of the Courts
Supreme Court of Arkansas

Ms. Marcia White
Administrative Services Division
Arkansas Department of Corrections

CALIFORNIA

Mr. Norman Holt, Parole Administrator I
Parole and Community Services Division
California Department of Corrections

Mr. John F. Monday, Executive Officer
Youthful Offender Parole Board
California Youth and Adult Correctional Agency

Mr. Ted Rich, Executive Officer
California Board of Prison Terms
California Department of Corrections

COLORADO

Ms. Kim English
Division of Criminal Justice
Colorado Department of Public Safety

Mr. Ben Griego, Director of Offender Services
Colorado Department of Corrections

Mr. Frank O. Gunter, Executive Director
Colorado Department of Corrections

Ms. Betty Marler, Director, Treatment Services
Division of Youth Services
Colorado Department of Institutions

CONNECTICUT

Mr. Todd N. Fisk
Connecticut Community Services Administrator

Dr. Larry R. Meachum, Commissioner
Connecticut Department of Corrections

Ms. Charlene Perkins, Director
Inmate Classification

DELAWARE

Mr. Howard R. Young, Director of Special Programs
Bureau of Adult Correction
Delaware Department of Correction

FLORIDA

Mr. Jeffrey S. Bryan, Administrative Assistant III
Chairman, Gene Hodge's Office
Florida Parole Commission

Mr. James G. Mitchell, Director
Adult Services Program Office
Florida Department of Corrections

Mr. Stephen B. Ray, Senior Human Services Program Specialist
Delinquency Program Services
State of Florida Department of Health and Rehabilitative Services

GEORGIA

Ms. Sue Aiken, Deputy Director
Research, Planning, Development and Evaluation
Georgia State Board of Pardons and Paroles

Mr. Robert A. Riols
Georgia Department of Children and Youth Services

HAWAII

Mr. Ken Hashi
Research and Statistics Section
Hawaii Department of Public Safety

Mr. George W. Sumner, Director
Hawaii Department of Public Safety

IDAHO

Ms. Olivia Craven, Executive Director
Idaho Commission of Pardons and Parole

Mr. Del Ray Holm, Chairman
Idaho Commission of Pardons and Parole

Ms. K. Ann Thompson, Senior Administrative Assistant
Administrative Offices
Idaho Department of Corrections

ILLINOIS

Mr. Jim E. Cunningham, Jr., Assistant Chief Probation Officer
Adult Probation Department
Circuit Court of Cook County

Ms. Nola Joyce, Manager
Planning and Research Unit
Illinois, Department of Corrections

Mr. Howard A. Peters III, Director
Illinois, Department of Corrections

INDIANA

Mr. Jeffrey Bercovitz, Director
Indiana Probation and Juvenile Services

IOWA

Ms. Jeannette Bucklew, Deputy Director
Division of Community Services
Iowa Department of Corrections

Mr. Douglas Dykstra, Co-Chair, Classification Steering Committee
First Judicial District
Department of Correctional Services

Mr. Gerald Spencer, Co-Chair, Classification Steering Committee
Seventh Judicial District
Department of Correctional Services

KANSAS

Ms. Elizabeth Gillespie, Deputy Director of Community and Field Services
Kansas Department of Corrections

Mr. Richard Koerner, Director
Policy, Planning, and Data Analysis
Kansas Department of Corrections

Mr. Gary Stotts, Secretary of Corrections
Kansas Department of Corrections

Mr. Ray Roberts, Deputy Secretary of Facility Management
Kansas Department of Corrections

KENTUCKY

Ms. Hazel M. Combs, Assistant Director
Kentucky Division of Probation and Parole

Ms. Judith G. Morris, Branch Manager
Assessment/Classification, Adult Institutions
Kentucky Department of Corrections, Division of Institutions

MAINE

Mr. Donald L. Allen, Commissioner
Maine Department of Corrections

Mr. A. L. Carlisle, Associate Commissioner
Maine Department of Corrections

Ms. Kim Ellis
Maine Department of Corrections

Mr. John Hines
Maine Department of Corrections

Mr. Phil Marston
Maine Department of Corrections

Mr. Michael J. Molloy, Director of Programs
Department of Programs
Maine Department of Corrections

Mr. Francis J. Westrack, Director of Classification
Maine Department of Corrections

MARYLAND

Dr. Anthony Swetz, Director of Treatment Services
Division of Correction
Department of Public Safety and Correctional Services

MASSACHUSETTS

Ms. Pamela A. Jonah, Commissioner's Program Manager
Commissioner's Office
Massachusetts Department of Corrections

Ms. Donna Lipson, Executive Assistant
Massachusetts Parole Board
Executive Office of Public Safety

Mr. Edward J. Loughran, Commissioner
Massachusetts Department of Youth Services
Executive Office of Human Services

Mr. Robert M. Mowatt, Director
Hennepin County Bureau of Community Corrections
Juvenile Probation Division

Mr. Scott Taberner, Assistant Commissioner
Executive Office of Human Services
Massachusetts Department of Youth Services

MICHIGAN

Mr. Ernie Boone, Director
Delinquency Policy and Program Development Division
Michigan Department of Social Services

Mr. J. Otis Davis
Michigan Department of Social Services

Mr. Terrence H. Murphy, Chief
Research Division
Michigan Department of Corrections

MINNESOTA

Ms. Deborah A. Eng, Deputy Executive Officer
Office of Juvenile Release
Minnesota Department of Corrections

Mr. Duane A. Erickson, Director
Field Services
Minnesota Department of Corrections

Mr. David Gustafson, Director
Region 3–Arrowhead Regional Corrections
Minnesota Department of Corrections

Mr. Robert E. Harrell, Executive Officer
Office of Adult Release
Minnesota Department of Corrections

Mr. James H. Hayes, M.S.W., Juvenile Division Director
Ramsey County Community Corrections Department
Juvenile Service Center
Minnesota Department of Corrections

Mr. Robert Mowatt, Manager
Juvenile Probation
Minnesota Department of Corrections

Mr. Richard T. Mulcrone, Deputy Commissioner
Minnesota Department of Corrections

Mr. Richard Quick, Exeuctive Officer
Office of Juvenile Release
Minnesota Department of Corrections

Ms. Kristin Tuenge, Supervisor
Washington County Department of Court Services
Juvenile Division
Minnesota Department of Corrections

Mr. Carl Wicklund, Director
Dodge/Fillmore/Olmsted Community Corrections

Mr. Frank W. Wood, Deputy Commissioner
Institutions Division
Minnesota Department of Corrections

MISSOURI

Mr. Robert K. Kauffman, Director
Management Information Services
Missouri Department of Social Service

Mr. George A. Lombardi, Director
Division of Adult Institutions
Missouri Department of Corrections

Mr. Dick D. Moore, Director
Department of Corrections

Mr. Cranston J. Mitchell, Chairman
Missouri Board of Probation and Parole

NEBRASKA

Mr. Harold W. Clark, Director
Nebraska Department of Correctional Services

NEVADA

Ms. Susan J. McCurdy, Executive Secretary for the Board Chairman
Nevada Board of Parole Commissioners

Mr. John Slansky, Chief
Nevada Department of Parole and Probation

NEW HAMPSHIRE

New Hampshire Department of Corrections
Division of Field Services

NEW JERSEY

Mr. Charles E. Fowler
Supervising Parole Officer
New Jersey Department of Corrections
Bureau of Parole

NEW MEXICO

Mr. Meliton E. Madrid, Region V Manager
Probation and Parole Division
New Mexico Corrections Department

Mr. Les Russell, Director
Probation and Parole Division
New Mexico Corrections Department

NEW YORK

Mr. Bill Baccaglini, Director of Program Evaluation and Research
Client Classification and Movement System, Division for Youth
New York State Executive Department

Ms. Gloria F. Conrad, Director
Classification and Movement
New York State Department of Correctional Services

Mr. Leonard G. Dunston, Director
Division for Youth
New York State Executive Department

NORTH CAROLINA

Ms. Gwendolyn C. Chunn, Division Director
North Carolina Department of Human Resources
Division of Youth Services

Mr. Paul Gross, Administrative Officer
Division of Adult Probation and Parole
North Carolina Department of Correction

Mr. Thomas E. Sutton, Correctional Planner II
Information Resources
North Carolina Department of Correction

NORTH DAKOTA

Mr. Daniel Christ, Programs Coordinator
North Dakota Department of Corrections and Rehabilitation

Mr. Charles R. Placek, Specialized Regional Supervisor
North Dakota Adult Parole and Probation Division

Mr. Ernest J. Reinhert, Parole Coordinator
North Dakota Parole and Probation Division

OHIO

Mr. Raymond E. Capots, Chairman
Ohio Parole Board

Ms. Elizabeth "Betty" Moore, Researcher
Bureau of Planning and Research
Ohio Department of Rehabilitation and Correction

OKLAHOMA

Ms. Mary L. Livers, Regional Director
Central Region
Oklahoma Department of Corrections

OREGON

Mr. Brian Bemus, Program Manager
Classification and Transfer Division
Oregon Department of Corrections

Mr. Frank A. Hall, Director
Oregon Department of Corrections

Ms. Tanna Reynolds, Executive Assistant
Community Services Branch
Oregon Department of Corrections

PENNSYLVANIA

Mr. James Alibrio, Director of Management Information Systems
Pennsylvania Board of Probation and Parole

Ms. Lee Ann S. Labecki, Director
Planning, Research, and Statistics
Pennsylvania Department of Corrections

Mr. Joseph D. Lehman, Commissioner
Pennsylvania Department of Corrections

Ms. Darlene E. Zelazny, Executive Assistant to the Chairman
Pennsylvania Board of Probation and Parole

SOUTH CAROLINA

Mr. Parker Evatt, Commissioner
South Carolina Department of Corrections

SOUTH DAKOTA

Ms. Lynne DeLano
Office of the Secretary
South Dakota Department of Corrections

TENNESSEE

Ms. Betty Adams, Commissioner
Tennessee Department of Youth Development

Mr. Charles B. Bass, Assistant Commissioner of Adult Institutions
Tennessee Department of Corrections

Mr. Howard G. Cook, Director
Classification Programs
Tennessee Department of Corrections

Mr. Paul Lewin, Director
Grants Management
Tennessee Department of Youth Development

Ms. Deborah L. Miller, Executive Director
Tennessee Board of Paroles

Mr. Charles Traughber, Chairman
Tennessee Board of Parole

TEXAS

Mr. Billy M. Birmingham, Chief
Operations and Statistical Analysis
Institutional Division
Texas Department of Criminal Justice

Mr. Jay Kantor, Assistant Chief Juvenile Probation Officer
Randall County Juvenile Probation Department
Texas Youth Commission

Mr. Jay Svinicki, Research Specialist
Texas Youth Commission and Intensive Supervision

UTAH

John Green, J.D., M.P.A., Administrative Coordinator
Utah State Board of Pardons

Ms. Colleen Gillett, Program Director of Field Operations
Utah State Department of Corrections

VERMONT

Mr. Richard A. Smith, Assistant Director of Program Services
Agency of Human Services
Vermont Department of Corrections

VIRGINIA

Mr. Dan Brown
Virginia Department of Youth and Family Services

Mr. Clarence L. Jackson, Chairman
Virginia Parole Board

Mr. Charles J. Kehoe, Director
Virginia Department of Youth and Family Services

Mr. E. C. Morris, Deputy Director
Division of Institutions
Virginia Department of Corrections

Mr. Walter L. Smiley, Deputy Director for Administration and Finance
Virginia Department of Youth and Family Services

WASHINGTON

Mr. David Bailey
Washington State Department of Corrections

Mr. Ruben Cedeño, Director
Division of Offender Programs
State of Washington Department of Corrections

Mr. David L. Fallen, Executive Officer
State of Washington Sentencing Guidelines Commission

Ms. Kathleen Gookin, Director
Division of Offender Programs
State of Washington Department of Corrections

Dr. Ron Jemelka, Ph.D.
School of Medicine
University of Washington

Mr. Robert Jones, Chief of Clinical Services
Division of Offender Programs
State of Washington Department of Corrections

Mr. Dennis Marsh, Executive Secretary
State of Washington Indeterminate Sentence Review Board

Mr. Dave Savage, Director
Division of Community Corrections
State of Washington Department of Corrections

Dr. John C. Steiger, Program Administrator
Division of Juvenile Rehabilitation
State of Washington Department of Social and Health Services

Mr. James E. Thatcher, Chief
Classification and Treatment Unit
Division of Offender Programs
State of Washington Department of Corrections

Mr. Jerome M. Wasson, Director
State of Washington Department of Social and Health Services

Mr. Ted M. Wilson
Corrections Mental Health Program Coordinator
Division of Offender Programs
State of Washington Department of Corrections

WEST VIRGINIA

Mr. Robert G. Casto, Staff Assistant, Programs
Division of Corrections
West Virginia Department of Public Safety

WISCONSIN

Mr. Russel L. Leik, Classification Chief
Division of Adult Institutions
Wisconsin Department of Corrections

Mr. Stephen M. Puckett, Director
Wisconsin Office of Offender Classification

WYOMING

Mr. Shane Sconce, Special Services Supervisor
Wyoming Department of Corrections
Probation and Parole

UNITED STATES

Mr. Peter B. Hoffman
United States Sentencing Commission

Mr. Thomas C. Kowalski, Director, Case Operations
United States Parole Commission
U.S. Department of Justice

Mr. J. Michael Quinlan, Director
Federal Bureau of Prisons

Name Index

Subject Index

About the Author

DEAN J. CHAMPION is Professor and Chair at the Department of Criminal Justice, Minot State University, North Dakota. His publications include sixteen texts, an edited work, and numerous articles. Among them are *Corrections in the United States: A Contemporary Perspective* (1989), *The U.S. Sentencing Guidelines* (Praeger, 1989), and *Felony Probation* (Praeger, 1988). His articles have appeared in several journals including *Journal of Criminal Justice, Crime and Justice, Journal of Contemporary Criminal Justice,* and *American Journal of Criminal Justice.* His professional interests revolve around judicial and prosecutorial decision making, juvenile rights, and jailhouse lawyers and correctional law.